D1789365

# Chewing The Cud
Alcibiades and Socrates talk life, love, and Nietzsche.

---

Incorrigibly 'old school', the author spent many years lecturing in Higher and Further Education trying, to borrow Socrates' words, to light flames rather than fill vessels. In its own way this book is an attempt to come to terms with the bitter fruit of this failure, albeit in a way sweetened by the comedic aspects. The idea for this dialogue arose from the reading of the passages in "The Twilight of the Idols" in which Nietzsche mounts a number of his trade-mark idiosyncratic, ad hominem arguments against Socrates. Initially intended as a means of reviewing and explicating the latest Nietzschean scholarship in respect of the 'shadows' still cast by Platonism, the fictionalised element of the dialogue evolved to form its own analogic critique on the way philosophy is written and practiced, especially as embodied here, by its all too human protagonists. To achieve this end, the book turns upon a number of conceits. Liberties are taken with certain dates, events, and, not least, the characters of the principals as they have come down to us from the quills of Plato, Aristophanes, Xenophon, and others. The Nietzschean aspects of the dialogue however, as voiced here by Alcibiades, are taken verbatim from the source texts. The dialogue takes place over the course of the following day of Plato's "Symposium". As the fates conspire to bring about the demise of ancient Athens, a sexually importunate and unwitting Socrates waylays a hapless Alcibiades to chew the cud in respect of life, love, and Nietzsche.

# Chewing The Cud

**Alcibiades and Socrates talk life, love and Nietzsche.**

John Taylor

**Arena Books**

Copyright © John Taylor 2013

The right of John Taylor to be identified as author of this book
has been asserted in accordance with the Copyright, Designs and
Patents Act 1988.

First published in 2013 by Arena Books

Arena Books
6 Southgate Green
Bury St. Edmunds
IP33 2BL


www.arenabooks.co.uk

Distributed in America by Ingram International, One Ingram Blvd., PO Box
3006, La Vergne, TN 37086-1985, USA.

All rights reserved. Except for the quotation of short passages for the
purposes of criticism and review, no part of this publication may be
reproduced, stored in a retrieval system, or transmitted, in any form or
by any means, electronic, mechanical, photocopying, recording or
otherwise, without the prior permission of the publisher.

John Taylor
**Chewing The Cud** *Alcibiades and Socrates talk life, love and Nietzsche*

British Library cataloguing in Publication Data. A Catalogue record for this
book is available from the British Library.



ISBN-13   978-1-909421-22-6

BIC classifications:-  HPX, HPQ, HPCA, HPCF3, HPM.

Printed and bound by Lightning Source UK


Cover design
By Jason Anscomb

Typeset in
Times New Roman

# Acknowledgements

"If the same indifference that attended the inception of this book greets its reception then its life will be mercifully short; according to Silenus the best thing being never to have been born, the next best to die young. On the other hand, should this thing get up on its legs and begin to run, this will be in no small measure due to the fostering it received from a variety of unwitting "soul physicians".

Among those to whom I owe a debt, and would encourage others to read, are; K. Ansell Pearce, Maudmarie Clark, Christophe Cox, Ulriche Haase, Lawrence J. Hatab, Kathleen Marie Higgins, Walter Kaufman, Alexander Nehemas, Kelly Oliver, David Owen, R.B. Pippin, John Richardson, Bernard Rossiter, Richard Schacht, Ivan Soll, Robert C Soloman, Dana R. Villa.

Needless to say, though some of their thoughts and ideas may have shaped what has issued here, they are in no way responsible for its resulting character."

# Preface

Written over the past two years, this book has been in the making for nigh on fifteen. Its genesis lies in the sudden collapse of a seemingly inviolate way of life. Sorely in need of a new friend, quite by chance, I came across an introduction to Nietzsche's work and had the uncanny feeling that one lay hidden behind the dazzling prose. Not the usual sort of friend, to be sure; rather one with "a heart of bronze", a heart that beat to a different rhythm and harboured certain beliefs that I regarded at the time, as pure anathema.

Early on there were many times when I nearly baled, but I was nonetheless hooked. Perhaps it was his rhetorical style? His insistence that you not merely read him, but feel and think with him. Psychology is always prior to philosophy. Perhaps it was his insistence with regard to first principles that the primary question is not: "What is the meaning of life?", but "Can there be meaning in life?". Put that way, the resounding answer down the ages - from Silenus to science, from religion to modern humanism all of its political manifestations – has been in respect of life, as found in the here and the now, an emphatic "No".

Suffice to say in next to no time I had read the canon and soon chasing down the paper trail ofexegesis and criticism. In more ways than the one, here I found proof positive of Nietzsche's adage: "You can only get out of a book what you put into it". On another level I found, time and again, that it was all too easy to underestimate Nietzsche. The coarser and more unpalatable stuff, on closer inspection, often turns out to more richly nuanced. Although not subject to the summary dismissal he once was, old habits die hard. A former philosophy tutor of mine, who I hadn't seen for years, took the mention of Nietzsche and "Truth" in the same breath as an affront to his amour-propre. "A minor cultural critic" was his tart verdict.

It was this intemperate response that set the wheels in motion. I began to look for a means of putting a full stop to my reading by bringing the more approachable aspects of my "friend" to be found in Increasingly voluminous exegesis to a wider audience. A.N. Whitehead's dictum to the effect that all philosophy is merely footnotes to Plato suggested the dialogue as the vehicle, especially as Nietzsche's ambition was nothing less than an attempt to take a wrecking ball to the entire Platonic tradition.

What follows is an attempt to honour a debt gratitude. Attentive readers might note that the last word is given to Socrates, and concludes with a question mark rather than a full stop. Something, I think, that both protagonists would agree is apposite, and, hopefully, the reader will too?

**John Taylor**

# CHAPTER 1
## The Early Bird Catches ...


A: Are you still following me? It won't be just be my shadow that takes offence.[1] But eh, who wants an ugly scene in a beauty parlour?

S: Very droll. I know - they're beauticians here, not miracle workers. I've heard it all a hundred times. Are you after one of those Minoan styles that are all the rage again?

A: What's it to you old man? The only thing you'd qualify for here is a comb-over.

S: Don't be like that. As I argued at last night's party, you should be looking for the beauty within.[2]

A: In your dreams! Beauty might be skin deep, but I fancy ugliness goes all the way down to the bone. As one of the hoi polloi, how could it be otherwise with you? You only get to put on airs [no pun intended] and mix with your social betters because of your connection with Plato. What the attraction is is beyond me? May be it's a case of "Why keep a dog?"

S. I don't always do as he says. That said I suspect I'll always end up saying what he thinks; like parchment my skin, these days – endlessly written over by him and others. My wife reckons I'll go down in history as the most famous ventriloquist's dummy ever.

A: That's the beauty of being a bit of a scribbler you can indulge in all sorts of make-believe, and who is there to contradict you? Given the animosity between Plato's family and my own, History will have it that I chased you rather than you me. It's a peculiar hypocrisy that inveighs against the poets and yet purveys its own nostrums and confabulations via the written word?

S: Totally agree, I much prefer an honest conversation.

A: As many a donkey minus a hind leg will attest.

S: No seriously, a matter of life and death to me – a good natter. They are getting harder and harder to come by. Without them I'm prey to mood swings; up and down like a whore's drawers. You probably won't get all of that – about the drawers, I mean. My daemon speaking, you see? Knows a lot more than you, or I.

A: I know what "drawers" are, though I don't share your disdain of the wearers of them.

S: You've still got a lot to learn. Have you learnt nothing from those Homeric heroes you are so keen to emulate - life as an expedition from innocence to experience, perhaps?

A: Enough to know that it is an ugly breech of form to patronize your social superior.

S: Still you have to admit he's got a point in speaking of Beauty as a Form, or Ideal

A: No, I Don't.

S: How else would you know that you are beautiful without reference to such an Ideal? 3

A: If I had any sense, I'd stop right now!

S: But you have, and charisma by the bucket load.

A: First, let's drop the sexual innuendo.

S: Must we? I'll try, but I can't promise. Proximity to you makes my heart race.

A: Don't!

S: Okay, I'll try harder! You were about to say…?

A: Anyway, I was going to decline the argument on your terms.

S: My terms?

A: Well you and Plato's; I'm never sure whose is who.
S: Me neither. He's so busy scribbling all the time, it's hard to keep with what I'm alleged to have said.

# CHEWING THE CUD

A: I was going to say I side with the nominalists. That my understanding of the concept "Dog", for example, is built up from acquaintanceship's with various breeds; Alsatians, Poodles, Dachshunds - even mongrels like yourself.4 Actually that's not really my view. Empiricism? Positivism? Whilst your metaphysics attest to anxiety in the face of finite becoming; positivism does no more than subdue such anxiety.

S: There's no need to pull rank.

A: What's rank is rank. Have you no "recollection" of that?

S: Now you want me to stand downwind?

A: Avail yourself of the facilities, why not?

S: There's nothing wrong with my hygiene.

A: No, - just trying to throw you off the scent!

S: Oh very funny I'm sure. You've not said why you dislike the idea of "Universals"?

A: Ah! Not so much a mongrel as a terrier – he won't let go of the bone. A rider on the storm.

S: I'm baffled.

A: [sings]. Riders on the storm
　　　Into this home we are born
　　　Into this world we are thrown
　　　A dog without a bone…

S: Must you - this dog thing?

A: Just outlining the parameters of our engagement, and, bye the bye, I prefer to keep my doors ajar so that others might be encouraged to push at them.
S: You probably know; I've something of a reputation in these parts. I'm a back-door man, you might say.

A: Well bugger me! Who would have believed it?

# CHEWING THE CUD

S: What most do you want me to take offense at? This is all very childish. If the "Dog" thing is meant to suggest I'm deficient in matters of hygiene then I'll have you know that I'm as particular in personal matters as in metaphysical ones. Its not the first time I've been here, and it's not just the ladies who take an interest in all things Brazilian!

A: Ugh! I'd prefer to think that all that bollocks the soothsayer said about a future namesake of yours being a dab-hand at kicking a pig's bladder was just that.5 Obviously he misidentified the bag of wind.

S: You're a fine one to cast aspersions. All the gossip in the agora is of your claim that you, or, rather, your thoughts will be born posthumously? 6 Anyway, you've still to answer?

A: Ah yes, the terrier and his bone. Are you sure you want to know? I warn you that once the genie is out of the bottle, they'll be no putting him back.

S: Ha, ha. On guard!

A: Lets begin with the cuts of meat that you and Plato serve up from that charnel house you call, "The Academy".

S: What? Why so sanguinary?

A: It's the way you choose to carve the world at its joints.7

S: Nature not the world. I should know. I said it, even if I didn't think it.8

A: More a butchery of "life" I'd say; for you two, philosophy is ever hacked from that grievous dichotomy: that between reality and appearance.9

S: And for good reason, the senses readily deceive us. If you want the truth you have to delve behind things. Talking of delving and "behinds", has any one told you…?

A: Enough!

S: Or what? You'll put me over your knee? Ha, ha. I like the idea of that.

# CHEWING THE CUD

A: Or I could simply swat you like a gad-fly.10There's many a man who'd think I'd performed a public service.

S: No doubt. This particular gadfly wants to know more of what you think before he's separated from his mortal coil though.

A: It's all so ahistorical, ... so imbued with ascetic values. The stuff you and Plato are forever preaching.

S: "Preaching"?

A. What else can you honestly call it? Since the highest values aren't realizable in this world, since the good life is to be lived elsewhere - in heaven, after death - then the only recourse in the here and now is ascetic self-denial. If one shifts the Centre of gravity of life out life into the "Beyond" - into nothingness - one has deprived life of its centre of gravity. [....] So to live that there is no longer any meaning in living; that now becomes the 'meaning' of life.11Put it this way, asceticism in the Platonic version is all about condemnation of the senses, and a quest for enlightenment. The Christian version on the other hand treats asceticism as an act of atonement - the muzzling, the stifling of the instincts and passions that typify life in the natural world.

S: Hold on. What's all this "Christian" stuff?

A: Its what you pair are the unwitting midwifes of. I'll explain later. Remember, I've lived posthumously.

S: Hmm, that's a big ask. Besides *lived*? - The gossip says *going* to live?

A: Well, that's the way things are, or will be. Nihilism wouldn't be such an issue otherwise.

S: "Nihilism"?

A: We'll come back to it I'm sure. It can't be ducked. Anyway, I was saying: historical refutation as the definitive refutation.
S: You were? All I know is that that sounds as if its written italics.

A: It is. Do keep up!

# CHEWING THE CUD

S: You cheeky monkey. I ought to put you over my knee.

A: Ha, ha.

S: I may be getting on in years but I can still give you a run for your money!

A: Try this for size then. By way of historical refutation: in former times, one sought to prove that there is no God - today one indicates how the belief that there is a God could arise and how this belief acquired its weight and importance: a counter-proof that there is no God thereby becomes superfluous. - When in former times one had refuted the "proofs of the existence of God put forward, there always remained the doubt whether better proofs might not be adduced than those just refuted: in those days, atheists did not know how to make a clean sweep.12

S: "Those days"? These days, more like. Softly, my friend, such impiety would not go unpunished. Such thoughts are even for me - well, frankly blasphemy! I mean, who but a madman, or that scoundrel Diogenes, would dare?

A: And me.

S: But didn't you say that arguments for or against are bye the bye - that agnosticism is the only position to adopt logically speaking?

A: That wasn't it at all!

S: Oh, I'd rather hoped it was. Hot bloodedness will be the death of you.

A: Coward!

S: "Coward"? No man can say that of me. Did I not fight to defend Athens' freedom? 13

A: Ok, ok. You can get down off of your high horse. We're even on that score. Remember? Or is it that your memory…?

S: Don't sneer!
A: Sneer? Me?

# CHEWING THE CUD

S: Yes you! If its not one insult its another. You know damn well I fought as a humble helot. Who here has gone up in the world? Would have me address you as "sir"?

A: Zeus. Talk about *amour propre*. It was just a figure of speech. Look we'll be here all day if we go on like this.

S: A truce then.

A: Good.

S: What are you then in the matter of religious belief then?

A: Atheist, but you are missing the point as to why. I think such beliefs arise out of a particular matrix of social and psychological needs. Moreover should the matrix change so, too, will the system of belief?

S What? Just like that?

A: No, after the Buddha was dead, …

S: The Buddha?

A: You won't have heard of him. the founding father of an Asiatic religion. The details don't matter now. The key point is that revered as a god when alive, his shadow was still shown for centuries in a cave - a tremendous, gruesome shadow. God is dead; but given the way of men, there may still be caves for thousands of years in which his shadow will be shown - and we - we still have to vanquish his shadow, too.14

S: Plato too, casts a long shadow it would seem. And these shadows, these spectres that prey upon the living, how do they manifest themselves? What kind of beliefs do they seek to propagate, perpetuate?

A: At last he's picked up the scent, and how?

S: And you'll find I have a bite to go with my bark if there's any more of that.
A: My genealogical investigations suggest we are still heavily invested in the pursuit of an ultimate reality, the idea of antithetical values - that good and evil are radically different values such that the one cannot be derived from the other -that…

15

S: Enough. That's more than enough to be going on with. How miserable life would be if there were no God, or Gods to believe in? No hope of a better life, or recompense for the injustices of this life.

A: Zeus! The concept of "God" invented as a counter-concept of life - everything harmful, poisonous, slanderous, the whole hostility unto death against life synthesized in this concept in a gruesome unity! The concept of the "beyond", the true world" invented in order to devaluate the only world there is - in order to retain no goal, no reason, no task for our earthly reality! [...] *Ecrasez l'infame*! 15

S: A noble lie nonetheless? 16 Even so, I'd like to press you on the issue of God's death. It's not the refutation of his existence that exercises you; isn't it rather what follows when such a belief is no longer available for us? Why are you smiling? Did I say something...?

A: No, no. Admiration. You're such a canny old bird.

S: Less of the old. Do I have to remind you what a bird in the hand is worth?

A: It's just that so many people miss the point when I try to discuss this, yet with you...

S: Perhaps Eupolis had a point: "The best of talkers, and speakers worst"? 17

A: Aye, but I can't cut off the dog's tail twice! 18

S: "How happily he lisped the truth". 19 It won't be just the dog that is glad to hear it.

A: Touché. To continue; you're right. It's not a question of having to suspend belief, but rather that such beliefs become unworthy of being held. Honesty as the youngest virtue; the ideal is not refuted - it freezes to death"20

S: A grievous philosophy, if true.21Without a God, or gods, wouldn't everything be permitted? 22
A: Some types of religious fanatics might think it's the other way around. Be that as it may, nihilism is still a problem that needs to be addressed.

S: And a nihilist is what?

# CHEWING THE CUD

A: A nihilist is a man who judges of the world as it is that it ought not to be, and of the world as it ought to be that it does not exist.23It threatens when one interpretation of the world collapses, especially if it was thought of as the interpretation.

S: You're implying that I might succumb?

A: You might were I to loosen Plato's grip on your imagination.

S: Fat chance! I'm not some starry- eyed acolyte. I'm more than capable of thinking for myself. I've influenced him as much as he I. Just because he's the one who wields the stylus doesn't say otherwise. It doesn't become you ....

A: You've said it!

S: Said what?

A: What it's all about for you and him. Return of the repressed: that's nihilism. Right from the off your philosophy was no more than an attempt to evade it - nihilism, that is.

S: I don't think I have said whatever "it" was, or is. And attempting to stone me into submission by flinging such alien sounding concepts at me is only going to leave me in the dark. I don't much like being left struggling to get a word in edge-ways.
A: See? You've learnt something that only others know already? Becoming! Or rather "Being". For you and him its a world of becoming - a world replete with deceptive appearances. Death, change, age, as well as procreation and growth, are for [you] objections - refutations even. What is does not become; what becomes is not... Now they all believe even to the point of despair, in that which is. But since they cannot get hold of it, they look for reasons why it is withheld from them. "It must be an illusion, a deception which prevents us from perceiving that which is [...]"24. One bolthole remains, an escape: - to pass sentence on this whole world of becoming as a deception and to invent a world beyond it, a true world.25
S: Just for reference, remind me - the Christian aspect that you want to lay at our door?
A: Ah yes. Mustn't forget that. The suffering that takes place is real enough as is the world in which it occurs, but the stick comes with a carrot – it's a transitory state. An after-life awaits, for the good, one free of the pain and suffering that mars a world of becoming. An ascetic vision; the ascetic treats life as a wrong road on

17

which one must finally walk back to the point where it begins, or as a mistake that is put right by deeds-that we ought to put right.

S: And I'm to think what? Some poetic nonsense or other cuts it? That you've taken the road less travelled? 26

A: I'll only say that if one shifts the centre of gravity out of life into the 'Beyond' - into nothingness - one has deprived life of its centre of gravity.[...]So to live that there is no longer any  meaning in living: that now becomes the 'meaning of life'.27

S: Interesting, but that's a lot for an old man to digest first thing in the morning. What say you that you have locks attended to and I'll wait for you over there by the pool? It'll give me time to catch up on a bit of beauty sleep. Hope springs eternal. Besides you still owe me an explanation of love, what with your turning up at the party last night already drunk. It was frustrating in more than the one way.

A: You've got Pandora all wrong, you know?

S: Have I? 28 Well anyway get them to save me a lock. I'll treasure it.

A: Can't you ever give it a rest? It 's all so wearing, so wearisome.

S: Blame it on my age. I'm in that awkward stage: not quite enough years to be "a dirty old man", but no longer young enough to be considered an erotic. Wearing them down is my best hope of success.

courtesy of www.parkeongerome.org

One hour later: at the poolside.

## CHEWING THE CUD

S: Oh, very nice. Very becoming! You'll look positively regal in your purple robe. Did you save me a lock? You promised!

A: Behave. I did no such thing!

S: Then I'll have to make do with that lovely colour that comes to your cheeks when they flush.

A: I could go home. Hipparete – Timandra - will be waiting.29 Still under my skin, Hipparete. Still miss her badly.

S: Didn't you tire of humping her about?

A: Is there any call for such callousness?

S: Some might suggest that it didn't take you long to replace her, and, yet others, that you were already sampling Timandra's wares. Not that anyone could be in any doubt about what's on offer; you are not by any stretch the first to shop at that stall. Anyway let's not waste time on gossip; we've got lots to talk about. We've hardly begun and I'm set on giving you my closest examination. I've been wondering. Your speaking of Hipparete reminds me. Don't you think appearances are deceptive, merely transitory; the result of fickle fortune - as transient as the rose's bloom? Real beauty, on the other hand lies within; properly cultivated the object of beauty becomes inured to the vagaries of fate?

A: A pretty speech. Oh, how one loves one's desires; rather more I fancy than the putative object of desire.30.

S: That's downright cynical! No wonder people are so divided about you. As to the slur upon my feelings for Xanthippe, I'll have you know that...

A: Well I'm relieved it's Xanthippe you're speaking of. But is it? Cynical, I mean? And don't think the sly asides concerning Hipparete went unnoticed - the "humping" and the appearance of beauty as opposed to the reality. So she gave nature a hand every now and again? Don't we all? Haven't I just? Besides, I don't see you've got that much to be cocksure about. Some might suspect that you and him in doors are overly in love with "Reason".

S: Well at least I can claim it was love that brought us together, and not just the two of us!

# CHEWING THE CUD

A: Can you? Marriage in the bourgeois sense of the word - I mean, in the most respectable sense of the word "marriage" - is not a matter of love, any more than it is a question of money; no institution can be foundered on love. It is a question of society's granting permission to two people to gratify their sexual desires with one another, under certain conditions, to be sure, but conditions that keep the interests of society in view. It is obvious that a certain attraction between the parties and very much good will - will to patience, compatibility, care for one another - will be among the presuppositions of such a contract; but one should not misuse the word love to describe this! For the two lovers in the complete and strong sense of the word sexual gratification is not essential and really is no more than a symbol: for one party, as already said, a symbol of unconditional submission, for the other a symbol of assent to this, a sign of taking possession.

In marriage in the aristocratic, old aristocratic sense of the word it was a question of the breeding of a race [is there still an aristocracy today, one asks?] - thus of the maintenance of a fixed, definite type of ruling man: man and woman were sacrificed to this point of view. It is obvious that love was not the first consideration here; on the contrary! And not even that measure of good will that is a condition of bourgeois marriage. What was decisive  was the interest of the family, and beyond that - the class. We would shiver a little at the coldness, severity, and calculating clarity of such a noble concept of such of marriage as has ruled in every healthy aristocracy, ... we warm-blooded animals with sensitive hearts, we "moderns"! Precisely this is why love as a passion - in the great meaning of the word - was invented for the aristocratic world and in it, where constraint and privation were greatest -31

S: I don't understand. "Bourgeois"? – That's new to me. Where are you going with this?

A: As I said, some might say that you and "he" indoors are too in love with "Reason".

S: Too, in love with "reason"? Don't be so ridiculous! Most suffer from a dearth of it!

A: Even so, I would want to ask: might the hyperfetation of reason be a sign that the instincts have gone astray? Might reason and happiness be in-commensurable values? Might reason be a universal acid that once uncorked has the power to scour and shrivel the tender shoots of affection? Might human life only be possible, supportable, by means of the very illusions that unbridled "Reason" threatens to trample under-foot?

# CHEWING THE CUD

S: Tsk! All that money spent on your education? You mustn't mix your metaphors if you want me to keep up.

A: You know enough what I mean; human kind can stand little truth.

S: If there's anyone here threatening to drive a coach and horses through people's cherished beliefs, it has to be you my friend.

A: Me? I don't know about coach and horses, but I know about would be charioteers and I'm looking at one! Or, on second thoughts, is it a dark horse I see?

S: You can be so snide.

A: I thought I was being ironic. Like you were being about Hipparete and me? You don't recognize your own stock in trade? It's quite a weapon in your hands.

S: Weapon?

A: Now who's playing the ingénue?

S: I don't...

A: Don't! It lies at the heart of your modus operandi. It's there to view in all of Plato's dialogues. First you elicit consent for a spurious definition from your intended victims, and then you chase them up hill and down dale till they're in a state of total confusion, and willing to admit to the circus-master their ignorance of everything.

S: But didn't the oracle say that I was the wisest in that I readily admit to knowing least? 32

A: So you put it about. You're not denying the ironist affects a position of social superiority visa -a -vis his victims, I notice.

S: Come on, a bit of charity wouldn't come amiss. Freethinking comes with risks for someone from my station in life. Not all us have the insurance a silver spoon brings.33

A: Some might say rabble is what rabble does.

# CHEWING THE CUD

S: "Rabble?"

A: Plebeian then. Take your pick. Either way the aim appears to be to give the well born a bad conscience.

S: "Bad conscience"? Are you making these terms up as you go along?

A: Never mind for now. Let's go back to Reason.

S: Good idea. I know where I am with that.

A: But do you; all that crude psychology - the tripartite division; soul, spirit, appetites? Cave dwellers in search of the sun. As a formula; Reason + Virtue = Goodness.34.

S: What's wrong with that as a summun bonum - an ideal to live by? Don't forget Beauty, for where Goodness is so, too, is Beauty.

A: And that you…No forget that.

S: Forget what?

A: I don't want to give offense… but that you should be the one to espouse all this?

S: Oh, because I'm plug ugly you mean. Haven't I said often that it's the beauty within that matters, even with regard to your good self.

A: I don't want to rain on the parade, but isn't it just the case, politeness notwithstanding that…Well, … ugliness incites fear?

S: I'm not sure I like where this is going.

A: None of us do.

S: All very well for you. What was it Euripides said about you and the seasons? 35

A: To be taken with more than a pinch of salt. Anyhow. Ugliness? It incites fear. Fear of the three sentinels that guard the gates of Hades.

S: Hades, yes; three sentinels, no.

# CHEWING THE CUD

A: My lame attempt at being literary: Fear of death, oblivion, and meaninglessness.

S: A sad wreath of floweriness, to be sure.

A: You see my point? Ugliness is a coarse and brutal reminder of what lies ahead for each and every one of us should we live long enough. Ugliness is implacably associated in the mind of creatures like us with decrepitude, decline, disease, and dissolution.

S: You sound like Silenus. "Miserable, ephemeral race, children of hazard and hardship, why do you force me to say what it would be much more fruitful for you not to hear? The best of all things is something entirely outside your grasp: not to be born, not to be, to be nothing. But the second best thing for you - is to die soon". Surely it is our task to provide hope? How else is life to be redeemed?

A: This is something the Dionysian man shares with Hamlet: both have truly seen into the essence of things, they have understood, and action repels; for them action can nothing in the eternal essence of things.

S: Hamlet?

A: A character in the future; don't worry about him now.

S: Ok. but what about those slings and arrows of outrageous misfortune? 36

A: Ha, ha.

S: What's so funny?

A: You even sound like him.

S: Him?

A: Hamlet.

S: The calamity of a long life; you get to speak with many voices.37

A: Stop! You're doing it again.

S: No I'm not. I was alluding to Plato's treatment of me: "To be, or, not to be"? 38 That's what he said to me last time I saw him. He's thinking about killing me off, you know? Not literally, of course. Still, it sent quite a chill down my spine: like someone walking over your grave.

A: Could we? Silenus?

S: Of course. Yes, yes. I've not forgotten - the slings and arrows? What's your answer?

A: Art.

S: "Art"! Ha, ha. It'll be you who's the death of me.

A: Not just any old art; tragic art; the Hellene is saved by art, and through art, life has saved him for itself.39Perhaps art is even a necessary corollary and supplement of science? 40.

S: Its just such nonsense that has impelled Plato and I to call for the prohibition of the arts. Are we not heard?

A: Indeed. It ...the influence of Socrates ... again and again leads to the regeneration of art.41

S: It does?

A: The sublime metaphysical delusion of yours is the very instinct that leads science ever again to its own limits - at which it must necessarily give way to art.42

S: Am I being flattered or flogged here?

A: In Socrates the one turning point ... of world history...For if one were to think of this whole incalculable sum of energy ... as not employed in the service of knowledge ... then the instinctive lust for life would probably have been so weakened in general wars of annihilation ... that suicide would have become the general custom, and individuals might have experienced the final remnant of a sense of duty when ...strangling their parents and friends.43

# CHEWING THE CUD

S: Zeus! That's one hell of a back-hander! Curiously that puts me in mind of that stranger in the agora who took one look at me and declared I was a cave of all the lusts.

A: What did you say?

S: "You know me, sir". What else could I have said?

A: A sword is always double-edged. The philosopher, as a necessary man of to-morrow ... always had to find himself, in opposition to his today ...Hitherto all these extraordinary promoters of man, who are called philosophers, and who have rarely felt themselves to be friends of wisdom, but rather disagreeable fools and dangerous question marks, have found their ... hard, unwanted, inescapable task ... in being the bad conscience of their time. By applying the knife vivisectionally to the very virtues of the time they betrayed their own secret: to know of a new greatness of man.
Each time they have uncovered how much hypocrisy, comfortableness, letting oneself go and letting oneself drop ... were concealed under the most honoured type of their contemporary morality...44

S: Couldn't have put it better myself. Nobody is, or ever was, as keenly aware of this predicament as I. We must speak of this further. Even so - with reference to Silenus - this no cause for "the glass is half-empty" attitudes. One must look to the future; that's why I'm an optimist. With the aid of reason we can do...

A: "We can do"? That's politics, not philosophy. More to the point it is asceticism writ large. One more of those shadows cast by the death of God.

S: Are you sure that its not the sun talking? It's getting hot and you're rambling.

A: I'm doing no such thing. If you could wait a couple of millennia, you'd see.

S: Point made.

A: No: seriously. Just as the religious believer defames the here and now by living in hope of some heavenly reward, the progressive of the future will likewise sacrifice his, or her, present for the sake of future generations, or some future better society. Believe me it'll be the stock in trade of politicians, and many another improver.

# CHEWING THE CUD

S: That sounds rather jaundiced, pessimistic even.

A: Not to those like I. Our pessimism: the world does not have the value we thought it had, [...]. Initial result: it seems worth less; that is how it is experienced initially. It is only in this sense that we are pessimists; i.e. in our determination to admit this revaluation to ourselves without any reservation, and to stop telling ourselves tales - lies - the old way. This is precisely how we find the pathos that impels us to seek new values. In sum: the world might be more valuable than we used to believe; we must see through the naiveté of our ideals, and while we thought we accorded it the highest interpretation, we may not have given our human existence a moderately fair value.45

S: I tell you, again; you'll be the death of me.

A: One always kills the thing one loves.46

S: Say that again!

A: No. You'll only twist it. Let's seek some shade by taking a stroll in the forest. We can't have you getting palpitations.

S: Too late, I always get palpitations when I'm with you.

A: You've gone quiet.
S: All that talk of death. Recently, consciousness of my mortality has become an ever- present thought. Hard to shake off, I'm down to eight now.

A: Eight?

S: Teeth. I used to think I'd lose them doing battle in the agora, but they seem to be leaving of their own accord. Where will I be without my winning smile?
[Sings]. Will you still love me when I'm old and losing my hair?

A: "Sans teeth, sans eyes, sans taste, sans everything". 47

S: You can be a right bastard sometimes. Have you no pity? And don't think, just because I didn't go to school, I didn't recognize that rhetorical figure you used to twist the knife! You've been spending altogether too much time with those scheming, shape shifting, Sophists.

# CHEWING THE CUD

A: Money well spent, considering the alliteration in which you've couched your clumsy calumny.48

S: Don't try to get clever with me you little...

A: But, I'm not anymore!

S: One could find oneself wishing you didn't exist.

A: That's better. As to the lack of pity, I'm at a bit of a loss. Your master doesn't rate it highly.

S: How many more times? He's not my master! 'Sides an argument from authority just begs further questions about the provenance of the said authority.

A: Pity, in so far as it induces suffering ... is a weakness as is any losing oneself to a harmful affect.49

S: I know for a fact that isn't Zopyrus' view.50

A: True, but one repays a teacher badly if one doesn't learn to think for oneself, don't you think? 51

S: Just because it's the fashion of the day, it doesn't automatically follow that it always the right thing to do.

A: Pah! The moral fashions.... These great wonders of classical morality - Epicurus, for example - did not know anything of the now customary glorification of thinking of others and living for others. In view of our moral fashion, one would have to call them flatly immoral; for they fought with all their energies for their ego and against sympathy for others [especially sympathy for their suffering and moral shortcomings]. Perhaps they would reply to us: "If have such a boring and ugly object in yourselves, by all means do think more of others than of yourselves". 52

S: Ha, ha. You can't help yourself can you? I've heard tell of men who've drowned in their own spittle. What are you advocating here - rank egoism?

A: No, but who anyway can avoid pursuing their interests?

S: There is no such thing as benevolence then.

A: Not all. However far a man may go in self-knowledge, nothing however can be more incomplete than his image of the totality of drives which constitute his being. He can scarcely name the cruder ones: their number and strength, their ebb and flow, their play and counter-play among one another, and above all the laws of their nutriment remain wholly unknown to him. This nutriment is therefore a work of chance: our daily experiences throw some prey in the way of now this, now that drive, and the drive seizes it eagerly, but the coming and going of these events as a whole stands in no rational relationship to the nutritional requirements of the totality of the drives...

One day recently at eleven o'clock in the morning in the morning a man suddenly collapsed right in front of me as if struck by lightening, and all the women in the vicinity screamed aloud; I myself raised him to his feet and attended to him until he recovered his speech - during this time not a muscle of my face moved and I felt nothing, neither fear nor sympathy, but I did what needed doing and went coolly on my way. Suppose someone had told the day before that at eleven o'clock in the morning a man would fall down beside me in this fashion - I would have suffered every kind of anticipatory torment, would have spent a sleepless night, and at the decisive moment instead of helping the man would perhaps have done what he did. For in the meantime all possible drives would have had time to imagine the experience and to comment upon it. - What then are our experiences? Much more that which we put into them than that which they already contain! Or must we go so far as to say: in themselves they contain nothing? To experience is to invent? -53

S: Let's not set two hares running at the same time. O.k. evidences enough of your own benevolence. Though, on second thoughts, is it that you responded without...? Oh never mind. Piety! I'm still not clear about what it is you're saying. Is your beef about the person displaying it or the object of his concern?

A: See! You must have been a dog, if not in this life then in another.

S: Well?

A: It's both. Pity often springs from ressentiment. Neurotics often feel that though all else is lost they at least have the one power, in spite of their weakness, the power to hurt.54Many a beggar would have starved without this power. Wherever responsibilities have been sought it was the instinct of revenge that sought. This instinct of revenge has so mastered mankind in the course of millennia that the whole of metaphysics, psychology, conception of history, but above all morality, is impregnated with it. As far as man has thought, he has introduced the bacillus of revenge into things. "Sweeter than honey" - old Homer called it: revenge that is.55

S: But nonetheless one does right by the beggar?

A: Does one? If one does good merely out of pity, it is oneself one really does good to, and not the other. Pity does not depend on maxims but upon affects; it is pathological. The suffering of others infects us; pity is an infection.56

S: Isn't that rather hard-hearted? That we identify with the suffering of others is surely what makes us human?

A: We come to the crux, I think. Psychological hedonism. The idea that we are "pleasure seeking: pain avoiding creatures".

S: And consequently suffering is viewed as an evil. Couldn't have put better myself. Now you're talking!

A: But that's the mistake; a prime example of the tyranny of antithetical values that I referred to earlier. You remember?

S: It's the short-term memory I'm having difficulty with, not the long term.
A: Irony?

S: An occupational hazard, I'm afraid, when you're conversing with me. Anyway, indulge me. Refresh my memory.

A: The idea that those opposite values are so radically different as to be underivable from one another. That's rather inelegantly put, but you know what I mean? The good cannot be derived from the bad, and vice versa.

S: Good and evil we must come back to.

A: Yes, if only to get beyond the pair of them.

S: I beg pardon?

A: A joke.

S: A joke? These are serious matters.

# CHEWING THE CUD

A: Oh, for pity's sake!

S: This is another of your jokes?

A: Serious, right? Let me try again, with different words.

S: Good. That first attempt didn't sound like you somehow.

A: Almost all the problems of philosophy ... pose the same form of question....: how can something originate out of its opposite, for example rationality in irrationality, the sentient in the dead, logic in un-logic, disinterested contemplation in covetous desire, living for others in egoism, truth in error? Metaphysical philosophy has hitherto surmounted this difficulty by denying that the one originates out of the other and assuming the more highly valued thing has a miraculous source in the very kernel and being of the "thing in itself". 57

S: "Thing in itself"?

A: Just a piece of cant.

S: "Cant"?
A: "Kant" with a "K", actually, we'll probably have to come back to him.

S: But doesn't Parmenides deny the possibility of change and motion. Doesn't he, in fact, argue that there is only unchanging being. Isn't this what defines our calling: our commitment to the absolute value of "truth", as manifest in our determination to isolate "being" from "becoming", "appearing", "seeming". Isn't this the very kernel of Plato's endeavour? 58

A: Indeed. His Idealist construction stands like a colossus over philosophical thought and will for centuries to come.59 Even our will to truth. An egregious error: - this pervasive attachment to dualism? "How could anything originate out of its opposite, for example, truth out of error; or the will to truth out of the will to deception; or selfless deeds out of selfishness? Or the pure and sun like gaze of the sage out of lust"?

S: More sarcasm?

A: Not intentionally. Let me finish. Where was I?

30

# CHEWING THE CUD

S: Lust.

A: Oh yes. "Such origins are impossible; whoever dreams of them is a fool, indeed worse; the things of the highest value must have another, peculiar origin - they cannot be derived from this transitory, seductive, deceptive, paltry world, from this turmoil of delusion and lust. Rather from the lap of Being, the intransitory, the hidden god, the "thing in itself" - there must be their basis, and nowhere else."

S: And what pray is wrong with that? Doesn't Parmenides say, "One cannot think of what is not"?

A: This way of judging constitutes the typical prejudgment and prejudice which give away the metaphysicians of all ages.60 As to Parmenides, we are at the other extreme; we might well reply: "What can be thought of must certainly be a fiction". 61

S: But are you not caught here in a contradiction of your own making? I've heard tell that in your view that "all life is based on semblance, art, deception, points of view, and the necessity of perspectives and error". 62 If so, it seems a forlorn hope to wish for truth within this life.

A: But that would be to suppose these antithetical values are distinct and discrete. What if they are co-mingled? Were this supposition rejected it might be said he who does betrays his own "hostility to life"' a metaphysical desire to negate "the world of life, nature, and history" in favour of "another world", which, however, remains "indemonstrable."63

S: "A deft piece of footwork" as the wrestler would say. It's one of his idiosyncrasies. The sport seasons his conversation.64

A: You ask me which of the philosophers' traits are really idiosyncrasies; their lack of historical sense; their hatred of the very idea of becoming. They think that they show their respect for a subject when they de-historicize it, sub specie aeterni - when they turn it into a mummy. All that philosophers have handled for thousands of years have been concept mummies; nothing real escaped their grasp alive, [...] Death, change, old age, as well as procreation and growth, are to their minds objections - even refutations. Whatever is does not become; whatever becomes is not ...Now they all believe, desperately even, in what has being. But since they never grasp it, they search for reasons why it is kept from them. "There must be mere appearances, there must be some deception which prevents us from perceiving that which has being: where is the deceiver? -We have found him," they cry ecstatical-ly; "It is the senses! These senses, which are so immoral in other ways too, deceive us concerning the true world". Moral: fixe let us free ourselves from the deception of the senses, from becoming, from history, from lies; - history is nothing but the faith in the senses, faith in lies. Moral: let us say No to all those who have faith in the senses, to all the rest of humanity; they are all "plebs". Let us be philosophers! Let us be mummies! Let us represent mono-theism by adopting the expression of a gravedigger! And above all, away with the body, this wretched idee fixe of the senses, disfigured by all the fallacies of logic, refuted, even impossible, although it is impudent enough to behave as if it were real!"65

S: That was said with a fine passion. Do you know that your nostrils flare...

A: Don't start that!

S: If you had nostrils like mine, you'd learn to take compliments with a good grace. Anyway, I was just buying myself some time. Once again there are an hundred and one questions one might pursue.

A: As the saying goes "a dog does not stop to scratch its fleas when its hunting".
S: Lest I lose the scent in all that verbiage, lets track back to pity. I'm sure your claims about antithetical values were meant to be illustrative of some point in this regard. And if I'm not mistaken this bears on the issue of -what did you call it? - Psychological hedonism?

A: Exactly. We treat suffering as an unmitigated evil. This is far from the case. It is often the spur that goads us to greater efforts and greater success.

S: So speaks the general, but then as flies are to wanton boys, so are the rank and file.

A: You mistake me for another. Not so long ago you claimed people are divided about me. And perhaps for the very reason I regard giving battle as a last resort. Armies are organizations of ill omen - utilize for too long a period and the result is calamity.

S: A far cry from the view of Zopyrus, - at least the non- militaristic sentiments.66 Now there was a pessimist of the first rank.

A: I didn't know you knew him.

32

# CHEWING THE CUD

S: I don't, or should I say, I didn't - only by reputation. A bit of a recluse and something of a misogynist, so I hear. Xanthippe ran into him once. Did a bit of cleaning at the palace where he was living. You know what he said? "Here comes the harbinger of sorrows". Xanthippe was of a mind to kick him down the stairs67 - all that stuff about suspension of the will as the only way of avoiding suffering - depressing. No wonder he had a face like a wet weekend. What was that other bon mot? "Life is like a business whose receipts did not match its expenses" or something like that? 68

A: Sounds about right. But the economics isn't the half of it. He's ultimately a moralist, like you!

S: What are you saying?

A: I'm saying he looked into the abyss - which nobody hitherto after us Greeks has dared do.

S: He, too, was another who lived posthumously?
A: As you implied, he kept himself to himself. Like you, in his own way, he drew a judgment on the world. Stepped back from the brink and declared "nothing is more certain than that generally speaking, it is the grievous sin of the world which gives rise to the manifold and great suffering of the world; whereby is meant not any physical-empirical connection but a metaphysical one."70

S: Say again "brink"?

A: He clearly saw that becoming has no goal, and, second, that there is no grand unity in which we as individuals can immerse ourselves as in an element of supreme value.71He baulked at what he saw. Passed sentence on this whole world of becoming as a deception and [invented] a world beyond it, a true world.72 Here we have the pessimism that leads to nihilism; pessimism that rejects the optimism that is part and parcel of the idea of an ordered universe. A pessimist, a world-denier and God-denier, who comes to a halt before morality and plays the flute, affirms *laede neminem* [harm no one] morality: what? - is that actually - a pessimist? 73

S: A flute player as well as a God-denier. I didn't know that. He has much to answer for in respect of your own education. If only I'd got to you sooner. The arts are forever corrupting the senses.

A: Don't be absurd. I'm more than capable of thinking for myself. 'Sides, I make it a matter of honour not to hide beneath the robes of priests.74Come to that, I deign to claim a daemon.

S: Prudence might, nonetheless, suggest you take a leaf out of Harpocrates' book.75

A: She might?

S:" Fools do by compulsion what they could have done by choice, but those with discretion immediately see what must be done sooner or later, and do it with pleasure and to their credit". 76

A: [sings] "I don't care anymore, I don't care anymore
        It's a secret I can't tell
        It's a wish down a well
        I don't care anymore, I don't care anymore."77

S: What are you saying? A pill can make your breath smell sweet, and to know how to sell air is one of life's subtlest skills. Most things are bought with words, and they're enough to achieve the impossible. All our dealings are in air, and the breath of a prince greatly inspires. So your mouth should always be full of sugar to sweeten your words so that they taste good even to your enemies. The only way to be loved is to be sweet natured.78

A: Oh, my sweet Lord! Next you'll be telling me all you need is love.79 Do you know that when Louise D'Epinay [you won't have heard of her, before you ask] - anyway when she set about educating herself she soon discovered two important lessons, which you won't find in any curriculum even today. First, that it is a mistake to judge your friends in terms of how kind they are to you. Second, that the great mistake she had been making with her friends and herself was in giving preference to their fancies, with no thought to her own wishes. "Owing to that little system", she says "I found that half of my 'friends' were in fact my masters. To have a will of my own seemed to me to be a crime. I was doing a thousand unsuitable things with a willingness that was equally unsuitable .I was a perpetual victim, inspiring gratitude in no one". And what does this marvellous woman resolve? Thereafter to dare to be herself; to have no regard for the caprices of others; to do only what she prefers, and " feel marvellously the better for it". 80 Doesn't it make you heart sing?

S: Not especially. By all means marry. If you get a good wife, you'll become happy; if you get a bad one, you'll become a philosopher.81

A: Ha, ha.

S: Least said; the perils of marrying a younger woman? My knees; I'm going to have a sit down soon; they are not what they once were.

A: And this has to do with Xanthippe how?

S: No, that's my back, and, believe me, you don't want to know.

A: On that we can agree!

S: Suffice to say, she gets very insistent when her so-called friends have plied her with drink.

A: No more! I need a clear head if I'm to think.

S: Me, too. Thoughts about higher things seem, all of a sudden, attractive.

A: Oh, yes. I was about to give expression to my reverence for my first and only educator, the great, Zopyrus.... I was already deep in the midst of moral scepticism and destructive analysis, that is to say in the critique and likewise the intensifying of pessimism as understood hitherto.82

S: Critique? Intensify?

A: Put it this way. Your optimism, not to say your morality, is rooted in your faith that ultimately the world has an order? Yes? Harm no one?   .

S: Yes. No man knowingly does wrong.83

A: Pessimism recognizes that becoming aims at nothing, and achieves nothing, and pessimism does not sit in judgment of this condition...84 what is the result? The innocence of becoming is restored.85

S: Say again. Where does Zopyrus go wrong?

# CHEWING THE CUD

A: He demonstrates that life lacks order, but he doesn't follow through. He baulks at the last fence and seeks a transcendental and uses morality as a means for condemning life in its entirety. Insofar as we [continue to] believe in morality we pass sentence on existence.86But a part cannot sit in judgment of a whole?

S: All very well for some, but what about the vast majority? Such pessimism is surely a counsel of despair?

A: The weak perish of it.87 One grants the reality of becoming as the only reality, forbids oneself every kind of clandestine access to after worlds and false divinities -but cannot endure this world though one does not want to deny it.88

S: Sometimes the way you speak in italics makes my blood boil! Must you rub your opponents nose in it? Have you any idea of how high-handed and arrogant you come across as? Some of what you say makes the blood run cold!

A: Of a sudden, you seem to be blowing all hot and cold. Don't you know when superior and subordinate are in harmony, equally brave in battle, that that makes for strength?

S: And clever remarks, deliberately designed to wrong foot people, don't help. The idea of, nay the necessity for, a "noble lie", was not the result of some naivety regarding the human condition - though I grant you its more Plato's idea than mine.89 Reason and good sense will always have the trump cards in any argument, but only a fool would think they constitute the well-springs of human affairs. Not my "official" view, I know, but one I'm driven to behind closed doors with Xanthippe. In fact, on occasion I find myself wondering if that ingrate Metic, Aristotle, might be the ideal guardian. But what do I know? You're not even listening are you?

A: Ripeness is all.90

S: Ripeness is all?

A: One doesn't see or hear the truth, unless one is already receptive to it. You'd think your "conversations" would have alerted you to that?

S: One of Plato's conceits. Lord knows, I told him often enough that this was the everyday reality of agora argy-bargey.

## CHEWING THE CUD

A: As to your beloved Xanthippe, I think you should ask of any woman's love and sympathy - is there anything more egotistic? - And if they sacrifice themselves, their honour, their reputation, to whom do they sacrifice themselves? To the man? Or is it not rather to an unbridled urge? - These desires are just as selfish even if they please others and implant gratitude -
To what extent this sort of hyperfetation of one valuation can sanctify everything else! 91

S: My first thought is of misogyny.

A: If it is, then set aside some time for a second. In the meantime though demolition is not an end in itself, it is a necessary prelude to reconstruction. Pessimism in the hand of the strongest becomes simply a hammer and an instrument with which one can make oneself a new pair of wings.92

S: That sought of purple prose might soften certain feminine hearts, but it cuts no ice with me.

A: And there I was thinking you thought me hot stuff? What a person is begins to betray it self when his talent declines – when he ceases to show what he can do, don't you think? Talent is also finery; finery is also a hiding place.93

S: Its cruel to tease!

A: That's something we can return to - cruelty" that is, not "teasing" - however tempting. Meantime let's see if we can forge a better understanding of strength and weakness in respect of pessimism.

S: You're a real shit you know; albeit a beguiling one, if that's not a contradiction in terms? Returning to things I'll accept; just so long as we are not moving in circles.

A: Ha, ha. I'm all for the eternal return. That's my view in a nutshell. You never know. The world might be far more valuable than we used to believe.94

S: Laugh, if you will? How's that going to happen if you've ruled universal solutions out of court?

A: Art. The great seduction to life, the great stimulant to life.95

## CHEWING THE CUD

S: I'm flabbergasted, - I mean incredulous. My father was a sculptor you know?

A: Word has it he was a stonemason.

S: That was his day job. In his head he was an undiscovered Phidias.96. Forever planning a new project; none of it ever came to fruition - well, rarely. He was a complete waste of space, according to my mother. If it hadn't been for her mid-wifery we'd have starved.97Had she met him at birth, she used to say, she'd made sure he'd been exposed and saved herself a lot of heartache! He spent a lot of time in taverns "coaching" his "models".

A: Not a marriage made in heaven, then? How come you didn't follow his trade?

S: Said, it was no use trying to cut against the grain. Reckoned that I didn't have an artistic bone in my body. I remember once in my teens trying to impress him with some poetry. I fancied myself as a possible Aesop.

A: That figures. What did he reckon?

S: "Moralistic hogwash!" Even now my cheeks still feel the sting of his derision.


A: Strange how many men end up marrying their mothers, don't you think?

S: I'm sorry? That was apropos? Did I miss something?

A: You always will, my friend. We knowers are unknown to ourselves, and for good reason: how can we ever hope to find what we have never looked for? There is a sound adage that runs: "Where a man's treasure lies, there lies his heart." Our treasure lies in the beehives of our knowledge. We are perpetually on way thither, being by nature, winged insects and honey gathers of the mind. The only thing that lies close to our heart is the desire to bring something home to the hive. As for the rest of life - so-called "experience" who among us is serious enough for that? Or has time enough? When it comes to such matters, our heart is simply not in it - we don't even lend our ear. Rather, as a man divinely abstracted and self-absorbed into whose ears the bell has just drummed the twelve strokes of noon will suddenly awake with a start and ask himself what hour has actually struck, we sometimes rub our ears after the event and ask ourselves, and at a loss, "What have we really experienced?" - or rather, "Who are we really?" And we recount the twelve tremu-lous strokes of experience, our life, our being, but unfortunately count wrong. The sad truth is that we remain necessarily strangers to ourselves, we don't understand our substance, we must mistake ourselves; the axiom, "Each man is farthest from himself", will hold for us to all eternity.  Of ourselves we are not "knowers" .98

S: Where did that come from?

A: Just something I wrote a while back. Something you said put me in mind of it. The unresolved dissonances between the characters and dispositions of the parents continue to resound in the nature of the child and constitute the history of his inner sufferings.99

S: What are you saying? I feel suddenly panicked. Is it all in vain? Am I in vain?

A: Pessimism? Morality? Ignorance? How many roads must a man walk down before you can call him a man?

S: Seven.

A: No, it's a rhetorical question.

S: Ok, eight then. It's some sort of guessing game, yes?

A: Do you even remember what rhetorical means?

S: Do I know what 'rhetorical' means? 100 What's your point?

A: That when it comes to having to take one's leave of this life, if he refuses to learn his lessons, even an ironist might find himself asking that a cock be sacrificed to Asclepius.101

S: Are we now reduced to making sick jokes?

A: Oh have your own way then!

S: I will indeed! All these digressions haven't thrown me off the scent. I'm still waiting to hear about your preposterous claims for the restorative powers of art. From what I heard, that sepulchral rogue of yours - Zopyrus - thought of it as a disinterested contemplation. A somewhat negative view, if you ask me.

A: How right you are, but probably for the wrong reasons.

39

# CHEWING THE CUD

S: Well you spent more than enough time closeted with the saturnine sage to know. Enlighten me.

A: We haven't got all day. To do him justice would take us too far afield.

S: The bare essentials will do, if only because his influence might be greater than you let on.102

A: I like to think of myself as something of a one off, if that doesn't sound too ...

S: See! That's just what...

A: All right, all right. Aesthetic pleasure for him - like any other pleasure for that matter - was essentially negative.

S: Oh my poor child! How did you survive him?

A: Listen. Don't be in such a hurry to dismiss what you don't understand. Losing yourself in a work of art was nothing more than a temporary relief from everyday suffering, - parole from the prison-house of our subjectivity.

S: Like a get out of jail free card, then?

A: Don't be facetious! It was you who wanted to know. "On the occurrence of an aesthetic appreciation, the will thereby vanishes from consciousness... This is the origin of that satisfaction and pleasure which accompany the apprehension of the beautiful... To become a pure subject of knowing means to be quit of oneself."103

S: You are quoting?

A: Yes; more or less.

S: Interesting. Pity our paths didn't cross.

A: Think yourself lucky. He wasn't renown for his patience.

S: To think I would deliberately try anyone's patience!

A: Take it from me cat and dog.

# CHEWING THE CUD

S: You do like to bring people to heel.

A: Discipline means organization, a chain of command, and logistics.

S: From where I stand it's not your most winning trait; another of those militaristic traits, no doubt? Have you noticed your jokes are always at the expense of others, and cruelly so - but never directed at yourself?

A: Not true; the whole of Part IV of "Zarathustra"? No? Then will you listen to yourself man? "Heaven and earth are not humanistic - they regard the myriad beings as straw dogs". I might say the same of a sage, but I'd probably be wasting my breath. Here's something else instead you'll find hard to swallow then. "Optimism", he - Zopy -used to say, "is not only a false but also a pernicious doctrine...; everybody then believes he has the most legitimate claim to happiness and enjoyment. If, as usually happens, these do not fall to his lot, he believes that he suffers an injustice". 104

S: That'd dampen anyone's mood.

A: But do you get it? Optimism, faith in reason and rationality, progressivism, - the lingua franca - of every soapbox orator; they demand we see our lives as a project or - what's the current cliché? – oh yes, a "journey" with success and happiness as everyone's entitlement. Pessimism rejects the narrative of historical progress that underpins this outlook. Whilst it cannot assure us of happiness, it assuages the unhappiness that optimism blithely seeks to generate and guarantee.

S: What did your man counsel, then?

A: Resignation. "It really is the greatest absurdity to try turn this scene of woe and lamentation into a pleasure resort..."105

S: "Pleasure resort"? What's one of those when it's at home?

A: An away from home, actually; time off, for good behaviour; a binge in the sun for the slaves of the future.

S: And that's progress? It's enough to give you second thoughts. Anyway you were saying, or rather Zopyrus was?

# CHEWING THE CUD

A: Yes. "Whoever takes a gloomy view regards this world as a kind of hell and is accordingly concerned only with procuring for himself a small fireproof room; such a man is much less mistaken". 106

S: There! I was right all along .He locked you up! For the best of intentions, I'm sure, but never the less? How did I know that? We must be simpatico, you and I.

A: Ha, ha. In your dreams!

S: In my dreams; most certainly!

A: Come on now! Let's stick with quotidian reality - you know, where everyone knows his or her place? The point I'm labouring to make is that for Zopyrus his "eudemonology" - if I might borrow one of the Metic's terms - is directed at maximizing freedom by reducing the opportunities for the growth of unhappiness.107 As the will is a desiring will, always thirsting for more?

S: Yes, I get it; happiness through peace of mind. He puts me in mind of those young Turks who style themselves as Stoics.

A: Hmm, they're not that far apart in some respects.
S: Did you know some of these young Turks list me as a key influence? See, not everyone sees me as Plato's "go-fer"? I might yet be a founder of schools, or do you consider me to be a one off - your very own cupcake?  Ha, ha, - just joshing. Seriously though, they have mistaken me for one of them.

A: Zopyrus knows that. He acknowledges that "the Stoic ethics is originally and essentially not a doctrine of virtue, but merely a guide to the rational life, whose end and aim is happiness through peace of mind. Virtuous conduct appears in it, so to speak, only by accident, as means, not as end". 108

S: Exactly so. Not so much a moral theory, as a eudemonia with moral consequences. That wouldn't do for me at all, but then neither does your take on all this.

A: It doesn't? Why haven't you said anything?

S: In part I love listing to you talk, and..

A: And the other part?

# CHEWING THE CUD

S: Sometimes I prefer to give a man enough rope.

A: You might say we're all dead men walking.

S: You might well! I've held my peace because I know you're want to disown your mentors - Zopyrus, in particular. I think you've imbibed more at his knee than you care to admit. All that stuff he regurgitates in respect of Silenus for a start. Things are just not that black. There's suffering and suffering. Life, living, might be unsupportable were we aiming for some once and for all situation of perfect happiness. But who does? Even if this is denied us, I don't see that that means there are no silver linings.

What was it your man said about said about boredom? Ah, yes. "Willing and striving are its [man or animal] whole existence, and can be fully compared to an unquenchable thirst. The basis of all willing is need, lack, pain. If, on the other hand, it lacks objects of willing because it is at once deprived of them by too easy a satisfaction, a fearful emptiness and boredom comes over it, in other words its being and existence become an intolerable burden for it. Hence life swings like a pendulum to and fro between pain and boredom, and these two are in fact its ultimate constituents. This has been expressed very quaintly by saying that, after man has placed all the pains and torments in hell, there was nothing left for heaven but the boredom". 109

A: I think you've been a little disingenuous. You're obviously more familiar with Zopyrus than you've been letting on.

S: It was along time ago, and only the once. We were both very young.

A: I didn't mean "familiar" like that. I mean - meant - in that sense.

S: I know, I know. Best that we don't start by having secrets, I find.

A: "We"? There is no "we"! If you're not careful, there will be no you either; I'll take some of that metaphorical rope of yours and hang you with it!

S: You're shouting. You can't do anything much with metaphorical rope, save perhaps to show someone isn't a Stoic?

A: It's a bloody good job that you're an old man.

S: Yes, it's by far the best armour, and not just for warding off blows from the outside. Still - the rope? Just because a satisfaction isn't permanent, it doesn't follow that it's unreal. Furthermore not all states of lack are states of suffering; some are decidedly minimal - thing we commonly undergo in realizing some goal or other. As to boredom, it is surely only the smaller, or should I say emptier satisfactions that quickly produce satiation, and are a prelude to boredom? Nothing is said of those satisfactions that you, yourself, allude to - those that are the result of considerable effort and sacrifice. Knowing your man, he'd simply reiterate his claim that the will, because of its ceaseless striving, is barred from any true satisfaction: hence the need to smother it.110 The more interesting question here, by far though, is how much of this you have swallowed?

A: Have I not already referred to the gulf that separates Zopyrus and me?

S: Indeed you have. It's when you flexed your muscles and spoke of pessimism of "strength" and "weakness" that my head began to reel. I'll tell you why.

A: Yes. Do me a favour, why don't you?

S: Oh my, don't tell me a little gadfly can still tweak my big, brave boy? 111

A: Get on with it!

S: My thought is that both types understand pessimism in the same way?

A: What of it?

S: Well, if so, what distinguishes strength from weakness must be something to do with their respective characters?

A: Yes, and your point is?

S: Well, not to beat about the bush, you seem in be-labouring the distinction to be unconcerned, uninterested, in the truth or otherwise of the pessimist thesis, and even of the evidence that might be adduced for or against it?

A: So?

S: I know I keep saying "Well", but I don't know how else to say it. The suspicion has been growing for some time.

A: Well, spit it out then!

# CHEWING THE CUD

S: Are we, or, rather, are you actually talking philosophy here? Ever since your earlier remarks about rhetoric, I've been wondering. Wondering, that is, whether you've somehow fallen under their spell? - The Sophists that is. You seem to be more concerned about why people come to believe whatever it is that they believe, than the - well - provenance of what they believe?

A: What a nose you have - four eyes upon the world, not just two like mere mortals.112

S: No, I'm being serious. You can't be cavalier about this. Truth matters!

A: But what if "Truth" was a woman?

S: Now you're just being silly for the sake of it.

A: No: emphatically not.
"You've travelled so far; the wind in your face
  You think you've found that one special place
  Where your dreams will walk out in line
  And follow the course you've set in your mind
  It isn't going to be that way
  No, it isn't going to be that way"113

S: Huh?

A: Just lines from a song that have got stuck in my head.

S: Ain't that the truth? Insidious; why we would ban them.

A: But yes, supposing truth to be a woman - what? - Is the suspicion not well founded that all philosophers, when they have been dogmatists, have had little understanding of women? The gruesome earnestness, the clumsy importunity with which they have hitherto been in the habit of approaching truth have been inept and improper means for winning a wench? Certainly she has not let herself be won - and today every kind of dogmatism stands sad and discouraged.114

S: You're rambling. Sometimes I wonder whether "philosopher" is a misnomer in your case. Traditionally the philosopher was thought of as someone who made plain what was unclear, or else as someone able to justify what otherwise goes without challenge in the pell-mell of ordinary life, or else as a bringer of light of presuppositions, of what lies hidden. You seem to come at every thing from a tangent.

A: To be sure, to speak of spirit and the good as Plato did meant standing truth on her head and denying perspective itself, the basic condition of all life; indeed one may ask as a physician: "how could such a malady attack this loveliest product of antiquity, Plato? Did the wicked Socrates corrupt him after all? Could Socrates have been a corrupter of youth after all? And have deserved his hemlock?" - But the struggle against Plato ... 115

S: Heh! Wait up! What was that about hemlock? I heard about the rest of the tittle-tattle, but what's this about hemlock? 116

A: Sorry. Forget it! I'm getting ahead of myself.

S: Talk about the obscure followed by the still more obscure. You gave me a really nasty turn there. Just like someone had stepped on my grave; and not for the first time? What are you? A philosopher? A psychologist? Usually the former is seeking to answer the age-old questions: what is the meaning of life? Why are we here, and that sort of thing?
A: For me it is more a case of: can there be meaning in life? After all the wisest of men of all ages have judged alike: it is no good.117Our immediate conditions of existence, whatever their positive aspects, are subject to the greater dominion of the negative - suffering, change, loss, and, most implacable of all, death.

S: You are preaching to the converted. Why else would Plato and I be espousing a means of escape from the cave of earthly existence?

A: Ah, but it is my contention that all such views of existence as deficient, fallen, base, and therefore in need of correction, if not outright transcendence are ultimately the expression of a latent nihilism.

S: You can't be serious?

A: Never more so. And I intend my remarks to apply not just to the religious outlook, but also to any moral, rationalist, or scientific outlook that is orientated to, guided by similar ends.

S: Then we have a hard day's labour ahead of us.

## CHEWING THE CUD

A: Well there's obviously plenty of life in the old dog yet.

S: Not to say bite. And no, it didn't escape my attention. Let's hope you are a better physician than you are a philosopher.

A: I ought to shout "ouch!" but this isn't as black and white as you'd like to believe.

S: "Belief"? Again?

A: "I write this to you, dear..."

S: Really? It's me you're talking to?

A: I know that. It put me in mind of a letter I wrote to my sister the other day. It's pertinent. "I write this to you ... only in order to counter the most usual proofs of believing people, who invoke the evidence of their inner experiences and deduce from it the infallibility of their faith. Every true faith is indeed infallible; it performs what the believing person hopes to find in it, but it does not offer the least support for the establishing of an objective truth". 118
S: So there is objective truth after all. All is not lost.

A: Ah, yes. The will to truth, which is still going to tempt us to many a hazardous enterprise; that celebrated veracity of which all philosophers have hitherto spoken with reverence: what questions this will to truth has already set before us! What strange, wicked, questionable questions! It is already a long story - yet does it not seem as if it has only just begun? Is it any wonder we should at last grow distrustful, lose our patience, and turn impatiently away? That this sphinx should teach us too to ask questions? Who really is it that here questions us? What really is it in us that wants "the truth"? - We did indeed pause for a long time before the origin of this will - until finally we came to a complete halt before an even more fundamental question. We asked after the value of this will. Granted we want truth; why not rather untruth? And uncertainty? Even ignorance? - The problem of the value of truth stepped before us - or was it we who stepped before this problem? Which of us is Oedipus here? Which of us sphinx? It is, it seems, a rendezvous of questions and question marks. - And, would you believe it, it has finally almost come to seem to us that this problem has never before been posed - that we have been the first to see it, to hazard it? For there is an hazard in it and perhaps there exists no greater hazard.119

# CHEWING THE CUD

S: In truth, I'm forced to admit that all this pain and suffering is getting the better of me. Can we take a break?

A: To be sure. We can talk about other things, if you don't feel you're up to it.

S: Why you haughty...! We'll do no such thing; not whilst there is breath in my body. It's my knees! They're killing me. It's as if any shock absorbers I had have collapsed.

A: I'm sorry. I had no idea.

S: No, you bloody well haven't. For all your airy talk about suffering and mortality, what do you really know? It's all very abstract at your age. And that's another thing, it can make you very bad tempered.

A: Rather than rage at the dying of the light, don't you think you'd be employed thinking about dying at the right time? 120

S: Sometimes I wonder whether you are a bit on the autistic side. People's feelings seem to be a matter of some indifference to you. To me, there is no better in all this. Let's sit on those rocks by the stream.

A: Don't mistake me in this matter. I say rather, if you have a suffering friend, be a resting place for his suffering, but a hard bed, as it were...: thus will you profit him best. And if a friend wrongs you, then say: "I forgive you what you did to me; but that you have done it to yourself - how could I forgive that?" Thus speaks all great love: it overcomes even forgiveness and pity ... all great love is even beyond all pity: for it still wants to - create the beloved. "Myself I sacrifice to my love, and my neighbour as myself" - thus runs the speech of all creators. But all creators are hard.121

S: More from the military manual? "Tough love" - is that what they call it? What was that neighbour stuff? It sounded as if you were making some kind of sarcastic allusion?

A: Never mind that for now. Just consider in respect of it, how difficult it is to stay on one's own path. Always someone crying calls us aside; our eye rarely sees a case where it does not become necessary to leave our own task immediately.... There is even a secret seduction in all this..: just our "own path" is too hard ... and

48

too far from the love and gratitude of others ... we do not mind at all escaping it.122

S: Ah, we're back with pity. There are some other loose ends I'd like to address in a bit. Anyway for now, what's the drift here? That pity is not unselfish?

A: That's just how things are. All our conduct is selfish.

S: It is? You've a hell of a way of taking the wind from a man's sails.

A: I'll twist. Pity is our bad love of us. Love for the friend and for our own self-perfection is a superior love.

S: Warm words for me? Whatever next?

A: Let me just say that in man creator and creature are united...And ...your pity is for the "creature in man", for that which must be formed, broken, forged, torn, burned, ...and purged - for that which necessarily must and shall suffer. And our pity - do you not grasp for who our converse is, when it protests against your pity as against the worst of all pampering and weaknesses? Thus it is pity versus pity.123

S: Any friend of yours would have a hard taskmaster.

A: Well so be it. Leadership is a matter of intelligence, trustworthiness, humane-ness, courage, and sternness. To those human beings in whom I have a stake, I wish suffering, being forsaken, sickness, maltreatment, humiliation - I wish that they should not remain unfamiliar with profound self-contempt, the torment of self-mistrust, and the misery of the vanquished: I have no pity for them because I wish them the only thing that can prove today whether one is worth anything or not - that one endures.124

S: Fearsome words, yet somehow beguiling. I suspect if you wrote it out, it would read as a challenge for some. Why are you smiling? There'd be no rest for the wicked once you'd got your hooks into them.

A: I'd only be interested in the wicked!

S: Hmm, what's that say about me I wonder?

A: Ah, friendship - you have to wonder. In classical antiquity, friendship was experienced deeply and strongly ... In this consists their head start before us: we, on the other side, have developed idealized love between the sexes. All the great virtues of the ancients were founded on this, that man stood next to man, and that no woman could claim to be the nearest, the highest, or ... the only one he loved.... Perhaps, our trees do not grow so high because of the ivy and the vines.125

S: Of a sudden, I feel quite drowsy. That sounded rather like the theme of last night's symposium, but somehow you sounded as if you were speaking from far away.

A: It'll keep. Sleep, my friend.

# CHAPTER 2
**Timely Thoughts**

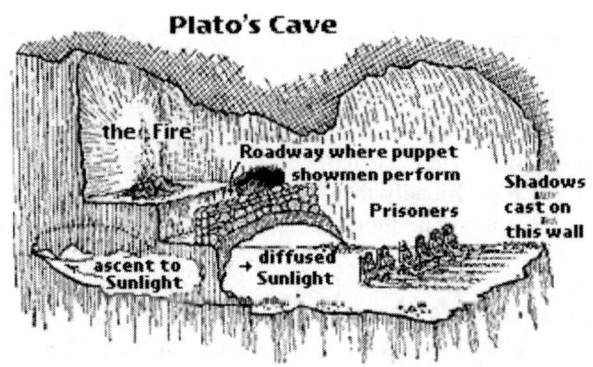

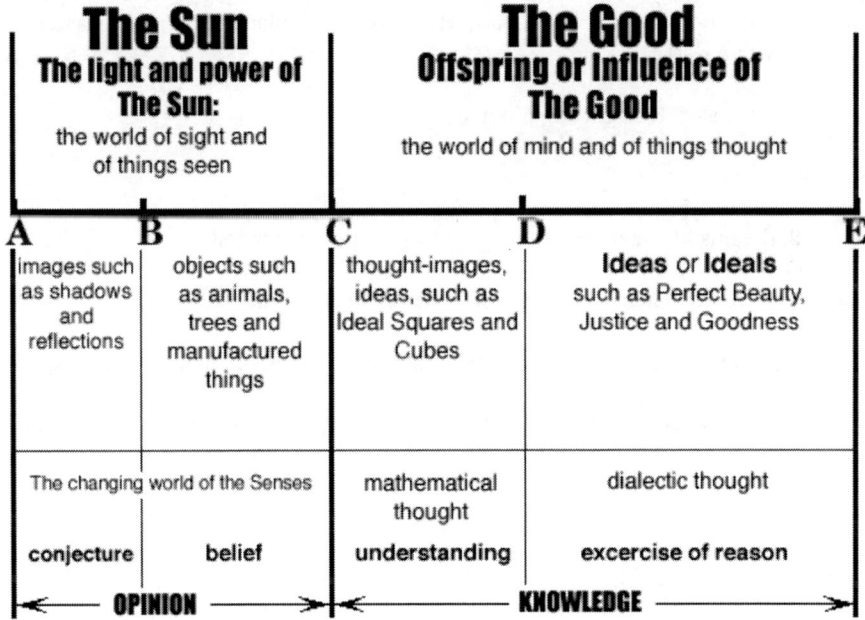

S: "No"!

# CHEWING THE CUD

A: So, you're awake? Are you all right? You look shaken.

S: I was dreaming. Wandering around in a big house, a palace I think, with a little boy. He was frightened. There were so many rooms and we couldn't find a way out. Suddenly we were in a room packed with people. They all started laughing and jeering when they saw us. I tried to speak, but as if by some signal they all put their hands over their ears. The boy, I was with, began to cry.

Anxious, I scanned the room for a friendly face. I saw Plato in the corner busily scribbling, as if he were taking notes. The thought hit me that he knew what was going on here, but when I shouted to gain his attention no words came. I was a mute. The crowd seeing this grew more hostile I caught sight of Xanthippe, who smiled contemptuously and tapped her forefinger against her temple - as if to say, "I told you all along you were mad; this is where it was bound to lead". Turning round I saw a raised bench at which sat three men sat with bowed heads, as if deliberating. Frantic, I began waving my arms to attract their attention. As those closest moved to pin my arms to my sides, the three raised their heads and began to crow mirthlessly. All three were cockerels capped with black cloth. That was when I awoke with a start.

A: What can I say? It might explain a lot.

S: How?

A: Well, dreams like that aren't going to do a lot for your mood.

S: Oh, very funny! Clearly nothing much has changed in the real world.

A: Sorry. That was flippant. Was the boy one of your sons - Lamprocles, perhaps?

S: No, I don't think so. See neither hide, nor hair of him. Loose rein. My father's ways coming out in me, I guess. Xanthippe thinks I'm as soft as cart-grease.

A: She wasn't much help to you in dream, if I might say?

S: No surprise there. She thinks I'd do better to stick with my own sort - no offense. And get a proper job, of course! No head, or patience, for the abstract. I've tried; believe you me. Thinks I ought to try living in the "REAL" world. Saying that's what you aspire to do one day just sends her into a fury.

# CHEWING THE CUD

A: She might have a point. I am afraid that old women are more sceptical in their secret heart of hearts than any man: they consider the superficiality of existence its essence, and all virtue and profundity is to them just a veil over this "truth", a very welcome veil over a pudendum - in other words, a matter of decency and shame, and no more than that.126

S: Never met anyone so literal minded. Anyway you wouldn't be taking her side if you heard what she says about 'your sort" as she puts it. She thinks Plato doesn't know his arse from his elbow: hence perhaps the "told you so" in the dream.

A: I wasn't taking sides. All women are subtle in exaggerating their weaknesses; they are inventive when it comes to weaknesses in order to appear as utterly fragile ornaments who are hurt even by a speck of dust. Their existence is supposed to make men feel clumsy, and guilty on that score. Thus they defend themselves against the strong and "the law of the jungle". 127

S: Subtlety and Xanthippe; now that would be an incongruous mix.

A: Only as a matter of tone, I think. Anyway your dream seems more about not being heard.

S: Odd that, don't you think? For as long as I can remember, I've had dreams about being suffocated; that and not being heard, or being able to make sense of things. My parents used to have the most frightful rows. Speaking of making sense reminds me; we've some unfinished business of our own.

A: Lord, give me strength.

S: See, sincerity is the key.

A: The key to what?

S: Having your prayers answered.

A: But I didn't say?

S: Then how did you know I was about to take you to task about "strength" and, not forgetting of course, "weakness".

A: Mad as a box of frogs.

# CHEWING THE CUD

S: You won't catch me on the hop.

A: Please! No more! Ask away, if you must.

S: Well you implied a while back that both groups saw your pessimism in the same way. Both agreed that the default position was a world in pain and suffering were humanity's lot. I think I get those who come at this from "strength". Of course, I'm assuming here that these are the sorts of brave souls who would like to play "follow my leader" with you.

A: That's a little on the pejorative side.

S: Yes, but you know who I mean. The "been there, done that, brought back the spoils" brigade. You know the "shit happens", "bring it on", "you won't see me back down" bunch.

A: And that's you eschewing rhetoric?

S: All I'm saying is that you can see the pay-off here in terms of a display of one's power, of one's self- control, in the face of adversity, that the majority would shy away from - at least the self-chosen kind. The problem is the pay-off for the "weak". What have they to gain?

A: One might say that for them pessimism offers a rationale for inaction. If things are bound to turn sour, why bother.

S: No. Actually that won't cut it. I'll tell you why. You've already implied, well admitted, that for you the merit of arguments for, or against, pessimism are bye the bye in terms of how people line up in respect of it. For you it's a more interesting question as to why people hold to a particular belief in a particular place or time.

A: Not that I'm disagreeing, but I didn't quite say all that.

S: It's ok. Really! It's a form of politeness some of us old-fashioned philosophers hold to; we like to make our adversary's argument as strong as possible....

A: Before you stick the knife in? Go on then. Don't sit there slavering.

# CHEWING THE CUD

S: Well regarding the character of the so-called "weak". If what defines them is their inaction, this will be so with all manner of beliefs. Take as an example, one diametrically opposite to pessimism - i.e. optimism. If it is for the "weak" always a matter of *que sera, sera* -whatever will be, will be - then things might well get better anyway. They might as well do nothing, once again.

A: All right, all right, I get it!

S: Not a problem for those who've passed the medical and enlisted in your band of friends, but even for them there's a further problem. If the pessimist is right, life is at best a poor thing. Sooner, or later, we must all stumble and fall. Death is as they say, a sexually transmitted disease. The best that can be hoped for is little victories; thin gruel, I know. Considered thus, most would surely conclude life was in vain - that pessimism was tantamount to nihilism?

A: I'll grant you that nihilism is a problem in itself, but can we put that to one side for now?

S: We'll come back to it though?

A: Yes, but let me address your immediate criticisms. I hadn't figured you as a hedonist.

S: But I'm not. You wouldn't catch me within a mile of Epicurus; I loathe the idea of gardening. And as to taking gardening leave ... well? 128

A: Ha, ha. Nonetheless a spade's a spade. Your assessment of pessimism proceeds from a hedonistic standpoint - in terms of the pleasure or pain to be had from it. Zopyrus proceeds in a like manner; it's just that the miserable old fart - forget that, its unkind - was always inclined to emphasize the painful aspects.

S: So? What are you proposing here?

A: Something I mentioned earlier; that we forsake psychological hedonism, and cleave instead to a different principle: the will to power. It is this will to power that enables the strong to affirm a pessimistic view of life, precisely because suffering is not - for them - the ultimate evil. It is in overcoming pain and difficulty that one experiences one's power. For my money, the strong actually seek out situations that will continuously test their power. We'll, no doubt, touch on it again, but it is the strong that seek beauty in the most inhospitable of places. Why else am I here with you?

S: But this is, by common consent, a pleasant wooded vale.
A: Now who's being stolid?

S: Zeus! Another of your backhanded compliments, I suppose. It must have driven poor Hipparete to distraction. How on earth did she know when you're coming on to her? Having married for love, at least Xanthippe knows where she stands with me.

A: Does she indeed? Many so-called love-matches, it seems to me, have error for their father and need for their mother.129 Your trouble is that you're unlikely to see any natural beauty outside of a window box!

S: I'll try to ignore that. Even if I grant you the plausibility of your case in respect of the strong...

A: What doesn't kill you; makes you stronger in the end.130

S: Hmm, but what debilitates you might weaken you so badly that... Anyway, you're still to tell how the weak fare in this brave new world of yours?

A: Trust you to worry about the under-dog.

S: Well, if this will to power is a universal principle it must apply to them too.

A: Quite so, but they are unlikely to acknowledge it. Most of the time they will cling to hedonistic views. Not just, I should hasten to add, because of laziness or a lack of drive, but rather because they want to avoid having to struggle. In short, embracing hedonism exempts them from having to accept a standard of value, namely power, in light of which they would be judged as having little worth.

S: A harsh creed, some might say.

A: My humanity does not consist of sympathizing with men but in enduring my sympathy for them. My humanity is a perpetual self-overcoming.131 The most spiritual men, as the strongest, find their happiness where others would find their destruction: in the labyrinth, in hardness against themselves and others, in experiments. Their joy is self-conquest: asceticism becomes in them nature, need, and in-

56

stinct. Difficult tasks are a privilege to them; to play with burdens that crush others, a recreation. Knowledge - a form of asceticism. They are the most venerable kind of man: that does not preclude their being the most cheerful and kindliest.132

S: It doesn't?

A: Not at all; when the exceptional human being treats the mediocre more tenderly than himself and his peers, this is not mere courtesy of the heart - it is simply his duty.133 When people deserve reward, this should be duly noted even if you personally detest them. When people deserve punishment, this should not be foregone even if they are close to you.

S: That's a strange word to be coming out of your mouth - duty?

A: Is it really? My chosen profession is all about duty. The people are the basis of a country; food is the heaven of the people. Those who rule over others should respect this and be sparing. A wise general always seeks to feed off the enemy. Have you been paying attention? Surely duty means: wanting a goal not for the sake of something else but for its own sake? 134 A man wants to be gracious for its own sake, but only the few, the most spiritual men may represent happiness, beauty, and graciousness on earth, and in them alone graciousness is not a weakness.135

S: Hmm.

A: Is that it? Can we put Pollyanna to bed and move on?

S: Who she? 136

A: Never mind; the eternally optimistic, eponymous, heroine of a series of novels, which became known as "glad books". You look lost in thought. What is it?

S: Plato's trip to the court of that tyrant, Dionysius 137

A: If ever there was an exercise in hubris that was it. Dionysius as a would be philosopher-king - what was he thinking of? Plato, I mean. Somebody should have forewarned him; if a military operation goes on too long without accomplishing anything, - and don't tell me it wasn't a military operation - your rivals will begin to get ideas.

# CHEWING THE CUD

S: Between you and me? - I had my doubts, but that wasn't what I was pondering. Rather I was mulling over what you've been saying in respect of the story of Damocles. What's the lesson that Dionysius is trying to teach his envious courtier?

A: By giving him all that wealth, but obliging him to live beneath a sword held aloft by only single horsehair?

S: Yes. My thought is that the lesson is that happiness hangs by a thread. Least-ways that is the accepted take. The crown sits uneasily on the head and all that.138 This, though, if we follow your line of reasoning, is to tell it from Damocles' point of view - or at least what was his likely point of view. What if Dionysius knew all along what seizing and holding power entailed? For him, the goal was not to be counted in terms of the happiness that the acquisition that untold wealth might accrue? Perhaps this ran in his mind as a poor second to the exercise of power. If so, perhaps the lesson was that the obverse side of the exercise of power is the willingness to live with the fear that others will try to wrest it away for themselves?

A: Wow! Now you're cooking. We'll make a philosopher of you yet.

S: Heh, you cheeky pip-squeak! One: I didn't say I actually believed this to be the case; rather, in comradely spirit I was trying it out for size. Second, I want to reserve the right to dispute that this how philosophy should be done. 'Sides before you interrupted me, I was about to raise another question that might be thought to be begged by taking sides with Damocles, namely why does the "happiness thesis" - for want of a better title - come to predominate?

A: That'll do fine as a title. Now we come to the not so little matter of the herd mentality.

S: That again sounds horribly denigrating. Before you grant me another occasion to think twice about your views, let me flesh out my thought here. It has to do with religion, or rather some religions, so you might approve? My thought is that some religions are "religions of lament", like that of the Egyptians - Isis having lost her husband, Osiris. Among the Babylonians, it is Ishtar who laments the loss of Tammuz; here Aphrodite the loss of Adonis. The same story in other words; in every case the death of someone before their time, often as the result of injustice. The dead being seen as paying the ultimate price for those are left behind. Those left behind thinking they owe the dead a debt, indeed wanting those deceased to live again. What do these people seek if not expiation of their own guilty deeds? By attaching themselves to one who has allegedly died for them, by lamenting, they

58

caste themselves as persecuted, as victims too, in hope death will not claim them too - that death will not be final.139
A: That's amazing; prescient, in fact. Soon such religions will span the world: Christianity, Islam, and Buddhism. Don't frown and shake your head, I've already told you I'm a man of the future.

S: I was rather hoping you'd think my musings were all rubbish. As to the herd, I take it that these are one and the same as the weak?
No doubt there'll be time enough to come back to these unfortunates, but in the interim there is a final loose end from our initial conversation that I'd like you to address.

A: Fire away. What's your query?

S: About art? As you know, we...

A: That'll be the royal "We", or the two heads are better than one "we"?

S: If you please? It's a difficult subject.

A: Hmm, so very difficult that you cannot fine a place for it in your precious Republic.

S: True. But you'd have to concede that the present situation is insupportable; the inflation of the artist's knowledge, and the reverence that now accompanies their practice. I'm as much a fan as the next man of Homer, but to treat him as all wise - an authority upon carpentry and generalship, to name but two of his many accomplishments - well that's just ridiculous. It's not as if these people are dealing in realities; at best it is a pale imitation.

A: Easier though to make your bed than to lie in it, much less paint it?

S: Are you taking the piss?

A: Me? As if? Merely observing that for the "we" - one "e" there by the way - the artists' efforts are not so much second-hand, as they are third-hand. "The tragic poet, if his art is representation, is by nature at third remove from the throne of truth; …"

S: "And the same is true of all other representative artists". 140 No need to ask about your bedtime reading?

A: No. A couple of pages, and I'm fast off. Works like a charm! Mind you that might be down to sleeping in the second type of bed. The work of a real crafts-man.141

S: Only a rich man can afford cheap sandals. Plato would more than pleased to have you fitted out for a Procrustian one!

A: He's already set upon that. That's my point. Mine's better than a God's bed, es-pecially if Timandra is in it, and I'd sooner cut my ear off than attempt to lie in an artist's bed. He's such a clod, that Glaucon, don't you think? So earnest: "Owl-eyed"? "Looking for wisdom"? There's a couple of misnomers right there in the name.142

S: Oh, come on. Bad-mouthing people is surely stooping too low even for you?

A: It's not bad-mouthing; it's an ad hominem;143 not the same thing at all. Who-ever heard of an owl that was awake in the day? All that stuff that comes in threes; use, manufacture, and representation. Read for them; knowledge, belief, and mere opinion. And always the artist bringing up the rear, or should that be viewed the other way about? Plato trying for a trompe l'oeil effect - the one and only true re-ality masked by, hidden behind everyday appearance - Parhasius outwitting Zeux-is? 144 You forget I've known Aristocles since childhood; long before he dreamt of Syracuse and becoming a wide-boy.145 As for poor, hapless Glaucon, it is all too easy for the pair of you to harness his credulity and have him gallop off after your speculations.146 That's one horse you never tire of leading to water it seems, for he'll swallow anything.147Once you've persuaded him that "representative art is an inferior child born from born of inferior parents", - and the hypocrisy of that image considering that you have forsworn the use of rhetoric, yes you might well blush - it is a simple matter to get the poor dupe to draw the same negative conclu-sion in respect of the tragic poet. The last being your real target from the first. "Oh, what a tangled web we weave, when first we practice to deceive". 148

S: Who said that?

A: One of your "liars". His name doesn't matter, since for you he'd have to be ban-ished.

# CHEWING THE CUD

S: But these people corrupt; they pander to the basest of feelings, to the lewd and licentious, to the vulgar, "You are giving rein to your comic instinct, which your reason has restrained for fear you may seem to be playing the fool, and bad taste in the theatre may insensibly lead you into becoming a buffoon at home".149 Doesn't even Aristotle tell us that comic imitation is concerned with the ridiculous "which is a species of the ugly"?150If I might quote myself, "...the only poetry that should be allowed in a state is hymns to the gods and paeans in praise of good men; once you go beyond that and admit the sweet lyric or epic muse, pleasure and pain become your rulers instead of law and rational principles commonly accepted as best".151

A: Now that is a first - the ventriloquist's dummy quotes himself.

S: And that's just what makes Aristophanes, and his ilk, so pathetic - they make mock even of their friends.

A: I wouldn't be so sure that you and your master are at one on this. You don't know what he keeps under his pillow for the weekend.152

S: I don't even know what a "weekend" is, but I suspect this insinuation only goes to prove my point about how corrupting this sort of humour is.

A: Seriously, it is said that Plato thought the three graces found a home in the soul of Aristophanes.

S: I don't believe it! Anyway you've been giving it large in respect of ridicule; I've yet to hear anything otherwise on the subject. Is that because you're no more than an empty husk?

A: Not at all, I just choose to be all ears for a while. Allowing others to speak is often quite revealing in itself. We, all of us, show more than we tell; likewise we often know more than we can say.

S: If, indeed, you were all ears, I would have thought some of what Plato has to say here would have chimed with you - especially his remarks concerning the deleterious effects of encouraging audiences to identify with pity. Or is it that you have a need to minimize the achievements of others, in order to magnify those of your own?

# CHEWING THE CUD

A: I'll say this ... Art in which precisely the lie is sanctified and the will to deception has a good conscience, is much more fundamentally opposed to the ascetic ideal than is science: this [is] instinctively sensed by Plato, the greatest enemy of art Europe has yet produced. Plato versus Homer: that is the complete, the genuine antagonism - there the sincerest advocate of the "beyond", the great slanderer of life; here the instinctive deifier, the golden nature.153

S: Mother of God! Is that what you really are? One of nature's incendiaries - in both senses - judging from the verbal pyrotechnics? I'm damn sure that that was none of Zopyrus' doing.

A: Quite right. He was much more interested in the products of art themselves. For my part the thing of interest is the process, more especially the values and affirmations of the artist; more specifically still, the championing of appearance. In the main, I agree more with the artists than with any philosopher hitherto: they have not lost the scent of life, they have loved the things of "this world" - they have loved their senses. To strive for 'desensualization" that seems to me a misunderstanding or an illness or a cure, where it is not merely a hypocrisy or self-deception. I desire for myself and for all who live, may live, without being tormented by a puritanical conscience, an ever greater spiritualization and multiplication of the senses; indeed, we should be grateful to the senses for their subtlety, plenitude and power and offer them in return the best we have in the way of spirit [...]: it is a sign that one has turned out well when [...] one clings with ever greater pleasure and warmth to the ' things of this world'. 154

S: No two ways about it, you're a strange one; some sort of hybrid. I've no words for how alien that all sounded. Solid ground is what I need. Let's go back to my father and Zopyrus.

A: They were acquainted?

S: No. What I meant was that for my father art was the product of genius. He was forever looking for inspiration, or so he claimed when I was sent by mother to haul him out of some tavern or other.

A: A bit of a romantic was he? I think I see where you are going with this, but you're wrong about Zopyrus if you think he shared the same view as your father?

S: I am?

A: Afraid so. Artistic genius has nothing to do with individualization; quite the opposite, in fact. As I remember, "Only through the pure contemplation ... which becomes entirely absorbed in the object, are the Ideas comprehended; and the nature of genius consists precisely in the pre-eminent ability for such contemplation. This demands a complete forgetting of one's own person". 155 A temporary state of affairs, he would add, for sooner or later the will and the body reassert themselves; the magic fades for we are bound to the world. Time-consciousness, you see, the fount of all our unhappiness. No, don't ask; it's another story. Anyway, aesthetic pleasure, whether in respect of art, or nature - a matter of losing yourself in it.

S: And you've no time for this view?

A: Nor patience; - The "idea" of the beautiful? The sublime? Do you require proof of how far the transfiguring power of intoxication can go? - "Love is this proof... In this case intoxication has done with reality to such a degree that in he consciousness of the lover the cause of it is extinguished and something else seems to have taken its place - a vibration and glittering of all the magic mirrors of Circe.

Here it makes no difference whether one is man or animal; even less whether one has spirit, goodness, and integrity. If one is subtle, one is fooled subtly; if one is coarse, one is fooled coarsely; but love, and even the love of God, the saintly love of "redeemed souls", remains the same in its roots: a fever that has good reason to transfigure itself, an intoxication that does well to lie about itself - And in any case, one lies well when one loves, about oneself and to oneself: one seems to oneself transfigured, stronger, richer, more perfect, one is more perfect - Here we discover art as an organic function: we discover it in the most angelic instinct, "love", we discover it as the greatest stimulus to life - art thus sublimely expedient even when it lies -.156

S: Do you take me for a fool, then?

A: Ha, ha. Are you feeling bruised? But we should do wrong if we interfered with its power to lie.

S: We would?

A: We would...It does more than merely imagine; it even transposes values. And it is not only that it transposes the feeling of values: the lover is more valuable, is stronger. In animals this condition produces new weapons, pigments, colours and forms; above all, new movements, new rhythms, new love calls and seductions. It is no different with man. His whole economy is richer than before, more powerful, more complete than in those who do not love. The lover becomes a squanderer: he is rich enough for it. Now he dares, becomes an adventurer, becomes an ass in magnanimity and innocence; he believes in God again, he believes in virtue, because he believes in love; and on the other hand, this happy idiot grows wings and new capabilities, and even the door of art is opened to him. If we subtracted all traces of this intestinal fever from lyricism in sound and word, what would be left of lyrical poetry and music? – art for art's sake perhaps: the virtuoso croaking of shivering frogs, despairing in their swamp - All the rest was created by love -.157

S: No, no, no! That will not stand. I know Plato speaks of man as the civilized animal, but it is reason that allows us to slough off our animal nature; reason that defines our humanity. Even Aristotle, who has been known to wile away the hours studying plant and animal life, concedes that man is akin to the Gods by virtue of being a thinking animal. You as per usual, have to go that one step further and read us all the way back into nature.

A: Didn't I hear tell that the wrestler had theorized us as "featherless bipeds"? 158

S: Not in the way that that scoundrel Diogenes took him to mean!

A: Dogs and philosophers do the greatest good and get the fewest rewards? 159

S: Should have been castrated at birth; then he'd sung a different song!

A: But he wouldn't have been such a barrel of laughs. You need teeth to make people really laugh.160 Ask Aristophanes.

S: Ah. Aristophanes, Diogenes, the lot of you! Sometimes you drive me to distraction. Always burrowing away, seeking to undermine, ridicule what's best and right thinking. You're no different with your back to nature malarkey. You'll be telling me next that we're evolved from a pool of warm slime! 161

A: Now there's an idea.

S: I've an idea to spit on you!

A: Come. Come. You have to be philosophical about these things.

S: Very droll, I'm sure. And if wit were shit, yours would be?

A: Socrates, please! Before you say something you later regret.

## CHEWING THE CUD

S: Ok. All right. Deep breathe.

A: Ok. For me the human being has become an animal, literally and without reservation and qualification, he who was according to his old faith, almost God ["child of God", "God-man"]. 162 We no longer derive the human from "the spirit" or "the deity"

S: Now who's availing himself of a royal "we"?

A: Indulge me a moment. I was going to say, "we have placed him back among the animals". 163 To translate man back into nature, to become master over the many vain and overly enthusiastic interpretations that have so far been scrawled and painted over that eternal basic text of Homo natura; to see to it that the human being henceforth stands before human beings as even today, hardened in the discipline of science, he stands before the rest of nature, with intrepid Oedipus eyes and sealed Oedipus ears, deaf to the siren songs of old metaphysical bird catchers who have been piping at him all too log, "you are more, you are higher, you are of a different origin" - that may be a strange and insane task, but it is a task - who would deny that?164

S: No. No matter what rhetorical flourishes you dress it up in - all that Oedipal this and that. No more than the blind leading the blind; I'm not buying it!

A: That's not really an argument is it?

S: What? Have I spent a lifetime in service to the truth in vain? What of the higher things - spirit, reason, goodness, beauty? Would you reduce them all to naught?

A: Would you have me persist in that fiction that human-kind possess some extra-natural faculty that sets them apart from, and above the rest of creation; - the choices have been many: mind, spirit, rationality, consciousness, language, morality. You pay your money, and take your pick.

S: Zeus! I've never witnessed such casual blasphemy, such insouciance, such ... I'm lost for words. It's all so deflationary, so...

A: Oh come now. There is no need to get your self in lather about all this. Only a fool would deny that there are signal differences between animal kind, and ourselves and I'm not that fool. All I'm claiming is the difference is not hierarchical.

Indeed, for me, the so called extra-natural features are not much more than the means by which the weaker, less robust individuals preserve themselves - since they have been denied the chance to wage the struggle for existence with horns or the sharp teeth of beasts of prey.165

S: This is all very difficult to swallow. I require bite-sized morsels if I'm going to get my five a day in. "Five-a-day"? I don't know where that came from. Anyway, bite-sized because of the teeth, or lack of them, you understand? Nothing to do with the red meat you are serving up. Anyhow, I was going to say. When we speak of humankind vis-a-vis animals, we do so by means of a series of oppositions - antinomies, if you prefer -; reason versus nature, mind versus body, consciousness versus instinct. Instead of explaining the latter in terms of the former, as we usually do, you're proposing what? That we seek to explain the former in terms of the latter?

A: Exactly so. Being conscious is not in any decisive sense the opposite of what is instinctive, 166 it is actually nothing but a certain behaviour of the instincts toward one another, 167 that thinking is merely a relation of [...] drives to each other,168 and that "reason" is rather a system of relations between various passions and desires.169

S: And the spirit? Would you make a meal of that too?

A: Body am I entirely, and nothing else; and soul is only a word for something about the body; 170 the "pure spirit" is a pure stupidity; if we subtract the nervous system and the senses - the "mortal shroud" - then we miscalculate - that is all! 171

S: Fuck! Is there no end to it? Throw me a bone; I need cheering up!

A: Man is the most intelligent of the animals - and the most silly.172

S: Not one of "his"? You don't know where they've been. 'Sides, I think I've had enough of this nature red in tooth and claw for one day. It's all so depressing.

A: How about, " A friend is but a single soul in two bodies"? 173

S: That's the nicest thing you've said all day.

A: Not me, I'm afraid. Him again!

# CHEWING THE CUD

S: Really? Still you thought of it, and said it. All of what you've been speaking of has left me feeling quite - well - deflated. Read in one light, alongside the stuff about pessimism, it appears nihilistic – I'm still not sure; less sure in fact. How one could avoid falling into that particular abyss. It's as if you drained life of its colour.

A: There's art, remember.

S: Ah, but what sort of consolation is that for the loss of that bright, over-arching, rainbow certainty by which the gods signal the passing of life's storms?

A: It is enough that we should be able to organize a small portion of life to our satisfaction. One thing is needful. - To "give style" to one's character - a great and rare art! It is practiced by those who survey all the strengths and weaknesses of their nature and then fit them into an artistic plan until every one of them appears as art and reason and even the weaknesses delight the eye. Here a large mass of second nature has been added; there a piece of original nature has been removed - both times through long practice and daily work at it. Here the ugly that could not be removed is concealed; there it has been reinterpreted and made sublime. Much that is vague and resisted shaping has been saved and exploited for distant views; it is meant to beckon toward the far and immeasurable. In the end, when the work is finished, it becomes evident how the constraint of a single taste governed and formed everything large and small. Whether this taste was good or bad is less important than one might suppose, if only that it was a single taste!

It will be the strong and domineering natures that enjoy their finest gaiety in such constraint and perfection under a law of their own; the passion of their tremendous will relents in the face of all stylized nature, of all conquered and serving nature. Even when they have to build palaces and design gardens they demur at giving nature freedom.

Conversely, it is the weak characters without power over themselves who hate the constraint of style. They feel that if this bitter and evil constraint were imposed upon them they would be demeaned; they become slaves as soon as they serve; they hate to serve. Such spirits - and they may be of the first rank - are always out of shape and interpret their environment as free nature: wild, arbitrary, fantastic, disorderly, and surprising. And they are advised because it is only in this way that they can give pleasure to themselves. For one thing is needful: that a human being should attain satisfaction with himself, whether it be by means of this or that poetry and art; only then is a human being at all tolerable to behold. Whoever is dissatisfied with himself is continually ready for revenge, and we others will be his victims, if only by having to endure his ugly sight. For the sight of what is ugly makes one bad and gloomy.174

# CHEWING THE CUD

S: Is that another dig at me?

A: Pure coincidence.

S: All that "strength and weakness" nonsense - yet again. All very well for those who think it's still all in front of them. Speaking personally, for a moment, I begin to wonder if I'm not too old for this game.

A: From where I stand there's clearly life in the old dog yet. Yes art as the great seduction to life, the great stimulant to life, but that's not to say its always uplifting. Sometimes the things the artist displays are ugly: but that they display them comes from their pleasure in the ugly. 175 Think here of Dostoevsky, Bacon, Goya. No, I forgot. You won't know them. But you know what I mean - joy in destruction can itself be a stimulant to life.

S: Can it? That's foreign to me.

A: Dionysus - "Pessimism of strength"? Recall? Man no longer needs a "justification of ills"; "justification" is precisely what he abhors: he enjoys ills pur, cru; he finds senseless ills the most interesting. If he formerly had need of a god, he now takes delight in a world disorder without God, a world of chance, to whose essence belong the terrible, the ambiguous, and the seductive. In such a state it is precisely the good that needs "justifying".176 Pessimism as a critique of existing morality both destroys and builds. If I might put it this way, my type of pessimism is the great point of departure; 177 it may even be necessary for a few millennia.178

S: And you'll raise me how much? That's what this feels like. You continually raise the stakes. I used to pride myself on thinking the unexamined life wasn't worth living, 179 but I keep getting this uncanny feeling that your agenda, whatever it is, is structured in terms of a contest with me. A sort of "anything you can do, I can do better".

A: And what if it was? What if you were the template against which subsequent free spirits had to take their measure, were obliged to take their measure? I'll cut you dead hereafter if you so much as whisper that to another.

S: A sort of intellectual conscience? Is that what you are saying?

A: Now you're fishing for compliments. Yes, the intellectual conscience. - I keep having the same experience and resisting it every time. I do not want to believe it although it is palpable: the great majority of people lack an intellectual conscience. Indeed, it has often seemed to me as if anyone calling for an intellectual conscience were as lonely in the most densely populated cities as he were in a desert. Everybody looks at you with strange eyes and goes right on handling scales, calling this good and that evil. Nobody even blushes when you intimate that their weights are underweight, nor do they...

S: Quite so! And who'd contradict the dog over that? "Blushing is the colour of virtue", I mean.180

A: ...Nor do people feel outraged; they merely laugh at your doubts.

S: Tell me about it!

A: I mean: the great majority of people does not consider it contemptible to believe this and that to and live accordingly, without first having given themselves an account of the final and most certain reasons pro and con, and without even troubling themselves about such reasons afterward: the most gifted men and the noblest women still belong to this "great majority".

S: Absolutely, though, that said, I wouldn't have troubled over even women in general.

A: I was going to say? But what is good heartedness, refinement, or genius to me, when the person who has these virtues tolerates slack feelings in his faith and judgments and when he does not account the desire for certainty as his inmost craving and deepest distress - as that which separates the higher human beings from the lower.

Among some pious people I found a hatred of reason and was well disposed to them for that; for this at least betrayed their bad intellectual conscience. But to stand in the midst of this rerum Concordia discors 181 and of this whole marvellous uncertainty and rich ambiguity of existence without questioning, without trembling with the craving and rapture of such questioning, without at least hating the person who questions, perhaps even finding him faintly amusing - that is what I feel to be contemptible, and this feeling for which I look first in everybody. Some folly keeps persuading me that every human being has this feeling, simply because he is human. This is my type of injustice.182

S: He is so right - the mangy dog! "A friend is one soul abiding in two bodies"! 183 Suddenly, I feel refreshed. Come; let's walk some more. Tell me more.

## CHAPTER 3
### On Time-servers

An example of the *trompe-l'oeil*. Euripedes pierces the veil to gaze upon the "real" world

A: As a "child of the good", you are obviously the person to talk to about morality.184

S: Take your tongue out of your cheek, and I'll do my best.

A: See, its your sunny personality; I knew I was talking to the right man.

S: Can we dispense with the clever allusions, please? 185

A: But don't you say, "Then what gives the objects of knowledge their truth and the knower's mind the power of knowing is the form of the good. It is the cause of knowledge and truth, and you will be right to think of it as being itself known, and yet as something other than, and even more splendid than, knowledge and truth, splendid as they are. And just as it was right to think of light and sight as being like the sun, but wrong to think of them as being the sun itself, so here again it is right to think of knowledge and truth as being like the good, but wrong to think of either of them being the good, whose position must be ranked still higher"? 186

S: How many more times? Plato has me say these things. Personally, - forgive the pun - I draw the line at some of this, but I'll do my best on his behalf.187He was a changed man when he got back from his trip to Sicily. It was all maths this, and maths that. Mathematics was to provide the basic model for our understanding of everything.188

Bloody Pythagoreans! If it wasn't maths, it was music, "music of the spheres" - and all sorts of speculations about its supposed influence. "Music gives a soul to the universe, wings to the mind, flight to the imagination, and life to every-thing", he used to say.189You know Perictione, his mother, was a disciple of Py-thagoras? 190

A: Yes, I'd heard.

S: There was quite a fashion of husbands sending him their wives to be educated. Mad as hatters, the lot of them, if you ask me. Veggies too, except for the beans of course. Thought they were made from the same material as you and I - prohibited their consumption. Honestly, you couldn't make it up if you tried! You heard about his death? His house set fire to by his enemies, he legged it only to find his line of flight blocked by a bean field. Afraid to transgress, he waited for his pursuers who without more of a do cut his throat. Talk about pathos! 191

A: I hadn't heard that.

S: It gets worse.

A: It does?

S: Where Plato's concerned, I mean. He refused to hear any of this. "I'm trying to think; don't confuse me with facts", he said. I reckon it was all those mushrooms they had him eat whilst he was there. It took him a while to get them out of his sys-tem. "Musical innovation is full of dangers to the State", he said to me one day, "for when modes of music change, the laws of the State always change with them". 192 That's when I knew he was on the mend. "Rock and roll", I wanted to exclaim, though only Zeus knows why. Fatuous expression.

A: "Most men are within a finger's breadth of being mad". 193

S: Who said that?

A: The "Dog".
S: Might have known. Anyway, my point was that I shouldn't be so readily identified with Plato, if only because he, himself, comes in many guises. After all is said and done you'd have it all on to show some consistency if you'd written thirty-six dialogues. Books are immortal sons defying their sire? 194 You might even find yourself agreeing with him. What was it he said to me the other day? Oh yes! " In practice people who study philosophy too long become very odd birds, not to say thoroughly vicious; while even those who are the best of them are reduced by ... philosophy to complete uselessness as members of society". 195

A: I bet that gave you a bit of a frisson?

S: Nah! I'm a simple soul, me. All this green around us does nothing for me. Landscapes and trees have nothing to teach me, only people in the city can do that.

A: Not even that the tallest trees have their roots in deepest hell? 196

S: Now you're beginning to sound like him on a bad day. One thing he is right about I guess is that "those who tell the stories run society". 197

A: And who could gainsay that, especially where the philosopher is concerned. Some stories have greater longevity than others; some last two millennia or more. Gossip aside, all that brings us neatly back to the question of morality.

S: It does?

A: The *summun bonum* - the chief good, the ultimate principle of an ethical system? We said earlier that with the death of belief in God, a number of other related ideas meet their demise, for example, the belief in an essentially moral order, or the true, valuable world beyond this one.198To "Er" is human, to forgive is divine, as they say? 199 Sorry couldn't resist that.

S: No you couldn't, could you. Neither could you resist the "we said". It was you who said it, not I. As to the present I hear you talking not of the death of God, but rather the death of belief in god.

A: I thought it better to dot the "i" s and cross the "t" s with you around. Strictly speaking a metaphysical concept such as "God" himself cannot die. What can die is the attendant beliefs about the make-up of the world. Of course that's not to say that the belief in God want be taken over by other notions. We still have to vanquish his shadow, too.200 Remember?
S: How do you mean "other notions"?

A: The continuing belief in, desire for teleology, for some sort of historical necessity that will make sense of it all. The Christian Second Coming, Hegel's " cunning of history", the advent of Socialism. No, don't ask; it'd take too long. Just take it from me, the whole idea still has legs. What are these people saying if not that this world is full of contradictions: consequently there is a world free from contradiction; - this world is a world of becoming: consequently there is a world of being: - all false conclusions [...] fundamentally they are desires that such a world should exist.201 Moral value judgments are ways of passing sentence, negations; morality is a way of turning one's back on the will to existence.202 Definition of morality: Morality- the idiosyncrasy of decadents, with the ulterior motive of revenging oneself against life - successfully.203

S: You aren't giving me a lot to get my gums into, apart that is from all this sloganizing pap.

A: Well let's start with the Sophists. It is a very remarkable moment: the Sophists verge upon the first critique of morality, the first insight into morality: - they juxtapose the multiplicity [the geographical relativity] of the moral value judgments; - they let it be known that every morality can be dialectically justified; i.e. they divine that all attempts to give reasons for morality are necessarily sophistical - a proposition later proved on a grand scale by the ancient philosophers from Plato onwards [down to Kant]; - they postulate the first truth that a "morality-in-itself", a "good-in-itself" do not exist, that it is a swindle to talk of truth in this field.204 In sum, they argue that there are no moral facts.

S: To be sure, "It is better in fact to be found guilty of manslaughter than of fraud about what is fair and just", but you're going to have to do better than that!205 The inference is invalid. The pluralism in this area might indicate no more than the myriad falsity of such views. Knowing the low cunning of these Sophists, they,

73

more than likely, intend their audience to draw the conclusion that the disagreement is itself proof that there are no facts about morality on which to adjudicate. Again such a conclusion would be premature. It might simply be that such facts have yet to be discovered.

A: Clever I'm sure, but I'm not buying that. In my view there are no absolute morals, indeed moral judgment is an illusion.206Let me speak plainly, there are altogether no moral facts.207 Moreover there are no moral phenomena, rather only a moral interpretation of such things which itself is of extra-moral origin.208
S: Whisper that softly. You wouldn't want all and sundry thinking they had carte blanche to do whatever they liked. The family silver might be imperilled, and what would you do without a silver spoon to put in your mouth?

A: I'll ignore that last crack, since you've no idea of the expectations under which I live. As for the family silver, Voltaire's worry was about the consequences of a loss of belief in God and thereby in divine retribution.

S: This Voltaire I've never met, but you can see his point.

A: Of course you've never met him! Sorry, you put me off my stroke for a moment. My point was a different one; namely, that there are two kinds of deniers of morality. First, those who deny that the moral motives which men claim have inspired their actions really have done so - it is thus the assertion that morality consists of words and is among the coarser or more subtle deceptions [especially self-deceptions] which men practice, and is perhaps so especially in precisely the case of those most famed for virtue.209

S: Why do you have to constantly needle me?

A: I'm not, unless of course you're telling me that Xenophon's version of you is the correct one. You know you come across as a bit of a prig in his pages?

S: That says more about him than it does me. For all that, he means well. One shouldn't gossip, but as a military man you should appreciate this morsel - it gives you the measure of the man. Last time we met he was telling me that estate management required much the same skills as generalship.

A: Ha, ha. Let's hope he sticks with the manure he knows. Anyway I would be the last to deny that the point of view of La Rochefoucauld and others who think like him may also be justified and in any event of great general applicability.210

# CHEWING THE CUD

S: La Rochefoucauld?

A: I'm sorry. Another one of those who come after – reading him is one of life's pleasures. Not actually my kind of denier. I belong to the second kind. To deny that moral judgments are based upon truths.

S: So you're still a cynic?
A: Not at all! I concede that moral judgments really are the motives of action, but that in this way it is errors, which, as the basis of all moral judgments impel men to their moral actions.... Thus, I deny morality as I deny alchemy, that is, I deny their premises: but I do not deny that there have been alchemists who believed in these premises and acted in accordance with them. - I also deny immorality: not that countless people feel their selves to be immoral but that there is any true reason so to feel. It goes without saying...

S: Then why say it?

A: It goes without saying that I do not deny - unless I'm a fool - that many actions called immoral ought to be avoided and resisted, or that many called moral ought to be done and encouraged - but I think the one should be encouraged and the other avoided for reasons other than hitherto. We have to learn to think differently - in order at last, perhaps very late on, to attain even more: to feel differently.211

S: So where does that leave us? In terms of moral motivation you want as the phrase has it "to read us back into nature"? Is that it?

A: Not in a simplistic fashion, no; for wherever we encounter a morality, we also encounter valuations and an order of rank of human impulses and actions. These valuations and orders of rank are always expressions of the needs of a community and herd.212

S: Calling "spades" spades will be the death of you.

A: It is surely no more than the truth? Man is par excellence the herd animal. One has to earn the right to be thought of as an individual. No, I'll re-phrase that, to be thought a singularity. Everyone in their cups, or not, will these days lay claim to being an "individual". I surely don't have to persuade you of all people of the cost of being willing to stand apart, to stand alone? Besides in suggesting these orders of rank I'm surely doing no more than what, in general terms, you and Plato are doing in the "Republic"? Perhaps we should come back to the creation of "individuals", or "singularities" as I prefer to call them

S: You mean to say such people are not just forces of nature as it were?

A: Not simply, no. A lot of things have to be in place before you start breeding individuals. Up until now they have been the exception, and they probably will remain so for the longest period. Anyhow, let's not get sidetracked. What was I saying? Oh, yes. The valuations and orders of rank are always expressions of the needs of a community and herd: whatever benefits it most - and second most, - and third most - that is also considered the first standard for the value of all individuals. Morality trains the individual to be a function of the herd and to ascribe value to himself only as a function. The conditions for the preservation of different communities were very different; hence there were very different communities.... Morality is the herd instinct in the individual.213

And before you say it, I mean by "herd" only that humankind live for the most part as members of collectivities. However I would insist that the imperatives at work to preserve the herd, the principles of social selection that ensure the survival and reproduction of the herd, run counter to those at work in natural selection. Riven by antithetical impulses, pulled in contradictory directions, man ends up the sickliest animal.

S: So what are you saying about individuals? You seem to imply these are fewer and farther between than we ordinarily think?

A: Quite. Every great civilization is at best a detour to produce half a dozen individuals.214

S: A depressing statistic, if true. That said, on grey days when I'm stuck in doors and Xanthippe is giving me earache about our modest means, I often fall to wondering what difference, if any, I've made. Not that I think of myself as one of your band of notables - far from it. Little victories, - Yes, I can get a few to lend an ear, but as to what they carry away, and for how long, who knows?

A: It would be a mistake, of course to confuse talk of culture and civilization here.

S: Sorry. Lost in reverie, for a moment.

A: Yes. The great moments of culture were always, morally speaking, times of corruption; and conversely, the periods when the taming of the human animal [civilization] was desired and enforced were times of intolerance against the boldest and most spiritual natures. Civilization has aims different from those of culture - perhaps they are even opposite -. Real individuals are few and far between - the product of great periods of gestation.215 I'd go so far as to say that contra the notion of civilization, the great epochs of our lives are the occasions when we gain the courage to re-baptize our evil qualities as our best qualities.

S: That last bit is insane.
A: Is it? Madness is something rare in individuals, - but in groups, parties, peoples, ages it is the rule.216 Our neighbours, the Spartans an example? In their civilization doesn't the preservation of the group come first, second, and third? Whether I view humans with a good or an evil eye, I find them always at one task, all of them and each one in particular: to do what helps the preservation of the human species. Not indeed from a feeling of love for this species, but simply because nothing in them is older, stronger, more inexorable and unconquerable than this instinct, - because this instinct is even the instinct the essence of our kind and herd.217

S: Am I missing something here? When I think of herd phrases like "herding together for warmth" leap to mind, or alternatively " conforming with one's kind in hope of support". You don't mean that kind of thing with your human herd, or do you?

A: Oh yes, that's all to the point. The tendency to seek out the average, to seek agreement. The humans who are more similar, more ordinary, have had, and always have an advantage: hence there has always been a natural, all too natural, continual development of humans toward the similar, ordinary, average, herd-like - common. As regards the second point, the greatest labour of humanity so far was to agree with one another about so many things and to impose upon itself a law of agreement - regardless of whether these things are true of false.218

S: Regardless?

A: Madness, remember? Early doors, it was, in all likelihood, utility that was at a premium. The origin of custom goes back to two thoughts: the community is worth more than the individual and enduring advantage is preferable to a fleeting one; from which the conclusion follows, that the enduring advantage of the community is to take unconditional precedence to the advantage of the individual. That is how education works, for example: one tries to condition an individual by various attractions and advantages to adopt a way of thinking and behaving that, once it has become a habit, instinct, and passion, will dominate him to his own ultimate disad-

77

vantage but "for the general good". 219 There's another thought about this nagging away in the back of my mind.

S: What's that then?

A: I can't quite get hold of it.

S: Zeus, that's frustrating isn't it? Thoughts can't be bidden; they come when they want to, eh? 220 Read Plato and you'd think I was some kind of oracle permanently primed to respond to whatever an interlocutor throws at me. The devil, you notice, reserves the best tunes for himself?

A: Not half. The argument reaches some hiatus and he reaches up to the sky and pulls down some mind-boggling myth or other; the "Cave", the "Divided Line", the "Ring, "Er". You've got to hand it to him in that regard!

S: I'm not much more than a poor winnower by comparison. Blood will out, I guess. My forebears were farmers you know? That's probably too grand a description by far, more the human equivalent of chickens scratching in the dirt.

A: Its not that you haven't made something of yourself.

S: Well Plato has, not forgetting the well-meaning Xenophon.

A: Zeus, he's dull. As soon as he opens his mouth, I want to sleep.

S: Ha, ha. Know what you mean. Narcolepsy on bandy legs, bless him.

A: Ha, ha. That will do the trick.

S: Xenophon as catalyst. Who'd have thought it? We'll have to stop pretending we don't know where the party is when he asks.

A: I was going to say in regard of the individual and society?

S: My very next question.

A: Well it seems to me that society, the herd, periodically reasserts itself against the individual. There is no linear, once and for all, progress here. In just the same way if the social imperatives lapse, our more original " animal nature" reasserts itself. Habit. Must say something about habit. Anyway; to continue? Yes, today it seems to do everyone good when they hear that society is on the way to adapting the individual to general requirements, and that the happiness and at the same time the sacrifice of the individual lies in feeling himself to be a useful member and instrument of the whole: except that one is at present very uncertain as to where this whole is to be sought, whether in an existing state or one to be created, or in the nation, or in a brotherhood of peoples, or communities. At present there is much reflection, doubt, controversy over this subject, and much excitement and passion; but there is a wonderful and fair sounding unanimity in the demand that the ego has to deny itself until, in the form of adaption to the whole, it again acquires its firmly set circle of rights and duties - until it has become something quite novel and different.

What is wanted - whether this is admitted or not - is nothing less than a fundamental re-moulding, indeed weakening and abolition of the individual: one never tires of enumerating and indicting all that is evil and inimical, prodigal, costly, extravagant in the form of individual existence has assumed hitherto, one hopes to manage more cheaply, more safely, more equitably, more uniformly if there exists only large bodies and their members. Everything that in any way corresponds to this body - and membership-building drive and its ancillary drives is felt to be good, this is the moral undercurrent of our age; individual empathy and social feeling here play into one another's hands.... 221

S: Very interesting, but there seems to be some slippage here. First off between what you call "natural selection" and "social selection", then, second, within the latter category between custom as evolution and habit, and custom as consciously imposed - if you see what I mean? A faint echo, as it were, of Plato and his aristocratic masters imposing their will upon society? I've heard tell of you saying something similar in this regard - a notorious phrase..?

A: All right, all right! I confess. Like a pack of blonde beasts of prey.222

S: Ah, bless! Diogenes' really was right. A blush really is the colour of virtue. Let's not forget the subordinate clause here - pun intended - "whose work is an instinctive form-creating, form-imposing"?

A: Guilty as charged; in mitigation - a blonde moment?

S: That's far from amusing. Who's to say what the wrong hands might do with such writing? All that stuff about life being about appropriation, exploitation, assimilation, etc.223

# CHEWING THE CUD

A: You are tarring with a broad brush there. Anyway I don't write books for everyone.

S: Even they were written for no one, and as things stand there are those who argue it would be a fate they merit, that's still no excuse.224
A: You are right. Ok? I think I can defend my position, but I need to give it some more thought. Can we come back to it later?

S: I won't forget, you know?

A: And I wouldn't want you to. Habit?

S: Habit, it is. Most of us want a quiet life, but then that doesn't sit well with what you were saying a while back about pursuit of pleasure and avoidance of pain.

A: Look closer. Paradoxical as it sounds, the self wants pleasure but not too much - too much, and over-excitement becomes a source of anxiety. As often as not it may be a case of reducing or eliminating such "un-pleasure". Take sex for example.225

S: You have my undivided attention.

A: I rather thought I might. Well it may be that what the self likes about it is not the climax, but the cessation of the desire it affords. Desire as such is perturbing and importunate.

S: That might be so. Can you believe that Plato considered having women exercise in the buff? 226I took a class of young men to see Praxiteles sculpting a nude Aphrodite the other day. I didn't know where to look. We had to get out of there double-quick. Complete waste of time trying to talk to them about beauty within after that! One of the blighters snuck back after dark, and having embraced the statue left a stain upon it. Praxiteles wasn't best pleased, and complained to Plato. Now he's wondering whether he should let me do any part-time teaching.

A: Can we forget about statues?

S: Why should we? Rumour has it you're not too fond of those depicting Hermes? 227

A: Zeus! You're a one for the gossip.

# CHEWING THE CUD

S: Well? The ithyphallic? Is it true you go off half cock at the sight of it?

A: All that for that punch line? You really oughtn't to believe everything you hear.

S: Have it your own way. Habit, then. If you'll pardon the observation, it seems as if the captain has jumped ship. We appear to be adrift.

A: Well let me set a new course. It is my contention that in so as at all times as long as there have been human beings, there have also been human herds [clans, communities, tribes, peoples, states, churches] and always a great many obeyers, compared with the small number of commanders, - considering then, obedience has been practiced and bred best and longest among humans, one may fairly assume that on average the need for it is innate in everyone, as a kind of formal conscience.228

S: Yet another military metaphor? Just so you know, I haven't drifted off? It's a bit of a problem of late. Fewer hours in the night, seem to require more in the day; one moment I'm here, the next I'm gone. Embarrassing. Trying to pass it off as a trance. Most adults keep a respectful distance, but the other day this kid sidled up to me and shouted at the top of his lungs, "Since when did a man in a trance snore?" You should have heard the crowd's derision. Talk about reputation's bubble bursting; I don't think I'll ever live that down. Still - you were saying? The herd instinct as you call it is another name for force of habit?

A: Right. Add to which the idea that social selection that is implicit in the herd instincts results in drives and practices that evolve over time. Put another way, preservation of the community is my correction for preservation of the species.229

S: So, the herd instinct: this desire to copy and imitate others doesn't end there. These "habits" serve to shape, produce, and reproduce a particular kind of society, and thus a particular kind of person?

A: Right on the button. Pleasure in the herd is older than pleasure in the I: and so long as good conscience means the herd, only bad conscience says "I". We gradually accustom ourselves to the way of feeling of our environment, and because sympathetic agreement and accommodation is so pleasant we soon bear all the marks and party colours of this environment.230

S: Is this why, for you, the individual is something rare?

81

# CHEWING THE CUD

A: Exactly! Throughout the longest time of humanity nothing was more terrible than to feel oneself individual. It has to be said, the herd instinct is antipathetical to individuals: it believes them evil. The strongest and most fortunate are enervated when they have ranged against them organized herd instincts, the timidity of the weak, the majority. Egoism is something late, and always still rare: the herd feelings are stronger and older.231

S: If that's so, it immediately raises the question of how the individual frees himself from the cocoon of social constraints. On the face of it, the struggle would seem to be in vain.

A: In large measure this is because we fail to see that individuals are created as organs, as functions of the whole.

S: Say again.

A: How can I best put this? ...This is important. A lot turns upon it. The human has begun as part of the whole, which has its organic properties and makes the individual into its organ - so that through unutterably long habituation humans immediately feel the effects of society against other societies and individuals and all the living and the dead, and not as individuals. The more un-freely one acted, the more the herd instinct rather than any personal sense spoke in the action, the more moral one esteemed oneself. Remember, as I said a moment ago, that throughout the longest time of humanity nothing was more terrible than to feel oneself individual.232

S: You keep alluding to time. Are you saying there are distinct phases to all this?

A: Yes and no. At the outset custom dominates, but that isn't to say its influence doesn't remain marked. It remains a back-clothe of which we are woefully ignorant, and will probably remain so.

S: But you speak of the individual as an organ and function. That would seem to imply the individual is something less, or different to, what he is ordinarily thought to be?

A: Come now. Don't look so crestfallen. It was you who declared the unexamined life is not worth living.233

S: Humph, but you have this knack of making what you say sound like you're taking dictation from heaven.

A: As if! Let's suppose it's all custom to begin with, and that later a moral phase appears. So long as social selection is dominant there are no individuals as such. Clearly neither the herd mentality, nor the individual, can develop in the absence of mental powers. But what if such mental powers were not only developed by social selection, but themselves under-went qualitative change such that they came to used by the very "individuals" created by this social evolution?

S: What sorts of mental powers are you thinking of here?

A: Principally, memory, consciousness, and language. Now since socialization is the key habit required for social cohesion, let's assume these mental powers served, first and foremost, to secure that end.

S: Stop there. There are now habits and habits? Such that some are what? Meta-habits?

A: Yes, why not? First proposition of civilization: among raw peoples there is a species of customs whose intention appears to be custom in general; painstaking and superfluous stipulations ... which however keep custom constantly close, keep the uninterrupted compulsion to practice customs constantly in consciousness: to strengthen the greater proposition, with which begins: any custom is better than no custom.234

S: But achieved how?

A: Punishment. We must seek the actual effect of punishment above all in a sharpening of prudence, in a lengthening of memory; it produces mastery of the desires: thus punishment tames human beings, but does not make them "better". 235

S: It doesn't?

A: Every prohibition worsens the character of those who do not submit to it willingly, but only because they are compelled.236 Forget that for now, anyway. We are getting ahead of ourselves, or rather you are.

S: I am?

A: Yes, teleology. You keep trying to look at all this through the eyes of a moralist. It is important to avoid the error of reading present purposes onto the past. Our own ends and goals, those which serve to interpret what we do, have been decided upon in that past. As I said earlier, we knowers are unknown to ourselves,...237 What we stand in need of is a genealogy to dig out these past commitments and reveal them to the light of day. The point needs to be laboured. There is no set of maxims more important for an historian than this: that the actual causes of a thing's origins and its eventual uses, the manner of its incorporation into a system of purposes, are worlds apart; that everything that exists, no matter what its origins, is periodically re-interpreted by those in power in terms of fresh intentions; that all processes in the organic world are processes of outstripping and overcoming, and that in turn, all outstripping and overcoming means re-interpretation, re-arrangement, in the course of which the earlier meaning and purpose are necessarily obscured or lost.238

S: And this applies across the board?

A: Yes. No matter how well we understand the utility of a certain physiological organ [or a legal institution, a custom, a political convention, an artistic genre, a cultural trait] we do not thereby understand anything of its origin. From time immemorial, the demonstrable purpose of a thing has been considered its causa fiendi - the eye is made for seeing, the hand for grasping. So likewise, punishment has been viewed as an invention for the purpose of punishing.239

S: I'm beginning to think I really do know next to nothing; punishment for my hubris, perhaps? Between you and me? Many a night I've lain awake pondering that incident with the oracle. What if she?

A: Was playing a straight bat?

S: Bastard. I might not fully understand the metaphor, but I can see the spin you're putting on it!

A: Well, probability being what it is, we must have the odd thought in common?

S: I've a good mind to take my ball and go home! But then I can at least pride myself on knowing the difference between right and wrong!

A: Ah, but seriously, can you?

## CHEWING THE CUD

S: You wouldn't catch me taking a prostitute home!

A: That's none of your business. Hipparete never wanted for anything whilst she lived. There are noble women who are afflicted with a certain poverty of spirit, and they know no better way to express their deepest devotion than to offer their virtue and shame. They own nothing higher. Often this present is accepted without establishing as profound an obligation as the donors had assumed. A very melancholy story! 240

S: That sounded suspiciously like a half-hearted admission of failure on your part? And Timandra? Wasn't she formerly a courtesan? Like father, like son, it appears.241

A: Your aspersion is directed at Aspasia, I take it? Finest woman I've ever known; worth more than any one hundred men, in fact. Are you such a prude as not to be able to see a person's worth for their past occupation?

S: Rumour has it, …

A: Honestly, you are no better than an old crone. Have you nothing better to do with your time?

S: Some say that, according to Aristophanes, that it was under her influence that Pericles started the Peloponnesian War.242

A: Utter balderdash, as I sure Aristophanes would tell you - if you cared enough to ask. If you weren't such a philistine you'd realize what Aristotle says is right. Comedies, and Aristophanes' are no exception; show people as worse than they are. You seem to have a talent for forgetting what you don't want to hear.243

S: Really? Isn't it that you and your lot are all the same? Look at Epicurus and Metrodorus and their motley consorts! Such a mellifluous bevy of names: Erokian, Hedeia, Mammarian ["Big Tits"! - I ask you? -], Nikidion. Especially coined for those lacking imagination, I shouldn't wonder. You give us real philosophers a bad name.

A: More salacious tittle-tattle. Who is telling the tales now? No mention here of Leontion here I notice.244 Are the clever ones beneath your attention, or is it that you simply can't see them from that moral high horse?

# CHEWING THE CUD

S: What moral high horse is that?

A: What of your straddling of Myrto - that was the mare's name wasn't it?

S: I was just doing my duty, my patriot duty.245
A: Twice, so I'm told. Not bad going for a moral paragon with no visible means of support. I bet Xanthippe had plenty to say about your success.

S: Yes, but none of it printable. Myrto was her choice. She insisted - a distant cousin of hers with a pronounced limp.

A: In a state of hatred women are more dangerous than men; first and foremost because, once their hostility has been aroused, they are hampered by no considerations of fairness, but allow their hatred to grow undisturbed to its ultimate consequences; then because they are practiced in discovering the wounded places every party possesses and striking at them: to which end their dagger-pointed intellect renders them excellent service [whereas at the sight of wounds men become restrained and often inclined to reconciliation and generosity].246

S: Tell me about it. I still haven't heard the last of it! 'Sides I wasn't the only one doing my duty. Euripides' was as slavish as I in doing his duties.

A: Just goes to show, a truth ceases to be true when more than one person believes it.247

S: Whatever that means. Look I've forgotten how we got into this. I never do know with you - you wind me up so - but can we stop the dirty laundry stuff?

A: Gladly, we'll never be whiter than white, however hard we try. Only he who had the imagination to picture a face, a figure twenty years older would perhaps pass through life undisturbed.248

86

# CHEWING THE CUD

Epicurus

S: So, where were we then; punishment -as an aide-memoire? Memory as a means of binding us to social rules and practices, in opposition to the yet more basic animal drives of natural selection. Talking of the latter reminds me. Xenophon believes our foreheads have been fringed with eyebrows to prevent damage to the eyes even from the sweat of the head?

A: So what; another example of teleological thinking. At root another Idealist, like Plato. Another believer in a mind led universe.

S: You make it sound like a statement of the obvious, but thus far you've said little about it, beyond your declaration that we should aim to read ourselves back into nature. Even so, this is not the whole answer since as you have been arguing these processes of natural selection are inhibited by [?], thwarted by {?}, appropriated by {?] other processes of social selection. To firm up my grip, I need to know a little more about the mechanics of natural selection, as you call it.

A: Ok. The very basics; we evolve by chance and adaptation from physical stuff.

S: Stupid stuff, don't you mean?

A: Yes.

S: So you hypothesize that intelligence, consciousness, are what {?] - supervenient on this essentially physical process?

# CHEWING THE CUD

A: Yes.

S: That doesn't sit well with that other phrase of yours that you keep doting about the place - "will to power. That all sounds very mentalist, but you want to insist that this evolutionary thing is entirely stochastic, determined by the random distribution of probabilities?

A: Yes, the whole process governed by the survival of the fittest.

S: Fittest how? The strongest?

A: No. Best adapted.

S: Best adapted, how? Best adapted to reproduce, or to survive?

A: Your point being?

S: Being adept at reproduction is no guarantee of survival in the general struggle thereafter.

A: Look how about we sound a retreat for now, and return to the issue of social selection?

S: A better general than I wouldn't allow you the opportunity to re-group.

A: I wasn't making some tacit admission of defeat; I was merely trying to move things along.

S: But if reading us back into nature is your default position, surely it is incumbent on a good general to secure his lines of supply?

A: I just said that...Oh, I give up.

S: Good. Glad to see that you've seen sense, at last. Although why you thought I'd accede to all that nonsense about the law of the jungle is beyond me. Thrasymachus isn't the kind of role model you should be seeking, my friend.249

A: No, not "give up" in the sense of "give in".

S: Well, you should have! If the animal kingdom is rightly described as red in tooth and claw, and we were just one animal among others, wouldn't be a case of every man for himself, a case of devil take the hindmost, a war of all against all? 250 If might is right, there would be a damn-sight more than thirty tyrants at play in your bloody scenario! I say again is any wonder that some of us worry about whose side you are really on? 251

A:  The issue of power we can return to, but let's not get into that now. All I was trying to say, before you got your knickers in a twist, is that it is nature that drives us at the biological level.

S: Knickers? What the bloody hell are "Knickers"? I'll have you know that I hang free. Twisted blood, more like. We are not in charge of all this?

A: No, the whole process is stochastic. You used the word not two minutes ago! Remember? In fact there isn't any us here in the sense of a unified ego. The process works from both without and within us, without our being aware of it. The subject is only a fiction: the ego of which one speaks when one censures egoism does not exist at all.252 We are a mass of competing drives and instincts. As every drive lacks intelligence, the viewpoint of "utility" cannot exist for it. Every drive, in as much as it is active, sacrifices force and other drives: finally it is checked; otherwise it would destroy everything through its excessiveness. Therefore: the "un-egoistic", self-sacrificing, imprudent, is nothing special - it is common to all the drives - they do not consider the advantage of the whole ego [because they do not consider at all!], they act contrary to our advantage, against the ego: and often for the ego - innocent in both cases.253

S: Hmm, humbling in so many ways. I'll have to take your word for all this, since science is not my strong suit. We remain though, at the every day level, social animals?

A: Herd animals guided by principles of social selection, yes.

S: Well what say you we repair to that tavern over yonder? As I recall you were seeking to flesh out the idea of meta-habits: certain habits that are conducive to the development of yet other habits. These meta-habits, or mental powers, I think you called them, were critical as regards the social cohesion of the herd - as you insist on calling them. You began with memory.

A: Nothing much wrong with yours.

S: And you left me on a promise!

## CHEWING THE CUD

A: I did? I'm sure I wouldn't be so rash.

S: If you want, I could leg it back to the beauty salon. They are pioneering a new treatment: anal bleaching!

A: Must you?

S: Only joking. Rough as a badger's arse, me. Oh, come now, don't look so disgusted; Socratic irony comes in many forms. I was on a promise though. You said you were going to use this discussion of meta-habits to explicate the transition from a society based on custom to one based on morality.

A: Yes, that's right. I was going to say a few words about consciousness and language.

S: Isn't consciousness - well obvious?

A: No. From where I stand consciousness plays no role in the total process of adaption and systemization. We could think, feel, will, and remember, and we could also "act" in every sense of that word, and yet none of this would have to "enter our consciousness" [as one says metaphorically]. The whole of life would be possible without, as it were, seeing itself in a mirror. Even now, for that matter, by far the greatest portion of our life actually takes place without this mirror effect; and all this is true even of our thinking, feeling, and willing life, however offensive this may sound to older philosophers.254

S: Always twisting the knife.

A: The genius of the species, you might say?

S: I'm proof against flattery, me.

A: Well and good. I was making a serious point.

S: And I'm not serious? Is that what you are implying?

A: Its what you're inferring to be sure, but that's not the same thing. No one in their right mind would regard you as other than serious, but as to whether they should take you seriously - well that's another matter altogether.

# CHEWING THE CUD

S: Ok. Smart, arse. Tell me how come we are conscious?

A: Consciousness has developed only under the pressure of the need for communication. My idea that consciousness does not really belong to man's individual existence but rather to his social, or herd, nature, that, as follows from this, it has developed subtlety only in so far as this is required by social or herd utility.

S: And language, then?

A: Similar pressures were at work here. Now supposing that need has at all times brought together only such human beings as could indicate similar requirements, similar experiences by means of similar signs, it follows that on the whole the easy communicability of need, that is to say ultimately the experiencing of only average and common experiences, must have been the most powerful of all powerful forces which have disposed of mankind hitherto. The more similar, more ordinary hunan beings have had and still have the advantage, the more select, subtle, rare and harder to understand are liable to remain alone, succumb to accidents in their isolation and seldom propagate themselves.255

S: Averse to the quotidian as you are, don't you think - not wishing to appear facetious, mind - well don't you think you should get out more?

A: That's as maybe. Tremendous forces have to be called upon to cross this natural, all too natural progressus in simile, the continuing development of mankind into the similar, ordinary, average, herd-like, - into the common.256

S: Pathos is what I hear, but what of the second phase?

A: Note though in respect of this first phase, these evaluations and rank orders are always expressions of the herd, of a community.... Morality is herd instinct in the individual. It is still the case that such social habits are primarily designed to lock the individual member more securely into the herd. A key difference separates the two phases. In the first phase the worth of an action is judged in terms of its consequences - whether these are beneficial or otherwise.

In the moral period a first attempt at self-knowledge is made. To be sure, a fateful new superstition, a peculiar narrowness of interpretation therewith became dominant: men interpreted the origin of an action in the most definite sense as origin in intention, men became unanimous in the belief that the value of an action resided in the value of the intention behind it. It is under the sway of this prejudice

91

that one has morally praised, blamed, judged and philosophized on earth almost to the present day.257

S: Solid ground, at last. But why all those crabbed words and phrases; "prejudice", 'narrowness of interpretation"?

A: But ought we not today to have arrived at the necessity of once again determining upon another inversion and shift of values, thanks to another self-examination and deepening on the part of man - ought we not to stand on the threshold of a period which should be called, negatively at first, the extra-moral; today when amongst us immoralists at least the suspicion has arisen that the decisive value of an action resides in precisely that which is not intentional in it, and that all that in it which is intentional, all of it that can be seen, known, "conscious", still belongs to its surface and skin - which like every skin, betrays something but conceals something more?258

S: What? You can't go around asking questions like that.

A: Why can't I?

S: Apart from it's being too long?

A: I'm not seeking a simple "yes" or "no".

S: Most want answers, not questions.

A: It's not my job to put things on a plate. I prefer to have my "friends" to engage with me.

S: They'll be few in number, that's for sure; like the Metic's - he's big on the idea of friends. Philia rather than Eros, as befits a cold-blooded creature. As for me, I'm more one of his hot-blooded mammals - very nice to snuggle up to.

A: I wouldn't be able to call them "friends" if they weren't. Besides, you of all people ought to appreciate that there is more art to asking the right question, than there ever is in the answer.

S: I'm not sure Plato would agree. For all his curiosity, he strikes me as more interested in providing unassailable answers - that sort that close an argument down for good. If it were comedy he was writing, I'd probably be his straight man. He saves the real laughs, the real pyrotechnics, for himself. Heh, but what do I know?

A: Forgive me saying, but I don't see how any of that last connects up. As to myself, I thought I'd been doing my level best to...

S: Look. Look over there: in the trees. The mud-bathes. I think they're open again. I don't know about you, but I'm hot as well as tired. Beginning to ramble in mind as well as body, no doubt. A lie-down is as good as a sit-down. Hang on, I'll ask that slave whose acting as a swineherd. He'll probably know if they are open. " Heh, slave!"259

P: You talking to me?

S: Well, I don't see anyone else.

P: I have a name, just like you.

S: Less of your lip, or it'll go the worse for you!

P: What's worse? As the man said: "If you can meet with Triumph and Disaster, and treat those two impostors the same". 260

S: You insolent so and so! I'll have your name.

P: Pyrrho.

S: You think you're clever, do you?

P: No, I know nothing.

S: Are you're taking the piss! That's my line.

P: If it is, and if you can say such a thing, I'd be wanting to add, "and I'm not even sure about that"261

S: For a slave, you've got a lot to say for yourself.

P: I didn't say I was a slave.

93

# CHEWING THE CUD

S: What sort of man would allow himself to be seen driving pigs?

P: When it comes to goodness and integrity "little people" are far superior to philosophers. Take my sister, with whom I live.262

S: Have you no pride? Can you credit this Alcibiades?

A: Leave me out of this.

P: I was going to say, my sister doesn't sit in judgment so why should I? Did I say? She's a mid-wife.... Why's your friend smiling?

A: I told you; I'm staying out of this.

S: "Doesn't sit in judgment"? Would you have us reduced to anarchy?

P: Who's to say the world needs governing? Good order results spontaneously when things are let alone.263

S: Well I never.

P: Those who realize their folly are not true fools.264

S: Why you patronizing little shit. I'll be buggered if I'm going to let someone else tell me what to think. I didn't mean "Well I never", as "I had never thought of that!".

P: Oh, I see. It was a clumsy attempt to patronize me, then?

S: Hand me that sword of yours Alcibiades. Alcibiades!

A: I rather think you ought to cut your losses. Who breaks a butterfly upon the wheel?

P: I once heard tell of a man who dreamt he was a butterfly. When he awoke he no longer knew whether he was himself, or a butterfly dreaming that it was him.265

A: Well you're certainly no butterfly, Socrates. On the other hand perhaps, as yet, you are only the caterpillar. That might explain a lot; the beauty within?

# CHEWING THE CUD

S: Oh, ha, ha.

P: I've heard it said that life forms have an innate ability or power to transform and adapt to their surroundings.

S: Well, well, the man's really a chameleon. Now he sounds like you. Perhaps I should just squash him like a bug?

A: Really, you so intemperate. First you have a mind to put the poor fellow to the sword; now you want to crush him underfoot. Why sweat it? Just supply Plato with the bare bones tomorrow, or whenever, and he'll see you right. You always win where he's concerned, don't you?

S: I like that: the pen mightier than the sword, eh? But what shall I say to Plato, other than complain about the man's temerity?

A: No, don't do that. People complain from weakness. You don't want to try Plato's patience in that regard. Perhaps you should start with his attempt to muddy the surface of your pond? Your notion of the philosopher as objective and in pursuit of disinterested knowledge. His mirror soul, eternally smoothing itself out, no longer knows how to affirm or negate: he does nor command, neither does he destroy ... neither is he a model man; he does not go before anyone, nor behind; altogether he places himself too far apart to have any reason to take sides for good or evil.266

S: Well o.k. Except for that last bit, but how's that going to help? This fellow seemed intent upon playing a game of "I'm more sceptical than you".

A: Exactly so. Look at him. He'll be at it all day. He can't decide whether he should be leading the pigs, or they him?

S: Ha, ha. More bell-end than bell-whether, eh? Yes, I know that's sheep, but you can see what I mean. How shall I put that to Plato? He can be easily affronted by any suggestion of smut?

A: You might say that when any philosopher suggests he is not a sceptic these days - as I hope is clear from what I just said about the objective spirit - everybody is annoyed ... It is as if at his rejection of scepticism they heard some evil, menacing rumbling in the distance, as if a new explosive was being tried somewhere, a dynamite of the spirit ... For the sceptic, being a delicate creature is frightened all too easily; his conscience is trained to quiver at every No, indeed even at a Yes that is decisive and hard, and to feel as if it had been bitten. Yes and No - that goes against his morality: conversely, he likes to treat his virtue to a feast of noble absti-nence, say, by repeating Montaigne' "What do I know? Or Socrates' "I know that I know nothing". 267

S: Have I let you walk me into a trap? This Montaigne? Oh, never mind.

A: Just joshing; with Plato as much as you. As I said, he'll see you right.

S: Shall we try out Archimedes ideas about displacement with a mud bath?

A: No, I think you've had enough displacement for one day. If you are hot and bothered we can probably get some refreshments here. Meantime we can wish your new, found friend adieu, as I'm sure he needs to make haste to get his pigs to the market.

## CHAPTER 4
### Time and place

A: Are you sitting comfortably? Ok, then. Where were we when the sceptic hooved into view? Oh, yes, the second phase. The period in which the social values evolve in ways that are more sickly, more hostile, to the body and its drives. The period in which the herd instinct finds new ways - not consciously you understand? - To use these new powers to inculcate a wider uniformity of social practices. Let me illus-trate by means of the meta-habits, I spoke of earlier. Memory serves to align cur-rent practice and future action with that of the past. Morality gives the whole thing a more sophisticated veneer in terms of a collective memory, a narrative with re-spect to our indebtedness to our ancestors, then later to the gods, and, later still a single God. Religion emerges as the dominant force tying us to the past. Tradition now continually becomes more venerable, the further away its origin lies and the more it is forgotten; the respect paid to it increases from generation to generation, the tradition at last becomes holy.26

S: I'm beginning to see where you are going with this. Self-consciousness? That too, gets moralized?

A: That too. In the first phase self-consciousness, self-awareness is selected pri-marily as an aid to communication. In the subsequent phase this becomes internal-ized as "bad conscience". We learn to hate our more basic animal instincts for their resistance to sharing. We blame ourselves for being anti-social. In a word, we don the mantel of asceticism.

S: You make it sound like a self-imposed cruelty.

A: Just imagine what it must have been like for these creatures having found their legs, having lived for untold centuries in another element. Of a sudden they found all their instincts devalued, unhinged. They must walk on legs and carry themselves where before water had carried them; a terrible heaviness weighed upon them. They felt inapt for the simplest manipulations, for in this new, unknown world they could no longer count upon the guidance of their unconscious drives. They were forced to think, deduce, calculate, weigh cause and effect - unhappy people, reduced to their weakest, most fallible organ, their consciousness.

I doubt that there has ever been on the earth such a feeling of misery, such a leaden discomfort. It was not that those old instincts had ceased making their demands; but now their satisfaction was rare and difficult. For the most part they had to depend on new, covert satisfactions. All instincts not allowed free play turn inward. This what I call man's interiorization; it alone provides the soil for the growth of what is later to be called man's soul.269

S: It has a certain gruesome fascination.

A: Man's interior world, originally meagre and tenuous, was expanding in every dimension, in proportion as the outward discharge of his feelings was curtailed. The formidable bulwarks by means of which the polity protected itself against the ancient instincts of freedom [punishment was the strongest of these bulwarks] caused those wild, extravagant instincts to turn in upon man. Hostility, cruelty, the delight in persecution, raids, excitement, and destruction, all turned against their begetter. Lacking external enemies and resistances, and confined within an oppressive narrowness and regularity, man began rendering, persecuting, terrifying himself like a wild beast hurling itself against the bars of its cage.270

S: Calm yourself.

A: This "languisher", devoured by nostalgia for the desert, who had to turn himself into an adventure, a torture chamber, an insecure and dangerous wilderness - this pining and desperate prisoner, became the inventor of bad conscience.

S: I'm almost afraid to ask about language.

97

# CHEWING THE CUD

A: Language from the first being simple signals for aligning projects and feelings within the herd evolves to provide ideologies supporting these practices. An elaborate narrative evolves to secure the hold of theses values upon us. One has built these social values over humans for the purpose of strengthening their voice, as if God, as "reality", as the "true world", as the hope and future world, commanded them. Such an ideology serves to intensify the memory and self-awareness by which we are bound to social values.271

S: Sometimes you speak as if there was a plan.

A: No, not at all. These adaptations work best by concealing their herd ends from the moral agent they, in fact, create. Whilst they bring -no, give - values to consciousness, memory, language, these processes operate, in the main, behind our backs. For the most part we are never really cognizant of why we have the values we have. It is that very ignorance that makes them so effective; indeed "directly questioning the subject about the subject, and all self-reflection of spirit has its dangers in this, that it could be useful and important for its activity to interpret it falsely.272Of a sudden, you look very hot and bothered. Was it something I said?

S: Listening to you is an unsettling activity. Sometimes I find myself thinking there's a kind of malice in the way you go about it - as if you're not satisfied unless people walk away wrapped in suspicion about themselves. Are you sure that you've never that Pyrrho before?

A: One begins, don't you think, to mistrust very clever people when they become embarrassed? 273

S: "You want to make him interested in you? Then pretend to be embarrassed in his presence"? 274

A: Now who's being sly, as well as clever? To be ashamed of one's immorality: that is a step on the ladder at the end of which one is also ashamed of one's morality.275

S: I know, I know. If I weren't capable of expressing thoughts of my own this is where I'd say, "Our vanity is hardest to wound precisely when our pride has just been wounded". Don't think I can't draw the inferences from all of this; the moralist is created to serve herd ends, but in ignorance of the service he performs. Would that I could just dismiss this as jaundice on your part, but don't the very same strictures, suspicions, apply to the "individual" whose creation you want to champion?

A: No, not the individual, rather the singularity. Individuals, as I've explained, are the product of social selection; singularities result from self-selection. Individuals be damned; they're all the same. No sense of shame. They differ, of course, depending upon societal need in particular periods. These days they'll tell you, hand on heart, that they're all, first and foremost, good team players. As full of wind as the ball they chase and kick about. But there you go. The default position is always that of the herd perspective - fitting in, showing you belong to the group. It's all pervasive. Listen to any politician, any demagogue, for five minutes.; as soon as he opens his mouth, it's all "we", "our", "us". His address is always to an assumed, an imagined community, and a fictive majority that reside therein.276

S: Nonetheless there are costs to be borne if you stand outside. The rewards are rewards for compliance, for being good.

A: Indeed, it raises some large questions about the sort of "good" as an Ideal Form that Plato has you proselytizing for in the "Republic". Leave that to one side though, and look at it the other way around.

S: How do you mean?

A: Well if our ultimate base line is our genetic make-up, what we are as biology, what we are as unique individuals; then the prerogatives of the herd will always be in conflict with this. This is why I call for us to become who we are. We want to become those who we are - human beings who are new, unique, and incomparable, who give themselves laws, who create themselves.277

S: But what we call human is human precisely because it is, or has been, divested of the animal? That is precisely what Plato and I are talking about with respect to the tripartite division of the soul; reason, spirit, and the appetites.278Our true nature is only realized by our disciplining and controlling, not to say extirpation sometimes, of the appetites. You are surely conversant with the image of the charioteer? Reason as charioteer, spirit as the white horse, and the appetites - the dark horse.279

A: Of course; I've always fancied you as a bit of a dark horse.

S: Fancied? This is serious - what we are discussing. There is a..

# CHEWING THE CUD

A: Time and place. I know. I didn't mean it like that you old "monster in face, monster in soul"[?] 280

S: Oh, ha ha. I'm serious! You seem intent on giving free rein to the appetites in the name of a return to nature.

A: Hasn't it always been so? When one speaks of humanity, the idea is fundamental that this is something that separates and distinguishes man from nature. In reality, however, there is no such separation: "natural" qualities and those called properly "human" are indivisibly grown together. Man, in his most noble capacities, is wholly nature and embodies its uncanny and dual character. Those of his abilities which are awesome and considered inhuman are perhaps the fertile soil out of which alone all humanity ... can grow.281

S: Whoa! Not so fast. Now you sound as if you've been taking lessons from the Metic.

A: A bit of a xenophobe are we? You can do him the honour of calling him by name. Just because he upped sticks and opened his own academy doesn't make him a traitor.

S: All right, then. But you sound like Aristotle; all that stuff about "potential". You know what I mean. Second nature as the realization of the intrinsic potential that lies within a first nature.282

A: No, I don't - at least, not to my ear. Aristotle's view is a teleological one. When he talks of potential he does so in the belief that we are meant to be virtuous, meant to achieve happiness. I don't hold with any of that. Neither do I subscribe to your view, that we are as we are - all we can do is control the dark horse. Its no more than the standard conservative view down the ages - human nature is fixed, unchanging and unchangeable.
   It is always a dangerous process, especially so for life itself: and men and ages that serve life by destroying a past are always dangerous and endangered men and ages. For since we are the outcome of earlier generations, we are also the outcome of their aberrations, passions, and errors, and indeed of their crimes; it is not possible to wholly free oneself from this chain. If we condemn these aberrations and regard ourselves as free of them, this does not alter the fact that we originate in them. The best we can do is confront our inherited nature with our knowledge of it, and through a new, stern discipline combat our inborn heritage and implant in ourselves a new habit, a new instinct, a second nature, so that our first nature withers away ...

- always a dangerous experiment because it is so hard to find a limit to the denial of the past, and because second natures are usually weaker than first natures ... Yet here and there a victory is nonetheless achieved, and for the combatants, for those who employ critical history for the sake of life, there is even a noteworthy consolation: that of knowing that this first nature was once a second nature and that every victorious second nature will become a first nature.283

S: Chains?

A: Chains and hearts. As I wrote to my friend Lou, just the other day, "First one has the difficulty of emancipating oneself from one's chains; and ultimately one has to emancipate oneself from this emancipation too! Each of us has to suffer, though in greatly different ways, from the chain sickness, even after he has broken the chains". 284 Old habits die hard.

S: You and your habits.
A: I know, but what can you do? Every habit lends our hand more wit but makes our wit less handy.285

S: Stop showing off would be a start. I've listened to you long enough. Now you can do me the courtesy of listening to me. All this so-called genealogy of yours; people have said it functions as a critique of morality...

A: Strictly speaking that's not quite true. The inquiry into the origin of our evaluations and tables of the good is in absolutely no way identical with a critique of them, as is so often believed: even though the insight into some pudenda origo certainly brings with it a feeling of a diminution in value of the thing that originates thus and prepares the way to a critical and attitude towards it.286

S: Hmm, that rather takes the rug from beneath what I was going to say next. If, as you say your "inquiry" merely "prepares" the way, you aren't guilty of any genetic fallacy - a moral truth remains a moral truth in spite of being discovered through immoral means.

A: Correct, though I say again that such knowledge would serve to foster a healthy suspicion. There is needed a knowledge of the condition and circumstances under which they - moral values, that is - grew, under which they evolved and changed [morality as a consequence, as symptom, as mask, as tartufferie, as illness, as misunderstanding; but also morality as cause, as remedy, as stimulant, as restraint, as poison], a knowledge of a kind that has never existed or even been desired.287

S: Let me try another tack then, human nature. A couple of things since it seems there are, with the greatest respect, a number of tensions in what you've been saying.

A: Have you noticed how, prior to attacking you, people trot out that "with the greatest respect" thing? Much the same thing is at work with peoples' "Excuse me". The "please" that's tacked on when a man is actually making a request - seeking permission, gets dropped rendering the "Excuse me?" more often than not an instruction. Sorry. Continue. Like a bent bow me - always in tension.

S: Highly strung, certainly. I need to go back to the beginning.

A: It is weariness to toil at the same tasks and be always beginning - don't you think? 28

S: Let's not muddy the pond with his dark thoughts. I was thinking more of your general aim, or rather your boast that you wish to effect "a revaluation of values". Is that even logically possible? Revaluation surely presupposes some overriding principle in respect of which it is carried out? Moreover, this principle cannot be an existing principle - one of the old established ones - since this is one of those that are to be re-evaluated.

A: I don't mean "all" in that sense.

S: The question is whether you can make words mean so many different things?

A: The question is who is master ...that is all.289 Moral values have hitherto been the highest values: would anybody call this into question? - If we remove these values from this position, we alter all values: the principle of their order of rank is overthrown.290

S: What are you saying, then?

A: That the highest values condition the value of the other values. The lower values only have their worth in light of the established higher values.

S: Not wishing to be mulish about this, but why make a song and dance about your "re-valuation"? If our values are simply what we ourselves create, then each and every re-valuation is - well - as arbitrary as the next. You see my point? Only sometimes it's hard to see where you are coming from - like all that stuff about "becoming who you are". Incautious souls might think that is part of that back to nature thesis – that...

A: There is nothing to life that has value, except the degree of power - assuming that life itself is the will to power.291

S: There you go then. How human kind ought to live is to be derived from how they are in nature. A strait-forward instance of the naturalist fallacy - illicitly deriving an "ought" from an "is": normative conclusions being drawn from descriptive premises?

A. No.

S: No?
A: "Yes", "No". All I'm saying is that is that anti-natural morality, that is virtually every morality that has hitherto been taught, reverenced and preached, turns on the contrary precisely against the instincts of life.292 On second thoughts though I doubt that it is possible to root any idea of human nature in the idea of a human good. Isn't this what the Stoics and others do when they attempt to live according to nature? In truth, the matter is altogether different: whilst you pretend rapturously to read the canon of your law in nature, you want something opposite, you strange actors and deceivers! Your pride wants to impose your morality, your ideal, on nature "according to the Stoa", and you would like all existence to exist only after your image - as an immense eternal glorification and generalization of Stoicism. [....]
    But this is an ancient, eternal story: what formerly happened with the Stoics still happens today too, as soon as any philosophy begins to believe in itself. It always creates the world in its own image; it cannot do otherwise. Philosophy is this tyrannical drive itself, the most spiritual will to power, to the "creation of the world", to the causa- prima.293

S: Wait up! If I've understood you correctly, this makes a difference. Now it seems as if this "will to power" of yours isn't intrinsic to nature as such, but rather the value you describe human in terms of.
    That then raises the question of why the rest of us should follow your lead? Why we, too, should make the will to power our primary value? What's the matter? You look as if you've got the whole wait of the world on your shoulders?

# CHEWING THE CUD

A: This! It's such hard work at times. Some times you devoutly wish you could leave it alone. Running around after certainty- ridiculous, really. All you end doing is chasing your own tail, creating a rack of your own making and rending apart whatever sense of well-being you otherwise attain; and for what? You lay yourself open to fear, isolation, doubt, discouragement, conflict. It's tantamount to a disease. Ask any anyone and they'll tell you that it's best not to think too much.

S: But haven't you said yourself, "One should not let oneself be misled: great intellects are sceptics. Zarathustra is a sceptic. A spirit which wants to do great things, which also wills the means for it is necessarily a sceptic". 294 And that "the ability to contradict, the attainment of a good conscience when one feels hostile to what is accustomed, traditional, and hallowed - that is still more excellent and constitutes what is really great, new, and amazing in our culture"? 295

A: I know. Nonetheless, sometimes you find yourself thinking it's all in vain.

S: What's brought this on then?

A: Tripped over something from a past life, quite literally as it happened. Out of the blue, I bumped into Pollydorus the other day. You probably don't know him, but he and I once worked together. He was walking with a pronounced limp, as if he had suffered a stroke. As I gained his shoulder, I asked how he was doing. He stopped and turned and thrust his face close to mind, as if looking for clues. "Ah, Alcibiades!" he said at last, "I don't know anything anymore". "How do you mean?" I asked not knowing whether to smile or be alarmed. Leaning close again, he blurted out, "Don't know anything! Confused!" .Now thoroughly alarmed, but trying to keep my voice even, I asked: "You know where you are now?" He shook his head. "You know where you are going, then? "His eyes having swivelled about him, there came another shake the head. "Shit!" I thought, "I'm going to have to take him with me and then find some way of ascertaining where he now living so as to get him home". "Have you seen a doctor, recently?" I asked.
  "Time-waster!" he shouted. Me, or the doctor's opinion of him, I wondered? Not sure, I ventured: "That cannot be true. Have you sought a second opinion?" "Waste of time!" says Pollydorus becoming agitated again. "I'm a loser!" " No, you're not", I say desperately thinking of some way of placating him. The passing crowd, I'm suddenly aware are giving us more elbowroom than is normal. "Nobody is a loser per se. It depends on high you've set the bar"; I'm aware I'm speaking more quickly than I would like. "Just because you don't have the most beautiful woman on your arm, or you don't have the highest paying job doesn't mean that you are a loser". Suddenly it's as if a light has been switched on behind Pollydorus'

eyes. His face wreathed in a smile he leans close again and tells me, "You're talking bollocks, Alcibiades!" Laughing, I seize the opportunity to escape, wondering if this is not cowardice on my part?

S: Ha, ha, ha. You're being too hard on yourself.

A: Am I? You think it's easy being me. It's hard enough making myself heard in my own day, let alone now. And yes, I'm well aware I'm the fall guy in five or six dialogues with you supposedly written by what's his face.

S: Then you've weighed the evidence, and found it to be light.296 Why worry?

A: Easy for you to say. I've read the eponymously titled One and Two. Straightforward hagiography where you're concerned: as for my reputation, well?

S: You could always pray that things might be different in the future.297
A: You're familiar with its content then? Number Two, I mean? All very well for you to tease. There would more chance of my praying that I got out of here alive, than of my successfully petitioning for a change of reputation.

S: I thought you were the strong one; the one prepared to stand-alone?

A: I am, most of the time! That doesn't mean that I resent any the less the vermin who make a living by feasting off the back of my reputation, more especially when its all lies.

S: Well, there's another thing where you and Plato are one.

A: Speaking of "One", he'll never have to endure the indignity of having his mother's lowly origins traduced as a measure of the vaulting ambition of the eponymous hero.

S: He wouldn't stoop so low.

A: No, but he wouldn't baulk at having me wet-nursed by you! 298 Being regarded as the heir apparent of Pericles is not a sign the gods have blessed that one. Not everyone thinks imperialism is the way to go. I have my doubts about the wisdom of the Sicilian venture.

S: You can't say that!

# CHEWING THE CUD

A: I just did, but of course I couldn't say that in public could I? Weight of expectation, and all that; it'll happen whatever I think in private, and you know why? People like you. Despite all the prattle about love of Athens, about the just state, you remain resolutely purblind. Pericles remains beyond criticism. You still want to believe that Athens has acquired an empire in a fit of absence of mind.299

S: My dear Alcibiades, I had no idea you felt like that. Actually, I agree with you, but I'm free to speak whereas you …

A: A general must see alone and know alone, meaning he must see what others do not see and know what others do not know.

S: You're speaking in riddles.

A: Am I? Appoint a commander and the civilian authorities have to step back and give him free rein. In martial arts, it is important that strategy be unfathomable, that form be concealed, and that movements be unexpected, so that preparedness against them be impossible.

S: But you're such a contentious figure, my friend, half love you, half mistrust you.

A: Too many factions vying for power is what it is; the consequences of the plague's indiscriminate scythe is what it is. When welfare and justice embrace the whole people, when public works are sufficient to meet national emergencies, when the policy of selection for office is satisfactory to the intelligent, when planning is sufficient to know strengths and weaknesses, that is the basis of certain victory.

S: Are you really opposed to the Sicilian venture then? Is that what you're arguing? If so, it is a bit late in the day. The plans of Nicias seem well advanced.

A: Strength is not just a matter of extensive territory and a large population, victory is not just a matter of high walls and deep moats, authority is not just a matter of strict orders and frequent punishments. Those who establish a viable organization will survive even if they are small, while those who establish a moribund organization will perish even if they are large.

S: Perhaps it is better that those who contend for power at home, fight others abroad? Besides who knows what glory they might win for Athens?

# CHEWING THE CUD

A: I say: have no hard feelings toward anyone who has not shown you enmity, do not fight with anyone who does not oppose you. You are half-right about Nicias driving this; he's a convenient figurehead for various factions behind the scene. A general who is not popular is not a help to the nation, not a leader of the army. All this very public display of preparation might serve to raise morale at home, but you can be sure the enemy will know that we will be coming, and will, in the interim afforded him, have laid his plans for defence. Planning should be secret; attack swift.

S: It's not just misgivings that you hold? There is, in what you say, a sense of foreboding?

A: A country is exhausted when it must buy its supplies at high prices, and is impoverished when it ships supplies long distances. Attacks should not be repeated; battles should not be multiplied. Use strength according to capacity, aware that it will be spent with excessive use. Get rid of the worthless, and the country can be peaceful; get rid of the incompetent, and the country can be profited.

S: My dear, Alcibiades, what can I say? I really had no idea that you harboured such doubts about the whole enterprise, or that you had thought so deeply about your chosen profession.

A: "Chosen"? Well, anyway some of us are obliged, one-way or another to live in the so-called "real world".

S: But all that pent up anger, frustration...

A: Some of us have been taught not to spend our emotions like small change. Bye the bye. Speaking of which, I still owe you an answer; human nature? Perhaps there will be an opportunity to honour the debt I owe to Zopyrus. One of the things that incensed me in that philosophical potboiler, "Alcibiades I, was the author's snobbish dismissal of him. What was it? Persian princes get to be educated by four specially chosen wise men? Whereas I get the Thracian slave of Pericles "who was past all other work"! It makes my blood boil, still!

S: Whilst your loyalty does you credit, he was, nonetheless, a slave. You seem, more generally, to have something of a soft spot for the upstart.

A: What? Have you heard yourself, lately? It just oozes out of you too, doesn't it? An aristocracy of talent is what's needful, not an aristocracy of birth! I don't suppose we'll ever know who wrote that sycophantic drivel, but I take some comfort from knowing that if that was the best he could do as an artist, then as a man he was an even poorer specimen.

S: I don't get that last point.

A: You will, or leastways I hope you will, when we've considered the issue of deliberation. It strikes me that this is a hidden reef upon which any hope of mutual understanding must founder. A certainty whilst you hold your present course, and I mine?

S: Well let's hope you navigate a course through this fog. Personally speaking, I find this sort of metaphoric language so dense that I begin to doubt my ability to see the nose in front of my face.

A: That's because what's wet and thick is always predisposed to ignore what is, in fact, the fog of war. I'm jesting, I'm jesting; though not about the fog of war.

S: What say you we resume our stroll? That way I'll have the freedom of movement to cuff you should you chose to insult me?

## CHAPTER 5
### Still marking time

S: You were about to say?

A: Give me a moment to gather the threads. ...Having kept a close eye on philosophers and read between their lines for a sufficient length of time, I tell myself: the greater part of conscious thinking must still be counted among the instinctive activates; ... being conscious is in no decisive sense the opposite of the instinctive - most of a philosopher's conscious thinking is secretly directed and compelled into definite channels by his instincts. Behind all logic too and its apparent autonomy there stand evaluations, in plainer terms physiological demands for the preservation of a certain species of life.300

S: And that has to do with? Fat lot you'd know about threads.

# CHEWING THE CUD

A: I'll pretend I didn't hear that I'm struggling, once again to pick up the threads and weave them into a coherent pattern. I feel like Hume in his rowing boat faced with striking out for the distant shore.301

S: I don't know about this Hume, but you are for certain doing a lot of humming and haring.

A: Well if that's the best you can do for a pun, I'd better get on with it.

S: Might I suggest you begin with some remarks the "good"? It strikes me as odd that nothing much has been said about it. How you can talk so airily about a so-called re-valuation without so much as ... I know we are outdoors, but isn't this the elephant in the room?

A: Fair enough, but enough of the heavy? Let's start by agreeing that de-ontological notions - the idea that there are things that are things that are good and bad in themselves is a fairy story, something for the children?

S: You know damn well that neither of us; neither Plato, nor I ...

A: Good, I see I've got your undivided attention.

S: How many more times? Silly puns won't cut it.
A: Let's further agree that we shouldn't waste any time over the idea that the greatest good is that which produces the greatest happiness for the greatest number.

S: I suspect you know very well that I would never accede to anything that licenses the majority running roughshod over the minority. As to the first I'll wait upon what you have to say.

A: Let me begin sketching out my view with a series of questions. What are our evaluations and moral tables really worth? What is the outcome of their rule? For whom? - In relation to what? - Answer: for life. But what is life? Here we need a new, more detailed formulation of the concept "life". My formula for it is: Life is will to power.
   Further, what is the meaning of the act of evaluation itself? ... In short: where did it originate? Or did it not "originate"? - Answer: moral evaluation is an exegesis, a way of interpreting. The exegesis itself is a symptom of certain physiological condition, likewise of a particular spiritual level of prevalent judgments: Who interprets? - Our affects.302

# CHEWING THE CUD

Do you see? Thoughts about moral prejudices, if they are not meant to be prejudices about prejudices, presuppose a position a position outside morality, some point beyond good and evil to which one has to rise, climb, or fly - and in the present case at least a point beyond our good and evil, a freedom from everything "European", by which I mean the sum of the imperious value judgments that have become part of our flesh and blood.

This may well be a minor madness - the question is whether one really can get up there... The human being of such a beyond who wants to behold the supreme measures of value of his time must first of all "overcome" this time in himself - this the test of his strength - and consequently not only his time but also his prior aversion and contradiction against this time, his suffering from this time, his untimeliness, his romanticism.303

S: It's got to be your upbringing; that or the malign influence of Zopyrus. All I hear is self, self, and self! We are supposedly talking morality? Selflessness?

A: You are missing the important point here. Still, if you insist? Think about it. A man's virtues are called good depending on their probable consequences not for him but for us and society: the praise of virtues has always been far from "selfless", far from "un-egoistic". Otherwise one would have had to notice that virtues [like industriousness, obedience, chastity, filial piety, and justice] are usually harmful to those who possess them, being instincts that dominate them too violently and covetously and resist the efforts of reason to keep them in balance with the other instincts. When you have a virtue, a real, whole virtue [and not merely a mini-instinct for some virtue], you are its victim.304

S: Such cynicism. I heard tell of a man only the other day that he was a " fully fledged human being with no sense of self ... the ultimate team player". 305

A: Well what can you say? Cynical? Is it really? Doesn't your neighbor praise your virtue on precisely that account? ... To be sure for educational purposes and to lead men to incorporate virtuous habits one emphasizes effects of virtue that make it appear as if virtue and private advantage were sisters; and some such relationship actually exists. Blindly ragging industriousness, for example - this typical virtue of an instrument- is represented as the way to wealth and honour and as the poison that best cures boredom and the passions, but one keeps silent about its dangers, its extreme dangerousness. That is how education always proceeds: one tries to condition an individual by various attractions and advantages to adopt a way of thinking and behaving that, once it has become a habit, instinct, and passion, will dominate him to his own ultimate disadvantage but "for the general good". ...This praise of the selfless, the self-sacrificial, the virtuous - that is, of those who do not apply their whole strength and reason to their own preservation, development, elevation, promotion, and the expansion of their power, but rather live, in relation to themselves, modestly and thoughtlessly, perhaps even with indifference or irony - this praise certainly was not born from the spirit of selflessness. The "neighbour" praises selflessness because it brings him advantages. If the neighbour himself were "selfless" in his thinking, he would repudiate this diminution of strength, this mutilation for his benefit; he would work against the development of such inclinations, and above all he would manifest his selflessness by not calling it good! 306

S: "Indifference or irony"?

A: Not everything is about you alone. My point is that the motives of this morality stand opposed to its principle.307 Don't you see, the faith preached so stubbornly and with so much conviction, that egoism is reprehensible, has on the whole harmed egoism [while benefitting, as I shall repeat a hundred times, the herd instincts!]- above all by depriving egoism of its good conscience and bidding us to find in it the true source of all unhappiness. "Your selfishness is the misfortune of your life" - that was preached for thousands of years and harmed, as I have said, selfishness and deprived it of much spirit, much cheerfulness, much sensitivity, much beauty; it made selfishness stupid and ugly and poisoned it.308

S: I feel bound to object, even if it takes off at a tangent. Your remarks about faith and convictions are so derogatory. Some of us feel its sometimes a case of, "Here I stand; I can do no other". 309

A: A very popular error: having the courage of one's convictions; rather it is a matter of having the courage for an attack on one's convictions!!! 310

S: I'm talking faith here, not reason.

A: So I thought. To prove a conviction is quite senseless; rather, it is important to prove that one has a right to be so convinced. In my book conviction is an objection, a question mark. Convictions are prisons.311

S: You go too far!

A: Do I? Every conviction has its history ... it becomes a conviction after not having been one for a long time, and after scarcely having been one for an even longer time ... In the son, that becomes a conviction which in the father was still a lie. By a lie I mean: wishing not to see something that one does see; wishing not to see as

111

one sees it ...The most common lie is that with which one lies to oneself; lying to others is relatively an exception. Now this wishing-not-to-see what one does see, this wishing not to see as one sees, is almost the first condition for all who are party in any sense: of necessity the party man becomes a liar.312

S: Are you done?

A: No; not quite. Freedom from all kinds of convictions, to be able to see freely, is a part of strength...313

S: I knew there was something going on between you and that Pyrrho fellow back there! Was it just this scepticism thing, or something more?

A: Socrates, please! Convictions as a means ... Great passion..

S: Great passion was it? What did he have that I can't give you? The state of him! His sister's pigs were better turned out.

A: Mother of god, do you have to keep going off on one? If you can't behave rationally for more than five minutes at a stretch, there's just no point in my...

S: I'm sorry. It's just that I attract them like flies; both the learned and the plain looney.

A: You might want to think about that simile, but another time eh? Grand passions?

S: Great passions.

A: Yes. Great passions uses, and uses up convictions, it does not succumb to them - it knows itself sovereign. Conversely: the need for faith, for some kind of unconditional Yes and No ... is born of weakness. The man of faith ... is necessarily a dependent man - one who cannot posit himself as an end ... does not belong to himself, he can only be a means; he must be used up, he requires somebody to use him up. His instinct gives the highest honour to a morality of self-abnegation. The man of faith is not free to have any conscience at all for questions of "True" and "Untrue": to have integrity on this point would at once destroy him. The pathological condition of his perspective turns the convinced into fanatics ... the opposition-type of the strong spirit who has become free. Yet the grand pose of these sick spirits, these epileptics of the concept, makes an impression on the great mass - the fanatics are picturesque; man prefers to see gestures rather than to hear reasons.314

S: Why is it then that this problem has escaped the attention of so many?

A: We are still too pious.

S: Pious? You say the strangest things. If I might avail myself of an anachronism here: what would constitute the litmus test?

A: A cliché?

S: But not in my time.

A: Nor mine, come to think of it. A yellowing metaphor, in the future one would guess.

S: Funny. I had it in my head that it was in black and white that it was either red or blue. That was supposed to put a smile on your face. You look glum.

A: Just the thought of dead metaphors - so many of them, so autumnal.

S· Think of what Euripides said of you and autumn, then. Haven't you already said something similar?

A: Have I? Stoicism reduced to, boiled down to a handful bare bones; "show a stiff upper lip", "keep your chin up", "you have to be philosophical".

S: Yes, it's the only way of dealing with life.

A: No, that's another of them: "you just have to be philosophical".

S: What are you saying? Philosophy gets reduced to an adjective?

A: For the many, yes; or, boiled down to so many unrecognized dead metaphors.

S: And for the few? They still have a use for it?

A: Yes, but only as a handmaiden to science.

S: Ha, ha. Now you're having me on. Let's get back to the serious stuff, and let's say I accept your argument that conviction wont pass muster as proof of anything. What say you about what we find useful?

A: Happiness and virtue are no arguments, but for that matter making unhappy and making evil are just as little counter-arguments.315 I rather think that truth and pleasure are not to be found in the same bed despite what the world and his wife would like to believe.

S: Zeus! Talk about turning a party into a wake?

A: The experience of all, severe, of all profoundly inclined, spirits teaches the opposite. At every step, one has to wrestle for truth; one has to surrender for it almost everything to which the heart, to which our love, our trust in life cling otherwise. That requires greatness of the soul: the service of the truth is the hardest service. What does it mean after all to have integrity in matters of the spirit? That one is severe against one's heart, that one despises "beautiful sentiments", that one makes of every Yes and No a matter of conscience! Faith makes blessed: consequently, it lies.316

S: Oh, but I love you still; a man after my own heart! Even so, "faith lies"? Must you go so far?
A: That faith makes blessed under certain circumstances, that blessedness does not make of a fixed idea a true idea, that faith moves no mountains but puts mountains where there are none: a quick walk through a madhouse enlightens one sufficiently about this.317

S: Hmm, yours would be a hard bed to lie in. Some might argue a pretty little lie is necessary for the preservation of life, leastways for its propagation. That's what we used to say, anyway, when we were busy re-seeding Athens after the war.

A: My! Aren't you the daddy?

S: There's no call for facetiousness.

A: You'll be telling me next that: a man's got to do, what a man's got to do.

S: Well, he had to.

A: And with what was her name?

# CHEWING THE CUD

S: Myrto was Xanthippe's idea.

A: Not exactly a labour of love, then?

S: No. I said; a cousin of hers several times removed. Walks with a limp, and has a lazy eye. Difficult to tell when she's looking at you.

A: Ha, ha. And who would blame her for looking away? Yes, you said as much earlier, but not about the eye.

S: It was no laughing matter at home.

A: I can see that.

S: Still isn't.

A: At risk of sounding like your kill-joy one might say, one must not let oneself be seduced by blue eyes and swelled bosoms: there is nothing romantic about great-ness of soul.318 How many people still make the inference: "one could not stand life if there were no God!" [Or, as they say in the circles of the Idealists: "one could not stand life if it lacked the ethical significance of its ground!"] - Conse-quently there must be a God [or an ethical significance of existence]! ... What pre-sumption to decree that all that is necessary for my preservation must also really be there! As if my preservation were anything necessary.319

S: Ouch.

A: Well? What do you want me to say? A belief may be a necessary condition of life and yet be false.320

S: What are you claiming here: that utility is no argument for truth?

A: Right. We have fixed a world for ourselves in which we can live - by assuming bodies, lines, planes, causes and effects, motion and rest, form and content: without these articles of faith nobody now could stand life. However, these are still not proven. Life is no argument; among the conditions of life might be error.321

S: Whoa! Don't forget I'm getting on in years. If you want me to keep up, you can't go galloping off into fresh pastures. I'm still chewing over your thoughts about morality and the idea of the good. Suppose we agree that utility, however useful, is no substitute for the truth. That still leaves me wondering about what you meant by saying, "we are still too pious"?

A: Well in science, convictions have no rights of citizenship ...only when that decide to descend to the modesty of an hypothesis, of a provisional experimental point of view, of a regulative fiction, may they be granted admission and a certain value ... though always with the restriction that they remain under police supervision, under the police of mistrust. Yet this does not mean ...: only when a conviction ceases to be a conviction may it attain admission to science? Would not the discipline of the scientific spirit begin with this, to no longer to permit oneself any convictions? Probably this is the case: but one must still ask whether, in order that this discipline could begin, there must not have been a conviction to begin with - and even such a commanding and unconditional one that it sacrificed all other convictions for its own sake. It is clear that science, too, rests on a faith, for there is no science "without presuppositions". The question whether truth is needed must not only nave been affirmed in advance, but affirmed to the extent that the principle, the faith, the conviction is expressed: "nothing is needed more than truth, and in relation to it all else has only a secondary value".

This unconditional will to truth - what is it? Is it the will not to allow oneself to be deceived? Or is it the will not to deceive? For the will to truth could be interpreted in the second way, too - if only the special case "I do not want to myself" is subsumed under the generalization "I do not want to deceive". But why not deceive? But why not allow one self to be deceived? 322

S: Which is it, then: the first, or second?

A: Note the reasons for the former principle belong to an altogether different realm from those for the second. One does not want to allow oneself to be deceived because one assumes that it is harmful, dangerous, and calamitous to be deceived. In this sense science would be a long-range prudence, a caution, a utility; but one could object in all fairness: How is that? Is wanting not to allow one self to be deceived really less harmful, less dangerous, and less calamitous? What do you know in advance of the character of existence to be able to decide whether the greater advantage is on the side of the unconditionally mistrustful or the unconditionally trusting? But if both should be required, much trust as well as much mistrust, from where would science then be permitted to take its unconditional faith or conviction on which it rests, that truth is more important than any other thing, including every other conviction? Precisely this conviction could never have come into being if both truth and untruth constantly proved to be useful, which is the case. Thus - the

116

faith in science, which after all exists undeniably, cannot owe its origin to such a calculus of utility; it must have originated in spite of the fact that the disutility and dangerousness of "the will to truth", of "truth at any price" is proved to it constantly. "At any price": how well we understand these words once we have offered and slaughtered one faith after another on this alter! 323

S: So, the second?

A: So, consequently, "will to truth" does not mean "I will not allow myself to be deceived", but - there is no alternative - "I will not deceive, not even myself"; and with that we stand on moral ground. For you only have to ask carefully, "Why do you not want to deceive?" especially if it should seem- and it does seem! - as if life aimed at semblance, meaning error, deception, simulation, delusion, self-delusion, and when the great sweep of life has always shown itself to be on the side of the most unscrupulous polytropoi. Charitably interpreted, such a resolve might perhaps be a quixotism, a minor slightly mad enthusiasm; but it might be something more serious, namely, a principle that is hostile t life and destructive, - "Will to truth" - that might be a concealed will to death.

Thus the question: "Why science?" leads back to the moral problem: Why have morality at all when life, nature, and history are "not moral"? No doubt, those who are truthful in that audacious and ultimate sense that is presupposed by the faith in science thus affirm another world than the world of life, nature, and history; and insofar as the affirm this "other world" - look, must they not by the same token negate its counterpart, this world, our world? - But you will have gathered what I am driving at, namely, it is still a metaphysical faith upon which our faith in science rests - that even we seekers after knowledge today, we godless anti-metaphysicians still take our fire, too, from the flame lit by a faith that is thousands of years old, that Christian faith which was also the faith of Plato that God is truth, that truth is divine. - But what if this should become more and more incredible, if nothing should prove to be divine any more unless it were error, blindness, the lie - if God himself should prove to be our most enduring lie? -324

S: Polytropos - Homer, eh. That's how he characterizes Odysseus, yes? And the will to truth is something more terrifying than that; a principle that is destructive and hostile to life?

A: Indeed. The strength of a spirit might be measured according to how much of the "truth" he would be able to stand - more clearly, to what degree it would need to be watered down, shrouded, sweetened, blunted, and falsified.325

# CHEWING THE CUD

S: There's really no need to lay it on so thick. You wouldn't ever catch me arguing truth as utility, or pragmatism. If I were to attempt to summarize your argument in respect of individuals as products of moralities, it might be to say: by their fruits, ye shall know them.326

A: Actually, I'd rather go one better. I'd say of every morality: it is a fruit by which I recognize the soil from which it sprang.327

S: Have it your own way then! Must you always have the last word?

A: There is a difference between what you said, and what I said in reply.

S: It wouldn't harm your cause to be gracious now and again.

A: Gracious? Like you?

S: Well if not gracious, then good-natured.

A: Beware of the good-natured, I say. Association with them makes one languid.328 Surely, a good conversation presumes leave is given to both give, and take, offence?
S: So, this is why you play hard to get. I've heard some excuses in my time, but that takes the biscuit.

A: Why? Is it not reasonable to surmise that all associations are good that make one practice the weapons of defence and offense that reside in one's instincts. All one's inventiveness toward testing one's strength of will - To see the distinguishing feature in this, and not in knowledge, astuteness, wit.329 What's wrong with that as a modus operandi?

S: Even those raised to command might do well to take lessons in modesty.

A: Really? For what does one have to atone most? For one's modesty; for having failed to listen to one's most personal requirements; for having mistaken oneself; for having under-estimated oneself; for having lost a good ear for one's instincts: this lack of reverence for oneself revenges itself through every kind of deprivation: health, friendship, well-being, pride, cheerfulness, freedom, firmness, courage. One never afterward forgives oneself for this lack of genuine egoism: one takes it as an objection, for a doubt about a real ego.330

## CHEWING THE CUD

S: And the good is? You still haven't said.

A: What is good? - All that heightens the feeling of power, the will to power, power itself in man. What is bad? - All that proceeds from weakness. What is happiness? - The feeling that power increases - that a resistance is overcome. Not contentment, but more power; not peace at all, but war; not virtue but proficiency [ virtue in the Renaissance style, virtu, virtue free of moralist acid].331

S: I didn't get that last bit. More important though is surely, what sort of value power is in your terms?

A: A tablet of good hangs over every people. Behold it is the tablet of their overcoming; behold, it is the voice of their will to power. Praiseworthy is whatever seems difficult to a people; whatever seems indispensable and difficult is called good; and whatever liberates even out of the deepest need, the rarest, the most difficult - that they call holy.332

S: Peculiar diction, that? You sounded for a moment as if you had assumed the persona of some prophet or other - lofty in other ways, too. it seems. You don't seem to have much regard for what we might hold in common.

A. Whatever can be common always has little value.333

S: Hmm, sweeten the pill why don't you? I'd be right in thinking that all this talk about strength - even reason itself, though we'll come back to that - is to be cashed in in favour of this "will to power" thing? Anyway I'd like to ask if this is relative to the strength or weakness of the actor, or do strength and weakness refer to the actor's capacity to overcome resistance?

A: I'm not going there.

S: Why not? It's a legitimate question.

A: Granted, but you just want to get me on that carousel of yours, and spin me round with pettifogging questions till I'm too dizzy to think straight.

S: Ha, ha. Nonetheless, the answer is?

A: The strength of those who attack can be measured in a way by the opposition they require.334

# CHEWING THE CUD

S: There, there. That wasn't so difficult was it? We've established that resistance belongs not to the respective strengths and weaknesses of the actors here, but is defined independently of them.

A: If you say so Socrates.

S: I do indeed. But we have yet to determine whether such greatness of which you speak in respect of overcoming resistance is a matter of surmounting internal or external factors. We might admire two men for their ability in climbing the greasy pole of politics, but admire the second more than the first because he came from a poor background. A great achievement isn't the same thing as a great individual. On the other hand, we might wonder whether the epithet "great" can be ascribed to just any difficult task. You do hear from time to time of individuals who claim to have eaten their own weight in boiled eggs.

A: Enough! Enough of this nit picking; God forbid that you should become the patron saint of future philosophers. Set your nose to the word and off you go. You can't help it, I know. You're like Finn. Spends his life head down chasing his nose; never sees the wood for the trees.

S: "Finn"?

A: One of my dogs.

S: Why "Finn", I meant?

A: You'd understand if you saw him quartering a field of corn; like a shark hunting down a leak even to its own side, as the poet says. Only it's pheasants he's after.

S: Don't speak to me of cornfields, I dreamt of one the other night.
I was in the countryside walking and chanced to look behind, and there it was silently, rising up behind me. Field, after field, of the stuff; like the massed ranks of some foreign army that began pressing in on me, all the while growing taller, pushing me forward, wanting to claim my place, swallow me up. I tried to protest that I was Socrates; no tare to be driven willy-nilly into the hedgerow to be gleaned by the hands of the importunate, but no words came.

A: Ah, sweet pea, what can I say?

# CHEWING THE CUD

S: Clearly nothing worth hearing until someone finds a way of putting a forty year old head on twenty- year old shoulders, and probably not even then.

A: Whilst you've got your legacy in mind I've got more to say about greatness. Think about it. What belongs to greatness [?] - Which will attain anything great if he does not find in himself the strength and the will to inflict great suffering? Being able to suffer is the least thing; weak women and even slaves often achieve virtuosity in that. But not to perish of internal distress and uncertainty when one inflicts great suffering and hears the cry of this suffering - that is great, that belongs to greatness.335

S: That's monstrous! Be nicer to everyone you meet! Everyone is fighting some kind of battle! 336

A: Self-pity doesn't become you.

S: Why you -! I'll live to see the day when your feathers are plucked yet, you proud peacock!

A: There's no call for you to go off half- cock, old cock!

S: What the fucks that mean? Half cock? Are you implying I've been circumcised? There's an easy way to disprove that!

A: No.

S: Yes there is!

A: No, I just forgot.

S: Forgot? How could you forget something like that?

A: I didn't mean that.

S: Well, you shouldn't say it then. Really: your lack of manners.

A: Please! Can we get back to what I really wasn't saying? Monsterous?

S: So you knew all along? I don't like to boast about such things, myself. Others can easily feel belittled by the comparison. Is that what this is all about? Do you, yourself, feel...?

A: Oh, for fucks sake! You are doing my head in!

S: I am? Have I missed a step in the argument? Oh well, the hottest love has the coldest end.337

A: Please, before you say something you regret.

S: I already have.

A: Then before we say something we both regret? " Let him who would move the world first move himself". That was one of yours, not Plato's right?

S: Right, kind of you to notice and say so.

A: My so-called monstrous comments about greatness? I most definitely did not say that greatness is only achieved by inflicting suffering on others.

S: But what if I'm suffering and you're in a position to do something about it? If you chose not to, aren't you inflicting suffering?
A: Ignoring your suffering is not the same as inflicting it.

S: There are sins of omission as well as of commission.

A: I know, but all I'm saying is that the morality of compassion does not always hold all the trump cards. One has taken the value of these "values" as given, as factual, as beyond all question; one has hitherto never doubted or hesitated in the slightest degree in supposing the "good man" to be of greater value than the "evil man", of greater value in the sense of furthering the advancement and prosperity of man in general [the future of man included]. But what if the reverse were true? What if a symptom of regression were inherent in the "good", likewise a danger, a seduction, a poison, a narcotic, through which the present was possibly living at the expense of the future?- perhaps, more comfortably, more dangerously, but at the same time in a meaner style, more basely? - So that precisely morality would be to blame if the highest power and splendour actually possible to the type man was never in fact attained.338

# CHEWING THE CUD

S: An interesting speculation, I'll grant you, but no ore than that.

A: What if I were to say, such men of great creativity, the really great men according to my understanding, will be sought in vain today and probably for a long time to come; until, after much disappointment, one most begin to comprehend why they are lacking and that nothing stands more malignantly in the way of their rise and evolution, today and for a long time to come, than what in Europe today is simply called "morality" - as if there were no other morality and could be no other - the aforementioned herd-animal morality which is striving with all its power for a universal green pasture happiness on earth, namely for security, absence of danger, comfort, the easy life [...].The two doctrines it preaches most often are: "equal rights" and "sympathy with that suffers" - and it takes suffering itself to be something that must be absolutely abolished.339

S: Hang about. Have we shifted disciplines? Creativity is surely to with aesthetics, but here you seem to have yoked it to you in respect of suffering?

A: Creation - that great redemption from all suffering, and life's growing light. But that the creator may be, suffering is needed.340

S: Needed, you say. Surely it is a matter of regret that an artist is made to suffer for his art. Even so, although we may admire and grit in overcoming obstacles we admire as a man in this regard: not as artist. The merit of his work is independent of the struggle that sees it bare fruition.

A: No offense, but that just goes to show how difficult it is to shrug off that whole mind-set. Suffering isn't incidental to creativity; it is its essential loom, its lifeblood. Creativity is the will to power made manifest. You can't see it because you're so wedded to the idea that happiness equates with the absence of suffering.

S: Well that the right six numbers should do it.

A: Don't be so flippant; I'm trying to be serious here.

S: I know. It's just that I've got a lotto things on my mind, ha, ha.

A: "When the debate is lost, slander becomes the tool of the loser" That's another of your wise-saws?

123

S: Slander? There's no slandering going on here. A bit of sledging, maybe, but your straight bat has taken all the fun out of that. You were saying before I got all silly and unnecessary? It's a weakness that sometimes gets the better of me when I'm in close proximity to the object of my...

A: Stop! Stop it right now. This is the very heart of the matter! The hedonism of the weary is here the supreme measure of value.341

S: That reeks of paradox: "the hedonism of the weary".

A: Shop around. You'll find it retails in many guises. Not just the English happiness of comfort and fashion, but that of Buddhist resignation, Christian acceptance, and other elixirs calculated to procure the cessation of suffering; contentment, pleasure, and above all - peace.
    Our happiness is not opposed to suffering. Parents may gag at the thought, but happiness and unhappiness are sisters and even twins that either grow up together or [...] remain small together.342
This is why I say you should choose enemies you can be proud of.343

S: You can't fight everyone though.

A: That's why I say that, " For the worthier enemy, O my friends, you shall save yourselves; therefore you must pass by much - especially much rabble who raise a din in your ears about the people and about peoples. Keep your eyes undefiled by their pros and cons! There is much justice, much injustice; and whoever looks on becomes angry. Sighting and smiting here become one; therefore go away into the woods and lay your sword to sleep". 344

S: Weird - that whole prophet misunderstood thing.

A: Never mind that. Understand this. The "well-born" simply felt themselves to be the "happy" [...]; and as full human beings, overloaded with strength and therefore necessarily active, they likewise did not know how to separate activity from happiness, for them being active is of necessity included in happiness [...] - all of this in opposition to "happiness" on the level of the impotent, oppressed, those festering with poisonous and hostile feelings, in whom it essentially appears as narcotic, anaesthetic, calm, peace, "Sabbath", relaxation of mind and stretching of the limbs.345

S: Tell me if I misunderstand you. Not only is your notion of "happiness" non-hedonistic, it is actually anti- hedonistic in that suffering is an inescapable element of happiness. Further you are now claiming that insofar as happiness is a matter of overcoming resistance it requires the agent to be active. And so saying we are back with those familiar antipodes of strength and weakness, unless I'm mistaken? Since kind of "happiness" is attainable only for those capable of over-coming resistances - indeed seeking out greater and greater resistances - ergo, it is the prerogative of the strong?

A: Couldn't have put it better myself. You'd make a good pupil. I ought to consider charging you.

S: You should mind you don't get your fingers burnt! Education is the kindling of a flame, not the filling of a vessel.346 I'm the eternal student, not some client or customer to be fobbed off with some "one size fits all" learning package with pre-determined outcomes. Which reminds me, I didn't say I assented to any of this. On which point, though I think I can guess the answer - what of the weak?

A: If only everyone had an enemy like you, my friend?

S: Less of the soft soap then. Answer the question!

A: Gladly. The weak, of course, will get meagre pickings where over-coming resistance is concerned; their very weakness will incline them to resent the fact of resistance. Rather they will be predisposed to conceive of "happiness" in terms of the cessation of struggle, of activity generally - see life as a beach, as they say.

S: As I thought.

A: You should seek your enemy and you wage your war - for your thoughts. And if your thought is vanquished, your honesty should still find cause for triumph in that. You should love peace as a means to new wars - and the short peace more than the long ... Let your work be a struggle, let your peace be a victory.347

S: Can we leave the military metaphors to one side? Another question. A while back you declared that happiness or goodness was "all that heightens the feeling of power, the will to power, power itself in man". Just the one question: any fool can feel powerful without actually being so?

# CHEWING THE CUD

A: Your father with his latest conquest? Here, or rather, there the feeling of intoxication proved misleading. This increases the feeling of power in the highest degree - therefore, naively judged, power itself.348

S: To describe it as naive would be an under-statement where he was concerned.

A: Forgive me. I ought to have used a different example. But I've addressed your point? There's no happiness for he who lacks the feeling of power, but neither is there any genuine happiness for he whose feeling of power is delusive.

S: Yes, I see that. You know what I don't hear in what say; nothing at all about reason or deliberation. Many would think that they are synonymous with moral argument. Even Xanthippe is big on "reasons". You have to make sure that you have them all in a row where she's concerned. Anything you do say will be taken down and used in evidence against you at a later date. And that includes, I might add, things you didn't say, but should have.

A: Must we talk of old clapper-claws?

S: Have a care! Termagant, scold, shrew, she may be; but she is my "sweet chilli". Just because you don't have any time for women, it...

A: I never said that. As a matter of fact, I regard the perfect woman as a higher type of human being than the perfect man: also something much rarer - The natural science of animals offers a means of demonstrating the truth of this proposition.349
S: Would you Adam and Eve it? And there was I thinking you hadn't a good word to say about them, and much less marriage.

A: Not so. However before marrying I think it prudent to ask oneself: do you believe you are going to enjoy talking with this woman into your old age? Everything else about marriage is transitory, but most of the time you are together will be devoted to conversation.350

S: And Timandra? Is she a talker, or a moaner? Does she have to jump to attention when yours truly comes to attention?

A: Do you have to be so lascivious?

S: Just wondered how these things are *handled* in a military household?

126

## CHEWING THE CUD

A: There are women who, however you may search them, prove to have no content but are purely masks. The man who associates with such spectral, necessarily dissatisfied beings is to be commiserated with, yet it is precisely they who are able to arouse the desire of the man most strongly for he seeks for her soul - and goes on seeking.351

S: Is that some sort of kack-handed way of excusing your "excursions"?

A: Ever the moralist, aren't you? No, that was not my intention. That said, a marriage proves itself a good marriage by being able to endure an occasional " exception". 352 Haven't you proved that to yourself?

S: As a man of consequence, if that doesn't sound too pompous, I had my duty to do as an Athenian.

A: Yes, it does. But then again, women love a man of consequence as though they want to have him for themselves alone. They would gladly keep him under lock and key if their vanity did not dissuade them: for this desires him to be of consequence before others as well.353

S: Xanthippe has to be the exception there. Not - I hasten to add - not the kind of exception you were speaking of a moment ago; she's far too modest to countenance such shenanigans.

A: Generally speaking, the more beautiful a woman is the more modest she is? 354
S: That's not very funny; it's cruel. I merely meant that had the door a lock, I'd find myself on the outside even more often.

A: And that's not, itself, cruel? Ah, "Sweet chilli" No. I don't want to know. By way of an answer to your question; no creature wants to deceive itself [a dubious premise in itself], no creature may deceive itself - consequently there is only a will to truth. As to "truth"? The law of contradiction provides the schema: the true world, to which one seeks the way, cannot contradict itself, cannot change, cannot become, has no beginning and no end. There! The greatest error ever committed. One believed - I should say by you and Plato both - one possessed a criterion of reality in the form of reason - while in fact one possessed them in order to become a master of reality, in order to misunderstand reality in a shrewd manner.355

S: Why "shrewd"?

# CHEWING THE CUD

A: Sometimes you have an alarming tendency to seek out the mote rather than the beam, you know?

S; A pride in the detail you know. Like as not, you find the devil there.

A: I'll admit that I used the word "shrew" advisedly.

S: There you go then. Perhaps you intended some allusion to my "sweet chilli". Etymologically speaking there must be some connection between shrew and shrewd.

A: Amour proper.

S: What's that got to do with the price of eggs? I don't follow.

A: Just that they say the timid have less of it than the arrogant.

S: Well you'd be the one to know.

A: Actually, I was going to say that its the other way around. Being timid, being afraid, they [the poor] take care not to hurt others. But not as you might think because that matters more to them than those who are arrogant - as you clearly think - but to avoid being hurt themselves, ... and this on account of the extreme pain they feel at every hurt they receive. You might say this is a feature of a degenerate nature - the inability to ward off even the faintest stimulus.356

S: And shrews?

A: Small, timid animals, whose long twitching snout serves to sniff out both opportunity and danger; hence, perhaps, the shrew as wife? The woman as second-class citizen: reactive - precluded from being active, she must seek out her opportunities, her advantage, as circumstances permit. On the negative, pejorative side, the woman comes to be seen as mean-spirited, calculating, a bit of a schemer and busybody. Note, however, the backhanded recognition in the sobriquet? "Shrewd" [?] - someone who is clever to a degree.

S: To a degree?

A: Yes, to a degree. If you speak of men as shrewd, what happens? To be sure, you lose the negative connotations but not the all-important one.

# CHEWING THE CUD

S: Which is?

A: The spirit of rancour, of ressentiment. I've not thought this through. Even so, I think the shrewd person is, above all, re-active. As shrewd, as re-active, he, or she, plays off somebody larger, more intelligent. Somebody with a better grip, as it were, of the larger picture. The shrew divines how to mine this larger whole in pursuit of its more limited, and self-interested wants without drawing unwanted attention to the weaknesses inherent in the host's mien. There is in all this a curious cowardice. The instinct of self-preservation bids the smaller not to confront head-on the larger.

S: Hmm, I'll give that some thought when I get home; something to deliberate about?

A: Yes, do. Every girl who thinks to employ her youthful charms alone to provide for her entire life, and whose cunning is in addition prompted by a wise mother, has precisely the same objective as a courtesan, only she pursues it more shrewdly and less honestly.357

S: I said I'd think about it. Xanthippe's mother is due for a visit soon, so I'm unlikely to forget. You think I can talk?

A: Ah, yes Kant. I'd not forgotten; an old sparring partner of Zopy's. He held, Kant that is, that deliberation is all about stepping back from and also looking down on ones inclination.
S: A man after my own heart. I am something over and above my desires.

A: What if the will to overcome an affect is ultimately only the will of another, or several other, affects?

S: Then there would no self to own these affects. What does this Kant say?

A: More or less exactly that. Unlike his "inclinations" which are typed "alien influences", the "proper self" is the agent's "intelligible self". 358

S: There you are then, great minds think alike.

A: But this is to misunderstand passion and reason, as if the latter were an independent entity and not a system of relations between various passions and desires; and as if every passion did not possess a quantum of reason -.359

129

# CHEWING THE CUD

S: Come on, you can't just make such declarations. Where's the reasoning?

A: Ok. What is clearly the case is that in this entire procedure our intellect is only the blind instrument of another drive which is the rival of the drive whose vehemence is tormenting us: whether it be the drive to restfulness, or the fear of disgrace and other evil consequences, or love. While "we" believe we are complaining about the vehemence of a drive, at bottom it is one drive which is complaining about another; that is to say: for us to become aware that we are suffering about the vehemence of a drive presupposes the existence of another equally vehement or even more vehement drive, and that a struggle is in prospect in which our intellect is going to have to take sides.360

S: But if it adjudicates, how does its work differ from this Kant's "pure reason"?

A: No, it's not like that. What I'm saying is that "we" as agents are constituted by our contingent inclinations, or, in my terms the drives we happen to have There is no such thing as the rational will that stands over and above the inclinations we happen to have. The "will" is in reality nothing other than the configuration of these drives.361

S: You've lost me.

A: Put it another way then. I owe this too, to dear old Zopy. It concerns motives. How can I best express this? According to Kant, deliberation is about my contingent inclinations and these are things said to shape my character.
For Zopy, on the other hand, we deliberate from our motives, and these are not inclinations but rather determinate features of the world. To use an example of his, one is moved help another in distress by his situation, not by one's inclinations. That one is responsive to his need is due one's character. Were one not so disposed by one's character the cries of he who is in distress might fall upon deaf
ears. In short, my inclinations are the things that mould the stance from which I deliberate in the first instance. Thus for Kant if I didn't have inclinations I'd have nothing to deliberate about, for Zopy I'd have nothing to deliberate from.362
    If I might add, it seems to me at the bottom of us, really "deep down", there is, of course, something un-teachable, some granite of spiritual fatum, of predetermined decision and answer to predetermined selected questions. Whenever a cardinal problem is at stake, there speaks an unchangeable "this is I", about a man and woman, for example, a thinker cannot relearn, but only finish learning - only discover ultimately how this is "settled in him" .363

S: I see your point, but does it do other than get us out of the fire and into the frying pan. If you and Zopyrus are right, there would be no limit to the number of what I might call perspectives on any occasion. Judgment in terms of any objective standard would have to go by the board?

A: It doesn't mean that some form of crude relativism will rule the roost. Haven't I said enough about the psychological, the physiological, and the ideological components of our perspectives to allay any such simplistic interpretation? Or is it something else that is lurking in the background here? Is there some desire to hold the whole of life to account? "Thoughts about moral prejudices," if they are not meant to be prejudices about prejudices, presuppose a position outside of morality ...364

S: I don't know what you mean.

A: Don't be so coy! A condemnation of life by the living is after all no more than the symptom of a certain kind of life: the question whether the condemnation is just or unjust has not been raised at all. One would have to be situated outside life [...] to be permitted to touch upon the problem of the value of life at all: sufficient reason for understanding that this problem is for us an inaccessible problem. When we speak of values we do so under the inspiration and from the perspective of life: life itself evaluates through us when we establish values.365

Do you see? Evaluation is only possible from the perspective of life: to stand outside of life is to deprive oneself of the tools required to make any value judgment whatsoever. In themselves such judgments are stupidities.366 Let me put a final nail in the coffin? We cease to think when we refuse to do so under the constraint of language; we barely reach the doubt that sees this limitation as a limitation. Rational thought is interpretation according to a scheme that we cannot throw off.367

S: You wouldn't deny that the power of value judgments lies in their being presented as objective normative facts?

A: Philosophers have never hesitated to affirm a world provided it contradicted this world and furnished them with a pretext for speaking ill of this world.368

S: That's a rum thing to say.

A: Is it? We have measured the value of the world according to categories that refer to a purely fictitious world. Our value judgments are nothing other than false

131

projections.369 We who think and feel at the same time are those who really continually fashion something that had not been there before: the whole eternally growing world of valuations, colours, accents, perspectives, scales, affirmations, and negations [....] But precisely this knowledge we lack, and when we occasionally catch it for a fleeting moment we always forget again immediately.370 If I might assume the crown, we have thought the matter over and finally decided that there is nothing good, nothing beautiful, nothing sublime, nothing evil in itself, but that there are states of the soul in which we impose such words upon things external to and within us.371

S: Walk on ahead will you? I need to relieve myself. Sorry, but the call of nature these days is quite peremptory. That's old age for you; one damn thing after another. Won't be long. There, what did I say - two shakes of a puppy-dog's tail. I could tell you a tale or two about my tail's failure to rise to the occasion recently, if you're interested? Don't pull faces. Didn't someone say, " I am a man; nothing human is foreign to me"? 372

A: Not yet, he hasn't, but he'll get around to it." Whilst there's life, there's hope". 373

S: There you are then; "from many a bad beginning ... great friendships have sprung up."374

A: Do you even know what you are saying?

S: Probably not, but that worries me less and less these days. Its a toss up between my daemon and a senior moment". As for myself, I rarely get a look in. Still, "fortune favours the brave", or so I'm told.375

A: Incredible.

S: Is it? "Nothing is so difficult that it may be found out by seeking". 376 Which reminds me. I was going to ask.

A: "According to how the man is, so you must humour him"377

S: Who said that then? No. Never mind. I was going to ask, - several things, actually. I'm still somewhat in the dark about your notion of the "self"; likewise who, or what it is, that is in command when we deliberate. And linked to the latter, it seems to me is the issue of freedom. There is, as in other areas of your thought, a tension between what appear to be conflicting commitments. In particular between your overt championing of emancipation and your frequent allusions to our being, in one way or another - fated?

Oh, yes. I nearly forgot. Another thing about morality; the idea that moral commands are thought to be universally binding. Is it for you a case of, "so many men, so many opinions: to each his own way"? 378 Sorry about this. My head is full of strange voices, speaking with strange accents.

A: Don't start that again. You'll have me wishing, "I [should have] took to my heels as fast as I [could]", as soon as I clapped eyes on you! 379

S: Don't be like that. You might be too young for a senior moment, but with that new haircut of yours some blonde moments can't be too far away! A man of fashion ought, at the very least, to make sure his collar and cuffs match! And while we are at it, you still owe me an account of love. You were late, and already the worst for ware last night, and therefore had little to say that was constructive.

A: Zeus! You are just like your wife! Talk about "birds of a feather". Not so drunk that I couldn't see that there was something wrong with both accounts; yours and that of Aristophanes' - yours in terms of love as lack, his in terms of love as loss. Can we forget about all that for now? Judging by the length of your shopping list there's more than enough room that elephantine skull of yours for a whole library of characters.

S: Is this where I say: being a pachyderm, sticks and stones may break...

A: No. This is where you shut up, and I oblige you.

S: Charmed, I'm sure.

A: Might I suggest we take your "shopping list" in reverse order, but that before we do we find another place where we can be seated? You are limping, and I don't know about you but I'm hungry.

# CHAPTER 6
## Keeping time

A: That stiff ado was lovely. It was a stroke of fortune; our alighting on those two shepherds and they're offering to share their meal.

S: Well you certainly enjoy your food, that's for sure.

A: But that sauce! Don't say you didn't enjoy that, even if you struggled with the meat?

S: Since I lost my teeth, I've decided one should eat to live rather than live to eat.380 There are so many people less fortunate than we.

A: Is that dyspepsia speaking? I was going to ask about the leg?

S: Since you ask, I'm not partial to lamb.

A: Your leg, I meant!

S: Oh, the sciatica. It's eased off. Did I tell you about this swelling I've...

A: No. And before you ask, seeking a second opinion about hypochondria
is not going to yield much.

S: Perhaps I'll have more luck with your philosophy, though what with you being a pessimist I doubt it.

A: If you're going to be so wilfully crabby?

S: Yes. Why not start there, the "two willies"? Not my sobriquet. That's how I've heard you, and Zopyrus, referred to behind your backs. Tell me about the will.

A: And there was I thinking on this Zopy and I were polls apart: my proposition being, that hitherto the will of psychology is an unjustified generalization, that this will does not exist at all.381

S: This is not how the man in the street sees it. For him the will is a capacity, some-thing effective.

A: I know. We believed ourselves to be causal in the act of willing: we thought that here at least we caught causality in the act ... Nevertheless, the "inner world" is full of phantoms and will-o'-the-wisps: the will is one of them.382 As well as an error, something propagated by priestly types intent on giving us a bad conscience. They want people to consider their selves "free" so that they be judged and punished.383

S: The issue of freedom of the will we shall have to return to. For now I merely observe that, in apparent contradiction to what you have just said, you freely avail yourself of the term - will, that is.

A: Indeed I do. In real life it is only a matter of strong and weak wills.384

S: You can't have it both ways. And I have my own view on the issue of the so-called weakness of will. One of Aristotle's nostrums, I believe. "I know what the good is, but when it comes to I choose the bad."385 Absolute rubbish. Talk about biting the hand that feeds you. No sooner is his stomach full and he's off to set himself up in competition. Even tried to filch some of Plato's students, you know.

A: I'm sure your loyalty does you credit, but you were about to say?

S: Was I? Oh yes, I was. Until one has acquired knowledge of good and evil one cannot be said to possess virtue. That's why I say: no one knowingly does wrong. Of first importance -just to make it crystal: if you knew the right thing to do, such knowledge would be enough to ensure you did it. Ergo, weakness of will is impossible. If memory serves Plato records me saying as much in his "Protagoras" .386

While I'm at it, may I remind you that it is from this thought that I derive yet other important propositions; namely, that one who has such knowledge of good and evil also possesses all the important virtues - courage, piety, temperance and justice. Not forgetting that the virtuous are also the happiest. No higher good than virtue, you see? Why ethics is the first and foremost matter for the philosopher, or should be. Moral excellence, that's the ticket! Without that success in this life is a chance affair; with it one becomes incapable of wrongful, or weak-willed action. There I've said it! I'm quite out of puff; a long time since I last nailed my colours to the mast with such vigour.

A: Weakness of will: that is a metaphor that can prove misleading. For there is no will, and consequently neither a strong nor a weak will. The multitude and disintegration of impulses and the lack of any systematic order among them result in a "weak will"; their co-ordination under a single predominant impulse results in a

135

"strong will": in the first case it is an oscillation and the lack of gravity; in the latter, the precision and clarity of direction.387

S: How does that constitute an answer; and to what exactly? Are you siding with me against the metic, or just making free with the concept of the will?

A: In relation to the first part of your complaint, I'll say again: the weakness of the will - or, to speak more definitely, the inability not to respond to a stimulus - is itself merely another form of degeneration.388 Compare what is un-philosophically called a strong will with the inability to resist a stimulus: one must react, one follows every impulse. What is the essential feature of the former? The ability to suspend decision in face of the provocation of immediate impulses, to nonetheless formulate and stick to long-range decisions.389

To return to your jibe about the "two willies"; I would want to say that here is evidence of the daylight between Zopy and I. For him, craving, instinct, drive were the essence of the will; for me, this is merely a symptom of the exhaustion or weakness of the will; for the will is precisely that which treats cravings as their master and appoints them their way and measure.390

And as to my playing fast and loose with the word "will", a word in my defence. Just because I deny the existence of a faculty of the will, its does follow that the word has no application. This would like saying that because there is no faculty of the intellect the word intelligence has no application. Clearly we can speak of people and actions as displaying more intelligence than others. In like manner with the will, so long as we remember that it serves only to denote a resultant, a kind of individual reaction, rather than a faculty that "acts" or "moves", or the operations of such a faculty.391

S: Not for the first time I'm left wondering if there isn't something perverse about you? I always thought that the actual wrestling was a kind of release for Plato; a way of letting off steam, a means of letting the competitive instincts off the leash, which otherwise - especially whilst writing - he kept on a tight rein. With you, its there in your thinking; it's not enough that you disagree with me, you have to disagree with everyone else as well.

A: Maybe, but am I right or not - that's the question? All I'm doing is pointing out that philosophers are accustomed to speak of the will as if it were the best-known thing in the world. Willing seems to me to be above all something complicated, something that is a unity only as a word - and it is precisely in this one word that the popular prejudice lurks, which has defeated the always inadequate caution of philosophers.392

S: There you go again. Talk about a " will to power", a "will to contestation" might have been more apt.

A: I'm getting heartily sick of your sniping. If it isn't jibes about silver spoons, its imputations of haughtiness. And, if not haughtiness, then it's crass egoism and in-difference to others. Yet having spent the better part of the day seeking to puncture these misconceptions, at least as I see them, it seems I'm no nearer to plugging that well of rancour from which you draw your bile. And, bye the bye, don't fool your-self – Plato is no less competitve writing than I am racing a chariot.

    Perhaps the mistake is mine, in thinking of you as a fellow spirit. Only great pain, the long, slow pain that takes its time - on which we are burned, as it were, with green wood - compels us philosophers to descend into our ultimate depths and to put aside all trust, everything good-natured, everything that would interpose a veil, that is mild, that is medium - things in which formerly we may have found our humanity. I doubt that such pain makes us "better"; but I know that it makes us more profound.393

S: That sounds a lonely and barren furrow to be ploughing.

A: Is it really? Aren't we always in our company? - Whatever in nature and in his-tory is of my own kind, speaks to me, spurs me on, and comforts me; the rest I do not hear or forget right away. We are always, to repeat, only in our company.394

S: Perhaps things would be different if you could bring yourself to accept the prof-fered hand?

A: Which hand would that be; the one that, moments before, wielded the dagger of resentment, or the one extended in friendship?

S: I was trying to make amends.

A: Not to worry. We, open-handed and rich in spirit, standing by the road like open wells with no intention to fend off anyone who feels like drawing from us - we unfortunately do not know how to defend ourselves where we want to: we have no way of preventing people from darkening us; the time in which we live throws into us what is most time-bound; its dirty birds drop their filth into us; boys their gewgaws; and exhausted wanders who come to us to rest, their little and large mis-eries. But we shall do what we have always done: whatever one casts into us, we take down into our depth - for we are deep, we do not forget - and become bright again.395

# CHEWING THE CUD

S: What am I to make of that? A rebuke? What then? A rueful regret that I, and others, can only muddy the waters by projecting our paltry interests on yours? A boast that however saddened you might be by this, you'll survive it - become bright again?

A: Those who know they are profound strive for clarity. Those who would like to seem profound to the crowd strive for obscurity. For the crowd believes that if it cannot see to the bottom of something it must be profound. It is so timid and dislikes going into the water.396

S: Small wonder the crowd has such mixed feelings about you. Have you no conscience about being so dismissive of our fellow citizens; proud they may be, but also honest and true.

A: Conscience? You ought to ask yourself my friend, and before it is too late, just how much slack the herd's conscience would cut you if the boot were on the other foot?

S: Have I missed something here? What are you alluding to?

A: All I'm saying is that the reproaches of conscience are weak even in the most conscientious people compared to feeling: "This or that is against the morals of your society". A cold look or a sneer on the face of those among whom and for whom one has been educated is feared even by the strongest. What is it that they are really afraid of? Growing solitude! This is the argument that rebuts even the best of arguments for a person or cause. - Thus the herd instinct speaks up in us.397

S: Well, I for one will continue to speak as I find.

A: Be it on your own head, then. What we know about ourselves and remember is not so decisive for the happiness of our life as people suppose. One day that which others know about us [or think they know] assaults us - and then we realize that this is more powerful. It is easier to cope with a bad conscience than to cope with a bad reputation.398

S: It seems to me that it is you who would profit most from lending an ear to your own words!

## CHEWING THE CUD

A: Have we ever complained because we are misunderstood, misjudged, misidentified, slandered, misheard, and not heard? Precisely this is our fate - oh, for a long time yet! Let us say, to be modest, until 1901 - it is also our distinction; we should not honour ourselves sufficiently if we wished that it were otherwise. We are misidentified - because we ourselves keep growing, keep changing, we shed our old bark, we shed our skins every spring, we keep becoming younger, fuller of future, taller, stronger, we push roots ever more powerfully into the depths - into evil - whilst at the same time we embrace the heavens more lovingly ...Like trees we grow - this is hard to understand as is all life - not in one place but everywhere, not in one direction but equally upward and outward and inward and downward; our energy is at work simultaneously in the trunk, branches, and roots; we are no longer free to do only one particular thing, to be only one particular thing.

This is our fate; it remains that which we do not wish to share, to make public- the fatality of the heights, our fatality.399

S: I'm not even going to ask you what all that bollocks about 1901 means. As for the rest, charity suggests if it wasn't delirium, it was Bacchus speaking.

A: Ha, ha. Trust you! - Dionysus, maybe?

S: What do mean, "Trust you"?

A: For the psychologist there are few questions that are as attractive as that concerning the relation of health and philosophy, and if he should himself become ill, he will bring all of his scientific curiosity into his illness. For assuming that one is a person, one might...

S: Sorry, but how could one fail to be a person?

A: One might be an actor - not now, ok? For assuming one is a person, one necessarily also has the philosophy that belongs to that person; but there is a big difference. In some it is their deprivations that philosophize; in others, their riches and strengths. The former need their philosophy, whether it be as a prop, a sedative, medicine, redemption, elevation, or self-alienation. For the latter it is merely a beautiful luxury - in the best cases, the voluptuousness of a triumphant gratitude that still has to inscribe itself in cosmic letters on the heaven of concepts. But in the case of the former, which is more common, when it is distress that philosophizes, as in the case with all sick thinkers - and perhaps sick thinkers are more numerous in the history of philosophy - what will become of the thought itself when it is subjected to the pressure of sickness? 400

## CHEWING THE CUD

S: There's something insidious about your philosophizing- if you can even call it that - you know? The way in which you plant the worm of doubt in your opponent causing him to lie awake at night wondering if he really is a good apple or not. I'm not going to play that game, so can we get back to that condescension of yours for ordinary folk, assuming that you have some more of spleen yet to vent? Then maybe we can get back to some real philosophy?

A: All right, for those with ears who wish to hear. Common natures consider all noble, magnanimous feelings inexpedient and therefore first of all incredible. They blink when they hear of such things and seem to feel like saying: "Surely, there must be some advantage involved; one cannot see through everything". They are suspicious of the noble person, as if he surreptitiously sought his advantage. When they are irresistibly persuaded of the absence of selfish intentions and gains, they see the noble person as a kind of fool; they despise him in his joy and laugh at his shining eyes. "How can one enjoy being at a disadvantage? How could one desire with one's eyes open to be disadvantaged? Some disease of reason must be associated with the noble affection". Thus they think and sneer, as they sneer at the pleasure that a madman derives from his fixed idea. What distinguish the common type is that it never loses sight of its advantage, and that this thought of purpose and advantage is even stronger than the strongest instincts; not to allow these instincts to lead one astray to perform inexpedient acts - that is their wisdom and their pride.
Compared to them, the higher type is more unreasonable, for those that are noble, magnanimous, and self-sacrificial do succumb to their instincts, and when they are at their best, their reason pauses. An animal that protects its young at the risk of its life, or that during the mating period follows the female even into death, does not think of danger and death; its reason also pauses, because the pleasure in its young or in the female and the fear of being deprived of this pleasure dominate it totally: the animal becomes more stupid than usual - just like those who are noble and magnanimous. They have some feelings of pleasure and displeasure that are so strong that they reduce the intellect to silence or to servitude: at that point their heart displaces the head, and one speaks of "passion".
The unreason or counter-reason of passion is what the common type despises in the noble, especially when this passion is directed toward objects whose value seems quite fantastic and arbitrary. One is annoyed with those who succumb to the passions of the belly, but at least one comprehends the attraction that plays the tyrant in such cases. But one cannot comprehend how anyone could risk his health and honour for the sake of a passion for knowledge. The taste of the higher type is for exceptions, for things that leave most people cold and seem to lack sweetness; ...401

140

# CHEWING THE CUD

S: Do you have to go on? All those rhetorical flourishes, I mean. What's your conclusion here?

A: Well, that the higher types live according to their own values inured to the way others live, and permanently puzzled as to why the world doesn't share their way of looking at things. - This is the eternal injustice of those who are noble.

S: There you go again - the dramatic finale. Stripped of the colourful verbiage, are you saying anything other than mutual incomprehension rules between your nobles and the common people?

A: Well not just that, obviously. The common people would insist upon one rule for all. Moreover, ...

S: Oblige me? If I were to call over a crowd to listen to this last discursive detour of yours, would they think I was helping to progress the argument if I, too, employed some rhetoric of my own?

A: It would obviously depend on what you said.

S: But if I said, "Do you have to go on?" or even, " Do you have to go on and on?"

A: Now you are being disingenuous. Obviously the second formulation would induce anxiety.

S: And if I were to say," Do you have to go on and on, and on?"

A: Then I'd damn well expect the crowd's anxiety in respect anything I further say to turn morbid. But this goes to show is, that contrary to what you were arguing that rhetoric is highly effective.

S: Ha, ha. Indeed it does. But judging from the look on your face, it also proves your observation that a man would sooner cope with a bad conscience than a bad reputation.

A: My, aren't you a sly one?

S: Aren't I just? Since I've got you on the back foot lets retrace our steps. There's something I've been waiting to ask; this Kant fellow? He's like me in thinking that morality to be morality has to be incumbent on us all?

A: Correct. The "categorical imperative" – it's derived from two thoughts. One: that the claims of morality are universally binding. Two: the moral value of any action is dependent on its motivation.

S: You trotted that off as if you had learned by rote.

A: That's Zopy speaking. He agreed with Kant's initial observations, but remained un-persuaded of the theory built on the back of them. For him the supreme principle of morality wasn't reason, but compassion. Anyway we've talked about that. The thing is that for Kant we would do better, "if in moral judgment [the agent] follows the rigorous method and takes as his basis the universal formula of the categorical imperative: Act according to that maxim which can at the same time make itself a universal law" .402 Actually to be strictly accurate the maim runs, "Act only according to that maxim whereby you can at the same time will that it should become a universal law". 403

It's a test of volitional consistency, do you see? To cut a long story short: a maxim of non-benevolence is not universalizable. In a world where assistance is not guaranteed, i might find myself deprived of help when it is required to fulfil my ends. By willing such a world I'd be guilty of practical inconsistency, says Kant, and thus non-universal maxims are to be morally prohibited; hence benevolence is seen as a moral duty.

Do I need to draw your attention to the presumption that all of this serves to firm up and articulate? - That each and everyone count as one. The corollary is that honouring rational agency implies that you never make an exception of yourself in the conduct of your life, or to borrow another of Kant's formulations - always treat others as ends in themselves, never as means.

S: Hmm, I'd quite to read this man's work. His ideas sound interesting.

A: Well they'll run and run; that's a sure fire certainty. Whether you'd actually enjoy reading him is an entirely different matter. Garrulous. Kant's joke, you see? Kant wanted to prove, in a way that would dumbfound the common man, that the common man was right: that was the secret joke of this soul. He wrote against the scholars in support of popular prejudice, but for the scholars and not for the people.404

S: If that's a joke, the punch line has gone way over my head.

## CHEWING THE CUD

A: The joke is that he set out to write a critical philosophy and ended up re-instating popular prejudice by the back-door: belief in God, freedom of the will, and the immortality of the soul.

S: I can't say I find any of that a laughing matter. Doesn't your conscience prick you when jest about such important matters, or are you so dissolute that the state of your soul is of no concern to you?

A: We've been here before; hereabouts anyway, remember? The intellectual con-science is actually a conscience behind your "conscience"? That you take this or that judgment for the voice of conscience - in other words, that you feel something to be right - may be due to the fact that you have never thought much about your-self and have simply accepted blindly that what you have been told ever since childhood was right; or it may be due to the fact that what you call your duty has up to this point brought you sustenance and honours - and you consider it "right" because it appears to you as your own "condition of existence" [and that you have a right to existence seems irrefutable to you].

For all that, the firmness of your moral judgment could be evidence of your per-sonal abjectness, of impersonality; your "moral strength" might have its source in your stubbornness - or in your inability to envisage new ideals. Need I go on?

S: And should I persist, and claim "here everyone must judge as I do"?

A: Anyone who so judges has not yet taken five steps toward self-knowledge. Oth-erwise he would know that there neither are nor can be actions that are the same; that every action that has been done was done in an altogether unique and irretriev-able way, and that this will be equally true of every future action; that all regula-tions about actions relate only to their coarse exterior [even the most inward and subtle regulations of all moralities so far]; that these regulations may lead to some semblance of sameness, but really only to some semblance; that as one contem-plates or looks back upon any action at all, it is and remains impenetrable; that our opinions about "good" and "noble" and "great" can never be proved true by our ac-tions because every action is unknowable; that our opinions, valuations, and tables of what is good certainly belong among the most powerful levers in the involved mechanism of our actions, but that in any particular case the law of their mechanics is indemonstrable.405What's the matter? Why are you so anxious?

S: I can feel the earth shifting beneath my feet, here. I hardly dare ask, but where does this leave "morality"?

143

## CHEWING THE CUD

A: Morality? I guess I'd want to say morality is just as "immoral" as anything on earth; morality is itself a form of immorality.406 Yes, - before you ask. It is immoral to treat another as the same.

S: I'm not having that!

A: Why not? All comparisons are odious, don't you think? 407 Besides, what is a thinker worth if he does not know how to escape from his own virtues occasionally, for he ought not to be "only a moral being". 408

S: Don't toy with me! I'm serious!

A: And who would have the temerity to say otherwise? There are those who go looking for immorality. When they judge: "This is wrong", they believe one should abolish and change it. I, on the contrary, cannot rest as long as I am not yet clear about the immorality of a thing. When I unearth it I recover my equanimity.409

S: You arrogant, haughty so and so! Is there no limit to your conceit? Do you think that that wry smile will save you from other's wrath? Who are you to act so high and mighty? Life will teach you remorse, yet. Count on it!

A: Remorse? Remorse? No, listen. I, too, am in earnest. It's pertinent to the argument, and addresses something you alluded to a while back. I do not like this cowardice toward one's deeds; one should not leave oneself in the lurch at the onset of unanticipated shame and embarrassment. An extreme pride, rather, is in order. After all, what is the good of it! No deed can be undone by being regretted; no more than being "forgiven" or "atoned for". One would have to be a theologian to believe in a power that annuls guilt: we immoralists prefer not to believe in "guilt". We hold instead that every action is of identical value at root - and that all actions that turn against us may, economically considered, be nonetheless useful, generally desirable actions.

In any particular case we will allow that an act could easily have been spared us - but circumstances favoured it. Which of us, if favoured by circumstance, would not have gone through the entire gamut of crime?

One should never say on that account: "You should not have done this or that", but always: "How strange that I should not have done that a hundred times before!"

After all, very few actions are typical actions and real epitomes of a personality and considering how little personality most men have, a man is seldom characterized by a single action. Acts of circumstance, merely epidermal, merely reflexes that respond to a stimulus: long before the depths of our being are touched by it, consulted about it. a rage, a reach, a knife thrust: what of personality is in that?410

S: Can I interrupt? That's a bit strong isn't it - "how little personality most men have"? You are obviously your father's son, rather than Pericles'. Politics is clearly not your strongest suit.

A: Maybe, but one should not assume [....] that many men are "persons"; most are none, some are several.411 Most are little more than tokens of the type "man"; minor variations of what is typical at the time within a given sociocultural order.

S: But didn't you say something to the effect of, "we want to become those we are - human beings who are new, unique, incomparable, who give themselves laws, who create themselves". 412 Doesn't that apply to all?

A: The first question concerning order and rank is how solitary or gregarious one is; that value is the highest quantum of power that a man is able to incorporate - a man: not mankind.413 As I said earlier, a single individual can under certain circumstances justify the existence of whole millennia - that is a full, rich, great, whole human being.414

S: Hyperbole to one side, you seem to be inferring that the herd, as you insist on calling them, have no value. Even in the "Republic", Plato and I don't go that far. And we are no lovers of the demos.

A: For future reference: "I" imply, "You" infer. Only that I'm doing no such thing; just because I want to insist that every enhancement of the type "man" has so far been the work of an aristocratic society; one that recognizes the long ladder of a order and differences in value between man and man, and that it will be so again and again.415

S: Now you remind me of Callicles.416

A: Will you stop this, "I remind you of". Thrasymachus, Calicle's. I've nothing in common with either of them; certainly not the former. I have never said the herd is unimportant. Society is built from a broad base. Without it there are no higher men; viewed from a height, both are necessary, as also is their antagonism necessary.38. Now can we can we please get back to what I was saying about willing before you completely blunt the point of it?

# CHEWING THE CUD

S: Ha, ha. That's very droll - the "Point of it". "A rage, a reach, a knife thrust". I remember, you see. Such a way with words –they are akin to weapons in your mouth.

A: A deed often brings with it a numbness and lack of freedom: so that the doer is as if spellbound at its recollection and feels as if he were an accessory of it. This spiritual disorder, a form of hypnotism, most be resisted at all cost: a single deed, whatever it may be, is, in comparison with everything one has done, a zero, and may be deducted without falsifying the account. The iniquitous interest that society may have in treating our entire existence from a single point of view, as if its meaning lay in bring forth one single deed, should not infect the doer himself: unfortunately this happens all the time. That stems from the fact that a spiritual disturbance follows every deed with unusual consequences, whether these consequences are good or ill. Observe a lover who has received a promise, or a poet applauded by an audience: so far as torpor intellectualis is concerned, they differ in no way from an anarchist confronted with a search warrant.

There are actions that are unworthy of us: actions that, if regarded as typical, would reduce us to a lower class of man. Here one has only to avoid the error of regarding them as typical. There are other kinds of actions of which we are unworthy: exceptions born of a particular abundance of happiness and health, our highest flood-tide driven so high for once by a storm, an accident: such actions and "works" are likewise not typical. One should never measure an artist by the standard of his works.417

S: And amen to that last. Bloody poets, artists; the whole supercilious, self-regarding circus should be thrown into the sea! What do they do, other than stir the pot of the appetites? No thought for the collective good of society as a whole. Eyes only for what is base, for what creeps and crawls upon the ground, for all that is evil, for all that is led by desire. Evil as privation, as lack of the good, you understand? As I see it, at the moment of creation there was an outpouring of goodness, which served to shape the creatures of the earth. Given that there was a first step there had to be a last. These last creatures received little or nothing of the good and are therefore lacking in reality. A new thought. I've yet to think it through, but anyway – one looks above to find goodness. Even the metic wouldn't disagree with that – the good life as one of contemplation. Those artists drive me to despair! Who do they think they are? Use that yardstick, my boy, in relation to my father's "works", and you really would obtain a measure of the man.

A: I dare say, but he would not be the only one with feet of clay. Plato? You? Me?

# CHEWING THE CUD

S: No, that's not right. The first I can vouch for; the second has no pretensions to be thought an artist; the third as piss-artist - well what more needs to be said? One last, thing - Zopyrus{?} I take it that he and this Kant fellow didn't see eye to eye in regard of benevolence as the supreme principle of morality?

A: Right. For him, compassion took the laurels.

S: On what grounds?

A: His belief that cessation of willing brought recognition of our common woe: that desire chains to misery, on his part. As against Kant, as I recall the argument was that benevolence as the supreme principle was out of kilter with the intuition of the ordinary man and woman. Whilst stealing is wrong for Kant, his view doesn't acknowledge that stealing from the very poor and old is thought more heinous than stealing from the very rich for example. Why are we so incensed? Because we are compassionate at heart.

To be fair, I really ought here to say something about Kant's ideas concerning "pure reason": the reason binding on all rational agents, but who wants to be fair, eh? Purity of practical reason a self-deceptive fraudulence - a means of shielding morality from critical inquiry.418

S: Just as I was revising my opinion of you.

A: The quick retort might be that whilst Kant's theories might be said to be binding on all rational agents, human beings are plainly not among their number. Anyway though he's not around to tell us time is marching on and its time we made a move.

S: Tell us what?

A: Oh, didn't I say. Zopy said he was so punctual, punctilious even, in respect of his habits that you could set a watch by him - if you had a watch or knew what one was that is.

S: Do you think I'm stupid or something? Of course I know what a watch is! What I want to know is why anyone would want to spy on him? Was he thought to be an enemy of the state?

A: No. Not in that sense.

S: If not in that sense, in what sense an enemy?

147

A: Watch, I meant. Not watched in that sense.

S: If I was interested in word play, then I ...

A: It's not word play.

S: Really? If I were a different kind of philosopher I'd be thinking of writing a paper on the difference between sense and reference. Your words have sense, but no reference that I can discern.

A: Jesus Christ and Mother of God!

S: This Jesus Christ? Should I know him?

A: Never mind. I suddenly felt in need of additional help.

S: What's he do then, - that the Mother of God can't?

A; Please God? All I wanted to say, or rather Zopy was saying was in respect of Kant's morning constitutional.

S: Ah! So he was some kind of political theorist. That was why he needed to be watched!

A: Oh, for God's sake. His walk! His "morning constitutional" - his morning walk.

S: This is all very strange. If he wasn't up to no good, why would you want to watch a man walk? Did he have a peculiar gait?

A: Saints preserve us!

S: That temper of yours, and over what? You've still not answered my question, by the way. If not the gait then, was it something about his dress?

A: Look, as I said, time is running on.

S: "I run to death, and death meets me as fast." 419 Sorry. Don't know where that came from. You were saying?

A: Can we move on; both literally as well as metaphorically? I'm sure you many other questions to ask. We haven't, as yet, said anything of freedom.

S: If you'll just loan me your sword-arm; I'll pull myself upright. I get set when I've been sitting awhile these days.

## CHAPTER 7
### Of will and freedom of will – something out of time?

S: See, now I'm moving, I'm more or less ok; still peripatetic, even if now a little pathetic. I might yet be a poet? Anyway, you were going to say? Alcibiades! Where are you?

A: Miles away. Sorry, thinking about Zopy at the lectern conducting his discourse as if it were music to his ears and my brother and me, rather than a gaggle of callow schoolboys, a full blown orchestra. To my brother it was an endless cacophony without form or structure, something he was obliged daily to endure on pain of having his ears punished twice over. Zopy was a dab hand at cuffing. Never opened his shoulders and used the full force of his arm. No, it was all in the wrist, and the speed of the flick.
   Anyway, I was going to say that for Zopy the will alone is truly known to us. As I saying back there the will is not only a complex of feeling and thinking, but above all an emotion: and in fact the emotion of command. What is called "freedom of the will" is essentially the emotion of superiority over him who must obey: "I am free, 'he' must obey" - this consciousness adheres to every will, as does that tense attention, that straight look which fixes itself exclusively on one thing, that unconditional valuation "this and nothing else is necessary now", that inner certainty that one will be obeyed, and whatever else pertains to the state of him who gives commands. A man who wills - commands something in himself which obeys or which he believes obeys.420

S: Is this something from the military school of life, only I feel a cliché coming on?

A: You're as bad as my brother! Pay attention, or you'll find out for real one of Zopy's cuffs doesn't kill you, but makes you stronger in the end.421 I was going to say? .... Observe the strangest thing of all about the will - about this so complex thing for which people have only one word: inasmuch as in the given circumstances we at the same time command and obey, and as the side which obeys know the sensations of constraint, compulsion, pressure, resistance, motion which usually

149

begin immediately after the act of will; inasmuch as, on the other hand, we are in the habit of disregarding and deceiving ourselves over this duality by means of the synthetic concept "I"; so a whole chain of erroneous conclusions and consequently of false evaluations of the will itself has become attached to the will as such - so that he who wills believes wholeheartedly that willing suffices for action. Because in the great majority of cases willing takes place only where the effect of command, that is to say obedience, that is to say the action, was to be expected, the appearance has translated itself into the sensation, as if there were here a necessity of effect. Enough: he who wills believes with a tolerable degree of certainty that will and action are somehow one - he attributes the success, the carrying out of the willing, to the will itself, and thereby enjoys an increase of the sensation of power that all success brings with it. "Freedom of the will" - is the expression for that complex condition of pleasure of the person who wills, who commands and at the same time identifies himself with the executor of the command - who as such also enjoys the triumph over resistances involved but who thinks it was his will itself which overcame these resistances. He who wills adds in this way the sensations of pleasure of the successful executive agents, the serviceable "under-wills" or under souls - for our body is only a social structure composed of many souls - to his sensations as commander. *L'effet, c'est moi*: what happens here is what happens in every well-constructed and happy commonwealth: the ruling class identifies itself with the successes of the commonwealth. In all willing it is absolutely a question of commanding and obeying, on the basis, as I have already said, of a social structure composed of many "souls": on which account a philosopher should claim the right to include willing as such within the field of morality: that is, of morality understood as the theory of the relations of domination under which the phenomenon "life" arises.422

S: There's altogether too much there for me to digest in one go. Bite-sized is what the doctor says has to be the rule. A lot of educators agree. Have you noticed? Mashed everything these days. Be that as it may - commanding and obeying? Is this drawn from your experience of military affairs, or are you speaking metaphorically as it were.

A: It seems to me that all that is living is obeying ... he who cannot obey himself is commanded ... commanding is harder than obeying ... Even when it [the living] commands itself: it must pay for its commanding. It must become the judge, the avenger, and the victim of its own law ... What persuades the living that it obeys, commands, and exercises obedience even when it commands [itself]? ...the will to power.423

# CHEWING THE CUD

S: That's too gnomic for me. There is such a word - "gnomic"? No matter, I know what I mean. What's with this "will to power" thing? Can we just stick with one thing at a time? Its hard enough keeping up with what it is you are saying, without being obliged to learn a new language at the same time.

A: Think of it this way then, the fundamental thing about what is living is that it is prepared to deny gratification of some of its impulses, even sacrifice life itself, for the sake of more life, more power.

S: Perhaps so in the case of the strong, but what about the weak? Are they just to be left to the deprivations wrought by the strong?

A. But it's not that black and white. To be sure all men obey certain laws; most obey because commanded so to do by others. That said, the reason that they do is that they want power, and they believe this the best way to increase their prospects; they worry that infraction of social norms will invite retaliation and a reduction of such power as they have. Only the strong can create new norms, the rest are dependent on the rules established by these others. That's why faith is always coveted most and needed most urgently where will is lacking.

S: Faith?

A: Yes. Will, as the effect of command, is the decisive sign of sovereignty and strength. In other words, the less one knows how to command, the more urgently one coverts someone who can command, who commands severely - a god, a prince, class, physician, father confessor, dogma, or party conscience. From this one might perhaps gather that the two world religions, Buddhism and Christianity, may have owed their origin and above all their sudden spread to a tremendous collapse and disease of the will. And that is what actually happened: both religions encountered a situation in which the will had become diseased, giving rise to a demand that had become utterly desperate for some "thou shalt". Both religions taught fanaticism in ages in which the will had become exhausted, and thus they offered innumerable people some support, a new possibility of willing, some delight in willing. For fanaticism is the only "strength of will" that even the weak and insecure can be brought to obtain, being a sort of hypnotism of the whole system of the senses and the intellect for the benefit of an excessive nourishment [hypertrophy] of a single point of view and feeling that henceforth becomes dominant - which the Christian calls his faith.424

151

## CHEWING THE CUD

S: Obviously I'll have to take on trust what you say in respect of the historical record, but might I ask whether this applies wherever submission is the name of the game?

A: Yes. Once a human being reaches the fundamental conviction that he must be commanded, he becomes a "believer". Conversely, one could conceive of such a pleasure and power of self-determination, such a freedom of the will that the spirit will take leave of all faith and every wish for certainty, being practiced in maintaining himself on insubstantial ropes and possibilities and dancing even near abysses. Such a spirit would be the free spirit par excellence.425

S: Nothing irenic in that. Puts me in mind of "the dark philosopher". What was it he said? "War is father of all; and some he has shown as gods, others men; some he has made slaves, others free". 426

A: Indeed, "One must realize that war is shared and Conflict is Justice, and that all things come to pass [and are ordained?] in accordance with conflict".427

S: Never could get on with the fellow, myself. All of that deliberate ambiguity and obscurity. I've known many a man carry away one of his sayings like a burr on his cloak, who five minutes after he's taken his leave of me can't recall a word I've said. Sometimes you find yourself wondering whether you have to be a certain age to catch his drift. What was that one that came to me the other night when I was awoken by my sciatica? Ah, yes. "It is not better for human beings to get all they want. It is disease that makes health sweet and good, hunger satiety, weariness rest.'428   Sorry, rambling. You were saying - about commanding and obeying?

A: "Obedience" and "commanding" are forms of struggle. The connection between the inorganic and the organic must lie in the repelling force exercised by every atom of force. "Life" would be defined as an enduring form of processes of the establishment of force, in which the different contenders grow unequally. To what extent resistance is present even in obedience: individual power is by no means surrendered. In the same way, there is in commanding an admission that the absolute power of the opponent has not been vanquished, incorporated, disintegrated.429
    Just speculating. What is "passive"? To be hindered from moving forward: thus an act of resistance and of reaction. What is "active"/ - reaching out for power.430 The aristocracy in the body, the majority of the rulers [struggle between cells and tissues]. Slavery and division of labour: the higher type possible only through the subjugation of the lower, so that it becomes a function.431

152

# CHEWING THE CUD

S: If I might summarize? The general must, before engaging the enemy in battle, first discipline his own troops, and - not least - himself.

A: So long as it is understood that "the fairest order in the world is a heap of random sweepings". 432
S: You might well smile. It's like trying to catch hold of a greased piglet. And freedom of the will; I've quite forgot where we had gotten to.

A: Oh yes. It is not the least charm of a theory that it is refutable: it is with precisely this charm that it entices subtler minds. It seems that the hundred refuted theory of "free will" owes its continued existence to this charm alone -: again and again there comes along someone who feels he is strong enough to refute it.433

S: There you go again. No actual argument. Just a mocking, "Go on! I dare you. You are bound to fail". If you are so certain the whole thing is a crock, then lets hear the arguments.

A: Haven't I said already? Free will: the foulest of all the theologian's artifices, aimed at making mankind "responsible" in their sense, that is, dependent upon them. Men are considered free so that they may judged and punished - so that they might become guilty.434

S: So, you side with the determinist, then?

A: What? With those who do not wish to be answerable for anything, or blamed for anything, and owing to an inward self-contempt, seek to lay the blame for themselves somewhere else? 435

S: Now, I'm really in a quandary; you subscribe to neither party?

A: If I can clarify? The causa sui is the best self-contradiction that has been conceived so far; it is a sort of rape and perversion of logic. Suppose someone were thus to see through the boorish simplicity of this celebrated concept of the "free will" and put it out of his head altogether, I beg him to carry this "enlightenment" a step further, and also put out of his head the contrary of this monstrous conception of "free will": I mean "unfree will", which amounts to a misuse of cause and effect ... In the 'in itself' there is nothing of 'causal connections', of 'necessity', or of 'psychological non-freedom'. 436

S: So - I want to be sure I'm following this - you find the psychological necessity that determinism trades on no more convincing than the advocate of free will claim that action can be created *ex nihilio*, out of nothing as it were? Now I have you! Hoist with your own petard as they say in military circles- or will say, is it? Strange that - I mean could you be hoist by breaking wind? Will they use gas as a weapon in future? Is that what will be meant when they speak of "the fog of war"? You must tell me about this sometime.

Anyway, I've got you here bang to rights. That's another funny expression. No, forget it. We'll be here all day. My real point; aren't you the one who wants to stress the importance of "promise keeping"? Was it Aristophanes who told me? No matter. I recall the words. Something about the breeding of an "emancipated individual, with the actual right to make promises, the master of a "free will", who has a proud awareness of how his mastery over himself also necessarily gives him mastery over circumstances' .437

A: Correct. But in saying so I don't deny that "freedom of the will" has real experiential significance. That which is termed the "freedom of the will" is essentially the affect of superiority in relation to him who must obey: "I am free, 'he' must obey" - this consciousness is inherent in every [act of] will ... "Freedom of will" - that is the expression for the complex state of delight of the person exercising volition, who commands and at the same time identifies with the executor of the order - who, as such, enjoys also the triumph over obstacles.438

S: This freedom of yours then has nothing to do with license?

A: Absolutely not. Abandonment to one's instincts is one calamity more. Our instincts contradict, disturb, destroy each other; 439 it is rather a matter of having the affects under control. For what is freedom? That one has the will to assume responsibility for oneself. That one maintains the distance that separates us. That one becomes indifferent to difficulties, hardships, privation, even to life itself ...

How is freedom measured in individuals and peoples? According to the resistance that must be overcome, according to the exertion required, to remain on top. The highest type of free men should be sought where the highest resistance is constantly overcome.440

S: You make it sound as if it has more to do with freedom of action, than freedom of thought. What with the "maintaining of the distance that separates us"?

A: Glad you asked, for the two things are related in my book. People often conceptualize the issue of freedom in terms of an opposition between freedom from and freedom to. Both though want, above all, more power. The pleasure of power is explained by the hundredfold experience of displeasure at dependence and impotence. If this experience is not there, then the pleasure is lacking, too.441 Power is enjoyed not for its possession, but for its increase. One strives for independence [freedom] for the sake of power, not the other way around.442 Freedom is a potential. Man does not want independence or freedom as such. What he wants is not primarily freedom from something, but rather the freedom to act, and in acting, to realize his self.

That was the point of my letter to my friend Lou that I mentioned earlier. Having emancipated herself, she ought now emancipate herself from the emancipation, or risk being swallowed up by the identity that the group has formed. Freedom should be understood as facility in self-direction.443 Independence is for the very few; it is a privilege of the strong.444One of the greatest dangers of our age is the absence of a feeling for the importance of knowledge.445 Proper education is about becoming human, not an objective observation of facts. Man is not free; he becomes free by stepping beyond the given, by means of education and political contestation within the community.

S: We are not that far apart here. Did I not say in the "Phaedrus" I investigate not these things [general questions about the nature of the universe, etc.], but myself to know whether I am a monster more complicated and more furious than Typhoon or a gentler and simpler creature, to whom a divine and quiet lot is given by nature?

Knowledge is thus not something ready-made, but something inherent to be coaxed out by the teacher as mid-wife. Isn't this why Plato speaks of human kind as half way between an animal and an angel, or to use your metaphor - a rope suspended over an abyss? 446 The knowledge of the animal binds it to the present; that of humankind frees it by giving it over to temporal duration. Which reminds me. This Kant, - what's his take on this? If I've understood you correctly, his emphasis on intentions in respect of morality serves to put out of court all those adverse factors such as bad luck that as our tragedians would be quick to point out might well turn a good intention into an evil outcome?

A: Ah, that one should dare to think?

S: Why the insult when I've found common ground?

A: No insult, my friend; an ironic compliment. It was Kant's motto - "dare to think"; the first humanist; the first to claim absolute value for every human being. The problem being that such value must necessarily be independent of what such a human being has done or could do. In thus grounding human experience on the idea of a transcendental subjectivity, he retracts this form of subjectivity from historical development and time generally.

And thus out of the ideology of humanism there arises the spectre of "the last man", the one who is everything and knows not which way to turn.447.I know. Let me explain. If the human being is of absolute worth then irrespective of what he does this worth cannot be won or lost. Nothing can change for he is is independent of time and circumstance. If one is born perfect then there is nothing left to do whilst one is still alive; life itself becomes indifferent - action and thought become more or less meaningless. And there's the rub, whilst this human being has clearly been made it feels that it can be understood from its present alone, and is indifferent to its past. Lacking a soul, it becomes, at one and the same time, of absolute worth and scientifically speaking one more animal among others to be understood as Descartes understood animals - as a mere mechanism.

S: This Descartes?

A: One of those who come after; one who tasked himself with legitimating the pursuit of science by drawing a boundary between the sacred and the profane, between the mind and the body. Forever after known principally for this summation of his thought: "I think, therefore I am". 448 Hubris, of course, we philosophers are not free to divide body from soul as the people do; we are even less free to divide soul from spirit. We are not thinking frogs, nor objectifying and registering mechanisms with their innards removed: constantly we have to give birth to our thoughts out of our pain and, like mothers endow them with all we have of blood, heart, fire, pleasure, passion, agony, conscience, fate, and catastrophe.449

S: Wait up. You are doing it again; you and your rhetorical flourishes. You know talk of midwives will win my uncritical assent, but don't think I've missed the sleight that that was intended to conceal. "We philosophers", indeed! So I'm to infer I'm no longer among their number because I identify the self with the soul? You'll have to do better than that young man.

A: "I am body and soul" - so speaks the child. And why should one not speak like children? But the awakened, the enlightened man says: I am body entirely, and nothing beside; and soul is only a word for something in the body. The body is a great reason, a multiplicity with one sense, a war and a peace, a herd and a herdsman. Your small reason, my brother, which you call 'spirit", is also an instrument of your body, a little instrument and toy of your great reason.450

# CHEWING THE CUD

S: So now you've swapped hats again. Is that because you think the mitre is mightier than the sword? Sorry, that was truly awful; back to business. What are you proposing here? That we should rather think of consciousness as ego in relation to a self which is not itself conscious?

A: Exactly. Consciousness, for me, is never self-consciousness. Consciousness usually only appears when a whole wants to subordinate itself to a superior whole ... Consciousness is born in relation to a being of which we could be a function.451 As I said before, the whole of life would be possible without ... seeing itself in a mirror. The great activity is unconscious.452 Consciousness is essentially reactive; consequently we neither know what a body can do, or what it is capable of.

Granted that the "soul" is an attractive and mysterious idea which philosophers have rightly abandoned only with reluctance - perhaps that which they have learned to put in its place is even more attractive, even more mysterious. The human body, in which the most distant and most recent past of all organic development again becomes living and corporeal, through which and over and beyond which a tremendous inaudible stream seems to flow: the body is a more astonishing idea than the old "soul". In all ages, there has been more faith in the body, as our most personal possession, our most certain being, in short our ego, than in the spirit [or the "soul", or the subject, as school language now has it instead of the soul]....

And after all, if belief in the body is only the result of a false inference, as the idealists assert, is it not a question mark against the spirit itself that it should be the cause of false inferences? 453

S: All very interesting, no doubt, but how does illuminate the question of free will?

A: Think of Leibnitz's incomparable insight.

S: Leibnitz? Oh, never mind. One of those who come after, I presume?

A: Yes. The insight: that consciousness is merely an accident of of experience and not its necessary and essential attribute ... and not by any means the whole of it.454 The body becomes the important thing. As Leibniz says from the scientific viewpoint the world is a deterministic play of forces; in such a world I'm no more than the passive victim of such forces.

S: You should hear Xanthippe on fate. She can't get that song out of her head:
  "When I grew up and fell in love,
   I asked my sweetheart what lies ahead.
   Will there be rainbows day after day?

157

# CHEWING THE CUD

Here's what my sweetheart said,
Que sera, sera,
Whatever will be, will be'
The future's not ours to see.
Que sera, sera."455

Not that I said any such thing, but you should see the baleful look she gives me - as if I'd deliberately led her up the garden path. Of course it's all smiles when the kids are around and she embarks on the second verse. A waste of breath to point out that "whatever will be, will be" is trivially tautological; I just end up picking up the pots and pans. A load of rubbish, if you ask me: nobody can do anything about anything.

A: But determinism and fatalism are not the same thing. Think of it in terms of the narrative structure. Fatalism begins at the end. Yes, I know that sounds paradoxical, but the focus is on the outcome. The outcome is necessary given the person's character: character as fate as Heraclitus would say. Whatever happens must happen. A determinist view is, by contrast, much narrower. It insists that whatever happens, in principle, can be explained by prior causes - whether these be particular states of affairs or laws of nature. That's not to say Oedipus's behaviour can't be explained as a series of this caused that's, but this would be to miss the point of the narrative. The thing is that whilst the outcome is fated, the route to the outcome is not. The pathos of the story is generated in no small measure by Oedipus's fruitless attempts to evade his fate.

S: Doesn't the Metic "explain" all this in terms of a "tragic flaw" - the hero's\heroine's obstinacy, or arrogance? Come to think of it, he's a lot like you. Oedipus I mean, not Aristotle. Not that you would ever confuse the two of you if you had seen Aristotle's arse.

A: Ah, that's my fate right there. People will say the nicest things about me, but only behind my back.

S: Ha, ha. I like it. Your jest I mean, but the other too. Puts me in mind of a ripe peach. You ought to be wary of that. Repeating your jest, I mean. It's just the sort of tasty morsel that that jackdaw, Aristophanes, would gobble up and claim as his own - totally without principle, him.

A: Serendipity.

S: Serendipity? What's that got to do with anything?

158

# CHEWING THE CUD

A: You were about to ask what room, if any, my notion of fate allows for liberty of action.

S: I was? ...Yes, come to think of it I was. Some might argue that a belief in fatalism lands us with an undesirable either/or: either a mute resignation that one can do nothing to change anything, or a capitulation to license and caprice on the grounds that since all is determined one can't make matters worse.

A: There you go then - serendipity. A couple of points, though: such Mohammedan fatalism as you describe embodies a fundamental error.

S: Mohammedan? Must you throw sand in my eyes? I could get the hump ...

A: Don't. You are getting warm.

S: Perceptive of you. I'm certainly about to get hot under the collar. Just tell me what the error is – all right?

A: It lies in setting man and fate over against one another. In reality man is a piece of fate: when he seeks to resist fate in the way suggested, it is precisely fate that is fulfilling itself here; the struggle is imaginary, but so too is the proposed resignation to fate; all these imaginings are enclosed within fate. As to the "fatal flaw", a highly moralistic take on tragedy, the origin of the Christian "misunderstanding" of tragedy, I fancy.
   One can dispose of one's drives like a gardener and, though few know it, cultivate the shoots of anger, pity, curiosity, vanity as productively and profitably as a beautiful tree on a trellis; one can do it with the good taste of a gardener and, as it were, in the French or English or Dutch or Chinese fashion: one can also let nature rule and only attend to a little embellishment and tidying up here and there: one can, finally, without paying attention to them at all, let the plants grow up and fight their fight out among themselves - indeed, one can take delight in such a wilderness, and desire precisely this delight, though it gives one some trouble, too. All this we are at liberty to do, but how many know that we are at liberty to do it? Do not the majority not believe in themselves as in complete fully developed facts? Have the great philosophers not put their seal on this prejudice with the doctrine of the un-changeability of character? 456

S: Let's extend your gardening metaphor and dig a little deeper. At risk of appearing like some hapless clodhopper I'd like to get my beans in a row. You've just weeded out the cruder forms of determinism, but doesn't your earlier remark about "granite of spiritual fatum, of predetermined decision", not to say - if I heard right - remarks to the effect of "everything has been directed along certain lines from the beginning" suggest a fatalism [a different thing from the fate you've been speaking of?] that renders matters of agency otiose, sterile?

A: Hm. That's more a pitchfork than a spade you are wielding there. What can I say - other than, you are right?

S: "In *fragrante delictio*"?

A: In *flagrante delictio*, I think you mean.

S: It could be in "*flagellatee delictio*"; it's all sweet to me. What would you say to a spot of "S and M"? I'm self-taught, so I'll leave the finer details - and the choice - to you.

A: Youthful exuberance, perhaps? Me; not you. No, I can't say that. That I would leave myself in the lurch after all I've said about personal hygiene with respect to one's thoughts. No, that will never do! Must have ran off at the mouth, - not thought it through. Not my considered view anyway.

Let me try again. I can't set myself up as a piece of destiny come to herald the re-valuation of values, and not get this right.

S: Before you do, let me say that, whilst your commitment to the truth is commendable, you really don't have to be so hard on yourself. To put it in the vernacular, as it were, you are a bit up your own arse about all this.

A: There you go again! It's all arse with you! What can I say? You yourself, poor fearful man, are the implacable moira enthroned even above the gods that governs all that happens; you are the blessing or the curse and in any event the fetters in which the strongest lies captive; in you the whole future of the world of man is predetermined: it is of no use for you to shudder when you look upon yourself.457

S: "Cave of all the monstrosities" me, remember? Mark my words, one day someone will come up with a theory as to why people hold on to their shit. If I were of a more psychological bent, I might be inclined to think you were trying to impress someone.

# CHEWING THE CUD

A: Fat chance of that. And who would that be anyway? You should try dealing with the shit that's thrown at me every day. A strict diet of military and logistical reports when Pericles is around is very dull fare. As to the rest of the men in the family, it's all about party advantage or more crudely personal gain. Who said what to whom. Endless conversations and speculations about whom might be used against whom to gain some degree of extra leverage. Any talk about "unexamined lives not being worth living" leaves them looking at you as if you've dropped a bad smell. Not that they don't nonetheless expect you to step up to the mark, for fear that it will otherwise all go shit; family honour and all that shit you see. "You know what thought did" and all that crap. You should hear them; hear what they say about you when they're in their cups.

S: Yes, yes, that's a lot of shit to deal with. What can I say? Shit happens. Nevertheless, my instinct says that you have to learn to let go of it; otherwise you risk contamination on the one hand, and ending up sounding pompous and unbending on the other. Anyway how can you write all that stuff about lightness of being and the conflict that results with the spirit of gravity, and not know this?

A: Once again, you're right. Pathetic isn't it? Must get a grip. Become who I am! I was saying, or was about to? One is insofar as one has predetermined and limited possibilities in respect of one's physical and psychological make-up, one's aptitudes and capacities. One becomes what one is however, by developing one's talents, by cultivating our characters. We are free to do, and responsible - or not - for so doing.

S: If I were to play the devil's advocate? There are parameters to this? You are obviously not free to become anything you like  - a great artist or scientist - out of nothing, through some super-human effort of the will. That whole *ex nihilio* idea would take us back to that Kant fellow, or the transcendental "I" of a bootstrapping Sartre.458

A: Sartre?

S: Is he beyond you? Well, well, well. I never thought I'd live to see the day when you'd admit a thinker's thought was beyond you. Is that some sort of existential angst that has furrowed your brow? Not that I've the foggiest about what I'm on about. If only you were writing all this down? You never know who might come along in the future?

161

# CHEWING THE CUD

A: Just irritation - with you and your so-called daemon. How come you've been "told" about some thinkers, but others - equally, or more important, you haven't the foggiest about?

S: Search me? I've been wondering about that during our little head to head. Clearly they all have something in common with me in that they are all thinkers. Some seem to be akin in terms of their preoccupations, but yet others seem complete strangers. My only guess is that there must be some sort of 'family resemblance" thing going on here, like that builder fellow Wittgenstein talks about.459 Beats me! And anyhow, why is a builder included in the set? Explain that!

A: I can't be arsed.

S: There! You've broken the dream; something to do with parking?

A: But you don't ride a bike.

S: No, true. But my father rode many a one.

A: Ours not reason why; ours but to do die - I guess.460

S: But if not people like us, who is going to do the thinking? Nobody is going to tell me to think or not. Come on. Courage my friend: "Once more into the breach".

A: That I do recognize. It's Shakespeare.

S: No, you're wrong there! It's some king called Henry, though that's not to say logically there couldn't be some sort of family relation between the two of them.

A: Oh, please God? Can we - the philosophy in real time?

S: By all means, but do you have to roll your eyes like that? It's not as if I'm talking complete rubbish.

A: Indeed, "Though this be madness, there is method in it". 461

S: Be like that then! I was trying to help you out. I was going to say that what you need here is a halfway house. The Kantian/Sartrean account is too extravagant, whilst the determinist view denies agency altogether. Now I've a mind to argue that having first-order desires - like wanting to run a marathon, for example, but these might be frustrated by your second-order desires, : whatever you do in life, don't sweat it. Might the possibilities for self-creation be more limited than we imagine?

A: I take your point, but so long as a person is able to act on his first-order desires and that these accord with his second-order desires, I don't see how he can be described as other than free. If I may I'd like to come at this from another direction by picking the notion of "agency". I'd like to avoid the notion of the "self" and all the baggage that comes with it. I'd also like to embroider here upon the notion of independence.

Let me begin with one or two observations regarding the passive conception of the free will thesis, as I think of it. Primarily the focus is upon from freedom from outside influences of one sort or another - states of affairs, things, or persons that result in suffering of one kind or another. In this regard the passive conception is essentially reactive and thus, not coincidentally, indifferent to how, and whether or not, the freedoms fought for in its name are used. In short, the important thing is the possession; the rest is a matter of indifference.

That said this type of freedom is also the one most consonant with herd values. Many the freedoms won beneath its banner are ones designed to hobble the rich and powerful, the well constituted who are considered the enemy of the ill constituted. A process already so entrenched and so far advanced that it; the masters have been disposed of; the morality of the common man has won.462 So much so as the master been reduced to silence that his voice and values are all but forgotten. Everything now serves to hide this fact: art, religion, morality, - the whole ideology of society. Even science. One places ... "adaptation" in the foreground, that is to say, an activity of the second rank, a mere reactivity; indeed, life itself has been defined as a more and more efficient inner adaptation to external conditions. Thus the essence of life, its Will to Power is ignored.463
S: Ignored? Aren't you saying this is all the expression of triumphant herd values, or - as near as makes no difference - their will to power?
A: Yes, but it is a debased will to power. It is reactive. The ill constituted always seek their power within a structured system of rules. It supplies, at one and the same time a means of defence and of attack. Most of those in revolt are not seeking to overthrow the system; their complaint is that they do not occupy the position in the pecking order that their own sense of entitlement leads them to think they deserve. Yesterday's revolutionary often turns out to be today's reactionary. A rolling stone gathers no moss, you might say.

This is why I wrote my "Genealogy". [The] diminution and levelling of European man constitutes our greatest danger ... We can see nothing today that wants to grow greater, we suspect that things will continue to go down, down to the thinner, more good natured, more prudent, more comfortable, more mediocre, more indifferent, ... more Christian - there is no doubt that man is getting "better" all the time. Here precisely is what has become a fatality for Europe - together with the fear of man we have also lost our love of him, our reverence for him, our hopes for him, even the will to him. The sight of man now makes us weary - what is nihilism today if it is not that? - We are weary of man.464

S: Your active conception of freedom then? How does that serve to keep the guttering candle alight? It's all very well your pouring scorn on the negative conception as you term it, but who's to say what constitutes an authentic act, and who's to prevent this, in its turn, being a new orthodoxy that would seek to smother your free thinkers at birth?

A: Why would you want to specify an authentic action for all? That would be the herd mentality speaking again. Surely you would be looking to let a hundred flowers bloom? Independence as a means to power, and yet more power, remember? Not power as a means to independence. Besides within this conception suffering is not regarded as an unalloyed evil, but rather as the spur to greater things, the grit that helps to create the oyster. For us it is all about overcoming of the self, about transcendence of our current selves; about us as potentialities who, the day after tomorrow, might realize ourselves. It is the negative conception that is modelled on the humanist conception of us as already of infinite worth, a secularized version of the Pelagian heresy that the feely-touchy kind of Christian subscribes to without knowing.465

S: The heresy you can tell me about another time. Before I forget though; the stuff about big and small reasons? How does that impinge on all this?

A: Ah yes, I nearly forgot myself. This is, again, a contrast that I wish to highlight; I would want to reduce the importance of talk of the "self". Such a concept is central to the negative conception, in that the whole notion of freedom is intimately bound up with consciousness, with a highly self- conscious self-awareness. A free action fails to count as such according to the paradigm here. We are ever safest when subject to the tutelage of our "small reason".

By way of contrast, I would hark back to my contention that the greater part of life is lived without reference to self-consciousness, without our seeing ourselves in a mirror. We rarely think in the way we imagine, we rather act and in a thousand and one little ways we follow the prompting of our great reason, he body. More often than we would ever care to admit, we have no idea what it is that is taking us down the line. If we are lucky, we wake up one day in the middle of our lives, amazed and surprised at what we have become and somewhat puzzled as to how we have arrived at this point. Even it is otherwise, and we wake to disappointment, the only choice on offer is acceptance of our fate.

S: Fascinating. I'm curious. As you know Plato and I spent a good deal of time and labour on working out a theory on which to base an ideal state.466 Although based on sound cosmological principles that mirror the tripartite division of the soul, this theory, despite Plato's best efforts to get it up and running, has yet to bare fruit. I'm not wrong in surmising that this Liberal theory and what you describe as its negative view of freedom doesn't end there? It has its own theory of the state, yes? And on the basis of "Anything you can do [Plato and I, that is.] I can do better", you have your very own criticisms to make of this.

A: Of course; what kind of philosopher would you be, if you evinced no consideration of the future welfare of society? Haven't such concerns, albeit sotto voce, run like a leitmotiv throughout our conversation. Just because I didn't see eye to eye with Zopy on the flute, doesn't mean that I'm not a dab hand at the lyre.

S: But the question here is what kind of liar? The one who would rule by the sword, or the one who aspires to convert swords to ploughshares?

A: Well, not the noble liar - that's for sure. As to that last crack - I'm assuming it's a gift from your daemon? - I think you'll find the man in question is reported as saying, "Think not that I am come to send peace on earth: I came not to send peace, but a sword". And yes, before you say it, context is all. Even so, what is irrefutably true is that self-perfection requires non-conformity and not the lazy peace, cowardly compromise, the whole virtuous uncleanliness of the modern Yes and No.467

S: Must it always be blood and thunder with you?

A: Not at all! It is the stillest words, which bring the storm. Thoughts that come on doves' feet guide the world.468

S: You know, I don't think I'm ever going to get you.

A: I should cocoa.

S: 'Cocoa"? You can move from the bombastic and plain silly to the profound and back again in the blink of an eye. Thoughts like that resonate – "the stillest words". Odd that, don't you think? Most of the time one uses words so carelessly. Not that you don't pay attention to their meaning, but rather they get caught up in the Hurley-burley of the utilitarian ends they are striving to articulate. Then on occasion, out of nowhere and nothing, you come across a form of words; so fresh, so novel, so incisive they'll cut you to the quick.

And before you start lecturing grandma on how to suck eggs, - no, I haven't missed the allusion to how the thoughts of the best of us philosophers shape and reshape the world, nor how the pillow talk of lovers likewise reshape theirs. Not that Xanthippe goes in for much of that. Altogether too literal minded. Told her in bed the other night that I'd seen a lovely pair of "jugs" in the agora, and she says ," I thought the Phoenician potter said he wouldn't be back until next Spring", and this whilst the wheel-wright's wife next door is "yodelling" away as if her life depended upon it.

A: Perhaps after all, love forgives the lover even his lust? 469

S: As I said the reverberations go on and on. Anyway, where were we? Political philosophy. Cosmology. This Liberalism. It's first principles?

A: "First principles". Now there's a phrase. I think you'll find in the distant future, the world will turn in a different way. People will come to think that the nemesis of science was ever religion and mysticism, when, in fact, its arch enemy was always rationalism - the belief that knowledge could be deduced from first principles. That's not to deny that Liberalism has first principles of a sort.

Unlike you and Plato, the state is not seen as benign. Individual freedom and equality are seen as sacrosanct. Thus the state is seen as a contractarian affair - the product of the consenting individuals who come together with a view to sacrificing some of their powers to the state in order to ensure the security of all. This state can take many different forms; a monarchy, a republic, etc., but whatever the form the general idea is that it is charged with holding the ring so that its citizens can go about their business [literally and metaphorically] under the rule of law with the bare minimum of interference.

All of which brings us to Liberalism's other foundation stone: the commitment to pluralism. This takes us back to the negative conception of freedom we were discussing earlier. For the Liberal, everyone should be free to pursue their lives in accordance with their own particular beliefs and values so long as these don't impinge in harmful ways of those of others.

S: Can I interject? This is a kind of myth, yes? And, if I may say, not dissimilar to the kind of thing that Plato would dream up, only a more literal-minded one, - one lacking the panache, the vibrancy of his. My question would always be when Plato bothered to inform me of one of these sorts of ideas: what was going on prior to this? He'd always wave such questions aside and insist that the important thing was what belief in the myth might achieve.

A: A good question, from where I stand. Early doors most Liberals were want to conceive of the prior circumstance as a state of nature, a period of utter lawlessness in which the devil took the hindmost - a war of all against all. Hence why for the first Liberal states that appeared, with an eye to the depredations previously wrought by assorted "tyrants", high on the list of the first priorities to be established were the freedoms of life, liberty, and property.

But in answer to your question, by severing the individual from his ends the Liberal conceives the person as a pre-existing chooser of ends, as antecedently individuated -that is to say the ends we choose are not constitutive of our identity, of who we are. Furthermore, there is another dubious assumption in all this. It assumes that our ends are formed prior to, and independently of, our association with others. In short, society does not inform a person's ends, values, of identity, but is rather the happy result of a contract arrived at by the a-socially individuated. It's nonsense.

S: Lets assume you are right; you have still to provide an alternative explanation.

A: Discipline and breeding!

S: What? Are you affecting to play the tyrant, again? Have you no regard as to how alien, how intimidating, that phrase will sound to ordinary folk?

A: Hatred for mediocrity is unworthy of a philosopher: it is almost a question mark against his "right to philosophy". Because he is an exception he has to take the rule under his protection; he has to keep the mediocre in good heart.470

S: I see what you're saying, but I doubt that that will cut it. You were going to say?

A: Yes, indeed. Well we've touched on a lot of this before, so I'll be brief. The Liberal gets it all back to front. There are no pre-existing individuals in need of protection from the state; individuals are products of a state or society; our affects and drives, our experiences and judgments are the fruit of our social history. Individuals are the belated products of a long history of prior socialization. The high points of culture and civilization do not coincide: one should not be deceived about the abysmal antagonism of culture and civilization. The great moments of culture were always, morally speaking, times of corruption; and conversely, the periods when the taming of the human animal ["civilization"] was desired and enforced

167

were times of intolerance against the boldest and most spiritual natures. Civilization has aims different from those of culture - perhaps they are even opposite -.471

S: So when do these individuals begin to appear?
A: I just said. The first experimental individuals - the transformation of an organ into an autonomous organism - appear when society breaks down. You might well figure as such a prototype.

S: Me? Am I to be so honoured? Wait until I've told Xanthippe. That'll give her pause. "The illustrious Alcibiades said that...". I can't wait to see her face. All that stuff this very morning about "I've given you the best years of my life, and for what?". Well, now she'll know! See me in the divorce courts will she?

A: I'm sorry. I didn't realize things were that bad. I thought, at first, it was irony at my expense.

S: It was, at first. Sorry. It didn't end well this morning.

A: How do you mean?

S: Lost my rag and told her that's what the divorce courts were there for: to negotiate the price of narcissism when it realizes it's been duped. Hard to believe, I know, but in her bloom?

A: That must have hurt. What did she say in reply?

S: Nothing. Well nothing polite company would want to hear. Once the pots and pans start flying, there's nothing to do but leave.

A: You know if someone cannot defend himself and therefore does not want to, we do not consider this is a disgrace; but we have little respect for anyone who lacks both the capacity and the goodwill for revenge - regardless of whether it is a man or a woman. Would a woman be able to hold us [or, as they say, "enthral" us] if we did not consider it quite possible under certain circumstances she could wield a dagger [any kind of dagger] against us? Or against herself - which in certain cases would be a crueller revenge [Chinese revenge] .472

S: All very well, if the thunder serves to clear the air, but lately...

168

# CHEWING THE CUD

A: Hmm - just pondering. What great philosopher hitherto has been married? Heraclitus, Plato, Descartes, Spinoza, Leibniz, Kant, Schopenhauer - these were not ....
A married philosopher belongs in comedy ...and that exception ... the sarcastic Socrates, it seems, married ironically just to demonstrate this proposition [?]473
S: Fat lot you believe you know! Mercurial, she was. A face like weather; - utterly beguiling. No crabbed thoughts, no pinched, expression back then.

A: Alas, what bewitched him was precisely that she seemed so utterly changeable and unfathomable. Of steady weather he found too much in himself. Wouldn't she do well to simulate her old character? To simulate a lack of love; is this not the counsel of - love? Long live comedy.474

S: Not that I'm not honoured to be considered a member of this pantheon of yours, but you're mistaken there. Mightn't it be the case that a good marriage, if such there be, avoids the company and conditions of love?475 Is that not a truth universally acknowledged that a single man in possession of a good fortune, must be in want of a wife?476

A: That's some sentence.

S: My daemon says a first sentence. Perhaps what you get if your previous behaviour was without blemish?

A: He cannot control himself, and from that the poor woman infers that it will be easy to control him and casts her net for him. Soon she will be his slave.477 Do you see? The desire for power others are often rooted in an absence of power over oneself?

S: Even so, given my experience at the sharp end of Plato's stylus, I wouldn't bet against some "Johnny come lately" chancing his arm by reducing me to a comic turn. That's the thing about parasites: they can live off you dead every bit as well as when you're alive.

A: Was that something you didn't wish to hear?

S: Talk of bodies reminds me. One last thing, implicit in what you've just been speaking of: - the question of asceticism and sexual abstinence. You'll forgive an old roué from putting his finger on so obvious a sore spot? Don't curl your lip, its a perfectly legitimate question. All that talk about listening to the body, attending to the body - well, it seems that it is still in thrall to the idea of continence. Forgive

169

the crudeness of the pun, but if I were your beloved Diogenes confronted by Alcibiades I'd be asking what kind of dog is it that confronted by his own bone seeks to live the ascetic ideal in his own flesh?

A: More old satyr than old roué, I think. Didn't I make it plain at the outset - the stuff about antithetical values? All that rot about "If thy eye offend thee, pluck it out". A load of old bollocks nonetheless, even if I've got Origen and "The Good Book" against me.

S: What's with this "Origen" and the book? 478 Is this a straight answer to my question, or just a means of throwing me off the scent?

A: Origen: A Christian ascetic who read the New Testament of love literally, and castrated himself so as not to be distracted by sexual desire. A short cut to paradise, you might say?

S: Sick, I'd say. I'm sure Hipparete would have something to say about that. This "New Testament" to which you allude; the holy book of the Christians, yes; Platonism for the masses, you said a while ago - if memory serves? Is it naive of me to ask about the relation of this religion of love to the "Symposium"?

A: Not so much a naivety as a mistake, for this is love as punishment. No sooner does this religion establish itself than it sets about persecuting all those who stand outside of it. "There is neither Jew nor Greek, there is neither slave nor free, there is neither male nor female" as its high priest declared.479The mantle of this of this love, both benign and malign is extended to all and sundry. All former distinctions are subsumed by it.

In the abstract, it is difficult to convey the enormity of all this. Suffice to say that its adherents hold that out of love for a suffering humanity their God sends his only son to earth to preach a message of love. Treated in the main with hostility and indifference, the son ends by being put to death on the cross like a common criminal.

S: Astounding! And the son and the God who is his father "permits" this to happen? It beggars belief.

A: Indeed, but thereafter it becomes a central tenet of the believer that this messiah died out of love for us in order to save us from our sins. A debt has thus been incurred that the believer is obliged to make good though it can never, actually, be repaid." God whom no one will ever repay what he, without owing anything, paid for us", says another of the flock, Augustine.480 And since the act was to redeem all of humanity all must be brought to bend the knee. Thus says Augustine, "The church persecutes out of love, and the impious out of cruelty ... The church persecutes its enemies and pursues them until it has reached them and destroyed them in their pride and vanity in order to make them enjoy the benefit of the truth ... The Church, in its charity, labours to deliver them from perdition in order to preserve them from death.481

S: Irony seems misplaced, but I never heard of a colder charity.

A: Ah, but there is, to say again, method in this madness; outside of this Church, this no salvation; no access to heaven, to immortality. Ipso facto, I do you the greatest service by forcing you to believe in this God of gods.

S: I'm appalled, and so, too, would Plato be if he heard of this. This is nothing short of a perversion of our beliefs. At best an egregious mistake. I'm bound to say, I'm glad I won't be around to see it! One cannot but hope this madness, because madness, will be short lived.

A: Then you'd be disappointed, I'm afraid. Two millennia hence, and humanity will still be struggling to get out from under the shadow cast over all cheerfulness.

S: Has all been in vain? Tell me, it hasn't all been in vain!

A: No, it hasn't. And you, as are as far as I'm permitted to see, are one reason why.

S: Well, thank the stars for small mercies. You gave me quite a turn there. I was in two minds about the worth of carrying on. Maybe something of worth might yet come of this quiet conversation of ours. On doves feet, as you say. Who knows? Perhaps this is not the place to pursue it though, this thing about asceticism - in light of what you've just said it might be of importance to be clear about it? Maybe we could talk further about this in respect of your ideas about the "self"? That's something we keep running up against without quite addressing full on.

A: O.k., but shall we put the world to rights first then?

S: Why not. We stand a better chance of doing that than ...Hey what do I know? I'm beginning to think that damn oracle was being ironical in ways that I couldn't imagine. Carry on.

A: The times when they emerge - people like your good self - are those of demoralization, of so-called corruption, that is, all drives now want to go it alone and, since they have not until now adapted to that personal utility [i.e. the interests of the individual], they destroy the individual through excess. Or they lacerate it in their struggle with one another.

It is then that the ethicists come forward and seek to show human beings how they can still live without suffering so from themselves - mostly by commending to them the old conditioned way of life under the yoke of society, only that in place of society it is [the yoke of] a concept - they are reactionaries.482...Their claim is that there is an eternal moral law; they will not acknowledge the individual law and call the effort to attain it immoral and destructive.483

S: This "individual law" of yours; is it not a contradiction in terms? Less a matter of freedom than of license to do what you damn well please, I'd say.

A: Not at all. "You call yourself free? Your governing thought is what I want to hear, and not that you have escaped your a yoke [...]. Free from what? What does Zarathustra care about that! But your eye should tell me clearly: free for what?"484

S: Zara' this, Zara' that. My daemon is a mere novice by comparison. Plain language, if you please?

A: Discombobulated are you?

S: Plain language, I said. Get on with it.

A: For the Liberal, as I said it is the absence of external obstacles that's the thing; it is a matter of what you can do if you wish. But then who would be so foolish as to think a political innovation would suffice to make men once and for all happy inhabitants of the earth? 485No, every gift or capacity must unfold through contestation.486 Hasn't every Greek felt from childhood on the burning wish within himself to be an instrument for the good of his city in the contest of other cities: therein was his egoism enflamed, therein it was also checked and bounded.487

S: "Checked and bounded" you say. Do I hear an echo of the metic here. Are you saying that freedom is only freedom, if it observes a mean? 488

A: No. Not a mean, but a measure. Perhaps our great virtue of the historical sense stands in a necessary opposition to good taste, at least the very best taste, so that we are only able to take up the small, brief and highest moments of good fortune and transfigurations of human life, as they appear every now and then, badly, hesitantly and only by forcing ourselves: those moments and miracles where a great force willingly held back in the face of that which is without measure or limits -, where a surplus of fine pleasure was taken in a sudden binding and petrifying, in standing fast and fixing oneself on a ground still trembling. Measure is alien to us, let us admit it; our thrill is precisely the thrill of the endless, unmeasured. Like a rider on a steed tearing at the bit, we let go our reins before the endless, we modern humans, we half-barbarians - and are only really in our element, where we are most - in danger.489

S: Hold fire a moment, before you go chasing the bubble reputation even down to the cannon's mouth - or not, as it would seem here.490 Sorry about that. I don't even know what a cannon is. Do you know what one is? No, scratch that - we'll be here all day! It must have been all those different time frames in your pretty peroration. They seem to have scrambled mine, too.

What was it I wanted to say, to clarify? Ah yes, freedom, for you, isn't so much a question of measure versus excess, as something that lies in the tension between measure and excess - the space between measure and the goad of hubris, as we Greeks might say?

A: That's it. The contest is the thing.

S: Yes, so I hear. Six teams entered in the chariot races at the coming Olympiad. Isn't that a tad excessive?

A: How so? Others are free to compete if they wish. You could enter yourself; my friends tell me you often to be seen exercising in the gymnasia.

S: A healthy body is the greatest of blessing.

A: In fact, you should have a word with Plato - you and he would make a great tag-team. If you found yourselves at a disadvantage, you could always talk your opponents into submission. I'll sponsor the pair of you, if you like?

S: How very whimsical. Personally I've always found poverty to be the short cut to self-control. You should try it sometime; nothing is to be said in favour of riches and high birth, which are easy roads to evil.

# CHEWING THE CUD

A: What's to be done with you? If you're going to exercise that chip on your shoulder at the first opportunity, and regale me with those horny homilies, we might as well go back to the philosophy. Where were we?

S: Something to do with Liberal values and their achievement?

A: Yes. Liberal institutions immediately cease to be liberal as soon as they are attained: subsequently there is nothing more thoroughly harmful to freedom than liberal institutions. One knows, indeed, what they bring about: they undermine the will to power, they are the levelling of the mountain and valley exalted to a moral principle, they make small, cowardly and smug - it is the herd animal that triumphs every time.[...] As long as they are still being fought for, these same institutions produce quite different effects; then they actually advance freedom in a powerful way. Seen more closely, it is war that brings forth these effects, the war for liberal institutions, which, as war, gives endurance to the liberal instincts. And war is a training in freedom.[...] The highest type of free man would have to be sought where the greatest resistance is continually being overcome: five steps from tyranny, up against the threshold of the danger of bondage. This is true psychologically, if under the "tyrant" one understands relentless and fearsome instincts which call for a maximum of authority and discipline towards themselves - finest type Julius Caesar -: this is also politically true, one has only to take a look at history.491

S: My salad days are long gone, but there's too much red meat in that for me - even if I had all my teeth. All that talk of war, of the measure of freedom as the greatest resistance overcome not just externally, but internally - I note. And yes, I can see where the logic points. The Liberal by abolishing external constraints on liberty ends up unwittingly promoting un-freedom.

A: Indeed, but you have to follow this through. Un-freedom in the sense of breeding a herd animal, which knows only how to obey, not to command. In conclusion, I would want to stress that, like the liberal, my notion of freedom is all about the individual as a singularity, in his difference from the plurality of others. And, finally, since there may come a time when this is not so, that as against the liberal it is conflict, resistance, obstacles, that engender singularity, difference and proper pluralism, not the protection against them - do you see?

S: You are doing it again.

A: What's that? It is just that I've been thinking a lot about the contradictions we are just lately. My growing conviction is that the herd fail to comprehend that it's

174

the whole deal or nothing. One can only play the cards one has been dealt. Most thing they can be one thing only. As believers in freewill, that they can appropriate the positive qualities of another's character whilst discarding the rest. Those Pauline conversions are a case in point. What do they display if not the adherent's slavery to the surface appearance of moral actions, their stupidity of judgment? Only vanity triumphs there. In trying to re-cast themselves as one thing only, they end up doing the same thing as before – only from a contrary perspective.

"No", my friend. What we witness here is a fundamental refusal to understand the necessity of the reverse side of things; a refusal to deal with anything that falls short of a false and corrupt ideal, of all that is harmful, dangerous, questionable, and destructive even. With every growth of man, his other side must grow too: that the highest man, if such a concept be allowed, would be the man who represented the antithetical character of existence most strongly, as its glory and sole justification.

Held in tension, like Heraclitus' bow, we grow or perish as the result of our contradictions. That a man must grow better and more evil is my formula for this inevitability.492

S: No, I meant you are doing it again. Rotating your left shoulder. Potidaea? 493

A: Sorry, habit - and perhaps thoughts of antagonism and the self. Where we ought to go next? Don't realize I'm doing it half of the time. Warding off your verbal thrusts. My shield arm, you see. Not so easy to raise it and keep it up these days. Stiffens up. Those precious seconds will be the death of me one day.

S: You should have a care. You never know when fate might come calling. If you'll permit the observation: most of the tragic heroes you esteem start off fully confident that they know what should be done.

## Interlude
## Passing Time

S: What say you we sit a while? My knees would welcome the respite.

A: Doesn't Plato say somewhere that old age brings with it a sense of peace and freedom? That when the passions lose their hold you escape not one mad master but many?

# CHEWING THE CUD

S: No; that was Sophocles celebrating his eightieth birthday. You've a lot to learn about all this. To be sure I exercise in hope of staying healthy, but not because I'm obsessed with the body beautiful. Being healthy is being able to forget about the body. Ask any of the old or the sick, and they'll tell you that real curse is not being able to forget about the body and its never ending complaints about what it's eaten, drunk, about being dragged hither and thither. Each day brings a new complaint.

That might be a worry about your so-called liberation of the body. There may come a day when this reveals itself as a new tyranny, as a new horizon - but one shorn of excuses. Everyone free and responsible for their own self-perfection: henceforth a refusal, a sign of moral turpitude. Now that would be a splendid? Were these denizens of this brave new age to look back on our own and deem it to be a kinder, gentler age - one in which failure, mediocrity, plainest of dress and appearance were seen as the hapless lot of the many, and exception could be celebrated with good conscience for what it is, without its becoming a stick to goad the rest in a fruitless quest to achieve the same?

A: Plato, I'm sure, says something similar. Though age blunts one's enjoyment of physical pleasures, one's desires for the things of the mind and one's delight in them increase accordingly?

S: If only I could remember. You're not listening. Oh, the condescension of what's still green. That's the worst thing about growing old: having to wear the patronage of "know-nothings"!

A: It's probably...

S: Irony is probably what it is! I've not lost my Elgin's just yet, - "Elgin's"? - Even if my daemon often neglects, these days, to remind me what exactly it is that I've lost, or why it is I've come upstairs. Not that the Metic would concur. Fifty and you are past it, in his book; fit only for garrulous repetition of past deeds. What was the caustic curmudgeon's mordant verdict? "Because they have lived for many years, because they have often been deceived, because they have made mistakes, and because human activities are usually bad, they have confidence in nothing, and all their efforts are far beneath what they ought to be". 494

A: A cold fish I grant you, and yes some of what he says leaves a sour after- taste. But your philosophical prejudices are showing here as well as your xenophobia. He has a name. Read his "On Rhetoric" and you'll find a different man. No doubt the coming of the plague, and the threat of expulsion have contributed to his current saturnine mood, but can you blame him?

## CHEWING THE CUD

S: Perhaps not, but others have suffered worse. Whole families have been decimated, or worse - yours not least. Teach him that you can't have a foot in two camps. Mark my words! Those Macedonian employers of his have designs, to say nothing of all those foreign disciples of his. Who's the one with a limp - Rufinus, the Cypriot? No one is more out of depth than a lame peripatetic, if you ask me.495

A: Even so, it must have hit him hard - having fought so hard to establish himself in a foreign city, to withstand the hostility and suspicion of we Athenians. His championing of rationality as our defining feature was no accident, I think - more a necessary aspiration than a simple matter of fact. Likewise, his ideal of the magnanimous man: 496 Pericles incarnate?

  Come the plague, what does he find? A city avid for revenge - for a culprit to blame and punish: someone must have provoked the gods. Athens at her apogee - mere hubris? All the great and the good of that high tide of human affairs now dragged before the tribunal of public opinion - Protagoras, Phidias, Thucydides, Anaxagoras, Aspasia, even Pericles, himself.497 These are febrile times, my friend. We must take care less we, too, are carried away by the ebb tide.

S: About you I wouldn't be so sure. As for me, I'll be fine. My daemon, long ago expressly forbade my involvement in politics. Whose going to trouble their selves over an old man whose express mission is to do no harm? And speaking of which, have heard Aeschylus on the subject?
  "What is an old man?
  His foliage withers
  He goes on three legs and
  No firmer than a child
  He wanders like a dream at noon"
A: If I have to choose, the Theban Sphinx's riddle is the one for me. What she asked, - you recall? - has one voice, and is four-footed, two-footed, and three-footed; and goes slowest when it has most feet? Oedipus answers...

S: No, don't tell me! Oedipus answers - a human being. It starts on all fours, is an adult on two, an old man on three - his cane? Oh, I do so enjoy riddles.

A: See, all you needed was a nudge. Maybe it'll all work out fine. Just to sure, you might encourage Lamprocles to stand for public office, though. You never know, he might develop a taste for the high life.

# CHEWING THE CUD

S: Yes, I get it. Penalty for abusing a parent: loss of public office. I wouldn't put a monkey on it.

A: Well, who'd want to risk being made a monkey out of? That'd be plain sloppy - or should I say, the slops?

S: Don't think I don't know what you are alluding to. So we had one our rows that serve periodically to clear the air, and Xanthippe emptied the slops over me - so what? After the thunder comes the rain; I'm sure most everyone appreciated the irony, even if you have difficulty with it.

A: Oh, I understand it well enough my pretty. My point is, and others understand this well enough - and without my having to spell it out - had Hipparete pulled such a stunt with me, she'd not have been able to sit down for a week.

S: Well, I prefer to turn the cheek than redden hers.

A: You are kind of missing the point here.

S: How; just because I "choose" not to strike back?

A: No. You are being a bit of a woman about this. The point is that it would never have gotten to that in my house.

S: "A soul which knows it is loved but does not itself love betrays its dregs - its lowest part comes up!"498 That's one of your aphorisms isn't it? Then, perhaps you should be eating your own words?
A: What? - You have chosen virtue and the heaving bosom, yet at the same time look with envy on the advantage enjoyed by those who live for the day? - But with virtue one renounces "advantage". 499

S: What? What kind of alpha-male shield beating is this nonsense?

A: I didn't say it was something to be forsworn. Where neither love nor hate is in the game a woman is a mediocre player - don't you think.500

S: That you can be a right shit; that's something I think!

A: Just enjoying the interlude, that's all. Sensuality often makes love grow too quickly, so that the root remains weak and easy to pull out? 501

## CHEWING THE CUD

S: I won't be toyed with! Any more of this, and I'll have your balls!

A: Ha, ha. See? It just goes to show; in revenge and love a woman is more barbarous than men.502 Ha, ha. Don't look so miffed. Love brings to light the exalted and the concealed qualities of a lover - what is rare and exceptional in him: to that extent it can easily deceive as to what is normal in him.503

S: Hmm, I suppose I have to be grateful for the change in gender, even though there remains the sting in the tail. A pity you were already the worst for wear when you arrived the other night; the others might have appreciated having something else to get their teeth into - however cynical.

A: Cynical? Me?

S: Cynical. You! "Ultimately one loves one's desires and not that which is desired"? 504

A: Where did you get that from?

S: From you - last night, before you passed out. Don't worry, the others didn't hear.

A: Why would I worry about that?

S: The cynicism, the egoism in back of it?

A: That's a shame. I took you for a cleverer man than that. Think about it.
Comparing man and woman in general one might say: woman would not have the genius for finery if she did not have the instinct for the secondary role, don't you think? 505

S: No, I don't think.

A: What would you say you do then, if you don't think?

S: I think! I think that you ought to apply your genealogical method, or whatever you call it, to statements like that previous one. It all sounded horribly essentialist, horribly ahistorical.

# CHEWING THE CUD

A: But then whence the origin of the sudden passion - the passion of the profound and inward kind - that a man feels for a woman? Least of all from sensuality alone: but when a man encounters weakness and need of assistance and at the same time high spirits together in the same being, then something takes place in him like the sensation of his soul wanting to gush over: he is at that moment moved and offended. Isn't it at this point there arises the source of great love? 506

S: Now there's a horny dilemma - pun intended. Half of me wants to accede, half wants to know why half of the world should have to wait upon the condescension of your kind of man?

A: But then again, suppose "truth" were a woman.507 What would that mean?

S: Stop! Stop! That's outlandish! Tell me later, if you must. Right now, I must sit!

A: Come on now. One seeks a mid-wife for his thoughts, another someone to whom he can be a mid-wife: thus originates a good conversation.508

S: Now it's my turn to be disappointed. Am I to be bought so cheaply? Or is it that I'm to deduce that imitation really is the sincerest form of flattery?

A: It's not like that.

S: Shall I pay you back in kind, instead? "You may lie with your mouth, but with the mouth you make as you do so you nonetheless tell the truth"? 509

A: Don't you know that that which is done out of love always takes place beyond good and evil? 510

S: You don't get it, do you? If I might avail myself of your own words again? "It's not that you lied to me, but that I no longer believe you - that is what has distressed me - ". 511

A: Please? Your imagination is running wild. If some of what I say sounds familiar, take it both as compliment and inadequacy on my part. Keep in mind what I said earlier about the importance of worthy enemies.

S: And the "inadequacy", to which you refer?

A: Once more, one repays a teacher badly if one always remains a pupil only.512

## CHEWING THE CUD

S: So you'll agree the franchise on the "midwifery metaphor" is mine alone; even if I appear pernickety, and even if I come across as some kind of closet pettifogger?

A: What better place for a man to deal with his shit than in a closet?

S: All very well for you to be so flippant about this. You don't have my problem. It's a matter of intellectual property. If you don't write anything down yourself, it's the devil's own work trying convince people what's yours, and what isn't.

A: You've said already. Anyway, I'm not so sure that I won't have the same problem. Some unscrupulous bastard is bound come along and having rifled through the bins and found unpublished notes, will then use them to claim these were in fact my final thoughts on this or that. I don't see that there is a way to stop it.
　　These woods are thick. Who knows, somebody might be eavesdropping right now in hopes of scratching together the "real" low- down on you and I?
God only knows what he might cast us as - You as the philosopher sage; me as cock-sure upstart? Whichever it is, it will probably say as much about him as us.
　　Have you noticed that: the more a man lives his life in the public eye, the more convinced people become that there must exist some private peccadillo that, once found, will lay bare his real intentionality. Sad to say there is an enduring avidity, cupidity, for this sort of thing. Yet here we are living our lives as if there were no end to them, struggling to impose some pattern on the warp and woof of experience as it touches our clumsy fingers, never knowing when fate might come calling. And should the curtain be wrung down today, in next to no time the carrion will be circling offering specious explanations along the lines of " because of this, therefore on account of that".

S: Bad enough those others will feel they have carte blanche to argue how your legacy is to be divvied up, I think. Suffice to say, the subject came up in discussion between Plato and me. I was telling him that, lately, I'd had this urge to get my house in order, and to that end I'd been giving some thought as to how I might manage the whole doleful business. I've rarely seen him so rapt; so many questions; such excitement. He was positively ablaze. A bit of what he calls a "writer's block", recently. Made me feel distinctly uncomfortable, - as if I were feeding him.

A: It makes you wonder if you ought to get your retaliation in first. Did I tell you I was thinking of writing an autobiography?

# CHEWING THE CUD

S: Don't you have to be of an age to write such things? Besides, isn't the whole genre self-serving?

A: That's why I'd have chapter headings like, "Why I'm so clever", "Why I'm so wise".

S: That would be sure to confirm some people's suspicions.

A: Oh, but I wouldn't want just anyone to be able to read it.

S: Hmm, as I said earlier, I think you might get your wish in that regard.

A: Anyway it's no more than a thought, for now. Given these straitened times we might be seeking exile the day after tomorrow?

S: Not me. Could you see me grafted upon a strange tree? No, for better or worse, I'm Athenian - root and branch. It is a matter of daily delight to me that a five minute walk, in whatever direction, will bring me to a well-spring and my first audience of the day.

A: Slim pickings, for a philosopher, like yourself, I would imagine.

S: I don't go to lecture; I go listen, and to observe the hustle and bustle of a city awakening and going about its business. Philosophy comes later - at a mid-morning break, or more likely over lunch while people chew over the news they have gleaned over the course of the morning round.
A: People complain from weakness, don't you find?

S: Maybe, but I try not to judge. Most seek a ready ear, but as much for their banter as for any grumbles they might have. In next to no time you become accepted as part of the furniture. Miss a day, and your absence will be commented upon. It's like being among friends. I love it.

A: Personally, I'm always surprised at how lonely I can feel even among friends.

S: Why doesn't that surprise me?

A: People bandy the term 'friends" about with such promiscuity. Ninety-nine percent of those they lay claim to, as friends are no more than ships passing in the night. Do you never stop and wonder about the price entailed by being friends?

# CHEWING THE CUD

Forget for the moment what you have to have in common to lay claim to the term. Think instead of how much must be left unsaid; how much you have to look past to retain the title? Not for nothing will a third party view them as birds of a feather.

S: There's a difference between you and I; I don't "think" about these matters at all. A simple smile, an open heart is the only passport I need to gain entry to another's world.

A: You say that now, but what if a better condition of life was in prospect?

S: Some of us may live in the gutter, but that doesn't mean we haven't got our eyes on the stars.513

A: Zeus! Must you always play that particular card?

S: Card?

A: The Jack of Hearts. [Sings],
"Why did you throw the Jack of Hearts away?
 It was the only card I had left to play".

S: What?

A: [Sings]: "I need a brand new friend who doesn't bother me,
      I need a brand new friend who doesn't trouble me,
      I need a brand new friend who doesn't need me".

S: Well I don't need you; I want you.

A: That door is shut.

S: So what was all that about?

A: Just some lines from "The Doors".

S: Forgiven my woodeness, but how can doors sing?

A: "The Doors" – they're a rock and roll band.

S: Like I said to Plato that time – "Rock 'n' roll"? Can anyone rock 'n' roll?

# CHEWING THE CUD

A: Well not quite. With your voice we would probably have to settle for "The Talking Heads".

S: You've stopped making sense. Can we go back to cards? With them I can figure out when the deck is marked.

A: That "holier than thou" stuff! For a start, it's just not true. You might have been born to a station lower than mine, but certainly not one bringing up the rear.

S: I think you'll find it's a matter of how one chooses to live that is the crucial thing. And I happen to think as Plato correctly reports in the Gorgias that it is better to suffer wrong than do it.514

A: Luke, 18: 14, corrected." He that humbleth himself wills to be exalted". 515

S: Luke? Who is this Luke?

A: Never mind. Life itself is essentially appropriation, injury, overpowering of what is alien and weaker; suppression, hardness, imposition of one's forms, incorporation and least, at its mildest, exploitation... Life is will to power.516

S: Ah, now we have it! At long last, your true colours!

A: Oh, come now. You are not now going to play the blushing bride. You heard Pericles' "funeral oration" as clearly as I. You can get a copy for the price of a mina from any bookseller.

S: What 's that got to do with anything?

A: Everything, I'd say; and especially with that vaunted "intellectual conscience" of yours. What was it that Pericles said? "We do not say that a man who takes no interest in politics minds his own business; we say that he has no business here at all".

S: Ah yes, those lines were the goad that led to Plato's "Republic". That was quite some polish that Thucydides gave to Pericles' words, eh? I'd bet Gorgias was green with envy.

A: And all that other stuff. 'Future ages will wonder at us, as the present age wonders at us now". What Athenian chest didn't swell upon hearing that; at the bluff apologia of imperial predation? "Our adventurous spirit has forced an entry into every sea and into every land; and everywhere we have left behind us everlasting immemorial of good done to friends or suffering inflicted upon our enemies". Not forgetting that proud boast and exhortation with which he brings the whole pulsating paean to its shuddering climax, "When you reflect upon her [Athens'] greatness, then reflect what her greatness was: men with a spirit of adventure, men who know their duty; men who were ashamed to fall below a certain standard.... It is for you to try to be like them!". Not much wriggle-room for an intellectual conscience such as yours? In a word, fucked, I'd say.

S: At the time, yes; but now? All things have a season, I guess. Just because I love my city and its citizens, and see it as my first duty to obey its laws, it doesn't follow that I always approve of them. Sometimes wisdom lies in knowing what you can and cannot change, and in being politic in respect thereof. Had I a say in the matter, I'd remove my name from the "Republic". Privately, I think the Metic has a point about the "Forms". Plato just can't help over-intellectualizing everything. Ties himself in knots of his own making. If there is a "Form" of the "Good", the "Beautiful", etc., doesn't there have to be one of the "Dirt"? 517
   Just between you and I, and the gatepost over yonder, - the issue of slavery? Can't say I'm comfortable about it. Never said word one about it, but its the customary spoils of war for our, and many another, people. Never kept a slave, nor would I want to; and this despite Xanthippe's protestations that her friends regard her as the only slave in our household. I've a theory of sorts about slave-holding. Whilst the society as a whole condones it, it's the middling and the lower orders who delight in the status that such ownership affords them. It's they who treat the slave most cruelly, as little more than a chattel. Your kind seem to be altogether more relaxed a bout the whole thing, willing to recognize merit where it is due, happy to confer responsibility on the more able, to allow them to tutor children - as in the case of Zopyrus -, even, on occasion, to take them in marriage, or grant them manumission.

A: One cannot erase out of the soul of a man what his ancestors have done most eagerly and often ... It is not at all possible that a man should not have in his body the qualities and preferences of his parents and ancestors - whatever appearances say against this. This is the problem of race.518

S: Race? Mightn't that be misunderstood? Speaking of " the qualities and preferences of his parents and ancestors", did I tell you that I ran into that creepy-crawler, Miletus, the other day.519 Still intent on climbing the greasy pole by studying the law, it seems. You think I'm conservative? You ought to meet him - positively antediluvian, him. Still arguing that the tragedian is the real custodian of wisdom, not the philosopher. To illustrate the point, he tells me he's writing his very own version of Oedipus. "A word to the wise", I said, "not even if you were to become a cannibal and swallow the combined brains of Aeschylus, Sophocles, and Euripides could you hope to be a match for Plato.

A: Do you think that was wise; to make an enemy of him? You realize that you've become quite irascible of late?

S: The privilege of the senior citizen, my boy! Can't be doing with all that pussyfooting around anymore. Time to speak my mind, while I can. Besides it was Plato I instanced as the point of comparison, not me. As I said before he stormed off shouting that he'd dine out on my brains before too long. As I told the crowd, if the comparison had been with me who, as everyone knows, knows nothing, logic would say he knows less than nothing. It made the crowd laugh, if not him.
A: Zeus. Have a care.

S: Well, I mean: to aspire to no more than being the lickspittle of Antylus - that's tragic.520 Don't get me started on what's tragic and what isn't. I know that you are in sympathy with the whole idea of tragedy as the great art form. He's the kind of big girl's blouse who would encourage the young and impressionable to blub like their so-called tragic heroes.

A: "I would rather be on earth as a servant, hired by a landless man with little to live on, than be king over all the dead and spent"? 521.

S: Homer, I know. And the answer is still the same. "We must beg Homer and the other poets, not to be angry if we strike out these and similar passages, not because they are un-poetical, or unattractive to the popular ear, but because the greater the poetical charm of them, the less are they meet for the ears of boys and men who are meant to be free, and who should fear slavery more than death". 522

A: You are not joking?

S: I never joke about serious matters like these. We're not opposed to he idea of myth as such; we just think that, especially where the young are concerned, the stories that are told them should be morally uplifting - with the emphasis on self-control and justice. Levity is out of place here. Jokes, too, would have to be excised.

A: What about elephants?

S: Elephants? Is this some myth to do with memory?

A: You know why they paint their toenails red? So they can hide in cherry trees. You are supposed to say; "I've never seen an elephant in a cherry tree", so that I can reply,...

S: That's precisely why jokes have to be banned.

A: That's the upside of having a friend with Alzheimer's: you can re-cycle the same joke over and over again.

S: If you are not going to take this seriously, then...
A: On the contrary, precisely because it is all so serious, I want to make a joke. Gallows humour. Quite apt in the presence of the metaphysics of the hangman.523

S: Deaths no laughing matter.

A: No, indeed. But I suspect many a one is going to have to swing for your metaphysics. Aeschylus "lied"?

S: Ah, now I see where these snide comments are coming from. Well he did. "God plants guilt among men when he desires utterly to destroy a house" – I ask you? 524You can't say God is the source of evil; you of all people as a member of Pericles' household at this present interregnum cannot believe that.

A: Why not?

S: The divine only does good, the divine never changes, the divine never lies, nor does it deceive.

A: Really? "Is it not from the mouth of the Most High that good and evil come?" "Shall we receive good at the hand of God, and shall we not receive evil?"525

S: I've never heard such, though it sounds much like our tragedians.

187

# CHEWING THE CUD

A: The Holy Book of the Jews, before their exile. Thereafter, and culminating in the Christian New Testament, God begins to be conceived of as perfect. In one and the same moment the problem of suffering is created, and created as insoluble, do you see?

S: You're flushed again, like last night. Strange, what occasioned it has just come back to me. Someone was arguing that Patroclus was Achilles' lover - "his lover and not his love [the notion that Patroclus was the beloved one is a foolish error into which Aeschylus has fallen, for Achilles was surely the fairer of the two, fairer also than all the other heroes; and, as Homer informs us, he was still beardless, and younger far]"526

A: And they say love is blind? Never before has that struck me as a euphemism. Truly, I don't know what's to be done with you, Socrates.

S: Strange how things come back to you, don't you think? Shot from the dark at the back of your mind. We've digressed somewhat. You were saying?

A: Yes, yes. We must get on, but a couple of other things with respect to Plato and the gods.

S: You'd be best off getting this from the horse's mouth, you know?

A: True, but the stable doors always ajar these days.

S: Well, there's not that much I can tell you about his current thought, for as you've just said he is rarely home these days. One thing I can say; this concern of yours to paint him in eschatological terms as a precursor of this Christian belief that is just over the horizon? His Myth of Er is more akin to that Eastern thought and the ideas of transmigration of souls. To be sure his concern here is, contrary to the tragedian, to sketch out a scenario in which human kind might perfect itself through the pursuit of the good. Hence the idea that what you do in this life has some bearing on what you appear as in the next; hence the need to keep the animalistic side of our natures, the emotional side on a tight rein.

A: "You live this life, as if it's real.
    A thousand kisses deep."527
Sorry. Some lines from a poem set to music.

S: There you see. That's the problem with poets. Always stirring the emotions. Not that I'm an authority on all this; too abstract for a simple man, like me. "Soul"? Yes. Immortality thereof? Yes. How? I can't say. My reason only takes me thus far.

No aptitude for math's you see; Plato's four levels - knowledge, thinking, opinion, and imagining. I'm stuck at the third level - opinion - with the rest of the numbties, according to His Highness. Need the maths in order to progress, and eh, what can I know because I'm marked as he who knows least? 528

A: Probably only in the fourth grade, then? Back of the class! "There are known knowns. These are things we know that we know. There are known unknowns. That is to say, there are things we know we don't know. But there are also unknown unknowns. These are things we don't know we don't know". 529

S: Ah, at last. All my life! A soul mate! And I'd thought such a one beyond my imagining.
A: Ha, ha. One other thing; "Everybody ought to perform the one function in the community for which his nature best suits him"? 530

S: What's your beef? That the proposed Republic is no more than a benevolent dictatorship? Well if the alternative is one in which the tragedian flourishes, perhaps the only way to guarantee a man's happiness is to limit his freedom?

A: I was minded of something else. Man reduced to a function; borne again as one thing only. A pathology, in my book, since a real man is many things. Besides, in such a regime there would be no place for the likes of you, my friend.

S: Absolutely. Now that would constitute a real tragedy!

A: Ha, ha. It's good to know that you haven't bought the shop.

S: No, I just happen to work there; some proper remuneration for loan of my persona, once in a while, wouldn't go amiss.

A: The fancy of contemplatives? Have you thought about it?
What distinguishes the higher beings from the lower is that the former see and hear immeasurably more, and see and hear thoughtfully - and precisely this distinguishes human beings from animals, and the higher animals from the lower. For anyone who grows up into the heights of humanity the world becomes ever fuller; ever more fishhooks are cast in his direction to capture his interest; the number of

things that stimulate him grows constantly, as does the number of different kinds of pleasure and displeasure. The higher human being always becomes at the same time happier and unhappier.

S: True enough.

A: But he can never shake off a delusion: He fancies that he is a spectator and a listener who has been placed before the great visual and acoustic spectacle that is life; he calls his own nature contemplative but overlooks that he himself is really the poet who keeps recreating this life. Of course, he is different from the actor of this drama, the so-called active type; but he is even less like a mere spectator and festive guest in front of the stage. As a poet, he certainly has vis contemplativa and the ability to look back upon his work, but at the same time also and above all creative power, which the active human being lacks, whatever visual appearances and the faith of all the world may say. We who think and feel at the same time are those who really continually fashion something that had not been there before: the whole eternally growing world of valuations, colours, accents, perspectives, scales, affirmations and negations. This poem, we have invented, is continually studied by the so-called practical human beings [our actors] who learn their roles and translate everything into flesh and actuality - into the everyday. Whatever has value in our world now does not have value in itself, according to its nature - nature is always value-less, but has been given value at some time as a present - and it was we who gave and bestowed it. Only we have created the world that concerns man ! - But precisely this knowledge we lack, and when we occasionally catch it for a fleeting moment we always forget it again immediately; we fail to recognize our best power and underestimate ourselves, the contemplatives, just a little. We are neither as proud nor as happy as we might be.531

S: Need you wonder I follow you around? Truly, the thoughts that change the world come on the feet of doves. That's Plato to a "T". And the irony of it, were it true. Plato, less a seeker after "Truth", than an artist providing us with the lines, the values, - pro and con- to which we like hapless puppets must speak. How does it go? "It is necessary also to consider un-comely persons and thoughts, and those which are intended to produce laughter in comedy ... For serious things cannot be understood without laughable things, nor opposites at all without opposites, if a man is really to have intelligence of either". 532

Speaking of things "pro and con" reminded me. In his later work he makes allowance for comedy in the republic of the future. That's not to say that a man of good repute should allow himself to be inveigled into participating in such. What's the stricture here? "He should command slaves and hired strangers to imitate such things, but he should never take any serious interest in them himself, nor should any freeman or freewoman be discovered taking pains to learn them". 533 It is incumbent on all such people that they maintain their dignity at all times; they are, after all, the role models to which the young will look for guidance and inspiration.

A: But that's the problem of the "actor"? I just alluded to it. What if you found yourself in one of Aristophanes' scenarios, or worse? Suppose we woke to find ourselves as the creatures of some stranger's scenario? I - the precocious philosopher/ warrior: handsome, debonair, with a wicked sense of humour. You a down at heel - if you had such – rather self- important autodidactic clown? I, as actor, wouldn't be free to say that I'm really a rather sad and pathetically lonely individual always on the move in search of relief from wretchedly incapacitating headaches. That would be for someone else's story. Likewise you could just throw your toys out of the pram and go about shouting, "Infamy! Infamy! He's got it in for me"! 534

S: That's not funny, that's satire.

A: That's why it might be funny.

S: No, it's not. The bastard has got it in for me.

A: But that wouldn't stop it being funny.

S: No, not the bastard in the wood, though he would seem no better! Aristophanes! He's got it in for me! You are missing the point. I quote, "A comic poet or maker of iambic or satirical verse shall not be permitted to ridicule any of the citizens". 535 Given that this is the bastard's stock in trade he'd soon find himself in search of other employment.

A: That'd be tragic. Still, he won't want for company in the dole queue.

S: "Dole queue"? Now you are being deliberately obtuse, and also missing the wider concern. Whatever the tragic poets say to the contrary, real life can produce a happy ending; we just have act on the principles that Plato has outlined for us. Anyway you were going to say, before we digressed from the digression?

A: It'll keep. What's one loose end more?

S: I've seen fewer loose ends in a sack of eels down at the docks.

# CHEWING THE CUD

A: All in good time. I was going to try to take you to task on not doing harm, but it can wait. It might be an idea to say some more about actors, since we're already broached the subject. This will enable us to say something more about the self, which as yet we have skirted around.

S: Sounds like a plan. First things, first; I must sit. We seem to have gone in a circle. That place where we took refreshment is over yonder. Old age, I'm afraid.

A: And there was I, thinking you'd planned to live forever.

S: Longevity, longevity. That's all I hear, these days. The seven ages, my boy; that's all there has been and will be. Longevity be damned! It's just a conspiracy to prolong old age. Now be a good fellow and fetch me a drink, whilst I settle my limbs in the shade.

A: All I want to say is that one pays heavily for coming to power: power makes stupid.536 I, too, have a theory in respect of all this. Only the weak man wishes to hurt and to see signs of suffering.537Many think of power only in binary terms: as something to be exercised over others, less it be exercised by others over oneself. For me the real power is that one exercises over oneself.

S: But that doesn't sit well with what you just said - all that threatening talk of appropriation, injury, suppression, and the like.

A: To refrain from mutual injury, mutual violence, mutual exploitation, to equate one's will with that of another: this may in a certain rough sense become good manners between individuals if the conditions for it are present [namely if their strengths and value standards are in fact similar and the both belong to one body]. As soon as there is a desire to take this principle further, however, and if possible as the fundamental principle of society, it at once reveals itself for what it is: as the will to the denial of life, as the principle of dissolution and decay.538

# CHAPTER 8
## Time is of the essence

A: Your drink's behind you. Don't worry. You went out like a light; and no; not for long. No troubling dreams, this time?

S: "Went out like a light"? No, I'm fine. Sorry about that. The less I sleep at night, the more I sleep in the day. It is getting difficult to pass it off as one of my trances.

A: Perhaps the gods are going to make you an owl in another life? The owl of Minerva takes flight at dusk?

S: That's Greek to me.

A: Sorry. Forgot you'd have to be Roman to know that. I was pondering on Hegel actually. "Wisdom takes flight at dusk". Going to hijack our gods wholesale. No culture of their own; you see?

S: Who? This Hegel?

A: No, the Romans. Give them different names - job done.

S: And they say it is Greeks bearing gifs you have to be chary of? Can we forget the history lessons of the future; I've only just managed to find my way back to the present from God knows where? I'm still all of a sweat. Zeus! It was hot in that room.

A: Room?

S: Do you think that's true: you choose your life and, in so doing, you choose your illness? I was presenting myself for examination. Someone had given me a mirror, as I'd wanted to check my look before entering the dock. The strange thing was that I didn't have the strength to lift the mirror.
Suddenly I became aware that there were others in the room observing me, some with malicious glee, others with looks of sad resignation. All, I realized in a panic, could see everything, knew everything, had decided that - in respect of myself - the die had been irrevocably past many years before. I was both the last to know that a verdict had been cast in regard of myself, and, most perturbing of all, the only one in the dark as to what this miscreant looked like, and who he actually was to others.

193

# CHEWING THE CUD

A: I thought you said your sleep was without dreams?

S: Did I? Perhaps it was one of those waking dreams. Do you know how many illnesses you can die of? I was asking Hippocrates. Even he didn't know for sure. He reckoned it must run into the tens of thousands. Weird, when you think about it. The numbers are so mind-boggling. Here we are sitting - where untold others down the years have sat, and yet others to come down the centuries will come to sit - in this sun dappled shade, the sky a sempiternal blue, the cicadas beating out their pulsing rhythm, not knowing what trifling change beneath our sun-kissed skin might be silently signalling future disaster. Disconcerting to think that even if others don't get you first, your own body harbours a potential killer who will see to it that you are dispatched sooner or later?

   Sorry, I'm rambling. I keep forgetting that thoughts of mortality will not have touched you yet.

A: Have I not bestridden many a battlefield?

S: Bestridden? You pompous, arse. I'm not speaking of that romantic nonsense of being half in love with life, and half with death - where one dreams of oneself as a fire-cracker, burning up hard and bright.539 There are no lightening offensives, no thrilling cavalry charges in old age. There are only dour regard actions in which ones energies are so many hapless infantry to be sacrificed in the fight for self-preservation.

   You should get out more. If you care to see it, there are fountains where these bedraggled armies gather to conduct an impromptu role call of their losses, and to welcome the latest recruits, to relate the latest prognosis, news of the latest remission granted, and so forth. Sickness, you see, gives such souls an identity, a history. Though the many are marginalized, and yet others are lost on the wayside, there are survivors to be feted as heroes for having defied the odds. It's a peculiar fraternity, but a fraternity nonetheless.

A: Please, my friend. You are very far form your dotage yet. You might walk with a bit of a stoop, but it'll be a while before you're knocking on that particular door.

S: "Youth is always dear to me but old age weighs on me heavier than Mount Aetna" - Euripides, you know? Got blotches on my legs. Went to bed one night; next morning they were there. Xanthippe, bless her, reckons it's a sign I ought to be thinking about making provision for her. She's been telling anyone who'll care to listen that Charon bit me in the night.

## CHEWING THE CUD

A: Why don't we go and sit by the pool? There is more to be said about actors and the self. It'll take your mind off of all this morbidity.

S: So long as you let your guard down a little. It's hard going if you can't see the man behind the thoughts, I find. Is it a deal?

A: OK. It's a deal. Between you and me, one day I'm going to live as a peripatetic like Diogenes, and move with the seasons.

S: Ha, ha. That'll be the day! I don't know which is the funnier image; you with a beard? Or your trying to beard the population, with only a lantern to see your way by?

A: Who said anything about a beard? I rather fancied myself wearing a moustache.

S: What? Ha, ha. Now we have a walrus hoping to beard a lion?

A: Talking of the ferryman, shall we begin at the shallow end, and then you can tell if you are getting out of your depth?

S: Very funny. You won't be the first pup I've had to drown.

A: If Piri were here, I'd have him make a meal of you for that remark alone. The actor then, as a metaphor for the self, yes? Two choices as we've already seen. One: the self as actor as a already individuated entity able to choose whatever role he wishes to play. Two: a view that denies as a fiction the idea of an indivisible self at the centre of action. Here we get into the metaphorics of performance. The self now modelled as effect rather than cause - the product of a stage-managed perfor-mance - a dramatic effect.

S: There would have to be a subject to take on the role, surely? I don't see where you are going with this. As you are already well aware such creatures are not our liking, Plato's and mine that is.

A: Ah, but you have to admire the falseness with good conscience; the delight in simulation exploding as a power that pushes aside one's so-called "character", flooding in and at times extinguishing it; the inner craving for a role and a mask, for appearance.540.Reflect on the whole history of women: do they not have to be first and above all else actresses? 541

195

S: But that's only because society has forced that role upon them. You shouldn't get Xanthippe started on this. Loathes all that face painting, and the women who go in for it. And when obliged by convention - attendance at a marriage or funeral – you should hear the self- loathing?

A: Yes, but this doesn't end with women. All those who are in a condition of dependency have to cut their coat according to the cloth, always have to adapt to new circumstances, always have to change their mien and posture, until they gradually learn to turn their coat with every wind and thus virtually become a coat.542 Not that the value of a thing is determined by its origin, but even today the care to make a living still compels almost all male Europeans to adopt a particular role, their so-called occupation. Indeed so much so, they forget the contingencies that led them to adopt the role, the vocation, and come to identify themselves with it: considered more deeply, the role has actually become character; and art, nature.543

S: Have I not said as much already in the "Republic"? "Have you not observed that imitations, if continued from youth far into life, settle down into habits and second nature in the body, the speech and the thought"? As I remember our concern was that the guardians would be corrupted if allowed to play roles that were below their intended station in life. You're teaching grandma to suck eggs.

A: Yes I am. I'm not making myself clear. I want to draw a distinction between actors and artists here. Put it this way. There are periods when men believed in their predestination for precisely this occupation [whatever it is or was], precisely this way of earning a living, and simply refused to acknowledge the element of accident, role, and caprice.544 There are also more democratic ages in which the individual become convinced that he can do just about everything and can manage almost any role, and everyone experiments with himself, improvises, makes new experiments, enjoys his experiments; and all nature ceases and becomes art. The first are actors, the second are artists, and here lies my concern - whenever a human being begins to discover how he is playing a role and how he can be an actor, he becomes an actor.545

S: No, I still don't get it. Aren't you the one who champions the artist?

A: As artists, yes - As the architects and builders, as bound by that fundamental faith that would enable us to calculate, to promise, to anticipate the future.546 Precisely this is lost when the artist becomes an actor. Perhaps all of us are no longer material for a society? Small men, you see? Some of them will, but most of them are only willed. Some of them are genuine, but most of them are bad actors. There are unconscious actors among them and involuntary actors; the genuine are always rare, especially genuine actors.547

S: Sort of.

A: You want faces to go with the props? My immediate general staff for this ill thought out Sicilian venture - genuine actors to a man. Filled with that simple piety that demands that they should fully inhabit their roles and perform their duty, come hell or high water. You could stake your life on such men. All they require is a man with a plan, a vision; the logistics you can leave to them.

Nicias is not such a one.548 A putative artist, but in reality a bad actor. Weak, indecisive, lacking the effect of command when the going gets tough. He wishes to be obeyed must know how to command. Laches - another of the same clothe. Tried and acquitted, I know, but the archetypical conservative when it comes to strategy.

S: Yes, I've spoken with him.549

A: Try explaining to him that it is best to win without giving battle, or that it is better, at the outset, to weaken prospective enemies by foiling their designs, or failing that isolating them and rendering them helpless?

S: Sometimes speed may be of the essence though.

A: Maybe so. Nonetheless speed does not mean haste. Thorough preparation is necessary. Victory needs to be complete otherwise one runs the risk of wasting resources damping down what should have been extinguished in the first instance.

S: And you wonder that the politicians distrust you?

A: That is the trouble with Laches; party through and through. To be sure the civilian government should be the ones who declare war, but absentee civilian leadership that involves itself in field command imperils victory.

S: Laches as soldier, then; a bad actor?

A: The point I was seeking to make is that the mere actor lacks any culturally embedded character; he lacks any commitment beyond his facile faith in his ability to handle any role. Best of all is to be an artist. That said, there is nothing more difficult to take in hand, more perilous to conduct, or more uncertain of success, than to take the lead in the introduction of a new order of things.550

# CHEWING THE CUD

S: Some might argue that you yourself are hardly the best role model. It has been said that your victories are achieved more often than not by subterfuge and treachery, than by force of arms?

A: A good general only seeks battle as a last resort. Why should I waste lives if I can achieve my objectives by other means? Lions have their uses, so long as donkeys do not lead them; but even so the fox is cleverer than the lion. No enterprise is more likely to succeed than the one concealed from the enemy until it is ripe for execution.551

S: And Mitylene? It is said you took one the women for your own and impregnated her.552

A: Not so, a slander. I opposed the ultimatum. As I said at the time, where's the profit in alienating the other cities, the other islands? As to both the slander and the policy, it is nonetheless safer to be feared than to be loved because love is preserved by the link of obligation, which, owing to the baseness of men, is broken at every opportunity.553

S: I never knew there was this side to you.

A: We are talking statecraft. Everyone sees what you appear to be, few experience what you really are.554

S: I meant I'm not so sure I like this side of you.

A: There's the problem. The key to victory is adaptability and inscrutability. When you know yourself and others you are never in danger, when you know yourself but not others you have half a chance of winning, and when you know neither yourself nor others you are in danger in every battle. Men are so simple of mind, and so much dominated by their immediate needs, that a deceitful man will always find plenty who are ready to be deceived.555

S: Have you heard yourself? My principle of harm, if I may call it such, says that those who live by the sword die by the sword.

A: Yes, I've heard myself, but have you? All courses of action are risky, so prudence is not avoiding danger [impossible anyhow], but calculating risk and acting decisively. Make mistakes of ambition and not mistakes of sloth, I say! 556 A man who is used to acting in one way never changes, he must come to ruin when the times, in changing, no longer are in harmony with his ways.557

S: You should have a care that those last bon mots don't come back to bite you.

A: They already have, but that is just the way of the world isn't it? Sooner, or later, it catches up with one. We run to run to death, and death greets us as fast; fate has its bag of tricks.558 Oh, come now, there's no need to look so crestfallen. Is it what we've been speaking of, or that you're no longer sure how you might get some purchase on me? Don't you know that to live in this world you need a heart of bronze? I'll take the blush as an affirmative. That should tell you, my friend, something about the perspective from which you come at your amorous adventures, and much else besides I shouldn't wonder?

S: "Perspective"?

A: Perspective? Did I say perspective? Ah well. I shall use the term interchangeably with "interpretation" in what follows, and both in the widest sense.

S: What is to follow then?

A: The self. Having dipped our toes in the shallow end, it is time we went deeper. But, how to begin? How about some general comments concerning the two terms?
   "Objectivity" [ought to be] understood not as "contemplation without interest" {which is a nonsensical absurdity}, but as the ability to have one's For and Against under control and to engage and disengage them, so that one knows how to employ a variety of perspectives and affective interpretations in the service of knowledge. Henceforth, my dear philosophers, let us be on our guard against the dangerous old conceptual fiction that posited a 'pure, will-less, painless, timeless knowing subject"; let us against the snares of such contradictory concepts as "pure reason", "absolute spirit", "knowledge in itself": these always demand we should think of an eye that is completely unthinkable, an eye turned in no particular direction, in which the active and interpreting forces, through which alone seeing becomes a seeing-something, are supposed to be lacking; these always demand of the eye an absurdity and a nonsense. There is only a perspective seeing, only a perspective "knowing"; and the more affects we allow to speak about a thing, the more eyes, different eyes, we can lend to the thing, the more complete will our "concept" of this thing, our "objectivity", be. But to eliminate the will altogether, to suspend each and every affect, supposing we were capable of this - what would that mean but to castrate the intellect? 559

199

# CHEWING THE CUD

One more. Whether the origin of our apparent " knowledge" is not to be sought solely in older evaluations that have become so a much part of us that they belong to our basic constitution? So that what really happens is only that younger needs grapple with the results of older needs? The world seen, felt, interpreted as thus and thus, so that organic life may preserve itself in this perspective of interpretation. Man is not only a single individual but one particular line of the total organic world. That he endures proves that a species of interpretation [even though accretions are still being added] has also endured, that the system of interpretation has not changed. "Adaptation". Our "dissatisfaction", our "ideal", etc., is perhaps the consequence of this incorporated piece of interpretation, of our perspective point of view; perhaps organic life will in the end perish through it.559

S: That was quite a wodge for me to get my gums around. Let's take the stuff about reading us back into nature as read. Let's begin instead with the perspectival metaphor. You want to dismiss the God's eye view of knowledge as a fiction, and in its place you are suggesting what - an aggregative view? One in which "objectivity" is never attained, but rather approached by dint of generating the number of perspectives that one brings to bare on the    object under review. You'd be better off talking epistemology with Plato, you know. The whole subject makes me yawn, if I'm honest. Still, I'll do my best. Seeing is not "believing"; it's knowing? I might be speaking out of turn here, but I think Plato entertains a hierarchical view of the senses. Sight being literally furthest from the ground, nearest to heaven, is the most important; "Windows upon the soul", and all that?

A: Not that any of that stopped from him thinking of the masses as an animals to be pacified.

S: What's that to do with this?

A: Nothing; really. It's just all that elitism. You know in a later age? No you wouldn't, would you. Anyway on the back of that some people came to believe that the soul of the poor, at death, left the body via the anus.

S: What are you telling me? That Pythagoras was right all along? Avoid beans?

A: Perhaps the moral - if moral there is - is that we philosophers also say the silliest things.

## CHEWING THE CUD

S: I'd not thought of it like that before, but I would have to be the exception here, if the oracle was right. Since I'm the one who knows he knows least, it stands to reason that I would be the one least likely to say anything stupid.

A: That's the best argument I've heard that that oracle should have been strangled at birth.

S: Have you never noticed how your sense of humour deserts you when you start to get self-important?

A: Ha, ha. I walked straight into that one, didn't I? That's not my view of a perspective, by the way. That starts from the assumption that we are already discrete and fully individuated beings creeping around our prey. My mistake; I find it hard to say no to a striking image - "the perspective optics of life". Odd how people get fixated by a phrase.560Still, I mean the term to be understood in the widest sense; perspective as the basic condition of all life. There would be no life at all if not on the basis of perspective estimates and appearances; the narrowing of our perspective is a condition of life and growth.560

S: Narrowing?

A: There is such a thing as the will to ignorance. We'll come back to that. Suffice to say for the moment that perspective is subsumed by interpretation, and that interpretation is the essence of life, its will to power, ... the essential priority of the spontaneous, aggressive, expansive, form giving forces that give new interpretations and directions.561All events in the organic world, indeed whatever exists, involves interpretation; not only their apprehension by subjects, but the subjects themselves along with the objects and events that are their concern. 562.

S: All very interesting, but I'm still none the wiser as to who or what it is that has these perspectives and interpretations. Are you claiming, arguing for, some sort of scepticism; that we are not able to apprehend the world as it is in itself? And then there's that so-called "naturalism" of yours. Were you to turn out a sceptic, would it have to apply to the animal kingdom as well? Wouldn't that oblige you to say that we have no apprehension of how they, too, view the world?

A: Absolutely. I should see about letting you loose on my critics. The human form of cognition can only be a difference of kind; a more complex form of the incorporation or assimilation to be found in the protoplasm. That aside, I'd be the last to argue that we human kind have a unified view. Have I not repeatedly pointed to the

201

plethora of antagonistic interpretations that continue to bewitch and bewilder our understanding of ourselves sowing concord and discord in equal measure - slave v master, Christian v pagan, faith v reason, and the derivatives thereof? 563

S: Granted. However, don't we end up on the other horn of the dilemma then? You, yourself say, "There is only a perspective seeing, only a perspective "knowing"; and the more affects we allow to speak about a thing, the
more eyes, different eyes, we can use to observe the thing, the more complete will our "concept" of this thing, our "objectivity", be".564 And that sounds bad enough even without the emphatic italics you're so fond of? Aren't we back with the other "I"?

A: Let me say again, loud and clear, I want no truck with the notion of an "ego substance", with that kind of theology that posits a "being" or subject-stratum "behind doing, effecting, becoming". 565 Describe it how you will, "the myth of the given", or "soul atomism": "the belief which regards the soul as something indestructible, eternal, indivisible, as a monad, as an atomon! 566

S: Ouch! That's told me.

A: Is it anything more than a seduction of language that leads us to posit a ""being' behind doing, effecting, becoming; 'the doer' is merely a fiction a fiction added to the deed - the deed is everything". 567 A peg on which we then hang, both metaphorically and literally, the black cap of responsibility and accountability as the malign products of the exercise of a free will.
    And before you start raising the usual suspects who'll claim to the contrary that here black is white, let me state that it is not all necessary to get rid of "the soul" ... and thus to renounce one of the most ancient and venerable hypotheses - as happens frequently to many clumsy naturalists who can barely touch on "the soul" without immediately losing it. But the way is open for new versions and refinements of the soul-hypothesis; and such conceptions as "mortal soul", soul as subjective multiplicity", and "soul as social structure of the drives and affects", want henceforth to have citizens' rights in science.568

S: Go on. The objection can wait; I'm intrigued. How do you propose to go about substantiating these claims?

A: For a start, by working backwards. Rather than starting with subjects, beings, doers, as is usual, I begin with deeds, actions, becomings. The subject is a created entity ... a capacity ... - fundamentally, action collectively considered with respect to all anticipated actions [action and the probability of similar actions.569

S: Excuse me. You're asserting that the subject is merely a relative unity?

A: Exactly. We've been here earlier. All unity is unity only as organization and co-operation: no differently than a human community is a unity - as opposed to an atomistic anarchy; it is a pattern of domination that signifies a unity but is not a unity.570 By the way I really appreciate the way you keep feeding me dolly-drops. Its just like living inside of one of your masters dialogues.

S: Let's wait and see as to who has the last laugh here. You were saying?

A: My idea is that every specific body strives to become master over all space and to extend its force [- its will to power:] and to thrust back all that resists its extension. But it continually encounters similar efforts on the part of other bodies and ends by coming to an arrangement {"union"] with those of them that are sufficiently related to it: thus they then conspire together for power. And the process goes on -.571

S: Don't try to tweak my nose by changing horses. The other one hasn't been led to water just yet.

A: Not that I want to get up your nose, but its considered bad form to mix your metaphors.

S: Well as long as I know what I mean. It'd take someone who is money as opposed to having money to want to make an issue of that.

A: An issue of what?

S: My vulgarity. Speaking personally, I'm not sure how much I'd willing to pay to have money - but then that's me.

A: "Everything that is precious is as difficult as it is rare", eh? 572

S: My question? Who interprets?

# CHEWING THE CUD

A: It is our needs that interpret the world: our drives and their For and Against. Every drive is a kind of lust to rule; each one has its perspective that it would like to compel all the other drives to accept as a norm.573

S: Morally speaking that seems to be a license for pure selfishness.

A: Moral evaluation is an interpretation, a way of interpreting. The interpretation itself is a symptom of certain physiological conditions, likewise of a certain level of ruling judgments: Who interprets? - Our affects.574

S: These affects, then - they constitute so sort of bottom line; your equivalent of Democritus' atoms?

A: No, no, no. The affects are primary, but they are not to be thought of as entities; no more than things such as fear, love, ressentiment, and the like. They are rather dynamic quanta of force and drive; moreover they are relational in that they relate one state of affairs to another. It is less a matter of individual affects, each with its own interpretation, than a case a union of affects conspiring together for power, as I said before.

S: But these perspectives, these interpretations, they can't float free - they must in-here in an individual?

A: Yes. Put it this way then. All estimation of value involves a certain perspective: that of the maintenance of the individual, a community, a race, a state, a church, a faith, a culture. The concept "individual" is an error because every being consti-tutes the entire process in its entire course [not merely as "inherited", but the pro-cess itself...]. We encounter perspectives within individuals, to be sure, but these individuals comprise - at one and the same time - aggregates of these perspectives and, to coin a phrase, their forms of life. The body you see is a political structure, an aristocracy, an aggregate ...575

S: Aggregates, aggregates? Where's the soul in all this. You've got to give me something concrete to build on here.

A: Be serious.

S: I am.

A: No, you're not. You're taking the piss.

# CHEWING THE CUD

S: Well, there might have been some irony in what I said.

A: Can you be ironic without taking the piss?

S: Me? Personally?

A: See, you're at it again! It was rhetorical.

S: If you've already made your mind up, why are you asking me?

A: Oh never mind. "Body am I, and soul" - thus speaks the child ...But the awakened and knowing say: body am I entirely, and nothing else; and soul is only a word for something about the body.576

S: And what of the character of this "self"?

A: That, too, is a more or less stable aggregate, a unity intimately related to the unity of the body. The body and physiology as the starting point: why? - We gain the correct idea of the nature of the subject-unity, namely as regents at the head of a communality [not as "souls" or "life-forces"], also of the dependence of these regents upon the ruled and of an order of rank and division of labour as the conditions that make possible the whole and its parts. In the same way, how living unites continually arise and die and how the "subject" is not eternal; in the same way, that the struggle expresses itself in obeying and commanding, and that a fluctuating assessment of the limits of power is part of life. The relative ignorance in which the regent is kept concerning individual activities and even disturbances within the community is among the conditions under which rule can be exercised ... The most important thing, however, is: that we understand that the ruler and his subjects are of the same kind, all feeling, willing, and thinking.577

You see? One may not ask: "Who then interprets?" for the interpretation itself, as a form of the will to power, has existence [but not as a "being", but rather as a process, a becoming] as an affect.578

S: May I?

A: Hold fire a moment, please. I've not finished.

All sorts of contradictory estimations and therefore contradictory drives swarm within one man. This is the expression of the diseased condition in mankind, in contrast to the animals, in which all existing instincts satisfy very specific tasks - this contradictory creature has however in its nature a great method of knowledge:

he feels many Fors and Againsts - he raises himself to justice - to a comprehension beyond the estimation of good and evil. The wisest man would be the richest in contradictions, who has feelers for all kinds of men: and, in the midst, his great moments of grandiose harmony - a rare occurrence even in us! - a sort of planetary movement -.579

In contrast to the animals, man has cultivated an abundance of contrary drives and impulses within himself: thanks to this synthesis he is master of the earth. Moralities are the expression of locally limited orders of rank in this multifarious world of drives: so that man should not perish through their contradictions. Thus a drive as master, its opposite weakened, refined, as the impulse that provides the stimulus for the activity of the chief drive. The highest man would have the greatest multiplicity of drives, in the relatively greatest strength that can be endured. Indeed, where the plant "man" shows itself strongest, one finds driving instincts that powerfully conflict with one another..., but are controlled.580

S: Your point as regards the complexity of our kind in respect of the animal kingdom is well made, but this very complexity would seem to be a fearsome thing?

A: It is. The richest and most complex forms - for the expression "higher type" means no more than this - perish more easily: only the lowest preserve an apparent indestructibility ... Among men, too, the higher types, the lucky strokes of evolution, perish most easily as fortunes change. They are exposed to every kind of decadence: they are extreme, and that almost means decadents ... This is not due to any special fatality or malevolence of nature, but simply to the concept 'higher type": the higher type represents an incomparably greater complexity - a greater sum of coordinated elements: so is disintegration is also incomparably more likely. The "genius" is the sublimest machine there is - consequently the most fragile.581

S: If things are thus for the "higher types", what of the "lower types"? You say their indestructibility is only apparent?

A: Hence morality. Unable to resist the prompting of the plethora of stimuli, they have sought relief in morality.

S: That's outrageous.

A: Is it? What has many a religious ascetic and rationalist philosopher done, if not to separate mind from body as a prelude to declaring war on a whole range of effects by declaring them evil and endeavouring to extirpate them? 582 Indeed, I'd go far as to say that for such ascetic types apart from the ascetic ideal, man, the

206

human animal, has had no meaning so far.583 A course of action that is in actuality self-defeating for it pits a will of life against life itself, nature against something that is also nature. 584All this the expression of the diseased condition in man, a symptom of nihilism, decadence, and the degeneration of life; proof that those who refuse combat are more seriously injured than those who engage in it.585

S: No, I'm not having that. Every human being who suffers is my fellow creature.586

A: And the contrary of that is?

S: Contrary? What do you mean contrary?

A: Just that. Only someone who suffers is my fellow creature, therefore someone who enjoys life is my enemy; ressentiment in a nutshell? Would it not be better to declare with Leibniz, "I take delight in other people's happiness. There is more nobility of the soul in rejoicing in the gaiety of others than in feeling sorry about their misfortunes".

S: Are we not all equal? Are we not all deserving of compassion?

A: No, we are not; and yes we are. However we should be wary of those who claim to adore the poor, the excluded, the defeated; they are in love with poverty. Their solicitude is no more than a disguised contempt, a means of reducing the wretched to their distress; a far cry from treating them all as equals.

S: And this preoccupation with suffering?

A: What can one say about the metaphysician in this respect? "Eternal bliss": psychological nonsense. Brave and creative men never consider pleasure and pain as ultimate values - they are epiphenomena: one must desire both if one is to achieve anything -That they see the problem of pleasure and pain in the foreground reveals something weary and sick in metaphysicians and religious people. Every morality is so important to them only because they see in it an essential condition for the abolition of suffering.587.

    In this situation, humankind are primarily reactive and negative. They think their contradictory nature evil and infer there must be a better life - a good, non-contradictory, extra-natural condition and world.588. Let us beware of that canard that would have us believe our happiness depends on others. What defines us is not our universality but our partiality. Our happiness is dependent upon our concourse with our intimates; our families, our friends, the people of our locale.

S: In the main, yes; but our happiness is such that it is a delight that we wish to share it with all and sundry?

A: An idle wish, just the same. There is no happiness save in innocence and insouciance. And that is not to say we are monsters. We simply take our happiness where we can find it, in spite of war, famine, pestilence and the myriad calamities that comprise our everyday backdrop.

S: An idle wish, in your eyes may be. Nonetheless, I, for one, wish to maintain that a properly unified life, a happy life, is achievable only by understanding the proper relations that pertain between reason, justice, and virtue.

A: Once again we have come full circle. I would have thought that if the "Republic" had taught you anything, it would be that politics is about prudence, - not least the art of balancing incommensurable values. You cannot everyday expect to swallow a piece of the late afternoon sun.589

S: Ok. A nod's as good as a wink. Time is running on, so I wont bore you re-iterating my position. Let me ask you something else, about your "justice" and "knowledge"? You were saying of your "higher types", a few moments ago, that they had to raise themselves to "knowledge", "justice". What was the phrase - To "an estimation beyond good and evil"? Doesn't all this imply some rewriting of our ordinary understanding of such concepts?

A: Indeed it does. The "highest human" is the one who incorporates the greatest multiplicity of perspectives, of affective interpretations. "Knowledge" can no longer be categorized as "objectivity ... understood as 'contemplation without interest'". It denies the very conditions of knowledge - affective perspectives and interpretations. In similar fashion "justice" as quietude, as equalization of power, comes to be seen as hostile to life - as a threat to the relations of supremacy under which the phenomenon of "life" comes to be.590 For the "higher types" its a matter of having one's For and Against under control and to engage and disengage them, so that one knows how to employ a variety of perspectives and affective interpretations in the service of knowledge.591 A human being who would be strong, highly educated, skilful in all bodily matters, self-controlled, reverent toward himself, and who might dare to the whole range and wealth of becoming natural, being strong enough for such freedom.592

## CHEWING THE CUD

S: All right. I've been patient long enough. My turn.

A: And there I was thinking that the very essence of a Platonic dialogue was that I, as principle speaker in this instance, try out various lines of argument, whilst you are restricted to the utterance of a "quite so" so as to prevent the flow from becoming a monologue, or seizing up altogether.

S: Trust you. Most are not so impolite as to remark on how stilted it often is. Anyway, I don't want to be funny, but I'm tired of playing the straight man.

A: Actually that sounds kind of funny.

S: If you have the waspish sense of humour of an Aristophanes perhaps.593 Although a little piqued myself, I really felt for Sophocles. And as you know I'm no fan of tragedy, though there I find myself in agreement with the Metic and at odds with Plato: tragedies being mercifully short in duration compared with epics.594

A: I don't thing Aristotle quite meant his remarks to be understood like that. You were going to say?

S: Ressentiment?

A: Ah, yes; "the slave revolt of values". Thanks to the counterfeit and self-deception of impotence the slave can act just as if the weakness of the weak - that is to say, their essence, their effects, their sole ineluctable, irremovable reality - were a voluntary achievement, willed, chosen, a deed, a meritorious act. This type of man needs to believe in a neutral, independent "subject", prompted by an instinct for self-preservation and self-affirmation.595. The slave revolt in morality begins when ressentiment itself becomes creative and gives birth to new values.596

S: Excuse me, but how can that be? Ressentiment, no more than history, say cannot do any such thing. It is men that move things, create things.

A: No, no. I want to insist that there is no such substratum; there is no " being" behind doing, effecting, becoming; "the doer" is merely a fiction added to the deed - the deed is everything.597

S: I don't see how that would even count as a deed. Common-sense dictates that a subject's intentions stand before or behind what he does. Your language seems to suggest that there are no actions, but just events. That can't be right.

A: But to demand of strength that it should not express itself as strength, that it should not be a desire to overcome, ... a desire to become master, a thirst ... for resistances and triumphs, is just as absurd as to demand of weakness that it should express itself as strength.598

S: There may be something in that. What do you say if I try to help you out here?

A: You want me to say "please"?

S: Not at all. No, I was thinking rather of a new kind of etiquette; one I've mentioned previously, one where you do your level best to make the best possible case for your opponent before you attempt to demolish his position.

A: Splendid. Makes it all the more a contest.

S: I thought that might appeal. So then your default position is a rejection of any intentional, or causal account of action. I threw in the causal thing, for free as it were, since this, too, would necessitate invoking a substratum in which the said causes are said to inhere. And anyway in rejecting the idea of free will earlier, you also expressed dissatisfaction with the standard deterministic explanations?

A: So far, so good. Where do we go from here?

S: Well you just spoke of expressive action, and it might be argued that the thing about expressive action is that intention can neither be separated from action, nor treated as discrete from the wider social and historical context that informs its construction. Eh voila! You find the subject in the deed, and, yet, you can still speak of there being actions.

A: Yes, I like it. What I fancy myself as doing in a deed need not be granted any special privilege.

S: If you find the thought of discussing the chaos in my heart uncongenial we could always talk instead of that other chaos that you hinted a while back provides the back-clothe to our efforts to impose order on our world. We have a lot of philosophical terrain without as yet saying much about the objects that people the world.

A: That's right; it wouldn't! I was pondering how the entire history of a "thing", an organ, a custom can in this way be a continuous sign-chain of ever new interpretations and adaptations whose causes do not even have to be relate to one another but, on the contrary, in some cases succeed and alternate with one another in a purely chance.599

S: There's another thing here. Down playing the role of intention shifts the focus to the person's character and life history and beyond. It invites consideration of the influence of community and culture as well.

A: Hence psychology as the queen of the sciences.

S: That's a bit previous. You can't go distributing laurels just yet. You've a problem that needs to be addressed. Haven't you here in denying the causal aspect of a deed more or less done away our everyday notion of responsibility? I take it that you want to hold these soldiers of yours responsible for what they do, or fail to do?

A: But via the soul hypothesis haven't we been arguing that everything about [an action] that is intentional, everything about it that can be seen, known, "consciousness", still belongs to its surface and skin; that the notion of an autonomous agent transcending our affective nature is a fiction; that morality in the traditional sense, the morality of intentions, was a prejudice, precipitate, and perhaps provisional - something on the order of astrology and alchemy - but in any case something that must be overcome?601 Have we not through a psychological misunderstanding ... invented an antithesis to the motivating forces, and believed one has described another kind of force: ... a *primum mobilum* that does not exist at all? 602

S: I didn't ask for another coat of that corrosive acid you use to strip away our certainties; I asked about guilt and responsibility.

A: What would figure as the sting of conscience? A sadness accompanied by a recollection of a past event that flouted all of our expectations ... Mischief-makers overtaken by punishments have for thousands of tears felt in respect of their "transgressions"...: "here something has unexpectedly gone wrong", not: "I ought not to have done that".603

S: I'm sorry. The sense of bathos doesn't merely attend to your words. Sadness replaces guilt?

A: Well the kind of guilt that turns on the claim that I could have done otherwise. Disappointment that I was not who I thought I was, sadness at what was expressed in the deed; the kind of regret that arises from my having no option of doing other than I did; the suspicion that had I done so, it just wouldn't have been me.

S: Hmm, I get your drift, I think. Even so, it raises more questions than it answers. How much of "who I am" can be said to be expressed in any deed? The things I do that might be said to be revelatory, either to me, or others, [and there would be room enough for disputation without end here], are few and far between. Much of the time my action is absentmindedly thoughtless, leastways according to Xanthippe. Then again deeds might reflect the changing purposes of the agent, perhaps far fewer of us than you imagine are characterized by that stability that would entitle us to boast that we, as you put it, have the right to bare promises?

That said, and this has nothing to do with that oracle, I wonder if the man in the street gets our line of business wrong. They always want to judge us in terms of our answers. They want rules to live by and think if they have them they can make a success of things. From where I sit most men are slaves and ever are likely to be. I may deserve only half-marks for the observation, but if you want a willing slave as opposed to the recalcitrant kind, then you'll prosper more by referring to him as your employee.604 Funny sense of deja vu in my saying that. Still, as you said convictions are prisons. More interesting by far is he who opens up a new line of questions.

A: If I might say? Good conscience has bad conscience as its precursor, not as its polarity. For all that is good has at one time been new and consequently strange, anti-moral, immoral, and has gnawed like a worm at the heart of its fortunate discoverer.

S: We are no longer talking philosophy here.

A: No, psychology as the queen of the sciences. A human being is a thing dark and veiled. One refutation is no refutation.

S: Now you're talking in riddles again.

A: Am I? All I'm trying to say is that reason can only take us thus far. I could provide you with chapter and verse in respect of the weakness of the various arguments for God's existence, but even then the logical possibility of God's would remain open. All I'm saying is: do not deride and befoul that which you want to do away with for good but respectfully lay it upon ice, and, in so much as ideas are very tenacious of life, do so again and again. Here it is necessary to act according to the maxim: "One refutation is no refutation". 605

S: Not for the first time I have this strange sensation of being invited to bear witness to my own aporetic practice, but as it were through a glass darkly?

# CHEWING THE CUD

A: There is method in all this. What have I to do with refutations? One error after another is laid quietly on ice: the ideal is not refuted - it freezes. Here for instance "the genius" freezes; round the corner "the saint" freezes; under a thick icicle "the hero" freezes; and in the end "faith" itself freezes.606

S: Brr. Your "blonde beasts" will be the death of me. I feel as if one of them has desecrated on my grave.

A: Just lately all manner of things give you a frisson. Is not clear that my overman is more a regulative ideal, a corrective to all that stuff about equality, objectivity and the like that characterizes our times; in short, all that champions the dissolution of the self. My free spirits are preoccupied with self-overcoming. One day, looking back, they will declare: those were steps for me, and I have climbed up them; to that end I had to pass over them. Yet they thought I wanted to retire on them.607

Your true nature lies, not concealed deep within you, but immeasurably high above you, or at least above that which you usually take yourself to be.608

S: This putting on ice? A ploy to cool the more sanguinary spirited?

A: Yes, but more than that. A means of breaking habitual responses, of socially taught and ingrained modes of thought and feeling. Just as individuals and nations too much given to seriousness have a need for frivolity, just as others too excitable and emotional require from time to time the pressure of a heavy burden if they are to stay healthy, ought we, the more spiritual men of an age which is visibly becoming more and more ignited, not to seize on every means there is of extinguishing and cooling, so that we can remain at least steady, inoffensive and moderate as we still are, and thus perhaps one day be able to serve this age as its mirror and self-reflection?- 609

S: Couldn't agree more. My heart melts for you, my dear boy. It is a hard task we have set ourselves. What use would we be as physicians if we didn't first look to our own health? That what you propose here can only be a first step? It is all well and good to advise the patient to refrain from this and that, but surely he would profit from some more positive encouragement?

A: The philosophers of the future might rightly, but perhaps also wrongly, be described as attempters. This name itself is in the end only an attempt and, if you will, a temptation.610

S: Must you revert to riddles?

# CHEWING THE CUD

A: What purpose would be served by proscribing panaceas? What serves the higher type of men as nourishment or delectation must also be poison for a very different and inferior type. There are recipes for the feeling of power, firstly for those who can control themselves and who are thereby accustomed to a feeling of power; then for those in whom precisely this is lacking.611

S: You are joking, right? Have you any idea how off-hand, how imperious, you sound?

A: No. Not joking, that is. If there is anything in which I am ahead of all psychologists, it is that my eye is sharper for that most difficult and captious kind of backward inference in which the most mistakes are made: the backward inference from the work to the maker, from the deed to the doer, from the ideal to him who needs it, and from every way of thinking and valuing to the want behind it that prompts it.612

S: Clearly you have no difficulty in locating your lantern.

A: And there is a drive to distinction - do not think too highly of it! For what kind of drive is that, and what thought lies behind it? We want to make the sight of us painful to another and awaken in him the feeling of his own impotence and degradation; by dropping on to his tongue a drop of our honey, and while doing him this supposed favour looking him keenly and mockingly in the eyes, we want him to savour the bitterness of his fate. This person has become humble and is now perfect in his humility - seek for those whom he has for long wished to torture with it! you will find them613 soon enough!

S: Fuck you!

A: Isn't that what you are trying to do? Negative power, no less than its positive antinomy, is nonetheless an expression of the will to power. Those who are at bottom flawed and failing seek compensation and self-recognition through cruelty and abuse of others. Suppose one conceived the attainment of mankind's "highest happiness" as being the to what and of what of morality: would one mean the highest degree of happiness that individual men could gradually attain to? That, or a necessarily incalculable average happiness that could finally be attained to by all? And why should the way to that have to be morality? Has morality not, broadly speaking, opened up such an abundance of sources of displeasure that one could say, rather, that with every refinement of morals mankind has hitherto become more discontented with himself, his neighbour and the lot of his existence? Did the hitherto

214

most moral man not entertain the belief that the only justified condition of mankind in the face of morality was the profoundest misery? 645

S: How would you know that? Who have you been talking to? I only vouchsafed that to...

A: It's of no consequence. My point is that the power of traditional morality because insecure generates an obscure anxiety and awe such that its adherents live permanently in fear of losing of losing control, and thus driven to seek ever new ways of reinforcing and enhancing their power over others.615 One needs to seek out more positive images of power such as that embodied in artistic sublimation.

S: Pah! "A curse on all artists", I say! Since when did they ever seek to carry the load of existence?

A: The spirit first becomes a camel; and the camel a lion; and the lion, finally a child. 616

S: Camels? Lions? What elephantine mumbo-jumbo is this?

A: Zarathustra. The lion, the individual, must first liberate himself from the load of socially produced duties that threaten to break the camel's back. Only then can the innocent child be set at liberty to create new values for himself.

S: "New" values? Aren't you the one who denies all creation ex nihilio?

A: There is nothing esoteric in all this. Many of the old values will suffice. What is important is that though we continue to do many of the same things, we do them differently.

S: As I said, mumbo-jumbo to me. You know where you are with philosophy. This?

A: Oh, the human soul and its limits, the range of human inner experience reached so far, the heights, depths, and distances of these experiences, the whole history of the soul so far and its yet unexhausted possibilities - that is the predestined hunting ground for a born psychologist and lover of the "great hunt". But how often he has to say to himself in despair: "One hunter! alas, only a single one! and look at this huge forest, this primeval forest!". And then he wishes he had a few hundred helpers and good, well-trained hounds that he could drive into the history of the human

215

soul to round up his game. In vain: it has proved to him again and again, thoroughly and bitterly, how helpers and hounds for all things that excite his curiosity cannot be found.617

S: Time we were heading back, I think. Perhaps you can say a little more about other matters as we go?

## CHAPTER 9
## Time Denied

S: Mention of psychology reminds me. Ressentiment? We've been putting it off. Would this be a good time? Clearly this plays an important role in your explanation of mankind as "diseased". The picture you paint of man torn asunder by competing drives and affects, unable not to respond to the myriad stimuli that assail him.

A: Why not? As you just described it, it must be a view with which you have some latent sympathy. Besides, it may serve to flesh out what we have just been speaking of. The concept of "God" invented as a counter-concept of life everything harmful, poisonous, slanderous, the whole hostility unto death against life synthesized in this concept in a gruesome unity! ...

S: Well as regards some religious types, certainly.

A: Oh, come now. You mustn't be so timid, so self-effacing. The concept of the "beyond", the "true world" invented to devaluate the only world there is - in order to retain no goal, no reason, no task for our earthly reality? 618Not just would be god-botherers, but all those philosophers, like you and yours, who draw an opposition between mind and body and are determined upon subordinating the latter to the former; not forgetting those of a scientific bent who strive for a spurious objectivity, a contemplation without interest.619 Isn't the lowest common denominator here a similar will to power: a desire to set one privileged affective interpretation and dominant set of affects against all others?

What is this, if not an expression of the diseased condition of man, a sign of nihilism, decadence, and the degeneration of life? In this condition human kind are primarily reactive and negative. They come to declare their contradictory nature evil, and to surmise there must be a better condition to be had. Ressentiment a powerful and dangerous explosive that in dexterous priestly hands is diverted away from its initial external objects of rancour, and internalized as "bad conscience" thereby providing the spring-board for an ascetic way of life.620

# CHEWING THE CUD

An act of the most spiritual revenge ... It was the Jews who, with awe-inspiring consistency, dared to invert the aristocratic equation [good = noble = powerful = beautiful = happy = beloved of God] and to hang on to this inversion with their teeth, the teeth of the most abysmal hatred [the hatred of impotence], saying "the wretched alone are the good; the suffering, deprived, sick, ugly alone are pious, alone are blessed by God ... - and you, the powerful and noble, are on the contrary the evil, the cruel, the lustful, the insatiable, the godless to all eternity, and you shall be in all eternity the unblessed, the accursed, and damned"!621

S: Yes, yes. So much I get. It's the issue of ressentiment, and probably the stuff about reactivity and negation that you slipped into the conversation there.

A: "You are evil; I am the opposite of what you are; therefore I am good". 622

S: Preposterous! That might suffice to sum you up, but not me.

A: Exactly.

S: What do you mean?

A: Your view of me.

S: Supposing I do think this, especially when you start freighting your words with all that gory stuff about will to power, life as exploitation, expropriation, and the like?

A: What does the lamb argue? "The birds of prey are evil; but I am the opposite of a bird of prey; therefore I am good"? 623

S: What's this. Some lost fable of Aesop?

A: No. The paralogism of ressentiment: the fiction that a force can separate itself from what it can do. In the minor premise it is assumed that the bird of prey is a force that cannot separate itself from its effects, but in the major premise that it can. It is evil because it does not. It is assumed that one and the same force is held back by the lamb, but given free rein by the bird of prey. Ergo, since the strong could prevent themselves from acting, the weak could act if they did not stop themselves; hence the reactive forces triumph.

S: Sorry. I was with you till that last bit: the triumph of these reactive forces?

217

# CHEWING THE CUD

A: It is not sufficient for the weak to hold back form activity. The weak must reverse the relation of forces that are at play if they are to present themselves as superior. Ressentiment is accusatory: the reactive forces presume a neutralized image of force; such a force separated from its effects is thought blameworthy if it acts, deserving if it does not. This need to direct one's view outward instead of back to oneself ... is of the essence of ressentiment: in order to exist, slave morality always first needs an hostile external world; it needs, physiologically speaking, external stimuli in order to act at all - its action is fundamentally reaction. The reverse is the case with the noble mode of evaluation: it acts and grows spontaneously. ...Should ressentiment appear in the noble man, it consumes and exhausts itself in an immediate reaction, and therefore does not poison.624

S: Always a get out for your kind. How I envy...

A: No, ressentiment isn't akin to envy. Envy is more specific: it wants even if it has no right to get. Ressentiment's desire, if you can say it has a desire, is for revenge, but even this is, more often than not, an imaginary wish for the humiliation and destruction of the object of its ire.

S: Pah! It's always the same with you lot. You think a privileged education entitles you to sit in judgment upon us lesser mortals. As I said earlier, only the rich can afford cheap sandals. If you are all so damn superior, how come you are reliant on literal slaves to impart some measure of cultivation into your otherwise feckless ways?

A: Did I omit to mention that the weapon of choice of the weak, of those lacking in power, is language - the sharpest tool in this box of tricks often proving to be irony? As to the powerful - well the coming to power can make for stupidity; and furthermore, and differently the ressentiment that carries many a man to the top of the heap often continues to glow and glower thereafter. The "master" and "slave" frequently inhabit the same soul, but let us acknowledge what the dialectian cannot: that when the "slave" here triumphs, he does so as slave, not as "master". 625

S: That was quite some broadside. I take it that was all aimed at me? No, don't bother answering that.

A: What else would I say? That ressentiment is the signature vice of the weak, who perforce define themselves by what is exterior to their selves, in terms of the other, by what they lack? In respect of "doer" and "deed", that the "doer" is here backloaded as it were?

218

# CHEWING THE CUD

S: Not content with a broadside, must you now bludgeon me to death?

A: You are as bad as Nicias. No matter how many times you tell him, he'll always look for ways to trim and tack. A misplaced sense of honour, I call it! If, as a last resort, you are forced to give battle where is the sense in risking having to fight the same battle twice?

S: Even I would quail at that.

A: Well that would be no surprise?

S: Must you be so sanguinary? Not for the first time I wonder whether your doubters are right to fear you more than the enemy?

A: Me sanguinary? War is not a game for children!

S: But even if it is politics by other means, it remains politics.

A: Perhaps, but one should not forget that politics is the lowest form of culture.626

S: I feel as if I've only gotten half of the story here - about the ressentiment, I mean. Can we let the other go for now? I assume there are some active forces that are what? - Thwarted some how?

A: As I see it ... Before I say, keep in mind the feeling thing. Ressentiment is after all about feeling; it is a spiritual, an imaginary form of revenge. Reaction ceases to be acted in order to become something felt. Let me put it this way? Lets go back to the body. Consciousness usually only appears when a whole wants to subordinate itself to a superior whole... Consciousness is born in relation to a being of which it would be a function. 627

S: We are back with your deflationary critique then? No doer behind the deed; but now consciousness is not self-consciousness? Is that what you are saying?

A: Yes and No. There is consciousness of an ego in relation to a self, which is not itself conscious. The great activity is unconscious.628 One overlooks the essential priority of the spontaneous, aggressive, expansive, form-giving forces that give new interpretations and directions, although "adaption" follows only after this; the dominant role of the highest functionaries within the organism itself ... is denied.629

S: But if as you say these active forces escape the surveillance of consciousness?

A: Yes, but we can speculate. Consciousness is essentially reactive; this why we do not know what a body can do, or what activity it is capable of. 630 What is active? - a reaching out for power. What is passive? -To be hindered from moving forward: thus an act of resistance and reaction.631 In a body the superior or dominant forces are the active ones, the inferior or dominated forces are the reactive ones. "Life" would be defined as an enduring form of processes of the establishment of force, in which the different contenders grow unequally. To what extent resistance is present even in obedience; individual power is by no means surrendered. In the same way, there is in all commanding an admission that the absolute power of the opponent has not been vanquished, incorporated, disintegrated. "Obedience" and "commanding" are forms of struggle.632Mere variations in power could not feel themselves to be such: there must be present something that wants to grow and interprets the value of whatever else wants to grow... In fact, interpretation is itself a means of becoming master of something. [The organic process constantly presupposes interpretations]. 633

S: Stop right there. This is no good. All this talk of action and reaction is clouding my mind. I just can't get a handle on it. Can we adopt a different approach? What about resignation?

A: What of it?

S: I find it easier to start from what I know. Having had my words constantly re-interpreted, re-hashed, and re-shaped by Plato, it has taught me everything I need to know about resignation. Speaking of which, you will have noticed how much more temperate I am in the dialogues than in real life? Another one of Plato's foibles; this desire to show us philosophers as more equable than other men. Anyway ressentiment? How does it differ from resignation? You see what I'm getting at. I might desire a certain kind of life that is beyond my means. Unable to achieve it, I become inhibited by my weakness. Why don't I choose to resign myself to its loss and adopt some other set of values through which I can re-figure myself as successful? Not that I would have to go this far. I mean as a slave I might attach no other value to myself than that my master attaches to me: "They are powerful; I am not. I have no expectation of living as they do".

A: True enough, but matters are different for those full of ressentiment. Their will to power remains intact. 634; they remain committed to political superiority, and are unable to resign themselves to their inability to achieve it. This is the impasse of the priest. As putative members of the warrior class in opposing their enemies and conquerors they found they could be satisfied with nothing less than a radical re-valuation of their enemies' values, that is to say, an act of the most spiritual revenge. 635 The self-deception of impotence: in the man of ressentiment vengefulness becomes repressed and submerged.

The man of ressentiment ... loves hiding places, secret paths and back doors, everything covert entices him as his world, his security, his refreshment; he understands how to keep silent, how not to forget, how to wait, how to be provisionally self-deprecating and humble. A race of such men of ressentiment is bound to become eventually clever than any noble race; it will also honour cleverness to a far greater degree. 636

S: That certainly goes some way to explaining hostility to those who are shrewd. It puts me in mind of something of something Plato said bout wrestling; something that he thought generally held true all competitors: that there were those who sought to win by expressing their skills, and then there were those who sought to win by making their opponents lose.

A: Not known as "the wide boy" for nothing then?

S: If he got hold of you, I'm sure he'd love to be the first to teach you a lesson in manners! Three falls wouldn't do; only a submission would suffice! Anyway I'm not here for you to set other hares for me to chase. I've not finished with your argument. These clever people who you scorn, are nonetheless clever, or have by hook or crock gotten clever. The circumstances from which they began may have been inauspicious, perhaps to use your prejudicial language - reactive and rebellious - but you cannot deny their achievements.

A: Now who's being shrewd? Only a fool would pretend otherwise. Slave morality from the outset says No to what is "outside", what is "different", what is "not itself"; and this No is its creative deed. This inversion of the value-positing eye is of the essence of ressentiment. 637

S: No, something does not chime here. You spoke just now as if this attitude were the product of conscious design, yet moments earlier you were speaking of ressentiment's revenge as "repressed and submerged", or words to that effect. The former I can well understand. We are all familiar with Aesop's fox and his sour grapes.

# CHEWING THE CUD

A: If not Aesop, then the sour grapes of certain moralists certainly.

S: What I was about to say was ... well, like the fox rationalizes his frustration at not being able to get the grapes by telling himself they are sour and not what he wanted anyway, your man of ressentiment might justify his doing no harm by saying that physical superiority is far from being a mark of real power which rather lies in the pursuit of spiritual goals.
A: Ha, ha. You would say that, wouldn't you?

S: I fail to see what's funny about that, but if you are going to resort to childish jibes every time you are in danger of losing an argument then...

A: Please, I was being serious.

S: Serious? How's laughing at someone serious?

A: Oh, laughing can be a very serious matter. You are missing the point about ressentiment. In your example such re-valuation as there is restricted to what brings about satisfaction. Just as not all grapes are sweet, so, too, not all power is "real power".

S: Yes, that's my point. So what am I missing?

A: The revaluation of the priest, of the man filled with ressentiment, goes much further. He abjures the value of political superiority altogether. He repudiates all those other attitudes that serve to sustain it - The lust to rule, hatred, haughtiness, vengeance, envy, whatever. Sounds familiar? The values themselves are changed, do you see? Rather as if your fox were to insist his grapes far from being sweet or sour, were rather evil.

S: "Sounds familiar"? What do you mean?

A: The priest, the man of ressentiment, now takes the line that superiority over one's fellow creatures is an unworthy pursuit; he now preaches the gospel of neighbourly love and equality. No longer deceived about the object of his aspirations, he remains deceived but now in respect of what his aspirations really are.
  When the oppressed, down-trodden, outraged, exhort one another with the vengeful cunning of impotence: "let us be different from the evil, namely good! And he is good who does not outrage, who harms nobody, who does not attack,..."

- this listened to calmly and without previous bias, really amounts to no more than: "we weak ones are, after all, weak; it would be good if we did nothing for which we are not strong enough".

See? What is repressed, submerged here is the ressentiment's actual ambition. By means of re-valuation, or rather de-valuation of his opponent's values, in light of which he appears to others as inferior, he now passes off weakness as virtue. Masterstroke: to deny and condemn the drive whose expression one is, to display continually, by word and by deed, the antithesis of this drive.638

S: Even if it is as you describe it, we have here an impasse. The slaves brimming with a ressentiment they are too weak to act upon, and the masters still powerful enough to impose their will on the rest?

A: When would men of ressentiment achieve the ultimate, subtlest, sublimest triumph of revenge? Undoubtedly if they succeeded in poisoning the consciences of the fortunate with their own misery, with all misery, so that one day the fortunate began to be ashamed of their good fortune and perhaps said to one another: "it is disgraceful to be fortunate: there is too much misery" .639

S: But why should the fortunate succumb?

A: All instincts that do not discharge themselves outwardly turn inward - that is what I call the internalization of man ... that is the origin of the "bad conscience". 640 This is the way active force becomes truly reactive; once separated from what can do it is turned back against itself, and interiorized. The master becomes slave.

S: The master becomes slave? And the priest - you have spoken of priestly ressentiment as if this were different? Where does the priest come into all this?

A: He ensures the triumph of reactive forces; it is he who took the side of all decadent instincts - not as being dominated by them because he ... divined in them a power by means of which one can prevail against "the world". 641 It is he who begins to preach that the wretched alone are good; the poor, the impotent, lowly alone are the good; the suffering, deprived, sick, ugly alone are pious, alone are blessed by God, blessedness is for them alone - and you, the powerful and the noble are on the contrary the evil, the cruel, the lustful, the insatiable, the godless to all eternity; and you shall be in all eternity the unblessed, accursed and damned! 642 If one wanted to express the value of the priestly existence in the briefest formula it would be: the priest alters the direction of ressentiment.

## CHEWING THE CUD

S: How so? Weren't you just arguing that this man of ressentiment of yours, this man simmering with pain, is always looking to blame some active, external cause for his plight?

A: Indeed, but ressentiment is explosive. To be sure the priest is initially complicit in the blame game, but soon he encourages the reactive man to seek the cause of his suffering within, in himself, in some guilt, in a piece of the past, he must understand his suffering as a punishment. And thus the priest introduces the idea of sin; sin has been the greatest event so far in the history of the sick soul: we possess in it the most dangerous and fateful artifice of religious interpretation. 643.

S: O.k., to re-cap: ressentiment says "it's your fault", bad conscience says "it is my fault".

A: Yes, but ressentiment wants not only to accuse, but that the accused be found guilty. It can only be appeased by spreading its miasma, and this is where bad conscience comes into its own by ensuring that all pronounce themselves guilty; hence the appearance of the ascetic life, the wholesale devaluation of existence in this world.
   The idea at issue here is the valuation the ascetic priest places upon our life: he juxtaposes it [along with what pertains to it: "nature", "world" the whole sphere of becoming and transitoriness] with a quite different mode of existence which opposes and excludes, unless it turn against itself, deny itself: in that case, the case of the acetic life, life counts as a bridge to that other mode of existence. The ascetic priest treats life as a wrong road on
on which one must finally walk back to the point where it begins, or as a mistake that is put right by deeds - that we ought to put right. 644
   A devaluation inspired by ressentiment. For an ascetic life is a self-contradiction: here a ressentiment without equal rules, that of an un-satiated instinct and power-will that would like to become lord not over something living, but over life itself, over its deepest, strongest, most fundamental preconditions; an attempt is made here to use energy to stop up the source of energy; here the gaze is directed greenly and maliciously against physiological flourishing itself, in particular against its expression, beauty, joy, ... This all highly paradoxical in the highest degree: we stand here before a conflict that wants itself to be conflict, that enjoys itself in this suffering and even becomes ever more self-assured and triumphant to the extent that its own presupposition, physiological viability, decreases.645

S: But it represents the pursuit of a kind of happiness, nonetheless?

224

# CHEWING THE CUD

A: A happiness though at the level of the impotent, the oppressed, and those in whom the poison and inimical feelings are festering, with whom it appears as a narcotic drug, rest, peace, "Sabbath", slackening of tension and relaxing of the limbs, in short passively. Lacking the strength to overcome it, for such as these, suffering becomes unacceptable, and only a life devoid of it is worth living.646

S: Its unusual for me to be at a loss for words. I have the feeling that a trap has been sprung and that I could very well tear myself to pieces extricating myself from it. Am I permitted to enquire as to the nature of the difficulty I am faced with? Clearly much of what you have just said had me in mind, and if not me - Plato; and further, and more strangely still, echoed with a charge you made earlier - that Plato and I bear a heavy responsibility for the way things turn out in the future. I might say that's a rum thing to assert: what people make of one's ideas is surely their responsibility and nobody else's? And only the gods know what those with dirty hands might make of what you've been saying today?

Just so that when we part I'll have some sort of context in which to think about all this, could we begin, at least, to spell out some of the ramifications? Could I begin by going back to the issue of resignation? I have often thought of myself as someone - a bit like your beloved Zopy - who is indifferent to the usual desires that beset the ordinary man. I expect that is why some of those who view themselves as sceptics see me as something of a role model for their resignation.

A: They are mistaken, if I have you right. To be resigned would surely mean being utterly indifferent to one's desires? If I'm not mistaken, that's not you. You are much more the ascetic in this regard; more engaged in an on-going battle to frustrate these desires in ever more cruel and imaginative ways. It would be a simple matter to ensure your desire for Charmides withers on the vine by avoiding his company, but No - you follow him to every watering hole. Likewise, you know I'm poison to you to both you and your beliefs, yet you shadow me like a dog. And I wouldn't be surprised to learn that something similar lies behind your letting yourself get hooked up with Xanthippe?

S: Not just a pretty face; cute as well. Let's start with this asceticism, then.

A: No, we have to begin with "bad conscience" as the consequence of ressentiment's slave victory of morals; there is a directional process at work here. In light of your remark about "dirty hands", I ought perhaps here disassociate myself from any who might interpret me as promulgating a view of history that suggests that the record is replete with ruptures and randomness. This would be to bend the stick farther than I would countenance. The slave won the ultimate, finest, sublimest triumph of revenge ... they succeeded in pushing their misery into the consciences of the fortunate.647A triumph of cunning over violence. It wasn't that the ruling nobles lost their power through a collapse of their physical strength, but rather that their instinctual modus operandi was no match for the priest's reasoning powers. Rule by violence is coarse and crude and served only to stoke the fires of ressentiment.

S: But how is the victory of the slaves a victory? They are after all is said and done, if I have understood aright, men of ressentiment - they take their identity from what they oppose.

A: Indeed. Man invented bad conscience in order to hurt himself after the more natural vent had been blocked.648 The animal soul turned back against itself, taking sides against itself, was something new, profound, unheard of, enigmatic, contradictory, and pregnant with a future that with it the aspect of the earth was essentially altered. 649 I take bad conscience as the profoundest sickness that man was bound to contract under the pressure of the most fundamental of all changes that he ever experienced - that change which occurred when he found himself definitively closed up inside the confines of society and peace. 650

This constituted a leap and a plunge into new situations and new circumstances of existence.651 Life now required one to be predictable and sociable. Whereas formerly life was a matter of exerting control over a natural environment, and others, now hostility came to be directed against the self. The creation of bad conscience signalled humankind's self-separation from nature. The restricted circumstances of city life meant that for the first time governance rather than environmental factors now began to shape our character, and that human character became an object of study and self-determination.

S: And this is where we are at now? If you'll forgive me for saying so, you might be construed as acknowledging that reason has come into its own here, especially as regards morality? I mean, what are Plato and I doing if not providing a rational foundation for the exercise of authority?

A: Whilst playing the lute, in secret with Zopy?

S: What do you mean by that?

A: Only that that was not what I meant by the advent of reason. as Zopy said, "the actual foundation of ethics ... has been sought for centuries like a philosopher's stone". 652This didn't stop him, any more than it has stopped you and Plato, from treating morality as a given.

# CHEWING THE CUD

S: So what do you mean by the advent of reason?

A: For any would be authority to obtain socially speaking it must appear rational, not so much in the sense of supplying means to given ends, as rather its being able to provide a rationale for its exercise of power. This the slaves could do and the nobles as blonde beasts could not. Hence why you were able to reduced Thrasymachus to anger.

S: That would certainly be one way to explain it.

A: Speaking of whom I should perhaps add that it was at this juncture that bad conscience also served to split apart inclination and behaviour, rendering human character and human action increasingly a matter of self-determination. That is the point of my genealogy: not to detail the genetic record - how we got here-, but to lay bare our attempts at self-creation, our attempts to determine what this freedom should consist of. The genealogy looks to the future precisely because man is the not yet determined animal. 653

S: Don't let me stop you now you are on a roll, but this "bad conscience" - how does it connect up with asceticism?

A: Ah yes, nihilism.

S: Nihilism? I asked about asceticism.

A: Bear with me. After all, knowledge, itself, is a form of asceticism. 654

S: Don't be tendentious, not when we are we are making such good progress.

A: Really, I'm not. Asceticism is ubiquitous. Consider whether sacrifice is not present in every action that is done with reflection? 655

S: One thing at a time - the nihilism?

A: Asceticism was to be the answer to the threat of nihilism.

S: Was?

A: Ultimately, the whole project failed.

# CHEWING THE CUD

S: What are doing? Trying to whet my appetite?

A: Its what you do with a jaded palate.

S: Would you like me to fetch another palette and paint you black and blue?
A: Ha, ha. There is another way of defining ignorance you know?

S: Get on with it!

A: To make ourselves self- governing and reflective creatures was the devil's own work. The impetus for the task did not come naturally, nor was it exogenous. The bad conscience obliged us to seek fault with ourselves, to look for the source of our dissatisfaction within. Remember man, under the direction of the priest, invented bad conscience in order to hurt himself after the more natural vent had been blocked? as a means of explaining why he suffered, in order to give his suffering a meaning, as a means of evading a collapse into nihilism. Hostility was unleashed against the self. Originally our cruelty was directed at others; we made a spectacle of their pain as a way of making our lives eventful. Denied this outlet, which anyway had limited returns, the self soon proved to be a more tractable medium. One could tyrannize not only over behaviour, but inclinations, impulses dispositions, and even thoughts.

Asceticism became habit and cumulative. Habit in that the adoption of a mechanical routine was wont to produce effects, but effects that were self-abnegating. A rat race began to gather pace in which familiar ideals came to be dismissed as arbitrary or artificial, or tainted with self-interest.

S: That's too abstract for me. Can't you clothe it in examples?

A: O.k. Bad conscience generates concerns that are seen as free standing, not reducible to subjective or prudential considerations, and with that you arrive at objectivity. Norms and values acquire weight as measures of integrity. The very fact that this pursuit of an internalized and private purity now has a public face invites scrutiny. Frequency of religious attendance invites suspicion that this is a merely an occasion to show off one's finery. Thereafter the fashion becomes one where the devout dress simply in the manner of the rural poor. But this too fails to allay suspicion of self-righteous, so hence the devoted banish dancing, drinking, sex other than for the purposes of procreation, or whatever. Greater and greater rigour demanded that all such norms and ideals be shorn of any human inclination or willing such that the only acceptable values were those of a metaphysical origin. That was

228

what was so inimical; it served to destroy any and every competing mode of evaluation. It became the sole horizon by means of which to make sense of the world and actions within it, all thought and conduct of whatever kind. When one places life's centre of gravity not in life but in the "Beyond", - in nothingness - one deprives life of its centre of gravity altogether. 656By cleaving to the ascetic ideal, we look to some apart, beyond, outside, above for reasons with which to shape our lives.

S: But nonetheless the ascetic ideal solved a problem for all that?

A: Yes. This is what the ascetic ideal means: that something was lacking, that man was surrounded by a monstrous void - he did not know how to justify, to account for, to affirm himself: he suffered from the problem of his meaning. He also suffered otherwise, he was in the main a sickly animal: but his problem was not suffering itself, but that there was no answer to the crying question, "Why suffer?"657

S: But there is a logic at work here in your story?

A: Well not so much a logic as a direction, as a result of the adherence to certain purposive commitments however inherently unstable in the long term. What I relate is the history of the next two centuries. I describe what is coming, what can longer come differently: the advent of nihilism. This history can be related even now, for necessity itself is at work here.

S: Necessity? The next two centuries? Most of the clairvoyants I've met rarely venture beyond next week. And to think that little old me set this all in train? As you tell it, each time this ascetic ideal is threatened with collapse it somehow gets up off of its knees and renews itself by means of some new or novel re-interpretation of the ideal. What finally finishes it off?

A: The will to truth that Plato and you, not forgetting Parmenides, brought into being, - or to be more precise its Christian manifestation.

S: Ah, we are back with Dionysus v Evangelical are we?

A: To be precise again Dionysus v Crucified.658

S: Am I missing something there?

A: Yes, Paul, but never mind. One sees what has really triumphed over the Christian god: Christian morality itself, the concept of truthfulness taken ever more rigorously, the father confessor's refinement of the Christian conscience translated and sublimated into a scientific conscience, into an intellectual cleanliness at any price. Truthfulness eventually turned against the very tenets of the beliefs that inspired it, and found them wanting.

And there's the irony; what was initially a means of averting nihilism, becomes the seedbed of it. The meaninglessness of suffering, not suffering itself, was the curse that lay over mankind so far - and the ascetic ideal offered man meaning! ... In it suffering was interpreted; the tremendous void seemed to have been filled; the door was closed on to any kind of suicidal nihilism.659

S: But nonetheless it offered the wretched hope?

A: But at what a price! A moral worldview in the necessary suffering of this world is treated as a punishment to be atoned for in order to gain access to a quite different mode of existence.

S: True enough, but as the light fades on a world lit by the flame of asceticism, what will we be left with if not with an encompassing sadness? To be sure, as you tell it, this quest for self-determination and greater freedom leads only to a pervasive insecurity or so it seems to me. In refuting this ascetic ideal the end result is surely only a new kind of misery?

A: Not refuting. That would require recourse to an ascetic ideal. Asceticism has collapsed, or will collapse, because of its own immanent instability.

S: But then once again we are back with the problem of interpretation, and if refutation is not possible because there is no external really existing reality against which to measure ... What about truth?

A: "Truth"? Don't make me laugh!

S: It's no laughing matter, at least not for me.

A: Nobody in the agora wants truth. Surely you have realized that by now. Our fallibility aside, our stupidity, our self-interest are the most redoubtable of defensive walls that your puny truth might attempt to breach.

S: Be that as it may, we philosophers know that thought seeks the truth.

# CHEWING THE CUD

A: You still haven't got it, have you? Truth was posited as being, as God, as the highest court of appeal ... Rather we should be asking: What really is it in us that wants "the truth"? - We did indeed pause for a long time before the origin of this will - until finally we came to a complete halt before an even more fundamental question. We asked the value of this will. Granted we want truth: why not rather untruth? And uncertainty? Even ignorance? ... And, would you believe it, it has finally almost come to seem to us that this problem has never been posed before - that we are the first to ... hazard it.660

S: This all sounds very strange to my ears. Not truth as such, but the value of truth - that is what interests you?

A: Please, can we drop this now? I'm sure we'll have occasion to come back to it.

S: No, no. You can't put into question my self-image, and then move on as if it is of no never mind!

A: I doubt I can satisfy you anyway, but look at it this way. In order to be able to imagine a world of truth and being it was first necessary to create the veracious man [including the fact that he believes himself veracious]. 661

S: Let's not forget I know nothing?

A: It ain't what a man doesn't know as makes a fool of him; it is what he knows as ain't so.662 The concept of truth serves to describe a "truthful world", does it not. Even in science the truth of phenomena constitutes a "world" distinct from the phenomena themselves. If someone wills the truth it is not in the name of the world; life, after all, aims to mislead, to dupe, to dissimulate, to dazzle, to blind.46. He who wills the truth always wants to make of this world an appearance. It has gradually become clear to me ... that the moral [or immoral] intentions in every philosophy have every time constituted the real germ of life out of which the entire plant has grown ... I accordingly do not believe a "drive to knowledge" to be the father of philosophy.663

S: So now the charge is that Plato and I are ultimately moralists?

A: Yes, but it doesn't end there. You are playing with fire!

S: So now we are arsonists?

## CHEWING THE CUD

A: Well might you joke. Life against life! He who wants another world wants to repudiate life, wants a diminished life, wants the triumph and conservation of his type. He would rather will nothingness, than not will at all. The ascetic ideal written large; "Everywhere ... this spirit is strong, mighty and at work without counterfeit today, it does without ideals of any kind ... except for its will to truth. But this, this remnant of an ideal is, if you will believe me, this ideal itself in its strictest, most spiritual formulation, esoteric through and through, with all external additions abolished.664

S: And if I nonetheless insisted that this is only your interpretation of events?

A: Yes, yes. And we, pressed this way, we who have put the same question to ourselves a hundred times, we have found no better answer. 665

S: Is that it? Is that all you can say?

A: Looking away shall be my only negation. 666

S: Oh, come on man! My appetite is not going to be sufficed by airy nothings.

A: I was trying not to be rude, but if you insist?

S: Do your worst

A: You are a decadent, and as such your beliefs stand between you and any hope of your becoming who you really are.

S: The "cave of the monstrosities", that's me. But answer me this: as cause or effect? I've heard tell that, on occasion you too have claimed to be a decadent?

A: Let us draw a distinction between decadence as cause - as suffering from oneself - and effect - the decadence that reveals itself as a commitment to idealism, or - in particular in your person, morality. What matters greatly here, in respect of the decadence caused by suffering from oneself, suffering from life, is the presence of an organizing idea such as to a totality whose incredible multiplicity ... is nonetheless the converse of chaos. In my own case the secret work and artistry of my instinct has produced the greater whole that I am. 667

232

# CHEWING THE CUD

S: Ho, ho, ho. Forgive my laughter, but have you no idea of how pompous that sounds?

A: Did I neglect to say that where the instincts have gone awry the sufferer is apt to be driven to idealism, to falsifying and devaluing the world?

S: Tart!
A: How does that make me a...?

S: Not you; your retort.

A: And not just you; degeneration is quietly gaining ground everywhere. Old Athens is coming to an end ... Everywhere the instincts are in anarchy.668

S: Couldn't agree more. But do I not offer a cure? Do I not advocate that one becomes master of his self, that a stronger counter-tyrant be opposed to the tyranny of the instincts? 669

A: Right. Rationality was seen as the saviour, neither Socrates nor his "patients" had any choice about being rational ... it was their last resort. They had only one option: be destroyed or - be absurdly rational. Socrates created a permanent state of daylight against all dark desires - the daylight of reason. You have to be clever, clear, and bright at any cost: any concession to the instincts ... leads downwards.670

S: A strange change of tense. You sound like you are speaking from the future. Not that I'm unappreciative of the testimonial.

A: Tsk! What does your conscience say?

S: What do you mean? My conscience is clear.

A: You shall become who you are.671

S: Have I missed something here? Never mind. Go on, this becoming who you are? Let's not go over old ground here visa-vie the intellectual conscience, and, for the sake of brevity, lets suppose I accept we go wrong in failing to acknowledge we are animals in a world without god, and furthermore that as pieces of "second nature" we are significantly shaped by culture.

# CHEWING THE CUD

A: Not bad. Perhaps I should set up a school?

S: I didn't say I believed any of that. "Let's suppose", I said. You clearly have more to say about "becoming who you are" that goes beyond our being honest in respect of the aforesaid?

A: Honest more in respect of our second nature. I want to learn more and more to see as beautiful what is necessary in things; then I shall be one of those who make things beautiful. Amor fati: let that be my love henceforth. We must learn to distinguish between what is and is not necessary in things, in ourselves.672

S: Yes, yes. All that talk about giving "style" to one's life, but what is the connection with that kind "self-creation" and this talk of necessity? That's what I want to know! And how does all this bear on morality?

A: Don't you see? Morality would have us pull ourselves up into existence by the hair, out of swamps of nothingness.673 It is the best self-contradiction that has been conceived thus far; it would have us perceive in every necessity something of constraint, need, compulsion to obey, pressure and un-freedom. It rides on the back of an impossible notion of freedom: the desire to bear the ultimate responsibility for one's actions, and to absolve God, the world, ancestors, chance and society.674

S: And this has what to do with necessity?

A: Necessity is the condition of effective action, rather than an impediment.

S: That sounds like the second best contradiction.

A: The master is someone who accepts the tyranny of of such capricious laws; in all seriousness, the probability is ... that this is "nature" and "natural" - and not that laisser aller.675Think of your namesake, the footballer. "On my head!" he shouts to his team-mate. Zino arcs in the perfect cross. Socrates leaps, hangs in the air, and neatly heads the ball in the back of the net. Substitute you for the footballing Socrates, and the ball bounces harmlessly out of play, leaving you to pick up your teeth. What's the difference? Wherein does the footballing Socrates' freedom of action lie? In his "understanding" of the laws of gravity as they effect the flight and velocity of a football such that he is able not to dispense with them, but rather to "bend" them to his will.

# CHEWING THE CUD

S: I'm at a loss to imagine the merit in being able to see the merit in being able to head a pig's bladder.

A: Don't be obtuse. The point is that to distain such "necessities" as menacing one's "responsibilities", as a threat to one's belief in oneself, to one's personal right to [one's own] merits at any price would be to render oneself powerless.676 But this kind of resentment is precisely what "morality" with its superlative metaphysical sense of freedom fosters. In short, "morality" gets in the way of our becoming who we are. To become who we are requires that we acknowledge necessity. Every artist knows how far from any feeling of letting himself go his most "natural" state is - the free ordering, placing ... giving form in the moment of "inspiration" - and how strictly and subtly he obeys thousand fold precisely then, laws that precisely on account of their hardness and determination defy all formulation through concepts.... 677

S: Yes, I remember; the business of self-creation; the surveying of strengths and weaknesses; the removal of weaknesses or ugliness's. What of the ugliness's that cannot be removed? 678

A: I repeat; then looking away shall be my only negation. 679

S: Wait up! Before we move on, I want to say something. All this talk of individuals and "singularities" has set my mind racing. I'm confused; both about what you are claiming and what your animus is with Plato and I in this matter. Sometimes you speak as if we could all be unique individuals, but then just as clearly you brutally assign the majority a herd status.

A: That nose of yours does you proud. Clearly we can't all be unique without the word failing to signify. It is, again, the way the pair of you carve the world at its joints. Put it this way; for us Greeks, here and now, the individual is not someone who can be known from the inside out as it were. Individuality does not exist apart from, and prior, to society. Rather for us the individual is someone understood against a given backdrop. Take Aristotle's "Poetics". He argues there that the characters of our stories, our tragedies, exist as props to articulate the logic of the narrative.

S: There are times, you know, when I wonder whether you are secretly infatuated with him. I just don't get it; I mean the size of his arse – and his ambition is just as gross. Don't look down your nose at me; I'm not ignoring the point. In fact, Plato and I don't differ that much on this. The basis of the "Republic" is a cosmological view; hence, the majority is treated as types defined by their social station. Do we not worry about the threat to social harmony when this model is imperilled?

A: Indeed, but you then proceed to lay the foundations of a new form of individuality with your tri-partite division of the soul.

S: So?
A: From such acorns do mighty oaks grow?

S: All very flattering, I'm sure – if I knew what you were driving at. Has this got to do with the Christians who come after?

A: Exactly. It is they who embroider upon your tri-partite psychology, and, in the process, begin to promulgate an entirely different conception of the individual. Don't get me wrong; humanity becomes more interesting as a result. Your form of storytelling aids and abets this.

S: Our storytelling? You make sound like we are engaged upon fiction rather than philosophy.

A: In a way it is just that; how reason comes to be born and through allying itself to virtue creates the conditions of its reward; classic realist novel writing.

S: And you know all this how?

A: Because I shall live posthumously.

S: A likely story. Even so, what is the worry here? Is it that those in the future will look back at us through the lens of their day and unwittingly mistake us for them?

A: Not so much mistake us for them, as think that we saw individuality in the same fashion. Think of it in terms of footballers.

S: Not pig's bladders again; I've had quite enough of pigs for one day. If I was that interested in the subject I'd be trailing around after Xenophon and listening to his homilies on farm management.

A: I was going to say that people in the future will lazily think of individuality as they do football stars – think that is that such people win the game on their own by expressing their individuality through their shooting skills, say. But of course the star expresses his talents only against the backdrop of a team effort and within the rules of the game.

S: It all sounds like a bit of a pig's breakfast to me, but I take your point. Whilst we are on tall stories – the business of storytelling? You said a while back that Plato and I were – how should I put it – shaping a world through telling a story?
A: Quite, as an art form the realist novel approaches ethics. By encouraging identification with character, it promotes empathy – privileged access to the interior of the other. Given these parameters, we are then invited to judge the merits of such work in terms of whether the characters are well drawn. Do the characters and the context in which they shape their destinies constitute a convincing scenario? Are the characters vividly drawn, or do they merely represent certain ideas that the author is concerned to explore? Of course all this presupposes that we live in a world where there are such discrete beginnings and endings, and not least that we, ourselves, are single, unified entities, that are in principle knowable. An illusion that is further bolstered by the seeming transparency of language, of it's providing us with express access to what it is dealing with.

S: A "for example"?

A: I don't know. Strange, but some lines from the bard are in my head. 'When my love swears she is made of truth, I do believe her, though I know she lies".

S: What am I to make of that?

A: Try running it past Xanthippe.

S: You're kidding. At the least I know that it's the sort of thing that'd make her hoot and cackle, though god only knows why. Oh no, I'm not going to do that. In next to no time she will have told her friends and then there'll be all those pitying looks and shaking of heads, not to mention all that whispered,"See how little he really knows?"

A: But wouldn't you have to know what the lines really mean to be able to anticipate the response?

S: No, and that's the damn thing about it. There are things I just don't get. All very peculiar, if such mental tics intrigue you, but we must get on. Time will not be denied. You know what I thinking then; that if we were two characters in such a story, I'd definitely be the one who was fully rounded, more fully present. You'd be

237

coming across as more of a talking head. You are so guarded. Does anyone – has anyone – ever get close to you?

A: Would you have me spend myself like loose change on strangers?

S: But that's my beef, my dear boy. I've known you on and off for many years now, and yet you still appear to me as a stranger. How must it be for all those others who look to you for leadership? To be sure they are drawn like flies around a honey pot by your physical charm and charisma, but the story thereafter is always one of disappointment and uncertainty – of a failure to connect.


## CHAPTER 10
### Time's two – men and women

S: Indeed. Let's talk about women for a while, if you don't mind.

A: It might be easier to set the world to rights, but if you want to get something off of your chest?

S: Observing Xanthippe can be instructive in this regard. She'll often begin by saying she did X, say because I forgot to do Y. Later she'll revise matters and argue that her intention was probably shaped by what the neighbours might think when they got to hear what it was that I forgot. And, yet later still, the revision itself is subject to revision; like the other week, when she threw the slops over me. At the time she thought she thought she hated me and wanted to humiliate me. Later, having spoken to her friends, she decided that her motivation in so showering me was a cry for help.

A: No shit. Is it not the case that, often after a quarrel between a man and a woman, one suffers most at the idea of having hurt the other, while the other suffers most at the idea of not having hurt the other enough, from which follow tears, sobs and distracted mien through which the heart of the other is made heavy even after the quarrel is over? 680

S: It's complicated, I know; but anyway you see its application to the issue at hand.

A: Not really: only that which has no history is definable. 681

# CHEWING THE CUD

S: Xanthippe has plenty of that, not that she cares to be reminded of it these days. Timandra is the same, no doubt?

A: I'll ignore the snide comment. You know there is something amazing and monstrous about the education of upper- class women. What could be more paradoxical? All the world is agreed that they are to be brought up as ignorant as possible of erotic matters, and that one has to imbue their souls with a profound sense of shame in such matter until the merest suggestion of such things triggers the most extreme impatience and flight. The "honour" of women really comes into play only here: what else would one not forgive them? But here they are supposed to remain ignorant even in their hearts; they are supposed to have neither eyes nor ears, nor words, nor thoughts for this - their "evil"; and mere knowledge is considered evil. And then to be hurled, as if by a gruesome lightening bolt, into reality and knowledge, by marriage - precisely by the man they love and esteem most! To catch love and shame in a contradiction and to be forced to experience at the same time delight, surrender, duty, pity, terror, and who knows what else, in the face of the unexpected neighbourliness of god and beast!

Thus a psychic knot has been tied that may have no equal. Even the compassionate curiosity of the wisest student of humanity is inadequate for guessing how this or that woman manages to accommodate herself to this solution of the riddle, and to the riddle of the solution, and what dreadful, far-reaching suspicions must stir in her poor, unhinged soul - and how the ultimate philosophy and skepsis of woman casts anchor at this point!

Afterward, the same deep silence as before. Often a silence directed at her self, too. She closes her eyes to herself.

Young women try hard to appear superficial and thoughtless. The most refined simulate a kind of impertinence.

Women easily experience their husbands as a question mark concerning their honour, and their children as an apology or atonement. They need children and wish for them in a way that is altogether different from that in which a man may wish for children.

In sum, one cannot be too kind about women. 682

S: Forgive me, but aren't you showing your age in saying that?

A: My age? It'll be a good few years till I catch up with yours, or are claiming there was some naivety in....

S: Neither. Diotima told me that she had seen it written that every man bears traces of his century. 683 After all, you can't mean that this how women are - no pun intended - period?

A: No, indeed. One of the lessons of the genealogy: that it is all contingent. Second natures. Forgive me if I don't share your fascination with Xanthippe. When a man stands in the midst of his own noise, in the midst of his own surf of plans and projects, then he is apt also to see quiet, magical beings gliding past him and to long for their happiness and seclusion: women. He almost thinks his better self dwells there among women, and that in these quiet regions even the loudest surf turns into deathly quiet, and life itself into a dream about life. Yet! Yet! Noble enthusiast, even on the most beautiful sailboat there is a lot of noise, and unfortunately much small and petty noise. The magic and the most powerful effect of women is, in philosophical language, action at a distance...; but this requires first of all and above all - distance. 684

S: You are a queer bird. For a moment, I was of a mind to say I feel sorry for you. Yes I know that wouldn't be appreciated. Nonetheless ... all this finer feeling..

A: Just because you are indifferent to the paradox ... We artists. - When we love a woman, we easily conceive a hatred for nature on account of all the repulsive natural functions to which every woman is subject. We prefer not to think of all this; but when our soul touches on these matters for once, it shrugs as it were and looks contemptuously at nature: we feel insulted; nature seems to encroach on our possessions, and with the profanest hands at that. Then we refuse to pay any heed to physiology and decree secretly: "I want to hear nothing about the fact that a human being is something more than soul and form." "The human being under the skin" is for all lovers a horror and unthinkable, a blasphemy against God and love.

S: You know what some wag in the agora said to me the other day? "How can you trust someone who bleeds every month, and refuses to die?"

A: Well, as lovers still feel about nature and natural functions, every worshipper of God and his "holy omnipotence" formerly felt: everything said about nature by astronomers, geologists, physiologists, or physicians, struck him as an encroachment into his precious possessions and hence an attack - and a shameless one at that. Even "natural law" sounded to him like a slander against God; really he would have much preferred to see all mechanics derived from acts of the moral will or an arbitrary will. But since nobody was able to render him this service, he ignored nature and mechanics as best he could and lived in a dream. Oh, these men of former times knew how to dream and did not find it necessary to go to sleep first. And we men of today still master this art all too well, despite all of our good will toward the day and staying awake. It is quite enough to love, to hate, to desire, simply to feel - and right away the spirit and power of the dream overcome us, and with our eyes open, coldly contemptuous of all danger, we climb up on the most hazardous paths to scale the roofs and spires of fantasy - without any sense of dizziness, as if we had been born to climb, we somnambulists of the day! We artists! We ignore what is natural. We are moonstruck and God-struck. We wander, still as death, unwearied, on heights that we do not see as heights but as plains, as our safety. 685

S: I'm lost.

A: No, we're on the right path, I'm sure.
S: No, I'm lost with respect to the path of our conversation. Was that aimed at me; at Plato, too? No beauty within; the very ides being one of your necessary illusions?

A: Neediness is needed. 686

S: Neediness is...! No, stop! Quite apart from anything else, this sounds almost misogynistic?

A: Never! - "Woman is our enemy" - out of the man who says that to other men there speaks an immoderate drive that hates not only itself but its means of satisfaction as well. 687

S: Well if not misogyny, then a scepticism toward the fairer sex?

A: I thought we had established that the word "fair" would have to blush in the context of talk of love?

S: There you go again. A stranger might think that at best you must kept company with too many women to speak with such acerbity about women's wiles, not to say your denigration of love. 688

A: Why? I'm just getting into my stride. You might be right that a certain jaundice results from being confined to the hen-house - all that constant rehearsing of the pecking order. It's every bit as bad as the male equivalent in the changing-room.
    As to love, it is far from simple; and denigration is not the name of my game. Rausch! Do you require the most astonishing proof of how far the transfiguring

power of intoxication can go? - "Love" is this proof: that which is called love in all languages and silences of the world. In this case, intoxication has done with reality to such a degree that in the consciousness of the lover the cause of it is extinguished and something else seems to have taken its place - a vibration and glittering of all the magic mirrors of Circe -

Here it makes no difference whether one is man or animal; even less whether one has spirit, goodness, and integrity. If one is subtle, one is fooled subtly: if one is coarse, one is fooled coarsely; but love, and even the love of God, the saintly of "redeemed souls", remains the same in its roots: a fever that has good reason to transfigure itself, an intoxication that does well to lie about itself - And in any case, one lies well when one loves, about oneself and to oneself: one seems to oneself transfigured, stronger, richer, more perfect, one is more perfect - Here we discover art as an organic function: we discover it in the most angelic instinct, "love", we discover it as the greatest stimulus of life - art thus sublimely expedient even it lies -

But we should do wrong if we stopped with its power to lie: it does more than merely imagine; it even transposes values. And it is not only that it transposes the feelings of values: the lover is more valuable, is stronger. In animals this condition produces new weapons, pigments, colours, and forms; above all, new movements, new rhythms, new love calls and seductions. It is no different with man. His whole economy is richer than before, more powerful, more complete than in those who do not love. The lover becomes a squanderer: he is rich enough for it. Now he dares, becomes an adventurer, becomes an ass in magnanimity and innocence; he believes in God again, he believes in virtue, because he believes in love; and on the other hand, this happy idiot grows wings and new capabilities, and even the door of art is opened to him. If we subtracted all traces of this intestinal fever from lyricism in sound and word, what would be left of lyrical poetry and music? - Art for art's sake, perhaps: the virtuoso croaking of shivering frogs, despairing in their swamp - All the rest was created by love - 689

S: Ambivalent at best; a long way form idolization.

A: The last is more a woman's thing. The idolization of love practiced by women is fundamentally and originally an invention of their shrewdness, in as much as it enhances their power and makes them seem ever more desirable in the eyes of men. But through the centuries-long habituation to this exaggerated evaluation of love it has come to pass that they have become entangled in their own net and forgotten how it originated. They themselves are now more deceived than men are and consequently suffer more from the disillusionment that is almost certain to come into the life of every woman - insofar as she has sufficient intelligence and imagination to be deceived and disillusioned at all.690

S: Well you'd definitely have Xanthippe support on that last point. She's often to be found lamenting what she sees as the waste of her life. Apparently if it wasn't "yours truly's" insatiable "urges" there's no telling where she might have ended up, what she might have achieved, what suitors she might have attracted. All in her head of course - the "insatiable urges". I've been on short rations as long as I can remember. Not that I'm complaining; it allows me the luxury of turning my mind to other things.

A: Like young Charmides? The son of Glaucon, Plato's nephew – talk about biting the hand that feeds you?
S: Haven't I set you right about that already? Things like the beauty within, I meant! Puzzling thing about Xanthippe in that respect. Try to talk to her about society women and get nothing but scorn and more than a dash of invective about their airs and graces, their - as she sees it - false modesty. And as for their dress, or undress, to her eye, least said the better.

A: Ha, ha. They believe in their tailors as they believe in their God - and who would dissuade them from this faith? This faith makes blessed! And self-admiration is healthy! Self-admiration protects against colds. Has a pretty woman who knows herself to be 691well dressed ever caught a cold? Never! I am assuming she was barely dressed.

S: Miaow?

A: Oh, come now! One must be accustomed to tolerating the most unusual opinions and points of view and even to take a certain pleasure in their counter-play; one must be able more or less to appreciate the art being applied. A little old woman once said to Zarathustra, "Are you visiting women? Do not forget your whip"? 692

S: Xanthippe? No, not even on a bad day; though, that said, there's little love lost some days even for her own kind. Nonetheless, you can't say things like that; it's monstrous.

A: Quite so. Behind all their personal vanity women themselves always have their impersonal contempt - for "woman" -. 693

# CHEWING THE CUD

S: Xanthippe's laughter - when she expresses these sorts of sentiments? Well - it makes my blood run cold.

A: Hmm, how and when a woman laughs is a mark of her culture: but in the sound of her laughter there is disclosed her nature, in the case very cultured women perhaps even the last inextinguishable remnant of her nature. - That is why the psychologist will say with Horace, though for a different reason: laugh maidens. 694

S: Ha, ha! Who's this Horace? No, never mind. Ha, ha. That's wicked.

A: And laughter means [?]: being Schadenfreude but with a good conscience. 695

S: What?

A: When a man neighs with laughter he excels any animal with his vulgarity. 696

S: I walked straight into that little trap didn't I?

A: Just evening up the score a little. Can't have you thinking I've a down on women?

S: You're still a shit; like a nasty irritant that won't go away. A stubborn piece of foot fungi to boot!

A: Ha, ha. There's no need to go all eloquent on me. Just making sure I have your full attention. The more abstract the truth you want to teach the more you must seduce the senses to it. 697 Man created woman - but out of what? Out of a rib of his God, of his "ideal". 698

S: But this misogyny, …

A: Didn't I say: "... Out of the man who says that to other men there speaks an immoderate "drive" which hates not only itself but the means to its own satisfaction"? Didn't I also say, a while back, that ultimately one loves one's desires and not that which is desired; and that one should ponder the meaning of this? 699...For nevertheless, a soul that knows it is loved but does not itself love betrays its dregs - its lowest part comes up.700 Even so, it remains the case that love of one is a piece of barbarism; for it is practiced at the expense of all others. Love of God likewise. 701

S: Stop! Stop! What are you trying to do here?

244

A: Show you that the sick and the weak have had fascination on their side; they are more interesting than the healthy: the fool and the saint - the two most interesting kinds of man - closely related to them, the "genius". The great "adventurers and criminals" and all men, especially the most healthy, are sick at certain periods in their lives: the great emotions, the passions of power, love, revenge, are accompanied by profound disturbances. And as for decadence, it is represented. in almost every sense, by every man who does not die too soon: - thus he also knows from experience the instincts that belong to it: - almost every man is decadent for half his life. 702

S: Lord knows what has got into you, but I have to ask: women?
A: Ah, finally: woman! One half of mankind is weak, typically sick, changeable, inconstant - woman needs strength in order to cleave to it: she needs a religion of weakness that glorifies being weak, loving, and being humble as divine: or better, she makes the strong weak - she rules when she succeeds in overcoming the strong. Woman has always conspired with the types of decadence, the priests, against the "powerful", the "strong", the men -.Woman brings the children to the cult of piety, pity, love: - the mother represents altruism convincingly.703

S: Madness.

A: Is it? Neediness is needed!

S: Mere wordplay. Saying something twice no more explains it than saying it once.

A: Think about it - the craving for suffering. - When I think of the craving to do something, which continually tickles and spurs those millions of young Europeans who cannot endure their boredom or themselves, then I realize that they must have a craving to suffer and to find in their suffering a probable reason for action, for deeds. Neediness is needed! Hence the politicians' clamour, hence the many false, fictitious, exaggerated "conditions of distress" of all sorts of classes and the blind readiness to believe in them. These young people demand that - not happiness but unhappiness should approach from the outside and become visible; and their imagination is busy in advance to turn into a monster so that afterward they can fight a monster. If these people who crave distress felt the strength inside themselves to benefit themselves and to do something for themselves internally, then they would also know how to create for themselves, internally, their very own authentic distress. Then their inventions might be more refined and their satisfactions might sound like good music, while at present they fill the world with their clamour about

245

distress and all too often introduce into it the feeling of distress. They do not know what to do with their selves - and therefore paint the distress of others on the wall; they always need others! And continually other others! - Pardon me, my friend, I have ventured to paint my happiness on the wall. 704

S: That I understand. With that I can concur. Self-sufficiency - yes? Many a one lacking a project of his, or her own battens him or herself like a barnacle on what they imagine is the distress of another but in reality is a means of alleviating their own. What I don't get here is what your so-called will to truth" has to do with women; much less your earlier provocative query: "Suppose truth were a woman?"
   I'm right in thinking that all this bears the hallmark of your proffered crab-like sallies against whatever it is that has aroused your suspicion; your signature method of attack when it comes to dualist concepts?

A: Metaphysics - the faith in opposite values? If one persists in championing these as a means of rectifying the superstitious errors of the past, one is still entangled in the problem of the truth - annihilation of the other.
Not just a pretty face, eh?

S: Not even.

A: I was just...

S: Never mind what you were just. Get on with it! Am I right, or am I right?

A: Right you are! Two doubts are always uppermost. One - whether there are any opposites at all. Two - whether the value attached to these purported opposites are accurate or are merely foreground estimates, only provisional perspectives.75. As you have deduced it's the same methodology that's in operation whether the duality is good v evil, mind v body, truth v falsity, consciousness v unconsciousness.

S: And man v woman?

A: Why not?

S: Before you broach this particular, may I point out that there are one or two on your list that we have barely touched upon - consciousness v unconsciousness, for instance?

A: I thought we had. Much conscious thought is instinctive? Thought comes when it wishes, and not when "I" wish? 705. Tangentially, most people don't think deeply at all? Its generally assumed, I know, that whilst most evince an interest in very little, each man will take a deeper interest in his hobby, or should I say hobby-horse? Too kind an estimation, if you ask me. And besides, consciousness is not the opposite of instinct but a refined expression of them - every philosopher is secretly guided ... into certain channels by his instincts.706

Still you were enquiring about my methods vis-a-vis the anti-dualism. Let me stress that I'm not advocating a monism that reduces one of the binaries to the other, as say the cruder materialist is wont to do with say Descartes nonsense about body as extended substance and mind as non-extended substance. Consciousness for me still awaits incorporation at the instinctual level. Saying which reminds me. A third aspect of my method: I always view the traditionally "higher" aspect of the binary as the more dubious one, as the Johnny-come-lately, and therefore the one more likely to be error prone, mistaken, - something yet to be properly incorporated. Perhaps, I should also add, values here are best thought of as refinements of one another, rather than strict opposites.

Put it this way, what does our faith in opposite values permit? The adopting of a perspective, but not as we think about the world as such; – rather, how we exercise our will to power on the world - because it simplifies life.707

S: "Simplifies life"? Hardly. Whatever it is that demands that certain of us pursue the truth, it is very far from making things simpler.

A: Clearly, I'm not expressing this at all well. All truth is simple ... is that not doubly a lie? No this bad taste, this will to "truth at any price", this youthful madness in the love of truth – has lost its charm for us.708

S: Perhaps, I would have done better to keep my big mouth shut?

A: Let me try again. Almost everything we call "higher culture" is based upon the spiritualization of cruelty, on its becoming more profound: this is my proposition.709As to you knowledge-seekers, any insistence on thoroughness and profundity in matters of knowledge, - any will to truth - is a violation, a desire to hurt the basic will of the spirit which unceasingly strives for the apparent and the superficial.710

S: Do I hear echoes of certain voices in Plato's grotto?

A: The very last thing I want here is any thoughts of imitation.

# CHEWING THE CUD

S: Oh, ha, ha.

A: No; seriously; joking aside. Contrary to common belief, what the knowledge-seeker is after is not the truth.

S: It isn't? Enlighten me then, for I appear to have spent the better part of my life traveling down a wrong road!

A: That commanding something which the people calls "spirit" wants to be master within itself and around itself and to feel itself master: out of multiplicity it has the will to simplicity, a will which binds together and tames, which is imperious and domineering. In this its needs and capacities are the same as those that physiologists posit for everything that lives, grows and multiplies. The power of the spirit to appropriate what is foreign to it is revealed in a strong inclination to assimilate the new to the old, to simplify the complex, to overlook or repel what is wholly contradictory: just as it arbitrarily emphasizes, extracts and falsifies to suit itself certain traits and lines in what is foreign to it, in every piece of "external world". Its intention in all this is the incorporation of new "experiences", the arrangement of new things within old divisions - growth, that is to say: more precisely, the feeling of growth, the feeling of increased power. The same will is served by an apparently antithetical drive of the spirit, a sudden decision for ignorance, for arbitrary shutting out, a closing of the windows, an inner denial of this or that thing, a refusal to let it approach, a kind of defensive posture against much that can be known, a contentment with the dark, with the closed horizon, an acceptance and approval of ignorance: all this being necessary according to the degree of its power to appropriate, its "digestive power", to speak in a metaphor - ...

S: Wait. My teeth, or lack thereof; let me see if I've properly digested this? This "contentment with the dark" as you put it? You are saying what? Our desire for knowledge is too easily satisfied with exhibiting its sense of power; that although we may stumble upon the truth, this is rarely the result of a will to truth - the insistence upon "profundity and thoroughness"?

A: That's a passable summary.

S: But that serves only to raise the question of why we philosophers should want not just knowledge but the truth?

A: It's our cruelty.

# CHEWING THE CUD

S: Not mine. I adhere to the principle of doing no harm.

A: Please? Don't get all self-righteous on me, especially when we are making progress.

S: We are?

A: Yes. It is a matter of cruelty to the self; not cruelty to others. Learning transforms us; it does that which all nourishment does which does not merely "preserve". Of course, at the bottom of us, "right deep down", there is, to be sure, something unteachable, a granite stratum of spiritual fate, of predetermined decision and answer to predetermined selected questions. In the case of every cardinal problem there speaks an unchangeable "this is I"; about man and woman, for example, a thinker cannot relearn but only learn fully - only discover all that is "firm and settled" within him on this subject. 711

S: You said as much earlier.

A: I know, but it bears repeating. One sometimes comes upon certain solutions to problems that inspire strong belief in us; perhaps one henceforth calls them one's "convictions". Later - one sees them only as footsteps to self-knowledge, signposts to the problem that we are - more correctly, to the great stupidity that we are, to our spiritual fate, to the unteachable "right down deep". - Having...

S: Hmm, I'll have my own repeating problems if I don't chew this over. This will to truth? It is only obtained by our depriving ourselves of what we most want - the sense of mastering the world? Isn't this the ascetic ideal in another guise? And haven't you been pouring scorn upon this from the outset?

A: Ah, but the difference is crucial. The ascetic ideal is life devaluing. Its what gives priests and philosophers of your ilk a sense of mastery over the material and temporal world by means of devaluing this world as a poor facsimile of an eternal, spiritual world. Have I not taken pains to point out that this very ideal, if pursued to its end, if its injunction to truth-telling is adhered to, finally leads its adherents to forbid the lie involved in belief in God himself, in any eternal world? That this then bequeaths us that "strange and insane task" of translating ourselves back into nature; that our youngest virtue - our honesty - demands this of us?

Wait up. There's some confusion here, and I think I know what is. So we make a distinction between life affirmation and life enhancement?

249

# CHEWING THE CUD

S: How would that help? My difficulty lies those categories of the "weak" and the "strong". Sooner or later the argument, whichever direction it takes, seems to circle back to them. No sooner do I feel I've got a grip on them, albeit in their crudest manifestation, than you seem to head off potential objections by adding further characteristics that threaten to collapse the previous polarity in respect of which they were initially defined. A prime example would be the "weak" becoming, "creative", "intelligent" and giving not just - what was it? - "new meaning to the earth", or some such, but suborning the power of the strong.

A: But that's just what I want you to understand. The "weak" and the "strong" are highly unstable entities.

S: But then how can you maintain the "weak" are still weak if they attain the whip-hand?

A: Think of "life affirmation" as the ability to affirm life as it is without resort to theology or some other teleology. Think of life enhancement as a local stratagem by which life is made bearable. Clearly rather than face up to the tragic implications of our finitude, humanity has chosen, time and again, when faced with catastrophes that threaten to render life as previously lived meaningless to opt for "solutions" which ward off nihilism by recourse to some new life enhancing narrative that remains constrained by local circumstances and unable to positively affirm life as it is. Hence why I might both applaud and criticize such stratagems without contradicting myself. Do you see?

S: As biological foundationalist rather than biological determinist, I assume? It's one thing though for me to see this project as insane, but quite another for you to commend it on the very same ground?

A: The will to truth - don't you see? The spirit has to give up what it most desires, what it most wants to believe - precisely because of what that sense of power such belief would give - for the sake of what it has reason to believe. For we thinkers the mastery we seek is mastery over ourselves rather than the world. Power over ourselves is power over the world. Previously we thinkers were only able to give up what we most wanted to believe for what we had reason to believe under the auspices of your ascetic ideal. Our task is insane by virtue of its desire to turn the very ground on which we stand, the ground upon which we are most sure of success - hence why our truthfulness requires our being cruel to ourselves.

# CHEWING THE CUD

S: Insane in another way. Wouldn't the course you would have us set entail our jettisoning all that taken - for - granted that lards and weatherproofs our most deeply held sentiments? Even then its hard to see how your will to truth could make headway against the swell of time encrusted conviction. That doesn't actually scan metaphorically, does it? Still you can see what I'm driving at? Yes? If I had your way with words, I'd have long ago made my fortune selling bulls without balls to the farmers hereabouts.

A: To answer your first point. Yes, for progress to be made sentiment would have to be dug out by the roots. Nothing less than a thorough poisoning of the very instincts that have served so well to preserve and protect and enhance our type would be required. Our instincts are the very last things to be incorporated by consciousness. To this end it may necessary for us to give our honesty a helping hand by summoning up whatever we have in us of devilry ... our subtlest, most disguised, most spiritual will to power and overcoming of the world ... let us come to the assistance of our "gods" with our "devils", if needs be by the no means unproblematic readiness of the spirit to deceive other spirits and to dissimulate in front of them. After all, the spirit enjoys the multiplicity of and craftiness of masks, it also enjoys the feeling of its security behind them: ... it is surely the most protean of arts that defend and conceal the best? 712

S: If I didn't know better, I might think you were advocating the adoption of the woman's wiles. Still, I interrupted you in mid- flow a minute or two ago. You were reiterating your thoughts about "the great stupidity we are" an otherwise making free with the collective noun. Ah, what it is to play the role of the friend who is in need? "Having" you were about to continue?

A: "Having". Oh, yes. Sounds even more self-satisfied now; - out of context that is. Having just paid myself such a deal of pretty compliments I may perhaps be permitted to utter a few truths about "woman as such": assuming it is now understood from the outset to how great an extent these are only - my truths. 713

S: All well, I won't pay too much attention if they are only your truths. And don't think all that verbal fluttering of the eyelashes has gone unnoticed. "Pretty compliments" indeed! That fine blue robe seems to have quite gone to your head.

A: Relational truths, not relative truths.

S: Isn't it all relative? I mean when it comes down to the ins and outs of a couple's relationship?

251

# CHEWING THE CUD

A: Highly symbiotic, maybe –but that's another story. Are you being deliberately obtuse, as well as salacious?

S: Me? I don't see what other kind of spin you could put on those words, ... unless ... Unless they express "the great stupidity that we [you?] are"?

A: Exactly. You always seek to hurt the one you love [?]. My very own ressenti-ment, you see?
S: I'm confused. Clearly it's no accident that you preface these remarks about women.

A: Not women, "women as such".

S: Ok. "Women as such" then; - and in light of those declarations concerning the virtues of your "free thinkers". Presumably the boast about honesty and the cautions about what we believe and that which we have reason to believe bear on this?

A: You old dog you. Trust you to find the scent.

S: Hmm, well if I have, I'd have to say that you've taken a deal of trouble to conceal it. Wouldn't be a damn sight simpler to just tell people what you believe?

A: You are forgetting what I said in regard of the need for masks. Besides some things are best learnt by means of riddles. Consider these seven proverbs for women? How the slowest tedium flees when a man comes on his knees! Age and scientific thought give even virtue some support. Social garb and total muteness dress a woman with - astuteness. Who has brought me luck today? God! - and my couturi-er. Young: a cavern decked about. Old: a dragon sallies out. Noble name, a leg that's fine, man as well: oh were he mine! Few words, much meaning - slippery ground, many a poor she-ass has found.714

S: For once I'm on Xanthippe's side - crude, dripping with the ressentiment that you claim to be opposed to, and the very misogyny that only a few minutes ago you scorned.

A: Have I so misunderstood Xanthippe?

S: Actually, no. Now you mention it, I can imagine her cackling over those sayings of yours.

# CHEWING THE CUD

A: Who said they were mine?

S: Be that as it may, as, too, Xanthippe's wicked sense of humour. She's not the best ambassador of womankind.

A: That's the thing here - "woman as such". Men have hitherto treated women like birds which have strayed down to them from the heights: as something more delicate, more fragile, more savage, stranger, sweeter, soulful - but as something which has to be caged up so that it shall not fly away. Remember? - It was man who created "woman" out of a rib of his God, of his ideal?

S: But these "maxims"; "How boredom flies..." Obviously "woman" is set up in such a fashion that life hinges on getting a man. "It is a truth universally acknowledged that a man ..." and the rest of them. She lives through the man, so to speak - is constrained to seek her life through of another rather than for herself. That chimes with other things you've said about freedom, this being the converse. Again the "cavern decked about" - I can't say the sexual allusion is to my taste - has echoes of that other maxim of yours, "woman learns to hate to the extent that she unlearns how - to charm"? 715
And the 'crack – the one about the couturier? Is that saying anything different from that other remark of yours about the woman's genius for finery being the consequence of her instinct for the secondary role? 718 All very misogynistic, I'd say.

A: We immoralists! - This world which concerns us, in which we have to love and fear, this almost invisible, inaudible world of subtle commanding, subtle obeying, a world of "almost" in every respect, sophistical, insidious, sharp, tender: it is well defended, indeed, against clumsy spectators and familiar curiosity! We are entwined in an austere shirt of duty and cannot get out of it - and in this we are "men of duty", we too! Sometimes, it is true, we may dance in our 'chains" and between our "swords"; often, it is no less true, we gnash our teeth at it and frown impatiently at the unseen hardship of our lot. But do what we will, fools and appearances speak against us and say "these are men without duty" - we always have fools and appearances against us! 716

S: What's this; something from a war manual? Attack as the best means of defence? Am I to infer that I belong to the ranks of the fools?

A: Sometime I find myself wondering whether what things are called is incomparably more important than what they are. The reputation, name, and appearance, the usual measure and weight of a thing, what it counts for - originally almost always wrong and arbitrary, thrown over things like a dress and altogether foreign to their nature and even to their skin - all this grows from generation unto generation, merely because people believe in it, until it gradually grows to be part of the thing and turns into its very body. What at first was appearance becomes in the end, almost invariably, the essence and is effective as such. ...it is enough to create new names and estimations and probabilities in order to create in the long run new "things".717

S: What's an old fool to infer from that then? That where man and woman are concerned its the man who has generally got to decide what things are called?

A: Among other things, yes; don't take all so personally. One seeks a midwife for his thoughts, another someone to whom he can be a mid-wife: thus originates a good conversation.718

S: Then you won't mind my insisting that I already have the franchise on the "mid-wife" metaphor?

A: Ok, Ok. Zeus. You can be hard work. Someone took a youth to a sage...

S: What is this, another of your traps?

A: God, you are a prickly pear.

S: What makes you think you can feed off my fruit for free?

A: May I? ... Someone took a youth to a sage and said: "Look he's being corrupted by women". The sage shook his head and smiled. "It is men", said he, "that corrupt women; and all the failings of women should be atoned by and improved in men. For it is man who creates for himself the image of woman, and woman who forms herself according to this image".

"You are too kind-hearted about women", said one of those present, "You do not know them". The sage replied: "Will is the manner of men; willingness that of women. That is the law of the sexes - truly, a hard law for women. All of humanity is innocent of its existence; but women are doubly innocent. Who could have enough oil and kindness for them?"

"Damn oil! Damn kindness!" someone else shouted out of the crowd; women need to be educated better!" - "Men need to be educated better", said the sage and beckoned the youth to follow him. - The youth, however, did not follow him.719

## CHEWING THE CUD

S: Hmm, I know that feeling; people walking away. Plato tells it as if success is always assured. Anyway, what's a woman to do - given the asymmetry [I take it that this is what you are drawing my attention to?] of the power relationship? Play the man at his own game?

A: No, her great heart is the lie, her highest concern is mere appearance and beauty.720 Seducing one's neighbour to a good opinion and afterwards believing piously in this opinion - who could equal women in this art? 721
S: Tsk. Ever the sophist, aren't you. Manipulating appearance in lieu of really seeking the truth. I'm glad to say that my Xanthippe has had done with all that face-painting malarkey, or have I already said that? Damn irritating that. Mind - beginning to play tricks on me, What was I saying? Oh yes. A paler shade of grey suits her just fine.

A: Not everything is a question of black or white. The "apparent" world is the only one, while being is an empty fiction, and the true world is merely added by a lie to our world of becoming, passing away and change.722 Hence, why I might say: woman far from being deep, is not even shallow.

S: Pah! You and your schoolboy riddles. You may affect, on occasion, to take the side of the woman but that does not mean, any more than they, that you can have it all. Don't think I didn't notice - in your little story about the sage? - those words about "the law of the sexes". If it's a law, then small wonder nobody pays heed to your sage?

A: And what if it's a constitutive law as opposed to a biological one?

S: How's that render the man innocent? And if he is innocent, for what must he atone? There are signs here that you've not thought this through. And as to the issue of "will" and "willingness", and who does which – well?

A: I'm not blind. Despite all the concessions that I'm willing to make to prejudice in favour of monogamy, I can't see that man and woman have equal rights in love. In love, mark you, not before the law - before you ask.
The former do not exist. They have different conceptions of love. A man who loves like a woman becomes a slave; whilst a woman who loves like a woman becomes a more perfect woman. There is no equal pathos, no equal will to renunciation; for if both parties felt impelled by love to renounce themselves, we should then get - I do not know what; perhaps an empty space?

# CHEWING THE CUD

Woman gives herself away, man acquires more - I do not see how one can get around this natural opposition by means of social contracts or with the best will in the world to be just, desirable as it may be not to remind oneself constantly how harsh, terrible, enigmatic, and immoral this antagonism is. For love, thought of in its entirety as great and full, is nature, and being nature it is in all eternity something "immoral". 723

S: Immoral? Some would argue that the fairer sex are the fairer morally speaking as well. Is it not the woman who best exemplifies the values of altruism, pity, kindness, and humility?

A: But as what? That's the question. Are they not the bitter fruit of best practice? - Palliatives, restoratives, against the harmful effects of being those who must bow the knee, those who must serve?

S: Oh well, where there is a lioness, there's got to be a cheese-grater!

A: You're showing your origins.

S: Am I? I thought I was well wrapped. Still a man cannot disguise "a prodigious burden" for long.

A: I thought we agreed? None of that!

S: Just referencing "Lysistrata" 724What if the women mounted a challenge - no pun intended? Fought for equal rights?

A: "Emancipation of women" - is the instinctive hatred of the woman who has turned out ill, that is to say incapable of bearing, for her who has turned out well - the struggle against "man" is always only means, subterfuge, tactic. When they elevate themselves as "woman in herself", as "higher woman", as "idealist" woman, they want to lower the general level of rank of woman; no surer means for achieving that than grammar school education, trousers and the political rights of voting cattle. 725

S: Sugar the pill, why don't you?

A: Speaking of "cattle", I'm no more referring to women than I am to men. Parliamentarianism - that is, public permission to choose between five basic political opinions - flatters and wins the favour of those who would like to seem independent and individual, as if they fought for their opinions. Ultimately, however, it is indifferent whether the herd is commanded to have one opinion or permitted to have five. Whoever deviates from the five public opinions and stands apart will always have the whole herd against him. 726

S: Thick as thieves, you and Aristophanes.
A: What? Because he knows as well as I that no one brings along the finest sense of his art to the theatre, nor does the artist who works for the theatre. There is one common people, audience, herd, female, Pharisee, voting cattle, democrat, neighbour, fellow man; there even the most personal conscience is vanquished by the levelling magic of the great number; their stupidity has the effect of lasciviousness and contagion; the neighbour reigns, one becomes a mere neighbour. 727

S: You're preaching to the converted here. Is it not clear that we are at one on the question of democracy?

A: Appearances can be very misleading.

S: What I don't get is why you are so agitated by all this? More especially, I can't see why you should be so excited by the question of the woman. Yes, I know some men find it hard to leave them alone, but even they'll tell you in private that this is every bit a curse as much as it is a blessing. In your case however, its as if women, or rather the question of women, was a kind of lightening rod, a means of deflecting some larger danger?

A: Not exactly - Suppose "truth" were a woman? 728

S: Yes, you said as much a while back. One of your riddles, I take it?

A: A matter of being born posthumously.

S: Yet another of your riddles I've heard before. Your attempt at trumping my daemon, - as I remember?

A: This isn't a contest!

S: Ah, but you said it was.

A: I did, but this isn't right now.

# CHEWING THE CUD

S: No doubt the other Socrates would have something to say about a playing field that isn't level.

A: Great as he was, he might have taken the ball and gone home had he lived to see Iniesta and Spain's first half display? Fabregas's pass to Silva's head for the first goal; what sublime invention? Had it been to Silva's feet as expected the defender might have blocked the shot. And Xavi's slide-rule pass for the second. Wonderful.

S: Where are you? Who are all these people? This Spain? What does he do? Where does he go in the second half? Home like my namesake?

A: Forget it. It would be easier to explain the Offside law.

S: It would? What's that then?

A: No, it wouldn't.

S: But you just said it would.

A: Zeus! You're just like the Spanish team. Once they get an opponent on their carousel, they pass the ball around till he's dizzy.

S: Carousel? Are you saying I've one of these?

A: Stop! You are making my head whirl.

S: I have then? Tell me what it is, and I'll get rid of it. I can't have a meaningful conversation with you if you are confused. It's difficult enough as it is.

A: Jesus and mother Mary!

S: That's one Spaniard too many, and no disrespect to his mother, but can we get back to what we were talking about?

A: Thank Christ.

S: Look, I'm trying to be patient here. You've mentioned him before - this Christ - but you didn't say anything about him being a Spaniard. If you don't mind could we stay away from Spaniards and their carousels?

# CHEWING THE CUD

A: Give me strength.

S: You're still confused? You won't mind me saying? Perhaps if you went more slowly; that was all sad in a rush?

A: No, I'm not the one who is confused. And as regards haste; my aim is actually to reduce to despair any man in a hurry. Let's get on with it. Modernity - two problems.

S: You can do that without hurrying; believe me. "Modernity"?

A: Cut me some slack. In actuality, I pride myself on being a teacher of slow reading.729 "Modernity"? - Just another way of saying, "in the future". Anyway two problems for society and its subsequent health; nihilism [the devaluation of all values}, and degeneration of mankind - the reduction of man to the perfect herd animal. The first of these questions bears upon the problem of overcoming the "will to truth"; the second, in overcoming the "will to equality".

S: Ha, ha. You are joking, yes? The same in terms of height, weight, maybe, but equal? Or are you talking politics here, the demos and their so-called right to equal consideration at the ballot box? Personally speaking I thought I would have hoped that I'd have demonstrated on sufficient occasions that even those who might be considered well born, and thus possessed of some sort of entitlement to rule, are woefully lacking of any real knowledge. Enough times that is for all and sundry to draw the appropriate inference when it comes to the prospect of the wielding of power by the majority who are manifestly ignorant to begin with?

A: Here, you and Plato - or is it rather just you? - go too far. I fancy that Plato would have his own reasons for not wanting to betray his own class. And as to "the Labour Question"? The stupidity, fundamentally the instinct of degeneration, which is the cause of every stupidity today, lies in the existence of a labour question at all. About certain things one does not ask questions: first imperative of instinct.

S: Is that reproof aimed at me?

A: Absolutely. - I simply cannot see what one wishes to do with the European worker now one has made a question of him. He finds himself far too well placed not to go on asking for more, or to ask more and more impudently. After all he has the great majority on his side. There is absolutely no hope left that a modest and self-sufficient kind of human being, a type of Chinaman, should here form itself

259

into a class: and this would have been sensible, this was actually a necessity. What has one done? Everything designed to nip in the bud even the prerequisites for it - through the most irresponsible thoughtlessness one has totally destroyed the instincts by virtue of which the worker becomes possible as a class possible for himself. The worker has been made liable for military service, he has been allowed to form unions and to vote: no wonder the worker already feels his existence to be a state of distress [express in moral terms as a state of injustice]. But what does one want? - to ask it again. If one wills an end, one must also will the means to it- if one wants slaves, one is a fool if one educates them to be masters. 730

S: For saying you have a top drawer full of grace notes, you've an alarming tendency, on occasion to give voice the harshest, and most jarring of sentiments. You speak as if the common man is just a slave by another name.

A: Most are.

S: Just because most are not fit to rule, it doesn't mean that they aren't entitled to a say in how they are governed. That's surely the beauty of "democracy", in practice it is rule by oligarchy, - that is to say by competing elites? Elites who perpetuate the illusion of "democracy" by asking the populace to periodically endorse the rule of one or other of the said elites? The people vote for manifestoes, and that's all. How these are implemented, indeed, whether these are implemented, is - like their construction - a matter for the elites alone.

A: I wasn't after a lesson on political theory. I was rather seeking to challenge the idea of equality.

S: That surely is a given. All are equal by dint of having a soul.

A: No. Thus blinks the mob - 'There are no higher men, we are all equal, man is man; before God we are all equal". Before God! But now this god has died. And before the mob we do not want to be equal.731 The siren songs of old metaphysical bird-catchers who have been piping ... all too long, 'you are more, you are higher, you are of a different origin" than all other forms of life. 732

S: You have lost me.

A: Have I? Human kind might have a common nature that sets them apart from the rest of animal life, but they themselves differ so radically from one another that the notion of their equality must be adjudged a myth - a myth that is rooted in an outmoded religious belief. I'll go further. The notion that everyone has an "immortal soul" has equal rank with everyone else is impertinence, a conceit that cannot be branded with too much contempt. This optical magnification of one's own importance to the point of insanity - nothing but insanely important souls, revolving about themselves with a frightening fear - has given rise to the extremist form of equality of rights, all souls being thought to possess the same importance. ... one has transferred the arrival of the "kingdom of God" into the future , on earth, in human form - but fundamentally one has held fast to the belief in the old ideal.733

Don't look so crestfallen. To be sure, it is daunting to ruminate upon how much most collapse now that this faith has been undermined because it was built upon this faith, propped up by it, grown into it; but when one looks afresh at humanity one sees not equals, but an enchanting wealth of types, the abundance of a lavish play and change of forms.734

S: Though I may not like what I'm hearing, I'm not crestfallen. I'm rather intrigued. Am I right to suppose there is a link of sorts here with respect to your scepticism about the struggle regarding female emancipation? It seeks support from the old props as you would put it?

A: Quite so. Woman wants to be independent: and to that end she is beginning to enlighten men about "woman as such" - this is one of the worst developments in the general uglification of Europe. 735

Since the French Revolution...

S: "Europe"? "The French Revolution"?

A: Never mind. I'm sure you'll get the gist. Since the French Revolution the influence of woman in Europe has grown less in the same proportion as her rights and claims have grown greater; and the "emancipation of woman", in so far as it has been demanded by women themselves [ and not merely by male shallow-pates], is thus revealed as a noteworthy symptom of the growing enfeeblement and blunting of the most feminine instincts ... To be sure, there are sufficient idiotic friends and corrupters of woman among the learned asses of the male sex who advise woman to defeminize herself in this fashion and to imitate all the stupidities with which "man" in Europe, European "manliness", is sick ... 736

S: As I thought. This feminist thing is, for you, but another example of what you see as the "collective degeneration of humanity to the level of the perfect herd animal?

# CHEWING THE CUD

A: The same mistake over and over again: man has made the means to life into a standard of life; instead of discovering the standard in the highest enhancement of life itself, in the problem of growth and exhaustion, he has employed the means to a quite distinct kind of life to exclude all other forms of life, in short to criticize and select life. I.e., man finally loves the means for their own sake and forgets they are means: so that they enter his consciousness as aims, as standards for aims - i.e., a certain species of man treats the conditions of its existence as conditions which ought to be imposed as law, as "truth", "good", "perfection": it tyrannizes - It is a form of faith, of instinct, that a species of man fails to perceive its conditionality, its relativity to other species. At least it seems to be all over for a species of man [people, races] when it becomes tolerant, allows equal rights and no longer thinks of wanting to be master - 737

S: That last bit is too strong.

A: Is it? What was it the Latuka chieftain said? 'All good people are weak: they are good because they are not strong enough to be evil"? 738

S: The what - chief? I'm appalled. How can you say...?

A: Don't be such a milksop! Has it been noticed that in heaven all interesting men are missing? - Just a hint to the girls as to where they can best find their salvation. 739

S: Now you are being outrageous just for the sake of it!

A: Am I? The strata and class struggle that aims at "equality of rights" - once it is more or less over, the war against the solitary personality will begin ...The strongest must be bound most firmly, watched, laid in chains, and guarded - if the instinct of the herd has its way. For them a regime of self-control, ascetic detachment, or "duty" in exhausting work in which one completely loses oneself. 740

S: Forgive me saying so, "the war against the solitary personality"? Isn't that - well a little paranoid?

A: Is it really? The instinct of the herd considers the middle and the mean as the highest and most valuable: the place where the majority finds itself. It is therefore an opponent of all orders of rank; it sees an ascent from beneath to above as a descent from the majority to the minority. The herd feels the exception, whether it be below or above it, as something opposed and harmful to it. Its artifice with refer-

262

ence to the exceptions above it, the stronger, more powerful, wiser, and more fruit-ful, is to persuade them to assume the role of guardians, herdsmen, watchmen - to become its first servants: it has therefore transformed a danger into something use-ful. Fear ceases in the middle: here one is never alone; here there is little room for misunderstanding; here there is equality; here one's own form of being is not felt as a reproach but as the right form of being; here contentment rules. Mistrust is felt towards the exceptions; to be an exception is experienced as guilt. 741

S: Well, I, for one, seem to have a little more faith in the good sense of my fellow citizens than you.

A: Well, more fool you. Even the ideals of science can be deeply, yet completely unconsciously influenced by decadence: our entire sociology is proof of that. The objection to it is that from experience it knows only the form of decay of society, and inevitably it takes its own instincts of decay for the norms of sociological judgment. It does not know any other instinct than that of the herd, i.e., that of the sum of zeroes - where every zero has "equal rights", where it is virtuous to be zero-742

S: Never having heard of this "Sociology", I'll let that pass; however if your intent is to demean every ideal, that's another matter.

A: Really? Don't you think one is deceived every time one expects "progress" from an ideal; every time so far the victory of an ideal has meant a retrograde movement?
Christianity, the revolution, the abolition of slavery, equal rights, justice, truth: all these big words have value only in a fight, as flags: not as realities but as showy words for something quite different [indeed, opposite!] 743

S: Are you quite finished? Yes? Then you'll allow me to reciprocate?

A: That's another one, I should add to my list.

S: What is?

A: "Reciprocity"

S: Why? What has reciprocity ever done to you? Did it try to teach you some man-ners?

263

# CHEWING THE CUD

A: Ah, sarcasm. Has your head gone? Do you feel you are losing? Have you been stung; by a gadfly, perhaps?

S: Why you ... The only kiss you are going to get from me is a Glaswegian one.
A: What's that when it's at home?

S: Ah, something you don't know, at last. Well maybe I'll surprise you. Make your point and I'll think about it.

A: I'd hate to think I was having this conversation only with myself.

S: Actually I meant ... Oh, never mind! Make your point.

A: I was going to, but you seemed to be in two minds.

S: That was about something else. I've made my mind up about that.

A: You have?

S: You've been a great help.

A: One good turn deserves another?

S: My thought, too.

A: Only it doesn't.

S: It doesn't? I'm sorry. What are we talking about here?

A: I thought you knew. You've had a crafty smile playing on your lips for the past couple of minutes.

S: I have? It must have been the anticipation of giving you a present.

A: I'm not sure I'd want a present from you.

S: That's o.k. You won't like what I've in mind for you.

A: Now who's being perverse?

## CHEWING THE CUD

S: Sweet, isn't it? One good turn deserves another.

A: I just said it doesn't.

S: It does!

A: No, it really doesn't. Reciprocity, the hidden intention to claim a reward: one of the most insidious forms of the diminution of the value of man. It brings with it that "equality" which depreciates the distancing gulf as immoral - 744

S: Are you saying you can read my mind?

A: What?

S: Never mind. I was thinking about something else entirely. You'll have to put some flesh on that.

A: Right. I have your attention?

S: Yes.

A: Puts me in mind of John Stuart Mill.

S: Do I? Who is he?

A: Not you as such; what you are thinking. It's his vulgarity.

S: So, now even my thinking is vulgar. 'Seems to me that the only thing that is rank around here is the one who is pulling it!

A: Get angry if you must, but get angry at the right things. Ultimately, for what its worth, what determines your rank is the quantum of power you are: the rest is cowardice. I abhor Mill's vulgarity which says: "What is right for one is for another"; "what you would not, etc., do unto others", which wants to establish all human intercourse and yours is presupposed; so that everything appears as a kind of payment for something done to us. The presupposition here is ignoble in the lowest sense; here an equivalence of value between my actions and yours is presupposed; here the most personal value of an action is simply annulled [that which cannot be balanced or paid in any way -].

265

# CHEWING THE CUD

"Reciprocity" is a piece of gross vulgarity; precisely that something I do may not and could not be done by another, that no balance is possible [except in the most select sphere of "my equals," inter pares -], that in a deeper sense one never gives back, because one is something unique and does only unique things - this fundamental conviction contains the cause of aristocratic segregation from the masses, because the masses believe in "equality" and consequently in equivalence and "reciprocity". 745

S: You won't rest until you've prized me apart from my principle of doing no harm, it seems.

A: No pathos of distance, no "self-overcoming of man", I'm afraid.746

S: You're a cold fish, you know?

A: Should one follow one's feelings? - That one should put one's life in danger, yielding to a generous feeling and under the impulse of a moment; that is of little value and does not even characterize one. Everyone is equally capable of that - and in this resolution a criminal, a bandit, and a Corsican certainly excel decent people.
    A higher stage is: to overcome even this pressure within us and to perform a heroic act not on impulse - but coldly, reasonably, without being overwhelmed by stormy feelings of pleasure - The same applies to compassion: it must first be habitually sifted by reason; otherwise it is just as dangerous as any other affect.
    Blind indulgence of an affect, totally regardless of whether it be a generous and compassionate or a hostile affect, is the cause of the greatest evils.
    Greatness of character does not consist in possessing these affects - on the contrary, one possesses them to the highest degree - but in having them under control. And that without any pleasure in this restraint, but merely because - 747

S: Otherwise the suspicion that the old ascetic spirit is at work behind the scene. You can leave it at that. I get it. Your worry is that female emancipation is but the latest ploy by means of which the herd mentality seeks to secure its sway over all aspects of social life.

A: The diminution of man into the perfect herd animal is the over-all danger.

S: Your vehemence about this issue seems to suggest a lack of confidence in your so-called free spirits. On occasion you speak as if these people's superiority and self-confidence can be taken as read and that the only problem for them is the continual efforts of the herd to curtail their freedom of action. Other times though -

and in spite of all the earlier braggadocio about strength and weakness - there seems to be a more fundamental worry as to whether these creatures might be, so to speak, strangled at birth?

A: Sad to say, but yes most potentially "higher" types succumb and end up among the excess of failures one encounters everywhere. 748The richest and most complex forms of human life, though attained, do not last for they perish more easily; they are achieved only rarely and maintain their superiority with difficulty, while only the lowest preserve an apparent indestructability.

The higher the type a man represents, the greater the improbability that he will turn out well. The accidental, the law of absurdity in the whole economy of mankind, manifests itself most horribly in its destructive effect on the higher men whose complicated conditions of life can only be calculated with great subtlety and difficulty. 749

S: No splendid blonde beast prowling about, avidly in search of spoil and victory", then?

A: Ha, ha. No; indeed. What is necessary is not sufficient. Strength, powerful drives, over-flowing vitality, are only preconditions, the splendid "animal" must be controlled and pressed into service. 750As I said to Lou in that letter, one must learn how to emancipate oneself from one's emancipation. But that's another story for another day perhaps? Have we done with women?

S: Not quite.

A: Not quite? You're looking browbeaten again.

S: Xanthippe. I was thinking of Xanthippe.

A: Clearly, you've not done with her quite yet; remarkable for a man of your years?

S: Is that what you are after - salacious tittle-tattle? Saluting one birthday a year suits me fine. Can we leave it at that?

A: That wasn't...

S: No? Actually, I was thinking, "I'll be late again". She still takes it as a personal sleight. Mark my words: there will be a whole list of things that require urgent attention. It's her way of taking both her revenge and the measure of my affection - she gets me running, or tries to. And all that, having had to eat my supper off of the floor! That's the truth of it. Which reminds me. We digress - "Supposing truth to be a woman"?

A: "Is the suspicion not well founded that all philosophers, when they have been dogmatists, have had little understanding of women? the gruesome earnestness, the clumsy importunity with which they have hitherto been in the habit of approaching truth have been inept and improper means for winning a wench? Certainly she has not let herself be won - and today every kind of dogmatism stands sad and discouraged. If it continues to stand at all! For there are scoffers who assert it has fallen down, that dogmatism lies on the floor, more, that dogmatism is at its last gasp.751

S: Up yours!

A: To speak seriously, there are good grounds for hoping that all dogmatizing in philosophy, the solemn air of finality it has given itself notwithstanding, may none the less have been no more than a noble childishness and tyronism; and the time is perhaps very close at hand when it will be grasped in case after case what has been sufficient to furnish the foundation-stone for such sublime and unconditional philosopher's edifices as the dogmatists have hitherto been constructing - some popular superstition or other from time immemorial [such as the soul superstition which, as the subject- and - ego superstition, has not yet ceased to do mischief even today], perhaps some play on words, a grammatical seduction, or an audacious generalization on the basis of a very narrow, very personal, very human all too human facts.752

S: That's quite some charge sheet. One or two new indictments, if I'm not mistaken? Be that as it may - the initial analogy, truth as a woman? It has the tone of some kind of introduction to an argument?

A: To a book I'm about to write entitled, 'Beyond Good and Evil".

S: And pray, what takes place beyond good and evil?

A: That which is done out of love? 753

S: Is it you or I who have lost the plot here?

## CHEWING THE CUD

A: Well it may the nineteenth century in my head sometimes, but this is no novel I'm writing.

S: But the plot is that there is no plot?

A: You could put it that way.

S: No plot, but nonetheless a conspiracy?

A: A conspiracy?

S: Yes! The aim is to subvert, to invert the entire Platonic understanding of truth as non-perspectival. That's what this is all about isn't it: the revaluing of woman - a kind of Trojan horse. The identification of woman with seduction, perspectivism, art, life are all sorties carried on in the name of this revaluation, this - what would you call it? – re-capturing of the affects. Plato's would be nemesis - that's whom I'm arguing with isn't it? You want to bring everything high low. Would that he were here to hear his suspicions of art and artists so well confirmed. I'm quite out of breath; I must sit down.

A: The struggle against purpose in art is always the struggle against the moralizing tendency in art, against the subordination of art to morality. ... A psychologist asks on the other hand: what does all art do? Does it not praise? Does it not glorify? Does it not select? does it not highlight? By doing all this it strengthens or weakens certain valuations ... Is this no more than an incidental? a accident? 754

S: That's as maybe. Come let's walk, I've changed my mind. We'll never get any-where if we keep stopping and starting. This "will to truth" thing – it's still going round in my head. I haven't got a handle on it yet. If you don't mind?

A: Fire away. Oft' times its difficult to know what you think until you hear what you say.

S: I sense that a lot of what you want to say turns on this. That stuff about woman and truth is still a bit of a fog. The sense escapes me, if sense there be? Perhaps it has something to do with the way you bandy the idea of "truth". Truth is truth, yes? Only you seem, on occasion to imply that - well, that the value we accord it is - well unwarranted somehow.

# CHEWING THE CUD

A: Within a herd, within any community, that is to say inter pares, the over estimation of truthfulness makes good sense. Not to be deceived - and consequently, as a personal point of morality, not to deceive! a mutual obligation between equals! In dealing with what lies outside, danger and caution demand that one should be on on's guard against deception: as a psychological preconditioning for this, also in dealing with what lies within. Mistrust as the source of truthfulness. 755

S: There you go again.

A: What do want me to say? Being serious about truth: what very different ideas people associate with these words! ... It can happen that a man's emphatic seriousness shows how superficial and modest his spirit has been all along when playing with knowledge. - And does not everything we take seriously betray us? It always shows what has weight for us and what does not. 756

S: Are you being facetious? Sometimes, it's hard to tell.

A: I leave that to you.

S: I'm trying to be serious about this, but you seem intent only on crossing up the transaction. Odd isn't it? You remind me of the Metic - he lost the plot when it came to talking about the plot. 757

A: Tragic. There's something we might agree on? It doesn't all turn on some supposed moral flaw, as both Aristotle and the Christian will later argue. As I said, I'll leave the facetiousness to you.

S: Being highborn, I would have thought you'd take a greater interest in this particular art form. Not wishing to be indelicate, the writers seem to have a marked predilection for showing the well-born coming to grief?

A: Aren't you the sly one? You most have spoken often enough to Euripides to know that, for him and his peers, the forces of life - nature, if you will - are both self-generative and self-destructive. Focusing on the family, and not least the well-born, family is merely a way to bring this home to duller minds that these contradictory forces are at work even amongst those apparently blessed. Fate, you see. Mortality and loss are ineluctably bound with human existence, which can neither be made good or reformed, nor transcended. Haven't I said as much already?

S: A little squib for his nibs and me? Why? - Because we live in hope of going to a better place?

# CHEWING THE CUD

A: Tragedy is surely both an affirmation of life, and recognition of its ultimate dissolution. Human kind must always confront a negative fate; one that limits their power, and, ultimately, brings death.

S: Affirmation! Where's the affirmation in what you've been saying; more a confirmation of Silenus' so-called wisdom, if you ask me. "Best: not to be born. Second: best to die soon". All worship of Dionysus should be proscribed forthwith; nothing more than an invitation to drink and debauchery; the erotic courting of pessimism and nihilism. Rampant romanticism; it is the delirium of those who believe themselves highly individuated that prompts the interest in dissolution as a worldly deliverance from pain. Some forms of eroticism can have a fatal allure.

A: Am I not looking at one?

S: With you I scarcely know whether I'm being insulted or complimented, and that's not to forget the "excluded middle" - whatever the Metic says - both at the same time? Anyway. You haven't answered me. Where is the affirmation to be found?

A: The world supports as well as undermining human achievement. Does not Apollo offer a sort of counter-balance for us Greeks?

S: Apollonian individuation as the deliverance from pain, you mean?

A: More the deliverance from the danger of life-denial, I'd say. In the final analysis, Apollo's forms are transient and ephemeral. Dionysus holds sway because of the tragic limits on formed conditions.

S: If that's the best that's on offer, remind me to offer a cock to the doctor.

A: Time waits for no man, I guess, but it would be sad if it came to that. Tragic? I'm not so sure.

S: I'll tell you what is tragic! Tragic is when I cut my little finger; comic is when you fall into a cesspit and drown!

A: Ha, ha , ha. Even so, I think you might have missed the mark there.

271

# CHEWING THE CUD

S: Really? Might the hubris belong to you? "Nothing in excess": aren't they the words inscribed over Apollo's temple at Delphi?

A: And there I was thinking you knew nothing about the subject.

S: I thought I'd said; Plato finds them, tragedies that is, mercifully short. On occasion he has me check them out. They differ from other types of story in that the hero fails to make a success in either sense; he neither sets the world to rights, nor does he win the heroine's hand thereby ensuring the generation of new life.

A: Has someone been reading Aristotle on the sly?

S: No, I have quite enough nous of my own; enough to recognize that the fatla flaw lies within rather than without the hero. Hubris - the overstepping of the bounds - Action that brings nemesis in its train. Nemesis - the allotting of a due proportion that serves to reestablish the order of the cosmos. 'Hamartia' less a literal missing of the mark than the result of a deficiency of character such as that revealed by a rampant egoism, excessive drinking and consorting with the wrong kind of women.

A: That's me told, then?

S: If you had my knees, you wouldn't be grinning!

A: Do you want to sit?

S: No, no. Let's get on.

A: The greatest danger that always hovered over mankind ... is the eruption of madness - arbitrariness in feeling, seeing, hearing, the enjoyment of the mind's lack of discipline, the joy in human unreason. Not truth and certainty are the opposite of the world of the madman, but the universality and the universal binding force of a faith; in sum, the non-arbitrary character of judgments. And man's greatest labour thus far has been to reach agreement about very many things and to submit to a law of agreement - regardless of whether these things are true or false.

S: Did I hear you aright? Regardless of their truth or falsity?

A: Yes. This is the discipline of the mind that mankind has received; but the contrary impulses are still so powerful that we cannot speak of the future of mankind with much confidence. ... Continually, precisely the most select spirits bristle at this universal binding force - the explorers of truth above all. ... It is in these impatient spirits that a veritable delight in madness erupts because madness has such a cheerful tempo. Thus the virtuous intellects are needed ... to make sure that the faithful of the great shared faith stay together and continue their dance. It is a first rate need that commands and demands this. We others are the exception and the danger - and we need to be eternally to be defended.

S: We do?

A: Well, there are actually things to be said in favour of the exception, provided that it never wants to become the rule. 758

S: Ha, ha. Less we get carried away by your own high spirits; most think you laud the exception, others that occasionally you can be found defending the rule. Here you seem intent on preserving it. Which is it?

A: Why can't it be all three? I could say: "It's a woman's prerogative to change her mind"? But of course there is no contradiction here, is there? That's rhetorical by the way.

S: Both claims, it would seem. Tell me about truth as a woman whilst I get my breath. Let's talk about one thing at a time. Not everything comes in threes, whatever old wives may say.

A: Ah, but this is an instance of "the three in one".

S: What are you smiling at? Is it some sort of private joke?
A: Never mind. Think of it - truth that is - as taking three forms; as a manifestation of the will to truth, the will to illusion, and the will to power. In age after age the same phenomena recurs. Over and over the avid will finds the means to maintain and perpetuate its creatures in life by spreading over existence the blandishments of illusion. One man is enthralled by the Socratic zest for knowledge and is persuaded that he can staunch the eternal wound of being with its help; the veil of art that flutters, tantalizing, before his eyes, beguiles another. Yet another is buoyed up by that metaphysical solace that life flows on, indestructible, beneath the whirlpool of appearances. Not to mention even commoner and more powerful illusions, which the will holds in readiness at any moment. The three kinds of illusion I have named answer only to more noble natures, which resent the burden of existence more deeply than the rest and who therefore require special beguilement to make them forget

this burden. What we call culture is entirely composed of such beguilements. Need I add, that depending on the mix we get particular cultures?

S: Before I gave way to the temptation to start preening myself, those words about compelling us to live on? Each position is a deception?

A: To be sure. And before you trot out the usual objections, think of it in these terms. Our concepts, our ideas, provide us with the tools with which to go about building our lives; what we rather need is to ask questions of the tools themselves.

S: But when you speak of truth as a tripartite will, as deception must you at some level hate the deception, want to be rid of it?

A: But if it is all illusion? Mustn't I both love and hate it?

S: Like women? Is that it? You both love and hate them?

A: Don't forget here that deception serves either an ascending or descending life. The degenerates need to discover value, rather than to create it for themselves; they seek a world beyond this world of appearance; like the coward who trades multiplicity for a false sense of security. As long as life is ascending, happiness is the same as instinct. Ascending life reflects its plenitude upon things - it transfigures, it embellishes, it rationalizes the world; declining life impoverishes, bleaches, mars the value of things; it suppresses the world. 759

S: And you know this how?

A: I know both sides, for I am both sides. No disrespect, but a philosopher recuperates differently and with different means: he recuperates, e.g., with nihilism. Belief that there is no truth at all, the nihilistic belief, is a great relaxation for one who, as a warrior of knowledge, is ceaselessly fighting ugly truths. For truth is ugly. 760

S: What? I'm not even to count as a philosopher now if I don't relax by showering in caustic acid! I prefer to come clean by acknowledging my ignorance.

A: Well you are just going to have scrub a lot harder.

S: There you go again! It's all so ad hominum!

## CHEWING THE CUD

A: Well it won't come out in the wash otherwise! And besides a good ad hominum is not be sniffed at. Ask that "Dog", Diogenes, he specialises in them. All I'm saying...

S: That's another of your ruses isn't it? - 'All I'm saying"! You can't play the little innocent. As if what then follows is so innocuous, and so lacking in contention as to be beyond cavil.

A: No type of pessimism known hitherto seems to have attained to this degree of malevolence.

S: What! Now you accuse me - me of all people? - of pessimism and malevolence?!

A: Not you! Me! I'm talking about me, for God's sake! All I'm saying - and don't say a word until I've finished - is that here the antithesis of a real world and an apparent world is lacking here - with me that is - : there is only one world, and this is false, cruel, contradictory, seductive, without meaning - A world thus constituted is the real world. We have need of lies in order to conquer this reality, this "truth", that is, in order to live - That lies are necessary in order to live is itself part of the terrifying and questionable character of existence.

Metaphysics, morality, religion, and science - those things merit consideration only as various forms of lies: with their help one can have faith in life. "Life ought to inspire confidence": the task thus imposed is tremendous. To solve it, man be a liar by nature, he must be above all an artist. And he is one: metaphysics, religion, morality, science - all of them only products of his will to art, to lie, to flight from the "truth", to negation of the "truth". This ability itself, thanks to which he violates reality by means of lies, this artistic of man par excellence - he has in common with everything that is. He himself is after all a piece of reality, truth, nature: how should he not also be a piece of genius in lying!

That the character of existence is to be so misunderstood - profoundest and supreme secret motive behind all that is virtue, science, pity, artistry. Never to see many things, to see many things falsely, to imagine many things: oh how shrewd one still is in circumstances in which one is furthest from thinking oneself shrewd! Love, enthusiasm, "God" - So many subtleties of ultimate self-deception, so many seductions to life, so much faith in life! In those moments in which man was deceived, in which he duped himself, in which he believes in life: oh how enraptured he feels! What delight! What a feeling of power! How much artist's triumph in the feeling of power! - Man has once again become master of "material" master of truth! - And whenever man rejoices, he is always the same in his rejoicing: he rejoices as an artist, he himself as power, he enjoys the lie as his form of power. - 761

S: Up yours! "No disrespect"? Such weasel words; how many times have I heard them? The only difference between you and the rest of the patronizing numbskulls is the number of insults you can smuggle in under your "excuse me, buts"! Hmm, and you are going to tell me you understand women? Go on then, Xanthippe likes a good laugh!

A: Understand that in identifying with each deception, I do so only in so far as it serves ascending life; I reject any deception that serves declining life. O.k.? I'm opposed to that feminist who uses the will to truth to enhance survival or dominate life. Such a woman seeks, like the metaphysician, to lay claim to an objective truth. The true world which is unattainable for the moment, is promised to the sage, to the pious man and to the man of virtue ... Progress of the idea: it becomes more subtle, more insidious, more evasive, - it becomes a woman.762 Woman wishes to becomes independent, and therefore she begins to enlighten men about "woman as she is" - this is one of the worst developments in the general uglifying of Europe. 763

S: What starts out as a means for ascending life turns into its opposite, and becomes the end of a descending life? Is that it?

A: Yes, deceiving oneself in a useful way. The means, the invention of formulas and signs by means of which one could reduce the confusing multiplicity to a purposive and manageable schema. But alas! now a moral category was brought into play: [namely] no creature wants to deceive itself, ... consequently there is only a will to truth ... This is the greatest error that has ever been committed, the essential fatality of error on earth, one believed one possessed a criterion of reality in the forms of reason - while in fact one possessed them in order to become master of reality, in order to misunderstand reality in a shrewd manner. 764

S: No. I still don't get it.

A: Only when the will to truth recognizes itself as an illusion, becomes a will to illusion does it serve an ascending life. Truth does not count as the supreme value ... The will to appearance, to illusion, to deception, to becoming and change [to objectified deception] here counts as more profound, primeval, metaphysics than the will to truth, to reality, to mere appearance; the last is itself merely a form of the will to illusion.765

## CHEWING THE CUD

S: Then it is a mistake to speak of "woman as such"?

A: Hence the scare quotes.

S: Because there's nothing more frightening than women? ...It was a joke.

A: Was it?

S: You tell me," Woman as the expression of the will to illusion"? "They give themselves airs even when 'they give themselves'". "Woman is so artistic". Isn't that what you said? Women's wiles; woman as chameleon; is this where we are at?

A: Yes, but after the inventive genius of the young female artist has run riot for some time in such indiscreet revelations of youth ... then they at last discover, time and again, that they have not been good judges of their own interest; that if they wish to have power over men the game of hide and seek with the beautiful body is more likely to win than naked or half-naked honesty. 766

S: So on the upside, as it were, - the ascendant, to use your terms, we have the woman - as manifestation of the will to illusion - doing what? Posing as a truth-seeker, but never taking herself seriously? A kind of Aristophanes in skirts, then?

A: Ha, ha. Clever people frequently have an aversion to science, as have ... all artists.

S: That's just what I mean. Nothing's sacred. They play fast and loose with everything; anyway, the downside in respect of these shysters?
A: They come to believe that the illusion they have created is the source of their power, and in so doing forget that it was they themselves that created it. Once again, the means - the illusion - is taken for an end.

S: Xanthippe's right about that; there's little that's more grievous than the sight of a woman who refuses to grow old gracefully.

A: Hmm, but I do believe your slip is beginning to show here.

S: "Slip"?

A: Female under-garment.

277

# CHEWING THE CUD

S: I'm a cross-dresser now! Is that your implication?

A: Mother of God! A venial sin - no more!

S: No more what?

A: Just a play on words. Forget it!

S: You ought to be more careful with them.

A: With what or whom? You've lost me.

S: Now you know how I feel - what its like to be me.

A: You?

S: Yes. There's many a slip between cup and labia.

A: Is that a joke?

S: I don't know. Is it, or is it perhaps the illusion of one?

A: You are a poor fool.

S: Is there any other kind?

A: You are mocking what you don't understand. Art is - illusions notwithstanding - the kind of woman it is impossible to live without. If we had not welcomed the arts and invented this kind of cult of the untrue, then the realization of general untruth and mendaciousness that now comes to us through science - the realization that delusion and error are conditions of human knowledge and sensation - would be unbearable. Honesty would lead to nausea and suicide. But now there is a counterforce against our honesty that helps us to avoid such consequences; art as the good will to appearance. ... As an aesthetic phenomenon existence is still bearable for us.767

S: Art - the will to illusion? You ought to be having this conversation with my father. He would have lapped it up. Each new floosy rationalized as yet another "seduction to life". How the old satyr would have loved that.

## CHEWING THE CUD

A: Nothing is elf-sufficient - neither ourselves, nor things. 768

S: And thus priapism is to be excused? You know how the sculpting fraternity used to refer to him: A chisel on a tripod. Revelled in it, when he found out. It became part of his chat-up lines. Charity bids me thank my mother for my own blessing in that regard. As for him, I can only surmise there must have been as many relieved as disappointed by the reality, and that for the latter this was merely a prelude to disappointment of another sort.

A: Must you always see things in moralistic terms? At times we need a rest from ourselves by looking upon, by looking down upon, ourselves and, from an artistic distance, laughing over ourselves or weeping over ourselves. We must discover the hero no less than the fool in our passion for knowledge; we must occasionally find pleasure in our folly, or we cannot continue to find pleasure in our wisdom. Precisely because we are at bottom grave and serious human beings - really more weights than human beings - nothing does us as much good as a fool's cap: we need it in relation to ourselves - we need all exuberant, floating, dancing, mocking, childish, and blissful art less we lose the freedom above things that our ideal demands of us. 769

S: Hmm, you said as much earlier. Metaphorically speaking that sums him up.

A: I hadn't finished. What sums him up?

S: Overheard him talking to a non-artistic friend one day. The friend asked him when he knew that a piece was finished. A reasonable question, I thought. I mean when you watch a painter at work, what makes the last dab the last dab, and something different to the second to last dab? – and, all the more so given that the painting consists of hundreds, nay thousands of such dabs? Anyway the thing was he threw his head back, and roared with laughter. I can still see him now. With a glance at the latest muse, he said, suddenly cold: "When I can walk away from it".

Of course when he did - walk away that is - there would follow weeks, sometimes months of inactivity. Not that he necessarily wanted for commissions. Just couldn't bring him self to "sculpt by rote". The lengths my mother used to go to get his friends to encourage him, when her own efforts invariably failed. "It's not friends I want for - its enemies!" I remember him shouting on one of these occasions.

A: Perhaps he had a point. A new creation needs enemies more than friends: in opposition alone does it feel itself necessary, in opposition alone does it become necessary. 770

It would mean a relapse for us, with our irritable honesty, to get involved entirely in morality and, for the sake of the over-severe demands that we make upon
ourselves in these matters, to become virtuous monsters and scarecrows. We
should be able to stand above morality - and not only to stand with the stiffness of
a man who is afraid of falling any moment, but also to float above it and play. How
then could we possibly dispense with art - and with the fool? 771

S: Just supposing I relent - just supposing, for with my looks whom else can I play
if not the scarecrow - where does that leave us? I feel giddy at the very thought, but
supposing as you say life cannot be justified by science or logic for there is no justification independent of our interpretations?

A: We hide the truth behind a bush and praise ourselves when we find it. 772

S: Huh? Don't play games now. I'm trying things for size .In front of others that's
embarrassing enough. Let me continue. Art, or rather the illusions of art give us
reasons to act, and, yes through art we create meaning rather than discover it as
science purports to do, - but this has what to do with the third aspect of your triad?
Will to power? Is the second here some sort of shield against the third?

A: Exactly. Artistic creation is a manifestation of the will to power as the will to
illusion - a means of temporarily stabilizing what is ultimately a world of endless
becoming. Because we have to be stable in our beliefs if we are to prosper, we have
made the "real" world a world not of change and becoming but one of being. Becoming does not aim at a final state, does not flow into "being". ... Becoming is of
equivalent value every moment; the sum of its values always remains the same; in
other words, it has no value at all, for anything to measure it against, and in relation
to which the word "value" would have meaning, is lacking.773

Do you know what "the world" is to me? ... A monster of energy, without beginning, without end; a firm, iron magnitude of force that does not grow bigger or
smaller, that does not expend itself but only transforms itself; as a whole, of unal-
terable size, a household without expenses or losses, but likewise without increase
or income; enclosed by "nothingness" as by a boundary; not something blurry or
wasted, not ... 774

S: Wait up. Remember my age. If you want me to keep up, you mustn't go racing
off. Smaller steps, if you please? All this talk of being and becoming is horribly

redolent of that "dark philosopher". An apt sobriquet for Heraclitus: so much murk. Never could see why Plato is so unsettled by him. Almost as if he was afraid of being made a fool of. Anyway, this "becoming" of yours that precedes "being"; I take it the former is equivalent to the chaos that underlies all things - this "monster of energy"? Or is it I now getting too far ahead of you?

A: Yes. My view is that becoming does not flow into being.

S: Spare me the technicalities for now. Plato feigns my interest in such. Can't you just say simply how this all bears on the third aspect of truth as will to power?

A: What shall I say? That man is a coward in the face of all that is eternally feminine? 775That those Apollonian masks - are necessary products of a deep look into the horror of nature: luminous spots, as it were, designed to cure an eye hurt by the ghastly night? 776 ...There are, after all, women who, wherever one examines them, have no inside, but are mere masks. 777The enchantment and the most powerful effect of woman is, to use the language of philosophers, an effect at a distance, an actio in distans: there belongs thereto, however, primarily and above all - distance. 778

Or shall I say that the affirming woman is Dionysian: pregnant with the future, a desire for change - both creative and destructive. Be like me, the Original Mother, who, constantly creating, finds satisfaction in the turbulent flux of appearances. 779 It is the constant flux, the ambiguity that unsettles us. Man thinks woman profound - why? Because he can never fathom her depths. Woman is not even shallow. 780

S: Is there no way to close the gap?
A: For seeing the ultimate beauties of a work, no knowledge or good will is sufficient; this requires the rarest of lucky accidents ... I mean to say that the world is overfull of beautiful thins but nevertheless poor, very poor when it comes to beautiful moments and unveilings of these things. But perhaps this is the most powerful magic of life: it is covered by a veil interwoven with gold, a veil of beautiful possibilities, sparkling with promise, resistance, bashfulness, mockery, pity, and seduction. Yes, life is a woman. 781

.... Is that it? Have you nothing to say?

S: Seduced by your words, by your metaphors; it seems I'm not the only one who aspires to be a mid-wife. That said I couldn't help but wonder here if, for all your ministrations, the child hasn't been stillborn. I've yet to meet the child not born of the union of man and woman, which is to say the metaphor you employed doesn't scan. Where your "Original Mother" is concerned this would presuppose that some human form of autogamy would have to be the rule, and hence what we have here is one myth more. Not that I, as Plato's hapless spokes-person, should object to the use of a myth from time to time in lieu of a manually crafted building block. Most edifices show signs of the folly that attended their construction. But that you should be reduced to the same stratagem - well it makes one wonder? To be frank, I find myself unsure as to whether, in the final analysis, there is for you any such thing as either truth or for that matter woman.

You'll forgive my perplexity in this, only everything seems in your philosophy to be seen through a glass darkly. At times it seems to be constructed as a mirror image of all that Plato and myself have attempted. Whereas we strive to show the beauty that lies within and behind what appears ugly, you appear to want to do nothing other than rub our noses in what is nauseating and noxious.

A: But don't you see? The beautiful exists just as little as the good, or the true. In every case it is a question of the conditions of preservation of a certain type of man: thus the herd man will experience the value feeling of the beautiful in the presence of different things than will the exceptional or over- man.

It is the perspective of the foreground, which concerns itself only with immediate consequences, from which the value of the beautiful {also of the good, also of the true} arises. Judgments concerning beauty and ugliness are shortsighted [they are always opposed by the understanding -] but persuasive in the highest degree; they appeal to our instincts where they decide most quickly and pronounce their Yes and No before the understanding can speak. The most habitual affirmations of beauty excite and stimulate each other; once the aesthetic drive is at work, a whole host of other perfections, originating elsewhere, crystallize around "the particular instance of beauty". It is not possible to remain objective, or to suspend the interpretive, additive, interpolating, poetizing power{- the latter is the forging of the chain of affirmations of beauty]. The sight of a beautiful woman" -

The judgment of beauty lavishes upon the object that inspires it a magic conditioned by the association of various beauty judgments - that are quite alien to the nature of that object. To experience a thing as beautiful means: to experience it necessarily wrongly - [which, incidentally, is why marriage for love is, from the point of view of society, the most unreasonable kind of marriage}. 782 What appears simple is without doubt on closer inspection complex.

S: I rest my case. Look! A stream. Being around you, for some reason, makes me quite hot and bothered. Do you mind? Five minutes? My feet are as thirsty as my lips.

A: Anything to cool your ardour.

## CHAPTER 11
### The Dionysian: a first sally for Time's being

A: About what you were saying a moment ago? About opening up new lines of enquiry? Dionysian wisdom is what is required here. The will henceforth to question further, more deeply, severely, harshly, evilly and quietly than one had questioned heretofore. The trust in life has gone: life itself has become a problem. Yet one should not jump to the conclusion that this necessarily makes one gloomy. Even love of life is still possible, one loves differently. It is the love for a woman that causes doubt in us.

The attraction of everything problematic, the delight in an x, however, is so great in such more spiritualized men that this delight flares up again and again like a bright blaze over all the distress of what is problematic, over all the danger of, and even over the jealous lover. We know a new happiness.783

S: That I can agree with, but what has that to do with that Dionysian wisdom of yours?

A: God created man happy, idle, innocent, and immortal - or so the story goes -: our actual life is false decayed, sinful existence, an existence of punishment - Suffering, struggle, work, death are considered objections and question marks against life, as something that ought not to last; for which one requires a cure - and has a cure! - From the time of Adam until now, man has been in an abnormal state. ... The true life is only a faith [i.e., a self-deception, a madness]. The whole of struggling, battling, actual existence, full of splendour and darkness, only a bad, false existence: the task is to be redeemed from it. "Man innocent, idle, immortal, happy" - this conception of "supreme desiderata" must be criticized above all. 784

S: Correct me if I'm wrong. This is the Jewish myth you are alluding to? The one in which mankind is punished for its curiosity, for eating from the "Tree of knowledge". A rum state of affairs, if you ask me?

A: My view, too. The secret for harvesting from existence the greatest fruitfulness and the greatest enjoyment is - to live dangerously! Build your cities on the slopes of Vesuvius! Send your ships into uncharted seas! Live at war with your peers and with yourselves! Be robbers and conquerors as long as you cannot be rulers and possessors you seekers of knowledge! 785

S: Stirring stuff, I sure, but I'm missing something here. You are plainly treating this Dionysian thing as an antithesis, but to what exactly?

A: You are right. I'm getting ahead of myself; after the Jewish thing, out of the Jewish thing, Christianity. Christianity ... is nihilistic in the most profound sense, while in the Dionysian symbol the ultimate limit of affirmation is attained.
 Dionysian versus the "Crucified": there you have the antithesis. It is not a difference in regard to their martyrdom - it is a difference in the meaning of it. Life itself, its eternal fruitfulness and recurrence, creates torment, destruction, the will to annihilation. In the other case, suffering - the "Crucified as the innocent one" counts as an objection to life, as a formula for its condemnation. - One will see that the problem is that of the meaning of suffering: whether a Christian meaning or a tragic meaning. In the former case, it is supposed to be the path to a holy existence; in the latter case, being is counted as holy enough to justify even a monstrous amount of suffering. The tragic man affirms even the harshest suffering: he is sufficiently strong, rich, and capable of deifying to do so. The Christian denies even the happiest lot on earth: he is sufficiently weak, poor, disinherited to suffer from life in whatever form he meets it. The god on the cross is a curse on life, a signpost to seek redemption from life; Dionysus cut to pieces is a promise of life: it will be eternally reborn and return again from destruction. 786
S: This is the Christ who will claim to be the son of the one and only God?

A: Yes.

S: That sounds risible on two counts, or would seem so to most of our contemporaries were they to hear of it. One god. Who'd believe that? As to his permitting his only son to be sacrificed, and in such an ignominious way – no Greek god would do such a thing? That beggars belief. As to the symbolism of his being innocent, that, too, will take some explaining. Even so, once again, I'd urge you to be a little more careful with your blasphemies.

A: Funny you should say that. Reminds me of getting caught short the other day. I had occasion to visit that public urinal Pericles had erected off the agora.

S: I know it well.

A: No jokes about a home from home, please.

# CHEWING THE CUD

S: Certainly not. At my age such places are a blessing. From a perspectival point of view though, you'd have to say the place has more glory holes than a gladiator's net.

A: Deadpan humour? I was going to say there was a piece of graffiti. Gave me quite a turn: Said God to Nietzsche, "I'll teach yer, you horrible creature".

S: I keep telling you not to blaspheme.

A: No, it wasn't that. It was the name: Nietzsche. Somehow I thought I knew him. What is that do you think? German?

S: Could be a member of the Polish aristocracy for all that I know.787 Anyway let's not get sidetracked by reverie. Both gods are suffering gods, but the difference between them is the response to this very suffering that they advocate, right? Forgive me saying, but haven't we already explored this track?

A: Ressentiment. We postponed discussion of it. Let me say by means of a preamble what my formula for greatness is. My formula for greatness in a human being is amor fati: that one wants nothing to be different, not forward, not backward, not in all eternity. Not merely to bear what is necessary, still less to conceal it - all idealism is mendaciousness in the face of what is necessary - but love it. 788
S: Bearing things, concealing things. Resignation, I think I understand. Concealment though?

A: Two forms; idealism, and Omni-satisfaction. The first acknowledges the reality of suffering and seeks to procure an escape: to pass sentence on this whole world of becoming as a deception and to invent a world beyond it, a true world. Suffering as no more than an illusion, you see? But verily, I also do not like those who consider everything good and this world the best. Such men I call the Omni-satisfied. Omni-satisfaction, which knows how to taste everything, that is not the best taste ... Always to bray "Yea-Yuh" - that only the ass has learned, and whoever is of his spirit. 789

S: Really, is the silly voice necessary? To be sure there are such "Hail fellow; well met" types. Always want to accentuate the positive, non-confrontational, never dissatisfied; always have you believe they get what they want, and what they don't get, they didn't want anyway. I've met them by the dozen over the years; you quickly learn that it's all water off the proverbial back where they are concerned.

# CHEWING THE CUD

Not my meat and drink, to be sure. But I still fail to see why we are re-warming the earlier stew.

A: Because ... Ok. I'll let you in on my secret: I am a disciple of the philosopher Dionysus. 790

S: Ha, ha. That's a new one. That'd explain why you're so pissed all of the time.

A: No I'm not, and I'm not saying I'm one of - much less at one with - the crowd at the rites. I'm serious.

S: Serious are you? How many fingers am I displaying?

A: And two to you, too. Seriously, creation is the great redemption from all suffering, and life's growing light. But that the creator may be, suffering is needed. In the teaching of the mysteries, pain is sanctified: the "pains of childbirth" sanctify pain in general - all becoming and growing, all that guarantees the future, postulates pain ... For the eternal joy on creating to exist, for the will to life eternally to affirm itself, the "torment of childbirth" must also exist eternally. 791

S: And the Apollonian? I'd heard that you had given due weight to the principles of form and order.

A: I changed my mind. My "forms" give beauty to the world, but are ultimately transient. Whatever I create and however much I love it - soon I must oppose it and my love: thus my will wills it. 792

S: Now I'm hearing echoes of my father.

A: Ah, yes. There must be much bitter dying in your life, you creators. 793

S: That's not the half of it though is it? This Dionysus of yours: doesn't he rejoice in, sanction even, destruction? I don't think my father would have gone that far. He meant his artefacts to last.

A: You misunderstand me. There's a difference. The desire for destruction, change, and becoming can be an expression of an overflowing energy that is pregnant with future, whilst at the same time affirming the value of that which it seeks to surpass or destroy. It can also be the hatred of the ill-constituted, disinherited, and underprivileged, who destroy, must destroy, because what exists, indeed all existence, all being, outrages and provokes them. Such as these destroy out of spite and vindictiveness. 794

Perhaps your father only got so far in this matter? The real joy attaches not to the thing created, but to the creative struggle itself. Unlike the other gods, he is first and foremost, the tempter god ... from whose touch everyone walks away richer, not having received grace and surprised, not as blessed and oppressed by alien goods, but richer in himself than before, broken open, blown at and sounded out by a thawing wind, perhaps more unsure, tenderer, more fragile, more broken, but full of hopes that have as yet no name, full of new will and currents, full of new dissatisfaction and undertows - ... namely no less a one than the god Dionysus, that great ambiguous one and tempter god. 795 The soul that, having being, dives into becoming; the soul that has, but wants to want and will.

S: This is all very contrary. For most happiness is rest, satiety, - to use a phrase of yours, I believe - "the Sabbath of Sabbaths".

A: What have I to do with happiness? All eternal joy longs for failures. For all joy wants itself, hence it also wants agony.

S: So what are you telling me -: "there's no success like failure, and failure's no success at all"? 796 Sorry, don't know where that came from.

A: I love him who wants to create over and beyond himself and thus perish.

S: Stop. My head's swimming. You'll cut me some slack if I've said this before? If it were Plato who was recording our conversation, he'd be trying to impose some order and structure upon. He spends endless hours re-writing. Most editing he tells me is a mattter of re-writing.

A: Ah, but this is real time. It lacks the polish precisely because we are trying to break new ground, forge new paths. There are no signposts, no boundary markers with which to orientate ourselves out here. There are bound to be false trails, wrong turnings.

S: That's my point. It's all green to me. I feel lost out here. It all looks the same to me. No order or structure. That's why cities have walls. They aren't there just to keep enemies at bay. They serve to keep nature at arms length. If it were within my power, I'd have nature paved over. Drives me to distraction, does Xanthippe. Always bringing some token of nature back from the market - flowers or else something in a pot. Always wanting to bring nature into the house.

Makes me sneeze, and my eyes run.

## CHAPTER 12
### Time's arrow

S: Ah, that's better. Sitting here with my feet in the water always puts me in mind of Heraclitus. You know the one: "one cannot step into the same river twice". 797

A: ..."nor can one grasp any mortal substance in a stable condition, but it scatters and again gathers; it forms and dissolves, and approaches and departs". You have to finish your quotes.

S: Poetic nonsense, if you ask me. As I said earlier Plato accords him such reverenc. It is quite beyond me.

A: Well don't forget the quote's sibling: "As they step into the same rivers, other and still other waters flow upon them". 798

S: Doubly Dutch. "Dutch"? Sorry, my mind gets clogged every now and again.

A: Weren't you there in the "Sophist"? Wasn't that where your master chose - fatefully I might say Parmenides' side over that of Heraclitus in the "battle of giants over being". 799 Calling them "giants" implies he took them - and Heraclitus, in particular - very seriously indeed.

S: Only in spirit; Plato explained it all after the event, as it were. "Literary license" I think he called it. Not that I could say I got the finer points. Not really my forte, you understand. A spade is a spade to me; I'm altogether happier dealing to the punters in the agora.

A: That's because they never notice the marked deck.

S: Very droll I'm sure; try explaining to them that the world is - what was the phrase you used a while back? - "a maelstrom of chaos"? They'd laugh in your face. And who could blame them?

A: But they, the ordinary people do not grasp how by being at variance it [the Logos, cosmos, or natural order] agrees with itself, a backward-turning adjustment like that of the bow or lyre". 800

# CHEWING THE CUD

S: "Doh"! You can only learn so much watching children play.801

A: How does Parmenides' prayer run? "Grant me, you gods, but one certainty even if it be but a log's breadth on which to lie, on which to ride upon the sea of uncertainty. Take away everything that becomes, everything lush, colourful, blossoming, deceptive, everything that charms and is alive. Take all these for yourselves and grant me but the one and only, poor empty certainty". 802

S: And upbraid me for impression?

A: But you've yet to hear the upshot of his solicitations.

S: And this was?

A: Experience nowhere offered him being as he imagined it, but he concluded its existence from the fact that he was able to think it.

S: Such a clever bastard, aren't you? And that was purely rhetorical.

A: Well and good then, since if I wasn't clever I should....

S: Oh, why don't you shut up, and answer me this,...

A: But if I shut up, then.

S: Zeus! "That which truly is must be eternally present; one cannot say of it that 'it was', or 'it will be'. What has being cannot become. [...] It is the same with passing away. Passing away is just as impossible as becoming, as is all change, all decrease, all increase. In fact the only valid proposition that can be stated is "Everything of which you can say 'it has been' or 'it will be" is not; of what has being you can never say 'it is not'". 803

A: For saying you didn't take much of an interest, you are surprisingly au faire with his thoughts.

S: Once words have been attributed to you, you begin to look a right fool if it becomes apparent that you have no understanding of them. In all probability I've read more of Plato's dialogues than you.

# CHEWING THE CUD

A: Now that's an image to conjure with! Ha, ha. I like it - Socrates swotting up on his doppelganger!

S: It's what happens when you write books for everyone, but then you've had no experience of this.

A: Oh, the real thing has claws! Personally, I've found if you try to write for everyone, you end up writing for no one. I hope that by writing for me I'll end up writing for everyone, not that I'd be comfortable if everyone thought they had understood me.

S: Well, you can rest easy on that score! Your perversity will see to that.

A: Perversity?

S: Well aren't you itching to tell me that Heraclitus had it right, whilst the rest of the world had it wrong?

A: If you mean that insofar as the senses show becoming, passing away, and change, they do not lie at all? - yes. 804Contrary to your master's claim that "that which is conceived by opinion with the help of sensation and without reason is always in the process of becoming and perishing and never really is", I take the side of Heraclitus and argue there is but nature, life, becoming and appearance and that any other kind of reality is absolutely indemonstrable.805

S: Oh, there's no need to be modest! Don't leave it there. You are no earthy empiricist seeking to dig up facts along with your turnips.

A: True. Whilst I'm partial to "the things of which there is seeing and hearing and perception - turnips among them - the eyes and ears are evil witnesses ... for men have souls that do not understand their language. 806 Put baldly, perception is already interpretation; "Pigs like mud, but men do not", and all that. 807 There is no one "true" description of the world but many. Everything is in continuous motion and change"; "the harmony of opposites"; - both "only different ways of explaining the same truth", don't you see? 808

S: I see only incompatible sentiments.

A: No what we are looking at here is self-change and aspect change. Self-change describes transformation over time; the usual sense of becoming. Whilst this describes the alteration of a particular object, aspect change refers to changes of viewpoint in its observation - variation in appearance. What they have in common is the rejection of being in its various forms.

S: But does not Plato, following Parmenides, teach that becoming and appearance are forms of alteriety?

A: Exactly. Parmenides arrived at his concept of Being by rejecting both becoming and appearance. The rest is history as they say - a history people will be struggling to free themselves from well beyond my time. The idea, that is, that the natural world is a derivative world of mere becoming, of appearance, in comparison to a metaphysical world characterized by true being.

It goes deeper still - this metaphysical tradition that you and yours are initiating. True being anchors origin, essence, substance, and also aim for the rest of existence. For what do Plato's "Forms" serve, if not as templates for empirical entities? as absolute standards of the true and the false in respect of people and their places? - All to be hierarchically assayed in relation to this yardstick of true being.

And not forgetting the Christian god; He, after all, is taken to be synonymous with "Being" itself: at one and the same time creator, essence, substance and providential overseer. The guarantor of all knowledge for Descartes; the assurance that this is the best of all possible worlds for Leibniz; the sole substance for Spinoza; the ground of all experience for Kant - it is a sorry catalogue. 809

S: Mere names to me, I afraid.

A: Heraclitus will remain eternally right with is assertion that being is an empty fiction. The "apparent" world is the only one: the "true" world is only added by a lie.

S: Yes, yes; but what does all this mean in terms of your view about the ultimate state of the world? This Kant - you've mentioned him before. Wasn't he the one who divided the world into a noumenal and a phenomenal world? The one who argued that we have knowledge only of the phenomenal and on this basis we have our science?

A: So what?

S: If I remember aright you described this earlier as a ploy by which Kant was able to reintroduce God, freedom, and immortality by the backdoor having made room for faith which though it lies beyond the scope of knowledge, remains accessible to Reason?

A: Must you always take the long way round the houses? Your point is?
S: Don't be so impatient. You've already lived before, or so you claim. If I'm to believe that kind of cant you have a duty to let me get a line on the other Kant. Its difficult enough not to get my consonants jumbled up, let alone the vowels. Anyway my point is that you deny all this side of his thought in the name of a more thorough going scepticism.

A: To be sure. Truths are illusions we have forgotten are illusions. Truth is the kind of error without which a certain species of life could not live.810

S: There! In your own words!

A: Despair of truth .... attends every thinker that sets out from the Kantian philosophy. 811 Indeed since Copernicus, man seems to have got himself on an inclined plane - now he is slipping away from the centre into - what? into nothingness? into a "penetrating sense of his nothingness"? 812

S: Copernicus?

A: A stargazer who found that the cosmos is heliocentric, not geocentric - our Earth being only the third rock from the sun.

S: That can't be true. What does [did?] this Kant think?

A: That Copernicus couldn't be gainsaid. Hence why he compared us to islands. Beyond our islands, we see only "a blind, empty, structure-less, "thereness" ... tossing blackly like the sea, chaotic relative to our distinctions and perhaps to all distinctions, but there nonetheless". 813Where are you going with this?

S: It is obvious isn't it? This is your view. Different words, maybe; but the world in itself, a world lacking definition and structure, a "chaos", a "will to power", a world of becoming?

A: Shall I help you out? A world of becoming could not, in the strict sense, be "comprehended" or "known"; only to the extent that the "comprehending" and "knowing" intellect encounters a coarse already-created world, built out of nothing but appearances but become firm to the extent that this kind of appearance has preserved life - only to this extent is there anything like "knowledge". 814 And from this you want to saddle me with what? You are clearly working yourself up to something. Oh, I get it. I'm just Kant with knobs on? Like Kant, like Plato before him, I have my own ultimate noumenal reality - the world of becoming - only I deem it a "false" world rather than a "true" world because I assert that it is a "self-contradictory world of becoming and change"?

S: Well in this light you make a better door than you do a window.

A: If anyone is being wooden here, it is you my friend. You constantly forget the anti-dualism that lies at the heart of my thinking. Do I have to go on repeating my self? Any distinction between a "true" and an "apparent" world - whether in the Christian manner or in the manner of Kant [in the end an underhand Christian] - is only a suggestion of decadence, a symptom of the decline of life. Have I not said it plainly? The true world - we have abolished. What world remained? The apparent one, perhaps? But no! With the true world we have also abolished the apparent one.815 Do you see? The antithesis of the apparent world and the true world is re- duced to the antithesis "World" and "nothing" 816 Translated into Kantian lingo: The antithesis "thing in itself" and "appearance" is untenable: with that, however, the concept "appearance" also disappears. 817

S: All right, all right! I hear the italics. Don't hector me.

A: Right. Just to be sure? Becoming is the most ordinary phenomenon; it lies in front of everyone's nose. 818

S: If you say so.

A: Say so. Haven't I just argued any other kind of realty is indemonstrable? 819 That whereas for Plato an you some sort of absolute reality is sought in timeless mental entities that remain always constant and invariable never admitting of any alteration in any respect or in any sense, for Heraclitus and me these mental entities are in fact derived from - the world of nature, experience, and becoming? 820

S: There is to speak "no world in itself"?

A: No. There are only perspectives, interpretations as I said earlier. The world as we know it is a world of relations. It becomes not just in the sense of being natural, but also of being subject to incessant change. It has a differing aspect from every point and therefore its being is essentially different from every point. 821 Whilst

Heraclitus' imagination saw this restless motion of the universe, this "reality", with the eyes of a blissful spectator who is watching innumerable pairs of contestants wrestling in joyous combat and refereed by stern judges, he was overcome by an even greater idea: he could no longer see the contesting pairs and their referees as separate; the judges themselves seemed to be striving in the contest and the contestants seemed to be judging them. 822

S: The allusion to my wide-boy I catch, but not the inference?

A: Once again, not chaos as some primary plenum, but rather the site of forces in struggle, the discordant concord of things. 823Not some pre-cosmic ragman's gleanings, but a brand new world of change and difference; not "Chaos or Nature", for Nature de-deified is "chaos". 824

The total character of the world.... is - in all eternity chaos - in the sense not of a lack of necessity but a lack of order, arrangement, [etc.]. Let us beware of saying there are laws in nature. There are only necessities: there is nobody who commands, nobody who obeys, no one who trespasses. 825

Do you see? Becoming must be explained without recourse to final intentions; becoming must appear justified at every moment [or incapable of being evaluated; which amounts to the same thing]. [...] "Necessity" not in the shape of an overreaching, dominating total force, or of that prime mover; even less as a necessary for something valuable. To this end, it is necessary a total consciousness of becoming, a "God". [...] Fortunately such a summarizing power is missing [ - a suffering and all-seeing God, a "total sensorium" and "cosmic spirit" would be the greatest objection to being]. More strictly one must admit nothing that has being - because then becoming would lose its value and actually appear meaningless and superfluous. [...] Becoming is of equivalent value every moment; the sum of its values always remains the same; in other words, it has no value at all, for anything against which to measure it and in relation to which the word "value" could have any meaning is lacking. The total value of the world cannot be evaluated. 826

S: Wait a minute. I'm beginning to think that unwittingly I've been resting on my laurels in more than the one way.

A: How do you mean?

S: Well I been sitting here dangling my legs in this Heraclitean stream and you haven't looked once, not even a covert glance.

# CHEWING THE CUD

A: You aren't going to start that again? I thought we had tacitly agreed to be serious?

S: Oh, this is serious. There comes a moment in a man's life where he drops off of the erotic map. He becomes invisible. All too frequently, he's the last to know; hence why he's prone to make a fool of himself. In this uncharted territory the undulating contours that served to orientate the desires of others lose their cachet, and his mien, his gait, herald the proliferation of so many sorry symbols of his decline to be read at a glance. It's a bad business. Think about it all too long and you can start to feel suicidal.

A: Look into the abyss and the abyss looks back? 827

S: I guess, but as much - and you'll appreciate this, though it pains me to admit it - the abiding thought that is that I'm no longer able to incite another man's fear, I must live by his indulgence. To become prey for the weak, and is the weak – it was always so with the strong -; its an unsettling thought. Who knows what calamities it will invite?

A: At the very least, you can claim to have made your mark.

S: Hmm, I might turn out to be just the mark; the marks I suspect will, in the end, be Plato's. Anyway, - let's forget this concern with laurels. I was thinking I'd got the hang of your claims in respect of "becoming" and "appearance", and "chaos" too, but then you bring the idea of "necessity" into play. You'll have to put some flesh on these old bones.

A: Ha, ha. I don't think that quite came out as you wanted it to, my friend.

S: I'm not so senile as to be unable to spot being patronized!

A: You're not.

S: What's so funny then?

A: Nothing.

S: You laugh at nothing. Are you sure you are quite right in the head?

A: Can a philosopher be such?

# CHEWING THE CUD

S: Search me; I'm a philosopher.

A: Ha, ha. Can we get on?

S: I'm not sure you are a philosopher, though.

A: Now the joke is wearing thin.

S: You could always try to eat more.

A: Necessity?

S: Ask your mother.

A: Enough, really! "Necessity".

S: Have you got your chisel to hand?

A: Chisel? Why do I need a chisel?

S: Because you seem to fashion your concepts to your specifications as we go along.

A: You've noticed?

S: Of course. Nothing wrong with that if you intend to build in a particular way, as long as you are consistent that is. Have you noticed that about us philosophers? We build our house out of the rubble of our predecessor's houses - houses we begin by inhabiting, and then demolish. But, and here's the remarkable thing, to the uninitiated the overall form is clearly different, but the conceptual bricks and mortar are the same. Look more closely and you find the architect has subtly re-fashioned many of these. And if you say I'm a chip off of the old block, I'll knock your block off.

A: It's always the scaffolding that gives your jokes away, you know?

S: Labour intensive, that's me I'm afraid. Xanthippe's always telling me she hasn't the time for my jokes. Anyway, you are withering on. "Necessity" in your book; not be confused with "determinism" judging by what you said earlier in the day?

# CHEWING THE CUD

A: Ha, ha. Mercurial, or what?

S: "And yet new waters flow". See? I need a cool head for your chatter, and my mercury has now fallen. I can say that, can't I? It's just that, what with my daemon and all that, I sometimes end up wondering if I have already forgotten more than you'll ever know even if, as you say, you'll live posthumously. Which reminds me. How come if you know so much about the future, you know nothing about what is about to happen?

A: I just don't. It's a blank. I just have to suck it and see, and, like you, live every momentous moment.

S: That's a very peculiar kind of conceit.

A: No more than your worrying, from time to time, whether you might be a figment of Plato's imagining.

S: Perhaps you are too? Could we be trapped in the same dialogue?

A: No, I don't think so. I'm not the kind of stooge he would put you up against.

S: True. It would be more business-like anyway. He wouldn't allow you to witter on about all sorts of personal stuff. It'd be a proper philosophical exchange. Still, that does not rule out the possibility that we are trapped in someone else's dialogue. Some nondescript nincompoop who is trying to cash in on our good name? Does it feel like you that he's writing about?

A: Who knows? It certainly feels like you, but then while you seem real enough to me, the Socrates I'm talking to seems very different to the one encountered on Plato's pages or for that matter those of Aristophanes.

S: He'd make mock of his own mother for a laugh. Still, I could run my hand through that mane of yours; if you want proof ... On the other that look of repugnance will stand surety instead.

A: As for me old man, I could bounce that rock off of your head? But what would that prove if this is indeed a fiction?

S: That my skull is nowhere near as thick as my hide?

# CHEWING THE CUD

A: You are missing the point. For the idealist there is no real world – therefore,...

S: That rock you are thinking about bouncing off my head seems real enough, heavy enough to do some damage.

A: Que idealist though I don't deny the existence of rocks. What I deny is that there are objects that exist independently of minds. "Idealist", - idea-ist. Get it? All that exists is minds and their ideas. There are not first rocks and then sense experiences of rocks that "copy" or resemble rocks, there is only the one thing, sense-experience.

S: That's just silly. It is sometimes muttered that Plato is one of these Idealists, on account of his "Forms" and all that, but even he wouldn't go so far as to claim ... I mean. Come on ... if we speak of rocks aren't we implying there are rocks to have experience of?

A: Our grammar misleads us perhaps? We have no way of describing the contents of our sense-experience other than by referring to the name of the physical object we believe this the experience to be of. But that doesn't mean the physical world exists. For the sake of clarity it would probably be better to talk of rock-experiences than experiences of a rock. That is all there is, rocks and other physical- -object words are but names for recurring patterns of sense-experiences and nothing else.

S: Is this where I say: you're off your rocker?

A: Berkeley would say, "If by 'physical objects' you mean things existing outside of us and causing our sense-experiences, I insist that they do not exist, nor could we know that they existed even if they did. But if by 'physical objects' you mean groups or complexes of sense-experiences, then they undoubtedly do exist - indeed, we are aware of them every waking moment of our lives, since we are constantly having sense-experiences that fall into ordered patterns or groups". 828

S: And this "Burke"? How did {does?] he differentiate between hallucinations - or, better still since you suspect we might be the inhabitants of someone else's confabulation - dreams and waking life?

A: Couldn't you resist, for a first time, mocking what you don't understand? Talk of bouncing rocks off peoples' heads is quite apt. There's quite a lot of difference between a real rock and an imaginary one, the heft of it for a start.

298

# CHEWING THE CUD

S: Do you mind putting that down? I find it difficult to think.

A: As I was saying? In respect of hallucination the rock would feel "real" because it would be part of a family of sense- experiences in a way an hallucination would not. As it happens, for Berkeley touch figured as perhaps the most important criterion in verifying the existence of "real objects". He had a point. One might have the visual sense-experiences to go with the thought that this is a rock, but you could be mistaken. What more often than not confirms your belief - in this case the existence of a rock - is the touch experience. Shall I demonstrate the truth of the argument by bouncing the rock off your head?

S: No, my head aches already from listening to you. Tell me instead about dreams. I've a mind to try and wake up from this one; it seems to be turning bad. I feel like I'm caught up in some strange loop. Didn't I hear tell that that warrior-poet, Shake Spear, thought that we were merely the stuff of dreams – our little lives rounded with a sleep?

A: When we first wake from a vivid dream we might momentarily be confused, not knowing what is dream and what actuality. The deciding factor is the mass and integration, to use a military metaphor, of the household troops. The familiar disposition of the furniture, the serried sounds of the morning hub-bub, of breakfast being cooked, and the like. Faced with the phalanx of our serried normalcy, lacking any fixed place in it, the figures of our dreams dissolve for want of support. Indeed, it could be claimed that the power to measure such fantasies against the ordered mass of experience is the definition of sanity, its disappearance to constitute insanity.

S: Speaking from an individual perspective, perhaps. Haven't you yourself said something to the effect that madness in respect of individuals is rare; among groups, tribes, and societies all too frighteningly common?

A: I did didn't I? Some more thought is required. It'll have to wait. We have digressed again. Where were we? Oh, yes! I was going to say. As for me, I guess when you subtract the common or garden biographical details that everyman and his dog foist on you in the belief that this makes you predictable, biddable, knowable, there are as many Alcibiades's as people who claim to know him. That said some will obviously be more right about him than others; some might even contend they are more right him than he is about himself. But there's the rub; at some point we all lose the right of reply.

# CHEWING THE CUD

S: Hmm, perhaps I ought to give Plato a good talking to whilst I can. Times marching on; time we did the same. Help me up. I've not forgotten. You can reprise the determinism stuff as we go.

A: Have I said, for me the total character of the world ... is in all eternity chaos - in the sense not of a lack of necessity but a lack of order, arrangement, form, beauty, wisdom, and whatever other names there are for our aesthetic anthropomorphisms?

S: I don't recall, but I'll put a mark against it.

A: Well, let us beware of saying that there are laws in nature. There are only necessities: there is nobody who commands, nobody who obeys, nobody who trespasses. 829 Do you see? One is necessary, one is a piece of fatefulness, one belongs to the whole; there is nothing which could judge, measure, compare, or sentence our being, for that would mean judging, comparing, sentencing the whole. But there is nothing besides the whole! 830

Think about it. If becoming could resolve itself into being or nothingness ... then [given infinite time] this state must have been reached. But it has not been reached: from which it follows [that it cannot and will not be reached]. 831

Look at it like this. I seek a conception of the world that takes this fact into account. Becoming must be explained without recourse to final intentions; becoming must appear justified at every moment [or incapable of being evaluated; which amounts to the same thing]. ... "Necessity" not in the shape of an overreaching, dominating total force, or of that prime mover; even less as a necessary condition for something valuable. To this end, it is necessary to deny a total consciousness to becoming, a "God". ...Fortunately such a summarizing power is missing [- a suffering and all-seeing God, a "total sensorium" and "cosmic spirit" would be the greatest objection to being]. More strictly one must admit nothing that has being - because then becoming would lose its value and actually appear meaningless and superfluous. ... Becoming is of equivalent value every moment; the sum of its values always remains the same; in other words, it has no value at all, for anything against which to measure it and in relation to which the word "value" could have any meaning, is lacking. The total value of the world cannot be evaluated. 832

S: That was a lot to swallow. Let's see if I've the gist of it? "Necessity" is one more concept to be stood alongside of "becoming" and "chaos"? Further this "necessity" of yours is to stand in lieu of any talk about divine intentions or purposes, and even the idea of human freedom of the will? This is a version of the determinism that Demosthenes preaches?

A: I'll take that as shorthand for Democritus?

# CHEWING THE CUD

S: Yes, one should certainly be of good cheer.

A: Ha, ha.833

S: At least you have forgotten about the rock. You had me worried for a minute. Accidents can easily happen.

A: There are no accidents.

S: No accidents?

A: The idea of accidents only makes sense in the context of some wider plan or order.

S: That's a strange thing about belief in freedom of the will, don't you think? If you are a determinist then the belief in freedom of the will must be determined, yet the determinist tell us that there is no such thing as ...

A: I rebut that great captious web of causality in back of which lies God as some alleged spider of purpose, and the a-theological versions of the same determinist doctrine. They would all subjugate becoming to being. Such a demand for certainty betrays a willed ignorance for the whole marvellous uncertainty and interpretive multiplicity of existence. 834
   The gods are dice-players and the earth is their table. Those iron hands of necessity which shake the dice-box of chance play their game for an infinite length of time, and we, ourselves, shake the dice-box with iron hands, ... we ourselves in our most intentional actions do no more than play the game of necessity. 835

S: Are you not dicing with meaning here? Most people understand "Chance" and "Necessity" as contraries; your chance and necessity appear to be unopposed.

A: Isn't the throw of the dice an act of freedom, but one that cannot determine the result - that is for necessity to decide? Everything, ourselves included, are combinations turned up in this game of chance.

S: But the regularities of the heavens and the earth surely speak against the operation of pure chance?

A: Indeed, but nor does it operate according to necessity whether immanent or transcendent. Both are indemonstrable. As for induction, at best it provides only probabilities.

S: Hmm, judgment will be witheld. You speak scathingly of metaphysics yet what you claim smacks suspiciously of the same.

A: But what is "appearance" to me now? Certainly not the opposite of some essence: what could I say about any essence except to name the attributes of its appearance! Certainly not a dead mask that one could place on an unknown x or removed from it! 836 Ah, the world viewed from the inside, the world defined and determined according to its "intelligible character" - it would be "will to power" and nothing besides. 837

S: Are you taunting me or simply casting a lure? No, don't bother answering that. I've been meaning to get chapter and verse about this notion from you for some time. Its run like a leitmotiv through so much of what you've said. Now is a good a time as any. Let's begin with your very last claim here: "a world viewed from the inside".

A: Precisely, a metaphysical theory claims to view the world from outside. Have I not vehemently denied the possibility of such? God is dead! The problem is that his shadow lives on; lives on in the shape of those other unquestioned parts of the litany; subjects, objects, knower and known, being, or epistemology, our ontology. Have I laboured in vain? Will to power as an explanatory principle instead, in place of the prevailing dualisms?

S: As some kind of empirical theory, then?

A: Yes – sort of. When I think of my philosophical genealogy, I feel myself connected with ... the mechanistic movement [reduction of all moral and aesthetic questions to physiological ones, of all physiological ones to chemical, of all chemical ones to mechanical ones]. 838 We no longer derive man from "the spirit" or "the deity"; we have placed him back among the animals. ... As regards the animals, Descartes was the first to have dared, with admirable boldness, to understand the animal as a machine: the whole of our physiology endeavours to prove this claim. And we are consistent enough not to except man, as Descartes still did: our knowledge of man today goes just as far as we understand him mechanistically.839

S: What is this false modesty. You've already intimated that you don't draw a line here. Did you not take issue with Democritus and his atoms?

# CHEWING THE CUD

A: As if I would be the one to hide my light beneath a bushel. Bite-sized portions, you said? As for materialistic atomism, what is that but a futile search for a last thing on earth to stand firm? The belief in "substance", in "matter", in the earth-residuum and particle atom: it was the greatest triumph over the senses hitherto achieved on earth. One must, however, go still further and also declare war ... on the "atomistic need" which, like that more famous "metaphysical need", still goes on living a dangerous after-life in regions where no one suspects it - one must also first of all finish off that other and more fateful atomism which Christianity has taught best and longest, the soul atomism. 840

All this rooted in the privileging of being, all this mirrored by the structure of our language. Everywhere language sees a doer and a doing; it believes in will as the cause; it believes in the "ego", in the ego as being, in the ego as substance, and it projects this faith in the ego-substance upon all things - only thereby does it first create the concept of "thing". Everywhere "being" is projected by thought, pushed underneath, as the cause; the concept of "being" follows, and is derivative of, the concept of "ego". In the beginning there is that great calamity of error that the will is something that is effective, that will is a capacity. Today we know that it is only a word.... I am afraid we are not rid of God because we still have faith in grammar. 841

S: Hence - how did it go? - "There is no such substratum: there is no "being" behind doing, effecting, becoming: "the doer" is merely a fiction added to the deed - the deed is everything"?

A: You've got it. You're a faster learner.

S: When did I say that I believed it? Just doing what I can to explicate the argument.

A: The point is: if we eliminate these additions, no things remain over but only dynamic quanta, in a relation of tension to all other dynamic quanta: their essence lies in their relation to all other quanta, in their "effect" upon the same.

S: And your will to power? It inheres in these individual entities?

A: There are no individual entities; there is no will to power as a capacity. There is no will: there are only treaty drafts of will that are constantly increasing or losing their power.842

My idea is that every specific body strives to become master over all space and to extend its force [- its will to power:] and to thrust back all that resists its extension. But it continually encounters similar efforts from other bodies and ends by coming to an arrangement ["union"] with those of them that are sufficiently related to it: thus they then conspire together for power. And the process goes on - .843

S: This is reminiscent of Heraclitus again: the world as war and strive?

A: Quite so. In place of atomic unities, if you will? - a holistic ontology of more or less stable power-complexes that exist in complex skeins of tension with those of their neighbours. Moreover the struggle is every bit as internal as external. Each power-complex struggles to retain its integrity, its control over its component parts to prevent their revolt or secession.

S: From the military school of life, again?

A: If I might soldier on? As I said earlier, I think, the body and physiology the starting point: why? - We gain the correct idea of the nature of our subject-unity, namely as regents at the head of a communality [not as "souls" or "life-forces"], also of the dependence of these regents upon the ruled and an order of rank and division of labour as the conditions that make possible the whole and its parts. In the same way, how living unities continually arise and die and how the "subject" is not eternal: in the same way, that the struggle expresses itself in obeying and commanding, and that a fluctuating assessment of the limits of power is part of life. The relative ignorance in which the regent is kept concerning individual activities and even disturbances within the communality is among the conditions under which rule can be exercised. In short, we also gain a valuation of not-knowing, of seeing things on a broad scale, of simplification and falsification, of perspectivity. The most important thing, however, is: that we understand that the ruler and his subjects are of the same kind, all feeling, willing, thinking - and that, wherever we see or divine a movement in the body, we learn to conclude that there is a subjective, invisible life appertaining to it. Movement is symbolism for the eye; it indicates that something has been felt, willed, thought.

The danger of the direct questioning of the subject about the subject and all self-reflection of the spirit lies is this, that it could be useful and important for one's activity to interpret oneself falsely. That is why we question the body and reject the evidence of the sharpened senses: we try, if you like, to see whether the inferior parts themselves cannot enter into communication with us.844

Socrates! Where are you?

# CHEWING THE CUD

S: Don't worry. I'm here again. A fleeting visit from my daemon; couldn't make any sense of it. She was talking about billiard- balls - whatever they are? Sorry. Can't see what that has to do with the price of bread.

A: That's the price you pay for being a doughboy.

S: Another endearment? Is that how you think of me - your little dumpling?

A: I should have known better.

S: Why? It's surely better out than in?

A: Than have attempted a joke.

S: It's a bit on the soppy side, I'll admit. But then you often find those with the hardest exteriors often have the softest of centres.

A: Zeus! Do you never give up?

S: "Onward, Christian soldiers", I say - though I don't know why. I wouldn't know one of them from a billiard-ball!

A: Billiard-ball model of causation. Two successive states, the one "cause", the other "effect": this is false. ... It is a question of a struggle between two elements of unequal power: a new arrangement of forces is achieved according to the measure of power of each of them. The second condition is something fundamentally different from the first [not its effect]: the essential thing is that the factions in struggle emerge with different quanta of power. 845
  I'll go further. It's not just a matter of qualitative alteration of enduring "substances", but the constant production of new entities. There are no durable ultimate units, no atoms, no monads: here, too, "beings" are only introduced by us ..."Forms of domination"; the sphere of that which is dominated continually growing or periodically increasing and decreasing according to the favourability or unfavourability of circumstances. ... "Value" is essentially the standpoint for the increase or decrease of these dominating centres ["multiplicities" in any case; but "units" are nowhere present in the nature of becoming] - a quantum of power, a becoming, in so far as none of it has the character of "being". 846

S: So "becoming" is what? - The outcome of this volatile mix of forces and powers.

## CHEWING THE CUD

A: Right in one.

S: Let's suppose, for a moment that I grant you that your argument against "Being" has some weight. May the gods preserve me for thinking so. And let's further suppose that without the notion of "being" we have to abandon the notion of an "origin" and "a divine creation", and thus we are as you put it left with the task of reading ourselves back into nature. Who's to say we shouldn't draw consolation from our position as the pinnacle of all this. Some might say vis-a-vis other cities, other nations, that we Greeks constitute the very acme of progress and civilized living?

A: No, no, no. You can't get away with such onto-theological nonsense.

S: "Onto-theological"? Is that a neologism or are you making this up as we go along?

A: Don't you see? You no sooner accept that I have a case than...

S: Might have a case?

A: O.k. - might have a case against back-loading the whole shebang, than you start front-loading the whole thing.

S: "Front-loading"?

A: Formerly, one sought the feeling of grandeur of man by pointing to his divine origin: this has now become a forbidden way, for at its portal stands the ape, together with other gruesome beasts, grinning knowingly as if to say: no further in this direction! One therefore now tries the opposite direction: the way mankind is going shall serve as proof of his grandeur and kinship with God. Alas this, too, is in vain! ... However high mankind may have evolved - and perhaps at the end it will stand lower than at the beginning! - it cannot pass over into an higher order, as little as the ant and earwig can at the end of its "earthly course" rise up to kinship with God and eternal life. 847

S: Why shouldn't man's adaptability count as progress?

A: We have become more modest in every way. We no longer derive man from "the spirit" or "the deity"; we have placed him back among the animals. We consider him the strongest animal because he is the most cunning: his intellectuality is a consequence of this. On the other hand, we oppose the vanity that would raise its head again here too - as if man had been the great hidden purpose of the evolution of the animals. Man is by no means the crown of creation: every living being stands beside him on the same level of perfection ... And even this is saying too much: relatively speaking, man is the most bungled of all the animals, the sickliest, the one who has strayed the most dangerously from its instincts. 848

S: But he is surely a success in so far as he is best evolved, best fitted for the environment in which he finds himself?

A: At risk of repeating myself, the cause of the origin of a thing and Its eventual utility, its actual employment and place in a system of purposes, lie worlds apart; whatever exists, having somehow come into being, is again and again reinterpreted to new ends, taken over, transformed, and redirected by some power superior to it; all events in the organic world are a subduing, becoming master, and all subduing and becoming master involves a fresh interpretation, an adjustment through which any previous "meaning" and "purpose" are necessarily obscured or even obliterated. However well one has understood the utility of a physiological organ ... this means nothing regarding its origin: however uncomfortable and disagreeable this may sound to older ears - for one had always believed that to understand the demonstrable purpose, the utility of a thing, a form, or an institution, was also to understand the reason why it originated - the eye being made for seeing, the hand made for grasping. ... Purposes and utilities are only signs that a will to power has become master of something less powerful and imposed upon it the character of a function; and the entire history of a "thing", an organ, a custom can in this way be a continuous sign-chain of ever new interpretation and adaptations whose cause do not even have to be related to one another but, on the contrary, in some cases succeed and alternate with one another in purely chance fashion. The "evolution" of a thing, a custom, an organ is thus by no means its progressus towards a goal, even less a logical progressus by the shortest route and with the smallest expenditure of force - but the succession of more of less profound, more or less mutually independent processes of subduing, plus the resistances they encounter, the attempts at transformation for the purpose of defence and reaction, and the results of successful counteractions.849

S: You make it sound as if it were a version of your dice game. Worst still, that it is all in vain.

A: True, mankind does not represent a development towards something better or stronger or higher in the sense accepted today. "Progress" is merely a modern idea, that is, a false idea. ... Further development is altogether not according to any necessity in the direction of elevation, enhancement, or strength. In another sense, success in individual cases is constantly encountered in the most widely different places and cultures: here we really do find a higher type, which is, in relation to mankind as a whole, a kind of Overman. Such lucky strokes of great success have always been possible and will perhaps always be possible. 850

S: But then, surely on your argument nature is indifferent to our values.

A: Quite so. All I'm saying is that greatness ought not to depend on success; the goal of humanity cannot lie in the end of history, but only in the highest exemplars. 851 The criteria that govern our values are not given by the nature of things, they are rather to be created and defended. The brief spell of beauty, genius, is sui generis : such things are not inherited. 852

S: Let me take you back a couple of steps. "Purposes and utilities are only signs that a will to power has become master of something less powerful, and imposed upon it the character of a function", I think you said? Two questions. First, this whole idea of reading us back into nature, treating us as pieces of nature ... - well since the story is told in terms of adaptation to a changing environment doesn't that suggest the animal's first priority is self- preservation? Second, if that is so, it is surely at odds with all the talk of some things mastering other things? That, in its turn, suggests that something other than the blind forces of nature is at play here?

A: Three things, then?

S: Three?

A: You said two questions.

S: Oh get on with it, will you!

A: Just to remind you that I'm paying as close an attention to you as I hope you are to me. In answer to your first point; physiologists should think before putting down the instinct of self-preservation as the cardinal instinct of an organic being. A living thing seeks above all to discharge its strength - life itself is will to power; self-preservation is only one of the indirect and most frequent   results. In short, here as everywhere else, let us beware of superfluous teleological principles! - one of which is the instinct of self-preservation. 853

S: At last, we have flushed our quarry out into the open - the will to power I mean.

A: Well let's see if it's going to bite you? Let me add to the above a codicil of sorts. The wish to preserve oneself is a symptom of distress, of a limitation of the really fundamental instinct of life that aims at the expansion of power and wishing for that, frequently risks and even sacrifices self-preservation. ... Our modern natural sciences have become so thoroughly entangled in this dogma concerning the instinct of self-preservation. ... But in nature it is not conditions of distress that are dominant but overflow and squandering, even to the point of absurdity. The struggle for existence is only an exception, a temporary restriction of the life-will. The great and small struggle always revolves around superiority, around growth and expansion, around power - in accordance with the will to power which is the will of life.854

S: Are you not guilty of a certain amount of equivocation here? Previously you have spoken of this "will to power" as if it is something to be acquired, but in what you have just said it is coupled with a rather different coterie of metaphors. You speak of it as a form of expenditure - discharge, sacrifice, squandering, and the like. You know what I'm going to say, don't you?

A: Well say it anyway! Having come this far, I'd not want to deprive you of your moment of glory - however short-lived.

S: Am I that transparent?

A: Positively salivating, I'd say. Well? Go on then.

S: Well having poured scorn on self-preservation as a covert teleological principle, as a superfluous, teleological principle, haven't you smuggled in one of your own making - the desire for power?

A: That's it? That's your best shot? You've been stalking me all day for that?

S: Well not just that. I had hoped other game might be afoot, but I guess you have to learn to take disappointment in your stride. Anyway, if the first shot doesn't prove fatal, perhaps a second will. Again it would appear that you are caught in some sort of self-contradiction here. On the one hand you imply that this desire for power is suggestive of a fundamental distress and indigence, that people - in particular - are driven by, to be explained by this lack, yet on the other hand you are prone to argue the fundamental condition is one of profligacy and surfeit?

A: Let me attempt to clarify matters? I think the problem is of your own making.

S: My making? How can that be? The words are yours.
A: Your being so wedded to teleological principles. You are still conceiving of the will to power in teleological fashion. I love him whose soul squanders itself, who wants no thanks and returns none: for he always gives away and does not want to preserve himself. 855 What have I said about self-overcoming? Did I not say of the will to power that it is the unexhausted pro-creative will of life; that life is always that, which must overcome itself? 856 Have I not spoken of the will to power as the instinct of freedom that must discharge and vent itself? 857 I had thought I'd made it plain for me superabundance is the norm. Further, in contradiction to your teleological tendencies, power is not primarily something the organism wants or needs but something the organism is or has and must exercise. The willing of will to power is not desiring, striving, demanding; rather it is that state of tension by virtue of which a force seeks to discharge itself. 858

S: You insist this profligacy is the norm, but from where I stand you could equally well describe most societies as acquisitive and conservative. Men are seldom as innocently employed as when they are making money saving for the proverbial rainy day, keeping indigence from the door. Some might argue that such self-discipline is the very life-blood of a healthy and fully functioning society; remove such brakes and the society careers out of control.

A: We come at this from opposite sides. I could tell you a story about this.

S: No, don't do that. Time is getting on. Give me a potted version.

A: Well, for my money, from the highest biological standpoint, legal conditions can never be other than exceptional conditions, since they constitute a partial restriction of the will of life, which is bent upon power, and are subordinate to its total goal as a single means: namely, as a means of creating greater units of power. A legal order thought of as sovereign and universal, not as a means in the struggle between power-complexes but as a means of preventing all struggle in general ... would be a principle hostile to life, an agent of the dissolution and destruction of man, an attempt to assassinate the future of man, a sign of weariness, a secret path to nothingness. 859

# CHEWING THE CUD

S: Ah, I see; it's of a piece; the opposition to equality, to democracy, to the legalistic form of women's emancipation.

A: And of much more besides, but only if it threatens to choke off the impulse to expenditure. "Emancipation from the emancipation", and all that; such restrictions can only ever be a temporary break, a prelude to a still greater squandering. You are, after all, the very exemplar of this. Denied outward expression, discharge, the will to power turns inward. The ascetic who tries to negate life and the will to power does no more than affirm them. What is asceticism except a perverse will of life against life itself, a will to nothingness that remains, nonetheless a will?

S: Ah! The will to truth as the will to power; the third aspect we never quite tidied up when we were discussing women? Truth as a manifestation of the will to truth, - as will to illusion, as will to power.

A: And your point is?

S: This will to power seems bent upon either its own destruction, or that of the object upon which its power is exercised?

A: Teleology, yet again! What can I say that'll convince you to abandon this prejudice? You seem to have annihilation on the brain. Think of the contest.
Power can only be acquired through expenditure - think of the athlete's training; growth and expansion in service of even greater expansion. The will to power seeks resistances; every contestant seeks that which resists it.860 The ideal contestant resists any ultimate peace, and wills instead the eternal recurrence of war and peace. 861 Hence the contestant seeks neither the total dissipation of his power, nor the destruction of his opponent. He desires not a final state, but rather the perpetuation of the contest.

S: Let's leave it there for the moment. I've another concern with your theory. A few moments ago you prefaced one of your remarks with the words, "from the highest biological standpoint". Yet just now the talk of this will to power was in terms of its cultural application. Am I to understand its application knows no bounds?

A: Right. The entire distinction between the organic and inorganic world is a prejudice.862The living is merely a type of what is dead, and a very rare type.863In short conscience of method demands we risk the hypothesis whether will does not affect will wherever "effects" are recognized - and whether all mechanical occurrences are not, insofar as force is active in them, will-force, will-effects. Indeed, if one grants this hypothesis, one would have gained the right to determine all efficient force univocally as - will to power. The world viewed from the inside, the world defined and determined according to its "intelligible character" - it would be "will to power" and nothing besides. 864 One would be obliged to understand all motion, all "appearances", all "laws", only as symptoms of an inner event and to employ man as an analogy to this end. 865

S: Whilst one can only admire the consistency of purpose and the scale of the ambition in what you claim, I'm still not sure that you are not prone to shipwreck from another quarter. Let me first reprise your argument to make sure I have it right. All my attempts to obtain three falls have failed, so I'll follow the best advice of my wrestling coach and seek a submission.

A: Go on then; stop hopping about and do your worst!

S: Well, it seems to me that you've inadvertently boxed yourself into a corner. In pursuit of your naturalist agenda you've argued that a mechanistic interpretation falls short in that it retains onto theological premises. In short, it offers a passive, reactive explanation of natural movement that originates in a divine watchmaker who sets the whole thing running. A similar objection pertains to the science that informs the biological view. Once again objection is made to the reactive principle, i.e. adaptation, which drives the evolutionary change here. All of which leaves you flailing about for some active principle capable of explaining both natural movement and change, and thus you are obliged to posit the will to power as a form of vitalism?

A: That's it?

S: You sound incredulous? Have you not understood what I've said? Have you done anything other than what you accuse that Kant fellow of doing: re-introducing the spirit by the backdoor?

A: Clearly I have failed to make myself plain. What truck have I with vitalism? I count it as one of man's principle errors that he endows himself with false attributes, and has placed himself in a false order of rank in relation to animals and nature. 866 My materialism requires that my active principle, as you term it, applies across the board, that is subsumes the mechanical, biological, and cultural change. As to this charge of vitalism, I'll say it once again and let that be an end of it: human beings and life itself must be translated back into nature, not the other way around - life is merely a special case of the will to power. 867 Vitalism arises from the belief that life is higher than, different from the rest of the material world.

S: Lessons in my "a, b, c's" are not required. This "active" principle of yours; it needs further explanation. As I re-call there was to be some explanation of exploitation. Latterly this notion has dropped out of view. Not that I'd blame you, the whole notion of life as exploitation is something that many would find repugnant in the extreme. Perhaps you've thought the better of endorsing it, in the meantime?

A: Aren't you the sly one? Once a moralist: always a moralist? You'd make a good Pharisee.

S: I don't know what you mean, but you haven't answered the question.

A: Oh, you want me to condemn myself by my own word of mouth? Why's that? So nobody can say hereafter that you tricked me, so no guilt can be attached to you?

S: If you refuse to answer, people will draw their own conclusions anyway.

A: "Exploitation" does not belong to a corrupt or imperfect and primitive society; it belongs to the essence of what lives, as a basic organic function, it is a consequence of the will to power, which is after all the will of life. 868 There. Happy?

S: No, but at least we have it out in the open. Is it any wonder that half of us don't trust you; that half of us think you a tyrant in the making?

A: Well the obtuse half can go hang if they lack the ears. It is wearisome to be ever at a beginning. For the last time! What does a will want, what does this one or that one want? I say again, this is not to be thought of as a search for a goal, or of as a motive, or of as an object for this will. What a will wants is to affirm its difference in relation to the "other"; the pleasure of knowing oneself different. 869 And, yes, as will to power life operates essentially, that is in its basic functions, through injury, assault, exploitation destruction, and simply cannot be thought of at all without this character. 870
No doubt you'll want to read this the wrong way, which is why I saved it till last -in hope that it might be otherwise. Let me remind you, for me, matter everywhere is characterized by motion and change, impelled by struggle and pathos: by attraction, repulsion, integration, dis-integration, tension, resistance, assimilation, incor-

poration, alliance, etc.: dynamic quanta, in a relation of tension to all other dynamic quanta? 871 This is all will to power, a will to power that interprets; interpretation means becoming master of something. And, to be sure, such interpretation involves forcing, adjusting, abbreviating, omitting, padding, inventing, and falsifying. 872 Whatever exists is essentially involved in processes of subduing, becoming master, and all subduing and becoming master involves a fresh interpretation. 873

S: And if one refused to play the game, refused to interpret, what then?

A: Que agoraphobic, you already know the answer to that.

S: Meaning?

A: You seek your prey elsewhere. The general renunciation of all interpretation would be tantamount to an ascetic renunciation of life and nature. Interpretation is the norm. A really serious naturalism obliges us to treat the soul as only a word for something about the body; 874 thinking is merely a relation of the drives to each other.875 The spirit is relatively similar to the stomach. 876

S: And you expect me to swallow that?

A: Yes. That commanding something which people call "spirit" wants to be master in and around its own house and wants to feel that it is master; it has the will from multiplicity to simplicity, a will that ties up, tames, and is domineering and truly masterful. Its needs and capacities are so far the same as those that physiologists posit for everything that lives, grows, and multiplies. The spirit's power to appropriate the foreign stands revealed in its inclination to assimilate the new to the old, to simplify the manifold, and to overlook or repulse whatever is totally contradictory - just as it involuntarily emphasizes certain features and lines in what is foreign, in every piece of the "external world", retouching and falsifying the whole to suit itself. Its intent in all this is to incorporate new "experiences", to file new things in old files - growth, in a word - or, more precisely, the feeling of growth, the feeling of increased power. 877

In sum, all existence is an interpreting existence from its highest intellectual forms to its lowest. 878 There is nothing other than this interpretive web...

S: So the will to power is of a piece with the anti-dualist motive that runs like a - shall we say, golden thread throughout your argument?

# CHEWING THE CUD

A: If you mean that without sarcasm?

S: I ask because it seems we are left with something of a paradox as to whether e describe the will to power as an epistemological or an ontological doctrine?

A: It is both and neither.

S: My thought, exactly.

A: Both in that it offers an account of knowing and being; neither in that -because as you say, anti-dualist - it seeks to collapse the very distinctions upon which epistemology and ontology, traditionally understood, are based i.e., subject and object, knower and known. But then you'll want to object...?

S: Of course I will!

A: I'll save you the bother. Supposing that this will to power also is only an interpretation, and you will be eager enough to make this objection? – Well, so much the better. 879

S: Couldn't have put it better, myself. But you can't leave it at that. Someone might come along and declare that it is all so obviously circular, that the whole caboodle doesn't rate a second thought. The very last thing you would want, I'm sure - especially if that person was I, or Plato.

A: True enough, but what would you have me do here? Reprise the arguments vis-a-vis correspondence as against coherence theories of truth, or those of foundationalism v holism? I don't see how that would take us forward. The circle here appears vicious for you because you start from the assumption that there must be a means of exiting it; for my part there is no escape, but that doesn't mean I lack a handle with which to make my critique. As holist, my critique must, perforce, take place as immanent, from within; that is, cull its resources from that which it wishes to criticize.

S: Agreed, but I think you can come at this another way. The real charge you want to avoid is that of being thought a mere relativist - of being thought of sanctioning the idea that all interpretations are, in the absence any external yardstick, of equal value.

# CHEWING THE CUD

A: Absolutely! I thank you. How remiss of me, not to mention it before. "The Eternal Return" might serve.

S: Not another vicious circle, I hope.

A: More a virtuous one, I think.
S: Tell me more.

A: The greatest weight. - What, if some day or night a demon were to steal after you into your loneliest, loneliness and say to you: "This life as you now live it and have lived it, you will have to live once more and innumerable times more; and there will be nothing new in it, but every pain and every joy and every thought and sigh and everything unutterably small or great in your life will have to return to you, all in the same succession and sequence - even this spider and this moonlight between the trees, and even this moment and I myself. The eternal hourglass of existence is turned upside down again and again, and you with it, speck of dust!"

Would you not throw yourself down and gnash your teeth and curse the demon who spoke thus? Or have you once experience a tremendous moment when you would have answered him: "You are a god and never have I heard anything more divine". If this thought gained possession of you, it would you as you are or perhaps crush you. The question in each and every thing, "Do you desire this once more and innumerable times more?" would lie upon your actions as the greatest weight. Or how well disposed would you have to become to yourself and life to crave nothing more fervently than this ultimate eternal confirmation and seal? 880

S: Ah, a riddle to unpick. Life is never easy around you. Are you sure it's a riddle rather than a maze?

A: It's a doctrine powerful enough to work as a breeding agent: strengthening the strong, paralyzing and destructive for the world-weary. 881

S: Well it doesn't want for hyperbole and drama. Am I to understand that in order to affirm the repetition of my life, I'd have to be willing to take the bad along with the good?

A: Have you ever said Yes to a single joy? O my friends, then you have said Yes too to all woe. All things are entangled, ensnared, enamoured,; if you ever wanted one thing twice, if you ever said "You please me, happiness! Abide, moment!" then you wanted all back. 882

# CHEWING THE CUD

S: You are doing it again; that priestly effect.

A: That's part and parcel of this. The Jews felt differently about anger from the way we do, and called it holy: thus they saw the gloomy majesty of the man with whom it showed itself associated at an elevation which a European is incapable of imagining; they modelled their angry holy Jehovah on their angry holy prophets. Measured against these, the great men of wrath among Europeans are as it were creations at second hand. 883 Ignore it if you want; just concentrate on the content.

S: So what are you saying here? Is it that the bombast of his Zarathustra pertains to his being a putative prophet, or is it something more besides? To the untutored ear this sometimes sounds as if this might be his ventriloquist's stock in trade too? Some quieter souls are putting it about that this is proof -all the ranting and raving - the ventriloquist is quite, well, - unhinged?

A: Agon in the grand style is what it is. Think Gorgias, think Thucydides, and the pathos of distance! Think Demosthenes and how the stormy air of Athenian democracy carries his oratory to new heights; just as it in turn makes this storm more violent and decisive. 884

S: I'm with Plato here. Wouldn't trust either Gorgias, or Demosthenes, further than I could throw them. Nonetheless, this seems an impossible ideal to live up to.

A: It is blessedness to write on the will of millennia as on bronze. 885

S: Zeus! There you go again. It's altogether too much and not enough.

A: You are not telling me you can't ignore a simple priestly inflection? We are the sum of affects: our reason is ever the puny part. Sometimes the only way to disturb a man's complacency is to get angry with angry with him.

S: No. Your riddle's import? I told you it was likely to prove a maze. I mean I have no control over the past. Everyone will have done something they have regretted, and which because they perhaps had no control over, would oblige them not to affirm their life - if that is we to be strict?

A: Powerless against what has been, he is an angry spectator of all that is past. The will cannot will backwards; and that it cannot break time and time's covetousness, that is the will's loneliest melancholy. ... To recreate all "it was" into "thus I willed it" - that alone I should call redemption. ...All "it was" is a fragment, a riddle, a dreadful accident - until the creative will says to it, "But thus I willed it". Until the creative will says to it, "But thus I willed it: thus shall I will it". 886

S: A wrong turning, already. It's a maze, and one in which I can't retrace my steps, can't will backwards. Unless what you are really saying here is something else? That the significance of certain facts about my life are yet to be determined? What I mean to say is that no one incident in a life has determinate significance independent of its relations to other aspects. A particular aspect of my life, thus far lived, may escape my control, but its significance is yet to be determined. Its significance in the context of one life might be very different in another.

A: Indeed. The future is yet to be determined. I taught them ... to create and carry together into what in human beings is fragment and riddle and dreadful accident; as creator, guesser of riddles, and redeemer of accidents, I taught them to work on the future and to redeem with their creation all that has been. 887

S: I'll take that as a Yes then. You never know, I might yet find my way to the heart of this thicket. Before I proceed; another question for the purposes of orientation. My being able to affirm my life; couldn't I do this in a prosaic fashion by simply ensuring I live it without regrets? To be sure if the world proves to be inhospitable to the values I hold, I would be obliged to re-think my values; but then it might be a case of "if you cannot have what you most value, then value what you have".

A: No, that sounds like ressentiment speaking! Eternal Return: The Revaluation Of All Values. Book 1: The Antichrist: Attempt At A Critique Of Christianity. Book 2: The Free.... 888

S: You are getting ahead of yourself there. If I understood you way back when, this Christianity thing is yet to happen.

A: Sorry, just thinking aloud.

S: No worries: the revaluation thing is obviously central to this "Eternal Return"; that being so, another question? You'll indulge me, if I go English on you – "English"? Where did that come from? Never mind. Definitions?

A: Boring.

# CHEWING THE CUD

S: Got to be done. "Eternal"? For instance, I believe in the idea of another life, in another world. Your eternal return would leave me in a strange sort of limbo; for my goal is the ultimate and lasting peace of heavenly peace being continually dragged back to your Heraclitean war and strife of this world would mean I couldn't affirm my life despite actually having made it to heaven. I'd hate to find I'd brought my pig to the wrong market.

A: No, no, no. I can't be doing with that. Zarathustra's fifth gospel is explicit: "I beseech you, my brothers, remain faithful to the earth, and do not believe those who speak to you of otherworldly hopes! ... To sin against the earth is now the most dreadful thing, and to esteem the entrails of the unknowable higher than the meaning of the earth". 889

S: So then, it's not just another and different life that is ruled out of court; more specifically it is the idea of an eternal life. Thinking about it you have a point. If our life is, indeed, eternal we can't have another after it. And further if it recurs then what your demon is saying is that it is also finite. A life couldn't recur if it were infinite since by definition it would go on forever.

A: Everything becomes and recurs eternally - escape is impossible! - The idea of recurrence as a selective principle.900 Living on earth is worthwhile: one day, one festival with Zarathustra, taught me to love the earth. "Was that life?" I want to say to death. "Well then! Once more!" 901

S: Right then, a problem for those such as I. We can't affirm the eternal return so long as we deny the finitude of death. Bye the bye, you realize that this puts a big question mark against your claim to have lived posthumously.

A: More evidence that this is a dream, or we are merely characters in someone else's imagining. You, yourself, are certainly and suspiciously acting out of character. All this forensic attention to the detail of my argument is very un-Socratic.

S: Ah, but you forget you only know me as the character that that other scribe created. That's why I'm here; so you can get to know the real me. And anyway, even if this isn't the real me, I'd have to say I'm quite enjoying being this version of me; much better lines! In fact, I've just thought of another, or should I say the person who is writing me has. Chances are, he, himself is cheating. Probably filching his lines from those of others. He seems to have got you to a "T", if I may so. Plagiarism is rife, though. That said, do you think it matters? I mean so long as the resulting story is interesting and challenges the reader to think afresh?

319

# CHEWING THE CUD

A: You're rambling.

S: Yes, I am. I was going to say. What was I going to say? Oh, yes. The thing about our finitude put it in my head. As you said, in so many words, the background assumption here is that eternity is thought of in terms of a life that never ends. But, of course, eternity might equally be thought of in terms of permanence, of escaping the temporal order, i.e. of change and becoming?

A: Now you seem to be doing my job for me?

S: We aim to please, we slaves. You see where I'm going with this?

A: Death, change, age, as well as procreation and growth, are for them - Plato and his cronies, that is - objections - refutations even. What is, does not become, what becomes, is not ... Now they all believe, even to the point of despair, in that which is. 902 Contempt, hatred for all that perishes, changes, varies - whence comes this valuation of that which remains constant? ... Happiness can be guaranteed only by being; change and happiness exclude one another. How could such as these desire this life once and innumerable times more? I should thank you for your help in allowing me to express it so.

S: My pleasure.

A: Ah, would it be your joy?

S: Joy?

A: All joy wants eternity. Joy, not pleasure. Wishing the eternal recurrence of the perfect moment, not that this moment could last for eternity. Creation - that is the great redemption from all suffering, and life's growing light. But that the creator may be, suffering is needed and much change. Indeed, there must be much bitter dying in your life, you creators. Thus are you advocates and justifiers of all impermanence. 903

S: Wait up!

A: My formula for greatness in a human being is *amor fati*: that one wants nothing to be different, not forwards, not backward, not in all eternity. Not merely bear what is necessary, still less conceal it - all idealism is mendacious in the face of what is necessary - but love it. 904 I say again: the highest stage a philosopher can

320

attain: to stand in a Dionysian relation to existence - my formula for this is *amor fati*. It is part of this state to perceive not merely the necessity of those sides of existence hitherto denied, but their desirability; and not their desirability in relation to sides hitherto affirmed [perhaps as their compliment or precondition], but for their own sake, as the more powerful, more fruitful, truer sides of existence, in which its will finds clearer expression. 905

I ask again, have I been understood? - "Dionysus versus the Crucified": there you have the antithesis. It is not difference in regard to their martyrdom - it is a difference in the meaning of it. Life itself, its eternal fruitfulness and recurrence, creates torment, destruction, the will to annihilation. In the other case, suffering - the "Crucified as the innocent one" - counts as an objection to this life, as a formula for its condemnation. - One will see that the problem is that of the meaning of suffering: whether a Christian meaning or a tragic meaning. In the former case, it is supposed to be the path to a holy existence; in the latter case, being is count as holy enough to justify even a monstrous amount of suffering. The tragic man affirms even the harshest suffering: he is sufficiently strong, rich, and capable of deifying to do so. The Christian denies even the happiest lot on earth: he is sufficiently weak, poor, disinherited to suffer from life in whatever form he meets it. The god on the cross is a curse on life, a signpost to seek redemption from life; Dionysus cut to pieces is a promise of life: it will be eternally reborn and return again from destruction.905

S: Zeus! Wait up. Don't go galloping off. Neither my legs, not the mind they carry can go at that pace anymore.

A: Sorry, I have things to attend to this evening; a meeting of the military council.

S: The war-horse darts into the fray.

A: That's not the way it works.

S: It's a spoonerism. Bad taste, I know. The rustic will out? Anyway, what do you mean: "not the way it works". I thought you "blonde beasts" wanted nothing other than glory.

A: Now who's been reading too much Homer? Single combat is a last resort; more force, more effect, is achieved by a disciplined and well-marshalled fighting unit.

S: No longer the "Hotspur" of yesteryear, I see. Give me a moment to re-group. The point of this sally of yours, "the eternal return"- its purpose, that is? Its less to do with eternity as it is usually conceived, than it is to do with differentiating your so-called free spirits from the rest of us in terms of affirming the re-instantiation of becoming, of impermanence? Is that it? You see Plato's nihilism as precluding such affirmation since it constitutes life as a lack, as encapsulating life-denying values; hence your insistence that a re-valuation of such values is a necessary condition of such an affirmation of life?

A: At last.

S: Short- cuts often prove not to be the most direct routes where knowledge is concerned; sometimes the circuitous route affords the best views.

A: And the wise-saw ends up cutting off the branch on which it is sitting?

S: Always the last word.

A: Well, the heaviest weight, and all that?

S: I'll ignore that.

A: Don't, you are doing so well.

S: Suffering Jesus!

A: Yes, by all means, let's turn our attention to him. Suffering is the very heart of nihilism after all.

S: It's a big ask of your free spirits - that they should see suffering as inevitable, and nonetheless see life as perfect, as leaving nothing to be desired? Perhaps I should remind you of our intention in setting off down this particular road? Was it not with a view to your escaping the charge of relativism, of being seen to endorse any and every choice of life-style.

A: We are getting there. You are forgetting the connection of all this to the will to power. What I want of my seekers of knowledge is that they become human beings who are bent on seeking all things for what in them must be overcome. For believe me: the secret for harvesting from existence the greatest fruitfulness and the greatest enjoyment is - to live dangerously! Build your cities on the slopes of Vesuvius! Send your ships into uncharted seas! Live at war with your peers and with yourselves! Be robbers and conquerors as long as you cannot be rulers and possessors, you seekers of knowledge. 906

Will to power. The will henceforth to question further, more deeply, severely, harshly, evilly and quietly than one had questioned heretofore. The trust in life is gone: life itself has become a problem. Yet one should not jump to the conclusion that this necessarily makes one gloomy. Even love of life is still possible, one loves differently. It is the love for a woman that causes doubt in us.

The attraction of everything problematic, the delight in an x, however, is so great in such more spiritual, more spiritualized men that this delight flares up again and again like a bright blaze over all distress of what is problematic, over all the danger of uncertainty, and even over the jealousy of the lover. We know a new happiness.907

S: You have someone in mind?

A: Yes, but let's not get sidetracked. The will to power as a principle of understanding; - a means of adjudicating between competing interpretations; - a means of rebutting the charge of relativism; and, if you will, eternal return as a principle of judgment? In so far as the word "knowledge" has any meaning, the world is knowable; but it is interpretable otherwise, it has no meaning behind it, but countless meanings. - "Perspectivism" - It is our needs that interpret the world; our drives and their For and Against. Every drive is a kind of lust to rule; each one has its perspective that it would like to compel all the other drives to accept as the norm. Remember, body am I entirely, and nothing else; and soul is only a word for something about the body? 908 The "pure spirit" is a pure stupidity; if we subtract the nervous system and the senses - the "mortal shroud" - then we miscalculate - that is all? 909

S: Yes, yes. There's no need for you to go back to square one. Likewise the stuff on suffering and strength and weakness, though, no doubt they'll loom large. Make your point.

A: We should start from the interests of the "lived body": the world seen from within, the world described and defined according to its "intelligible character" - it would be "will to power" and nothing else.

S: You've said as much already, but how does that elucidate your assertion concerning the "eternal return"?

# CHEWING THE CUD

A: I was pondering the difference between Kant and myself concerning freedom and necessity.

S: Kant? He's the one who divides the world into a noumenal and phenomenal world, a world of the mind and a world of nature, an intelligible world which is the province of a free, rational will, where moral freedom reigns; and a sensible world determined by heteronomous interests such as instinct, desire, pleasure, and the like?

A: Like shit to a blanket, your memory. No offense, intended. But think about the contrast here. For me the division between past and future is one between the "lived body" as it was and as it will be from this moment forward. The moment of acting affirms both the action and the momentariness of the action: the right to make promises.

S: I'm not sure I follow.

A: Kant's maxim: act always according to that maxim you can at the same time will as a universal law. My maxim would be: act always according to that interpretation you can at the same time desire as eternally returning.

S: O.k. Just to be sure. Both maxims are universal in form, but differ in content?

A: Exactly. Kant's maxim demands that actions be universal in content irrespective of time or context. For my part, the content of any willed return cannot be universal, since each life, each becoming is unique. Put another way. Kant's notion of autonomy is moral; mine is extra-moral insofar as it presupposes singularity relative to content.

S: Hence why, for you, imposing one's morality upon another is itself a form of immorality. Yes, I see. You know, you and I are not that different.

A: We're not? I thought we had just spent the better part of the day establishing that we are as different as chalk and cheese?

S: Oh no, we are most definitely in love with the same mistress. Speaking of which reminds me, before we go our separate ways, that you still owe me an account of what the brewer's droop failed to deliver last night.

## CHEWING THE CUD

A: Gadfly? More like a ... Oh, never mind. Let's not start that again. More to the point, what, if anything, I've just said leads you to suppose we are alike.

S: Your comments about the desire for knowledge for one. You persist in treating me as one and the same as Plato's sounding board.

A: Well, aren't you the one who claims to know nothing?

S: But that might be understood very differently. After all, it is still the greatest good for a man to discuss virtue everyday and those other things about which you hear me conversing and testing myself and others, for the unexamined life is not worth living for man. 910

A: Haven't you tied yourself into a bit of a knot there? On the one hand you, or you and your daemon, want to maintain you know nothing; but on the other, far from this giving you cause for pause, you make it your business to go about telling everyone that what they believe they know they don't.

S: Given that we have just spent a pleasant day chewing the cud about such issues, I would have thought that you of all people would be appreciative of my claim that the greater part of mankind are mired in the illusion of knowledge. "We knowers are unknown to ourselves", - didn't you say? 911 Self-conscious ignorance is surely preferable to illusion, maybe a first step toward proper knowledge even?

A: Hmm, even were that so, many a clever man could say to you - and he probably has - that ignorance and illusion might be constitutive of bliss. After all, you freely admit that you have nothing to teach any one about the good life? 912

S: Ah, but you missing a step in all this. In fact, you are taking it all from Plato's perspective.

A: I am? That'll never do. Enlighten me then.

S: It's not often that I get to insist that he quotes me verbatim, though a fat lot of good it did me in the end. The passage you quoted a moment ago? "It is the greatest good for a man to discuss virtue everyday". "Discuss", note. I didn't say anything about doing this as a means of practicing any good life. As you say I freely admit not to know what such a good life would entail. To be sure to live an unexamined life might very well imperil us, but I'm not in the business of finding answers to this, if indeed answers there are - which, personally I doubt. Besides if there were such, I'd be out of business.

You see, my friend, I'm more at one with you in this matter than you realize. Answers are anathema to me, the means by which - whether justified, or not, you put an end to dialogue. Uncertainty, doubt, they are the lodestar by which this ship sails; it is the asking of the questions that creates new interests, new horizons as you might say.

A: A friend, indeed. A splendid note to finish upon? You really are far from just being a pretty face.

S: And there I was thinking that I'd never seen such cruelty in so cute a package?

A: Come; let me fulfil my promise. Let's sit in the shade for a last time and mull over last night's conversation, for I must soon be away.

## CHAPTER 13
### What makes the world go around?

S: I take it that since you were already the worse for wear when you finally arrived; you need me to reprise some of the argument you missed?

A: Some of it, no doubt. That said, I've wondered since about the unspoken pre-supposition in which it was framed, or leastways that part of it I recall.

S: What presupposition is that then?

A: That love is only love if it benefits the lover.913

S: How could it be otherwise than a pursuit of goodness and beauty? Perhaps you missed that rogue Aristophanes' contribution. He was arguing love as loss, whilst I was arguing for love as lack. 914

A: Yes, I know. I'll come back to that. My point was a different one concerning we Greeks. Love is a natural desire to cultivate and possess what is deemed good and virtuous whether we are mere mortals or gods. And whether as mortals or gods we are circumscribed and constrained by nature.

S: That much is obvious.

# CHEWING THE CUD

A: Is it? Not to the Jew, or to those who subscribe to the Abrahamic religions that come after. For such as these one is commanded to love God, and yes a single all-powerful, omniscient, God who exists outside of nature, and prior to nature. Moreover one is commanded to love this God irrespective of considerations of personal welfare and in principled opposition to many of the competing goods that nature offers human kind.

S: Job! He was a Jew. His story I've heard tell by seamen down at the docks; a hard pillow on which to rest one's head. This God would seem to require of his adherents nothing short of complete submission. For the life of me I cannot see what Job has done wrong.

A: And in so saying you declare yourself your master's disciple.

S: Meaning?
A: For Plato the divine is responsible only for the good, never evil; the divine never changes; nor does it lie or deceive. It is all so moralistic.

S: As you keep saying. Well, so much the better. It is surely of the first importance what a man has reason to believe.

A: Ah, but now you are treating it all as a matter of assenting or not to particular beliefs. This is something new, something you and yours, and the early Christians following your lead insist upon. Prior to this a man was just born a Jew or an adherent of some sect or other. As in Homeric times, and before, your duty lay in honouring the relevant god in rites, not in questioning the veracity of the belief that behind the rite. The very idea of a supernatural separate from the sensible world is itself dependent upon a dualism that arises with the separation of body and soul. Only when this visible body is thought not to be my real self does this visible world come to be subordinated to another, more real world. What was it Plato said in ""Cratylus", or was it "Gorgias?" When the body becomes the tomb of the soul, the true home of the soul is sought beyond this world"? 915

S: Yes, yes, but where are you going with all this?

A: Presuppositions. All talk of love originates in conceptions of the divine.

S: Granted, but what has this to with the Jews and others and their ideas of submission?

## CHEWING THE CUD

A: We are still in thrall to Plato's moralism: that genuine love is only evoked by the good. If we love the rogue it is only because of the spark of good within him, or if we seduced by those bent on destruction this is to be explained by poor parenting or some such; never that quite simply that we are drawn to those whose power is such that they can take or give life on a whim. People have ever loved tyrants, even the most murderous of them, and wept copious tears at their passing. 916 Love is evoked, as often as not, not by goodness and beauty but by the promise of the loved one to anchor one's life, such that one may feel at home in the world.

S: But what of justice?

A: There you go again. Moralism. You can't see past it. Where is the justice in your loving Xanthippe and not another who is kind and considerate in ways that Xanthippe is not?

S: Well put like that.

A: Perhaps love is only genuine when matters of justice do not interpose? That's not to deny that we want fervently to believe that the object of our love is wholly on our side, has only our best interests at heart, that his or her love is unconditional, even if this is rarely so. More often than not this pill is sweetened by the pretence that the beloved is the fount of all virtues. Nonetheless the deep need to believe all this is such that we are exposed to disappointment and deception, but should such offer us a sense of the why of our lives we quickly fall in content thereafter to restrict ourselves to the delineation of the how of it all; the faith that we have in the loved one to deliver having already forged the trust that lies at the core of every intense love. A trust that will in many instances be willingly to look past the most flagrant of betrayals for the sake of maintaining that sense of rootedness in one's life.

S: Not for the first time I'm left wondering whether you've espoused a truth or the cruellest cynicism? Speaking of cynicism, I must ask: what you made of that scoundrel Aristophanes and his idea of the "split-aparts"? Everyone found it amusing at the time, and I suppose you have to give the fellow his due as an "icebreaker", but as a philosopher he really is pretentious don't you think? - Each of us looking for our lost half? 917

A: What do you want me to say? That this would only apply to the original "split-aparts", and not to us descendants?

328

S: Yes, exactly so. Not that I said so at the time; not wishing to appear a killjoy.

A: What makes you think that Aristophanes doesn't know that? Mightn't his point in recounting "myth" have been that in love we look for an impossible perfection. As I recall he didn't demur when Hephaestus pointed out that if such perfection were attained we might find ourselves saddled with a sterile satisfaction rather than ongoing bliss?

S: Trust you to come up with some sort of defence for that sacrilegious knave.

A: Poetic license, if you like. But knowing Aristophanes that was perhaps his whole point: the "myth" recounts a joke made at the expense of tiresome and importunate humankind by the gods. Humanity can never be satisfied?

S: So, now he is cleverer than then the rest of us put together? Is that where this is leading?

A: I don't know. You'll have to ask Plato what he keeps under his pillow for bed-time reading? 918

S: I'll do no such thing! Though why you should suggest he is a reader of pornography I've no idea. And not for the first time!

A: Just wondering. Had he a guilty secret? Had he recognised what was implicit in Aristophanes' chosen medium; that comedy as tragedy's other was structured in terms of its outcome – a resolution in respect of the re-birth of life and love? More to the point still; had he perceived that he, himself, might constitute the malign force?

S: "Malign force"? What are you inferring – implying?

A: Only that in a lot of comedy the confusion that precedes the moment of reversal, or recognition, - what's Aristotle's term? - is instigated by some malign, reactionary, force: one who has his own agenda and is intent upon keeping the lovers at the heart of the story apart. Hence all the business with masks, and the failure of the characters to recognise whom it is they truly love. I might add, if I were allowed to borrow a metaphor, that the dastardly designs of the dark force are more often than not thwarted by those who live below the line – that is by the disinherited, the disenfranchised, the weak. It is they who become clever and divise the strategem to

329

break the logjam that has occured above the line, thus allowing life to flow once more.

S: You want to know what I infer from all that? Well that was no philosopher speaking; merely someone intent upon seducing me, by underhand means, to un-kind conclusions.

A: Your inferences are running away with you again, but as regards Aristophanes and his would-be myth? Is he to be taken as implying that the lovers in seeking to make themselves whole again might be stirring up trouble of a different type. After all the "split-aparts" don't actually know what it is they want, and only "recognize" what is entailed by this "loss" when they come upon it by chance.

S: What are you saying? More cynicism? Many a slip between cup and lip?

A: There is room enough for that to be sure, but my point was the probable cause for such. Having lost their other half in a different life, how would they recognize, let alone understand it in this?

S: "Understand"?

A: The man what femininity is; the woman what masculinity is. All either party would understand is that they are drawn to what in each is mutually incomprehensible.

S: So, forget patriarchy and the world historical defeat of women? 919Did I say "World historical defeat of women"? I'm sorry. I don't know where that came from, much less what I'm talking about.

A: Honesty is refreshing don't you find, perhaps because its the youngest of our virtue? 920

S: I didn't mean it like that, as you well know. As for the Empedoclean image of trouble and strife, what can you do but shake your head and thank the gods that real loves are reserved for men alone? 921

A: I wouldn't exult too soon if I were you.

S: Ah, but I never do. Ask around. I never disappoint. Just because I've failed to tempt you thus far, there's no need to be shy.

A: I meant that Aristophanes allows that the "split-aparts" in their original state are of three kinds; as well as hermaphrodite, also male and female.

S: And your point is?

A: That they too, perhaps, male and female "split-aparts", suffer the same problems of recognition. The men go in search of the men they are not, and likewise the lesbian. Ample room for confusion and misrecognition given that each is drawn to representatives of their own sex, but representatives who are paradigmatically drawn to the opposite sex and thus beyond their reach.

S: Sex, sex, and sex. That's all you get with Aristophanes. We're not all two humped beasts rutting in the dirt. Love is about more than sex.

A: Quite so. One must learn to love. - This is what happens to us in music: First one has to learn to hear a figure and melody at all, to detect and distinguish it, to isolate it and delimit it as a separate life. Then it requires some exertion and good will to tolerate it in spite of its strangeness, to be patient with its appearance and expression, and kind-hearted about its oddity. Finally there comes a moment when we are used to it, when we wait for it, when we sense we should miss it if it were missing; and now it continues to compel and enchant us relentlessly until we have become its humble and enraptured lovers who desire nothing better from the world than it and only it.
　But that is what happens to us not only in music. That is how we have learned to love all things that we now love. In the end we always rewarded for our good will, our patience, fair-mindedness, and gentleness with what is strange; gradually, it sheds its veil and turns out to be a new and indescribable beauty. That is its thanks for our hospitality. Even those who love themselves will have learned it in this way; for there is no other way. Love, too, has to be learned.922

S: Then you should know what I speak of? You weren't so completely oblivious that you can recall nothing of what I said last night love's importunity?

A: Remind me.

S: About its having Contrivance for his father and Poverty for his mother ... always poor, and from being sensitive and beautiful, ... shoeless and homeless ... Like his

331

mother he lives in want ..., also his father's son he schemes and lays traps to capture what is good and beautiful. 923

A: Not the best of starts - having poverty as your mother I mean. Many a man finds that an impossible chasm to fill, no matter how rich he becomes.

S: Can you hold fire for a moment? The state you were in; I doubt you were able to appreciate the subtlety of the argument. On some points we are close. Loving is something to be learnt. Though initially rooted in the physical, love is about procreation in the beautiful.; such procreation, moreover, can be either physical or spiritual. 924

A: Oh, come on man! Do you have to be so pompous, so pious about it all? Raucsh, I say! In the beautiful, man posits himself as the measure of perfection. A species cannot do otherwise than thus say yes to itself alone. Its lowest instinct, that of self-preservation and self-expansion, still radiates in such sublimities. 925 The "aesthetic" states in which [this] world is seen fuller, rounder, more perfect.926 On the origin of the beautiful and the ugly. What instinctively repels us, aesthetically, is proved by humanity's longest experience to be the harmful, dangerous, worthy of distrust: the suddenly voiced aesthetic instinct [in disgust, e.g.] contains a judgment. 927

S: A judgment? What judgment would that be? The one my father found at the bottom of every goatskin: this floosy today; that one tomorrow?

A: I've said nothing about error. Clearly, here the experience of Raucsh was misleading .../ this increases in the highest degree the feeling of power / therefore, naively judged power, power ... there are two starting-points of Rausch: the overgreat fullness of life and a state of pathological nourishment of the brain. 928 Besides to experience a thing as beautiful means: to experience it necessarily falsely; but that's a different story. 929

S: Can we dispense with all this paradoxical piffle about this so-called Raucsh?

A: Paradoxical it may be, but piffle it is most certainly not. We can come back to it. If you like we could go back to what the world and his dog believes? We are divine through love, we become the "children of God"; God loves us and wants nothing whatever from us save love"; this means: no morality, obedience, or activity produces that feeling of power that love produces; one does nothing bad from love, one does much more than one would do from obedience and virtue.

# CHEWING THE CUD

Here is the happiness of the herd, the feeling of community in great and small things, the living feeling of unity experienced as the sum of the feeling of life. Being helpful and useful and caring for others continually arouses the feeling of power; visible success, the expression of pleasure underlines the feeling of power; pride is not lacking, in the form of community, the abode of God, the "chosen". Love gives the greatest feeling of power. To grasp to what extent not man in general but a certain species of man speaks here? 930

S: Zeus! Is nothing holy?

A: Holy? You have no idea of what you and his nibs got started! Love has been falsified as surrender {and altruism], while it is an appropriation or a bestowal following from a superabundance of personality. Only the most complete persons can love; the de-personalized, the "objective", are the worst lovers [- one has only to ask the girls!]. This applies also to the love of God or of the fatherland; one must be firmly rooted in oneself.931

S: What? Love, real love, is a form of egotism?

A: Think about it! Look into it; women's love and sympathy - is there any thing more egotistic? - And if they sacrifice themselves, their honour, their reputation, to whom do they sacrifice themselves? To the man? Or is it not to an unbridled urge? - These desires are just as selfish even if they please others and implant gratitude -
    To what extent this sort of hyperfetation of one valuation can sanctify everything else! 932
    No, don't say anything. Just think about it. That love may be felt as love - We need to be honest with ourselves and know ourselves very well if we are to be able to practice towards others that philanthropic dissimulation called goodness and love. 933

S: Honestly, this bombastic phrasing of yours - "the philanthropic dissimulation called goodness and love".

A: Ah, you want flesh on the bare bones, so as to better perceive the form? I can draw you a sketch from two different perspectives if you wish?

S: Whatever. They'll both reveal the form of the arrogant, no doubt?

A: You think? A little thought tells us that the causes of error lie just as much in the good will [as in the ill will] of man -: in a thousand cases he conceals reality from himself, he falsifies it, so as not to suffer from his good [or ill will]. E.g., God as the director of human destiny: or the interpretation of his own petty destiny as if everything were contrived and sent with a view to the salvation of his soul - this lack of "philology", which to a more subtle intellect would have to count as uncleanness and counterfeiting is, on the average, performed under the inspiration of good will. Good will, "noble feelings", "lofty states" are in the means they employ just as much counterfeiters and deceivers as the affects repudiated and called egoistic: love, hate, and revenge.

Errors are what mankind has had to pay for most dearly: and on the whole, it is the errors of "good will" which have harmed it most profoundly. The illusion that makes happy is more pernicious than that which has immediate bad consequences: the latter sharpens and purifies reason and makes it more mistrustful - the former lulls it to sleep -934

S: Hmm, something similar was said a while back. Your second point, or illustration?

A: Oh, yes - our prejudices concerning love. Despite all the concessions that I am willing to make to the prejudice in favour of monogamy, I will never admit the claim that man and woman have equal rights in love; these do not exist. For men and women have different conceptions of love; and it is one of the conditions of love in both sexes that neither sex presupposes the same feeling and the same concept of "love" in the other. What the woman means by love is clear enough: total devotion {not mere surrender] with body and soul, without any consideration or reserve, rather with shame and horror at the thought of a devotion that might be subject to special clauses or conditions. In this absence of conditions her love is a faith; woman has no other faith.

Man, when he loves a woman, wants precisely this love from her and is thus himself as far as can be from the presupposition of feminine love. Supposing, however, that there should also be men to whom the desire for total devotion is not alien; well, then they simply are - not men. A man who loves like a woman becomes a slave; whilst a woman who loves like a woman becomes a more perfect woman.

A woman's passion in its unconditional renunciation of rights of her own presupposes precisely on the other side there is no equal pathos, no equal will to renunciation; for if both parties felt impelled by love to renounce themselves, we should then get - I do not know what; perhaps an empty space?

Woman wants to be taken and accepted as a possession, wants to be absorbed into the concept of possession, possessed. Consequently, she wants someone who takes, who does not give himself or give himself away; on the contrary, he is supposed to become richer in "himself" - through the accretion of strength, happiness, and faith given him by the woman who gives herself. Woman gives herself away, man acquires more - I do not see how one gets around this natural opposition by means of social contracts or with the best will in the world to be just, desirable as it may be not to remind oneself constantly how harsh, terrible, enigmatic, and immoral this antagonism is. For love, thought of in its entirety as great and full, is nature, and being nature it is in all eternity something "immoral".

Faithfulness is accordingly included in woman's love; it follows from the definition. In man, it can easily develop in the wake of his love, perhaps as gratitude or as an idiosyncratic taste and so-called elective affinity; but it is not an essential element of his love - so definitely not that one might almost speak with some justification of a natural counter play of love and faithfulness in man. For his love consists of wanting to have and not of renunciation and giving away, but wanting to have always comes to an end with having.

It is actually man's more refined and suspicious lust for possession that rarely admits his "having", and then only late, and thus permits his love to persist. It is even possible for his love to increase after the surrender; he will not readily concede that a woman should have nothing more to give him. - 935

S: So what am I to infer from all this? That love, far from being about mutuality, sharing, altruism, is rather to be thought of as irremediably stained by egoism and possessive lust?

A: Well let's not forget what we artists are up against here? When we love a woman, we easily conceive a hatred for nature on account of all the repulsive natural functions to which every woman is subject. We prefer not to think of all this; but when our soul touches on these matters for once, it shrugs as it were and looks contemptuously at nature: we feel insulted; nature seems to encroach on our possessions, and with the profanest hands at that. Then we refuse to pay any heed to physiology and decree secretly: "I want to hear nothing about the fact that a human being is something more than soul and form". The human being under the skin" is for all lovers a horror and unthinkable, a blasphemy against God and love.

Well, as lovers still feel about nature and natural functions, every worshiper of God and his "holy omnipotence" formerly felt: everything said about nature by astronomers, geologists, physiologists, or physicians, struck him as an encroachment into his precious possessions and hence as an attack - and a shameless one at that. Even "natural law" sounded to him like a slander against God; really he would have much preferred to see all mechanics derived acts of a moral will or an arbitrary will. But since nobody was able to render him this service, he ignored nature and mechanics as best he could and lived in a dream. Oh these men of former times knew how to dream and did not feel it necessary to go to sleep first. And we men of today still master this art all too well, despite all of our good will toward the day and staying awake. It is quite enough to love, to hate, to desire, simply to feel - and right away the spirit and power of dreams overcome us, and with our eyes open, coldly contemptuous of all danger, we climb up on the most hazardous paths to scale the roofs and spires of fantasy - without any sense of dizziness, as if we had been born to climb, we somnambulists of the day! We artists! We ignore what is natural. We are moonstruck and God-struck. We wander, still as death, unwearied, on heights that we do not see as heights but as plains, as our safety. 936

S: A perilous business to be sure, if one allows oneself to be deceived by appearances. Thank the stars I have Xanthippe. The sex doesn't last, you know?

A: I've heard it said that when entering into marriage one ought to ask oneself: do you believe you are going to enjoy talking with this woman up into your old age? Everything else in marriage is transitory but most of the time you are together will be devoted to conversation.937

S: In our case, if not exactly a conversation, then a perpetual exchange of words.

A: By "our" you mean you and...?

S: Same difference, but whilst we are talking "friendship" we are not - are we? - talking the language of the Metic?

A: 'Here and there on earth we may encounter a kind of continuation of love in which this possessive craving of two people gives way to a new desire and lust for possession - a shared higher thirst for an ideal above them. But knows such love? Who has experienced it? Its right name is friendship.26.

S: Sounds like him.

A: Come now, don't distress yourself fussing and fighting over the Metic. There. See? You've got me at it. Aristotle! The man deserves a name.

S: Ungrateful wretch is what he is.

A: My dear friend, what is this our life? A boat that swims in the sea, and all one knows for certain about it is that one day it will capsize. Here we are, two good old boats that have been faithful neighbours, and above all your hand has done its best to keep me from "capsizing"! Let us then continue our voyage - each for the other's sake, for a long time yet, a long time! We should miss each other so much! Tolerably calm seas and good winds and above all sun - what I wish for myself, I wish for you, too, and am sorry my gratitude can find expression only in such a wish and has no influence at all on wind or weather. 939

S: Sometimes I think there is nothing I wouldn't forgive you for. Whilst I've never known anyone as adept at speaking the head as Plato, neither have I met anyone as adept as you in speaking the heart. I'm sorry; I think I've got something in my eye. Give me a moment.

A: A mote, I hope; rather than a beam. At any rate, nothing I've said?

S: No, no, not at all. Nothing that prevented me from seeing the sting in the tail of what you said.

A: It is as well to remind oneself of the rule: amor fati - love of fate. Passivity in face of it is tantamount to defeat. Got to actively embrace it, don't you know? Not exactly Aristotle's view; in fact not his view at all. Noticeably absent last night.

S: Same reasons, sort of, as for Xenophon. You know what he's about - moderation in all things - half a beer and a hand full of nuts; hardly the life and soul of a party. No sense in trying to graft hops on a vine, I say. That's not to say we shouldn't give his anaemic theories the once over. He sometimes puts me in mind of you".
  What is it he says in that "Magna Moralia" of his? "Just as when we wish to see our own face, we do so by looking in the mirror, in the same way when we wish to know ourselves we can obtain that knowledge by looking at our friend. For the friend is, as we assert, a second self. If, then, it is pleasant to know oneself, and it is not possible to know this without having someone else for a friend, the self-sufficing man will require friendship in order to know himself". 940

A: And this has to do with me how?

S: "We seekers of knowledge are unknown to ourselves": isn't that what you say? 941 All a bit of a blind if you ask me, this supposed love of the other for his own sake. It's all highly conditional when you get close up to it. "If one friend remained a child in intellect while the other became a fully developed man, how could they [continue to] be friends when they neither approved of the same things nor delighted in and were pained by the same things? For not even with regard to each other will their tastes agree, and without this ... they cannot be friends..." 942

337

## CHEWING THE CUD

Empedocles? You see the parallel? What was it he said? Like attracts like? That like cannot be known except by like? "Perfect friendship is the friendship of men who are good, and alike in excellence" 943

A: And your complaint, here?

S: It's so un-Greek!

A: Ha, ha. Does that really count as an objection? Don't you mean on Aristotle's criteria your putative relationship with Charmides would be deemed inappropriate?

S: But not only that; also many another tutored by Eros -not least, those between spouses. He has an especially low opinion of women, you know?

A: Yes, I know. Still, whatever our prejudices in favour of erotic love, at the top level you would have to concede in practice, in love, people are remarkably conservative. They tend to cleave to their own kind, racially, socially, and educationally. The warmth of familiarity and settled habit, the everyday easement of the "taken-for-granted" which, though largely ignorant of, guides our waking commerce with one another. A peace of mind beyond price; one that suggests [does it not?] that Aristotle's pre-occupation with Philia is close to the mark in some respects.

S: A little florid, but I take your point. That said, the Metic point is surely a more circumscribed one: namely, we can only "love" certain people - those whose character, concerns, interests reflect or mirror our own? And this is no accident, since for all the talk of altruistic concern, the beloved is - if well chosen - primarily a vehicle for the furtherance of the lover's own self-love and self-knowledge.

A: Apart from my agreeing with Aristotle that the pursuit of self-interest and altruism are not mutually exclusive, I still don't see how you see us as two peas in a pod?

S: Well, the self-knowledge thing. Neither of you believe that the good can be found by simple introspection. In fact, thinking about it the Metic is less interested in the "good" than he is the "right". Yes, that's it! Doing the right thing for the reasons at the right time. 944 Can't remember where he says this. Probably in that book dedicated to that errant, emission of his. But that's the function of the beloved; he acts as a kind of mirror by means of which we can get to understand the motives that drive our own actions, precisely because he and I are alike.

# CHEWING THE CUD

Hence again why the friend must be well chosen and the relationship must endure if such fruit is to be gathered. In loving and valuing the beloved for his own sake, one learns to love and value oneself.945"By oneself it is not easy to be continuously active but with others and towards others it is easier". 946 In the vernacular, a really close friend of this kind enables us to be the best we can.

A: Given how you feel about him that's a fair summation of his view.

S: I guess philosophical etiquette must extend even to him.

A: So what's your objection? After all this is a very moralistic take on love, shouldn't it be right up your street?

S: I've been wondering about that as I was speaking. Its not just the substitution of what is right for what is good, it is the absence of the erotic element, any concern for the pursuit of the beautiful. It's all so lacking in passion.

A: On that we can agree. The criteria for beauty have here metamorphosed; the most beautiful is no longer flourishing physicality beloved of the aesthetic drives; now it is moral or ethical virtue. It puts me in mind of your assertion that the Aesopian fable is the proper form of poetry. 947

S: You've lost me. Why are we suddenly talking about art again?

A: Because art is the only superior counterforce against all will to the denial of life, as the antichristian, anti-Buddhist, anti-nihilistic par excellence"948

S: Using the more obscure to explain the obscure doesn't help any.

A: Christianity gave Eros poison to drink - he did not die of it, to be sure, but degenerated into vice. 949An artistic-servitude in service of the ascetic ideal is therefore the most genuine artist-corruption there can be, sadly also one of the most common.950

S: No help, I'm afraid.

A: And mention of fear reminds me we have said nothing about it and love. After all fear as promoted knowledge of men more than love has, for fear wants to divine who the other is, what he can do, what he wants: to deceive oneself in this would be disadvantageous and dangerous. On the other hand, love contains a secret impulse to see as much beauty as possible in the other or to elevate him as high as possible: to deceive oneself here would be a joy and an advantage - and so one does so.951

S: It's not just my legs that find it hard to keep up with you.

A: Sorry. Do you want to stop a while?

S: That fallen tree trunk that last week's storm seems to have brought down will do.

A: Do you think it made a sound when it fell if there was no one to hear it? 952

S: Oh, for God's sake man! No brainteasers, please. I'm well and truly in the wars as it is, what with these cursed ache and pains. I've yet to get a handle on your claim about love as self-deceit. Fall we may and must, but love is surely our means of ascent to a better world?

A: Have you noticed that? As soon as any war breaks out anywhere, there also breaks out precisely among the noblest people a pleasure that, to be sure, is kept secret: rapturously, they throw themselves into the new danger of death because the sacrifice for the fatherland seems to them to offer the long desired permission - to dodge their goal; war offers them a detour to suicide, but a detour with a good conscience. 953

S: That's grotesque!

A: Is it? How else do we generals win battles, if not by capitalizing on this desire? How else did Miltiades triumph at Marathon than seeming to launch a frontal assault on the vastly superior Persian force and then catching the Persians in a pincer movement?

S: Seeming?

A: The numbers in the frontal assault were deliberately thinned so as to allow the Persians by weight of their superior numbers to easily punch a hole through the initial Greek assault and thereby fatefully extending and exposing their lines to the full force of the Greek pincer movement. The huge Persian losses compared to our own bare testimony to the success of Miltiades' strategy; a strategy, nonetheless, dependent on the suicidal sacrifice of the few for the sake of the many? 954

## CHEWING THE CUD

S: All right, all right. But why are you telling me all this? So far you seem intent, if intent on anything at all, on detailing the negatives on creating a picture of love as blind, reckless, selfish, amoral even? One might be forgiven for thinking that for you the whole thing is a mirage, a charade acted out by the foolish.

A: Ah, but whence is the origin of the sudden passion - the passion of the profound and inward kind - that a man feels for a woman? Least of all from sensuality alone: but when a man encounters weakness and need of assistance and at the same time high spirits together in the same being, then something takes place in him like the sensation of his soul wanting to gush over: he is at the same moment moved and offended. At this point there arises the source of great love. 955

S: Just to be clear; this is not an endorsement of the Metic's view?

A: No. This is basically a question of taste and aesthetics: would it be desirable, that the "most respectable", i.e., the most boring species of human should be left? 956

S: Ha, ha. Well said. Even so, just to be doubly clear? A few moments ago you spoke of Eros being poisoned by these Christians who are yet to appear? You seemed to imply that Plato and I were in some way culpable?

A: For stockpiling "trouble in store".

S: Meaning? I am wrong to declare that it is the duty of every man to honour love? 957

A: It's this amalgamation of love with beauty, goodness and truth that's the problem; that and the whole business of "ascent". We are to think that sex is the means and not the end; that sex is merely the gateway to higher things, to some sort blessed union such as prefigures what awaits beyond the grave - to some unchanging essence free of loss and suffering.
Don't you see it makes a vice of the very thing that is the very hallmark of human, all too human love: the singular attention to the particularity of the beloved? We love altogether fewer people than we find beautiful, and all too often those who are far from good. Hephaestus was right: love cannot know exactly what it wants. All this striving after something unchanging and eternal; this pursuit of wholeness, of beauty in itself; this obsession with the good that particular good things are claimed to instantiate, threatens to corrupt and pervert what is life-giving about Eros into a death drive.

S: Run that by me again.

A: Love becomes a force for destruction from the noblest of ideals, and this not because of any jealousy or possessiveness. Rather Eros desires a consummation that subjugates human life as we know it: that is to say, as people whose lives cannot be otherwise than framed by time and transience, and by the permanent peril of loss and loneliness.

S: But that's not to say that youth has the monopoly when it comes to love. An older man might teacher a younger to avoid many of the pit-falls?

A: Trust you to try a last throw of the dice. The un-Socratic irony here is surely that the opening up of the beloved to the lover makes him, or her, more vulnerable to loss and luck - not less.
     Come. Let's get you back on your legs. There's more to be said about this.

S: There is?

A: Most certainly. Only as an aesthetic phenomenon is reality and the world eternally justified. 958

S: Yet more of the oblique, if my ears don't deceive me? You said something to this effect earlier. I've been wanting to address it, for there seems to be something of a tension, perhaps an irresolvable one, between your commitment to truth on the one hand and your commitment to beauty on the other - between the epistemic and the aesthetic?


CHAPTER 14
**Rausch! – and in double quick time**

A: Its more apparent than real - the tension you refer to. If you don't mind, could we address that last. The whole issue appears less innocuous if you'll allow me to clarify what I understand by "beauty"?

S: You are beginning to appear something of a tease in respect of all this. Right from the outset you've been promising an answer, yet on every occasion we approach the point of consummation I find you with one foot out of the bed. There's always some excuse as to why you are not quite ready, not yet fully in the mood. There was once a time when I was minded to complain that Xanthippe kept me on short rations. Compared to you she now seems, with hindsight, to have been generous beyond compare!

A: Its only because its difficult to articulate. Art, ... in which precisely the lie is sanctified and the will to deception has a good conscience, is much more fundamentally opposed to the ascetic ideal than is science: this was instinctively sensed by Plato, the greatest enemy of art Europe has yet produced. Plato versus Homer: that is the complete, the genuine antagonism - there the sincerest advocate of the "beyond", the great slanderer of life; here the instinctive deifier, the golden nature. 959My idea of the philosopher of the future is that of an artistic Socrates.

S: Now you really are playing the coquette.

A: No, I'm serious.

S: Taking the piss more like, as I'm sure I'm going to find to my cost. But go on, I'll try it on for size since you've whetted my appetite once more. Before you do, let me say, having spent a lifetime honing it, I'd rather go down as the "truthful Socrates". As far as I can make out you lack any commitment in this regard.

A: Not to any particular theory of truth to be sure, but that's not to say I'm uninterested in the truth. The "Truthful Socrates". now that would be a fine thing to behold. Man is very well defended against himself ... he is usually able to perceive only his outer walls. The actual fortress is inaccessible, even invisible to him, unless his friends and enemies play the traitor and conduct him by a secret path. The thing is that I don't share your faith in what lies behind such commitments to "Truth" - the belief that there is some stable, enduring reality, or, as in your case, a metaphysical reality. As a consequence truth and knowledge has to re-situated within "the world of life, nature, and history". 960 Moreover, all of life is based upon semblance, art, deception, points of view, and the necessity of perspectives and error."961

S: Not the sort of place then where truth is to be found?

A: Sly old goat! Have I not said many times that nonetheless the desire to reject this supposition betrays a hostility to life, a metaphysical desire to negate the world of life, nature and history in favour of what? - another world, and one that remains forever indemonstrable. 962Enough, I am still living; and life is, after all, not a product of morality: it wants deception, it lives on deception ... but there you are, I am already off again, am I not, and doing what I have always done, old immoralist and bird-catcher that I am - speaking unmorally, extra-morally, "beyond good and evil'? 963

S: Yes, let's stick to the beaten path; as yet I've still to decide whether it is a friend or an enemy who might be leading me up the garden path.

A: Ah, that's where Piri would come in handy; he's got a nose. If you and he could swap noses, you'd find it a sight easier to hunt yourself.

S: Hmm, some say that if a hound is to be biddable, he's got to find you more interesting than any other dog's arse. As to the issue at hand, I've yet to hear how aesthetic judgments which are notoriously febrile, not to say subjective, may be relied upon when it comes to the creation of values to live by.

A: For a philosopher to say," the good and the beautiful are one", is infamy; if he goes on to add, "also the true", one ought to thrash him. Truth is ugly. 964

S: Instead of trying to get me to rise tell me about this "Rausch" of yours - a pet name for Eros, for the pursuit of beauty?

A: The condition of pleasure called Rausch is precisely a high feeling of power - /the sensations of space and time altered: tremendous distances are surveyed and as it were first apprehended .../ the refinement of the organ for the apprehension of much that is very small and fleeting / divination, the power of understanding with only the slightest of aids, from any suggestion, "intelligent" sensuality - strength as a feeling of mastery in the muscles, as suppleness and pleasure in movement, as dance, as levity and presto. 965

S: So then a feeling of potency, of heightened awareness, but to what end?
A while back you conceded that this feeling could be errant. 966

A: The capacity for Rausch can be active or passive; creative [making beauty] or receptive [the enjoying of beauty].

S: But not a yardstick for the judging of beauty?

A: Oh no, that too. I'll come to that. For the moment, observe that our aesthetics has, up to now, been a woman's aesthetics insofar as only the receivers of art have formulated their experience of "what is beautiful". In all philosophy up to now the artist is lacking. 967

S: So, the spectator's aesthetic experience is a paler version of that of the artist, or creator but one that nonetheless activates this feeling of Rausch? Different in intensity, it doesn't preclude enjoyment of higher feelings.

A: Art reminds us of states of animal vigour; it is on the one hand an excess and overflowing of blooming physicality into the world of images and desires; on the other, an excitation of the animal function through the images and desires of intensified life; - an enhancement of the feeling of life, a stimulant to it". 968

S: Must you always drag everything back to bestial origins? It puts in mind of the tawdry excuses my old man used to offer my long, suffering mother. I used to try to mediate, you know? I got into my head that reason would placate the wild words they exchanged. In fact, looking back on it may well be when philosophy began to take hold of me. The desire for clarity, certainty, order and what have you probably made me a little smug back then.
Every success I remember was always greeted by, "What do you know? When you grow up you'll realize you don't know nothing about the world!" Ironic given the way things turned out, but peculiarly dis-spiriting at the time. The really weird thing was that I never gave up. Every rebuff just served to drive me to make shore I got it right the next time - not that I ever did to her satisfaction. Curiously, my dad - always out of earshot - would always offer a consoling word, some mollification: "That's just your mother's way", or some such. "There will come a day when you'll have to wake your ideas up!" That was another of hers.

A: What can I say? As artist a man in this state transforms things until they mirror his power - until they are reflections of his perfection. This having to transform into perfection is - art. 969 He counts everything beautiful that reminds him of the feeling of perfection; the states in which we lay a transfiguration and fullness into things and poetize about them until they mirror back our fullness and joy in life. 970

S: Zeus. You won't be deflected will you?

A: You want me to address the stones you carry in your heart?

S: Oh, never mind. It's not that important. As I said before, he, my father, thought he was always working against grain with me.

# CHEWING THE CUD

A: Sad to say, the sober, the weary, the exhausted, the dried-up [the scholars] can receive absolutely nothing from art, because they do not have the artistic ur-force, the pressure of riches: whoever cannot give, also receives nothing. 971

S: Well, thank Zeus it takes all sorts to create a world.

A: Isn't that the truth. To experience a thing as beautiful means: to experience it necessarily falsely. 972

S: Isn't that the truth.

A: Not as you understand it, but we'll come back to that. Artists have an interest in the existence of a belief in the sudden occurrence of ideas, in so-called inspirations; as though the idea of a work of art, a poem, the basic presupposition of a philosophy flashed down from heaven like a ray of divine grace. In reality a good artist or thinker is productive continually, of good, mediocre and bad things, but his power of judgment, sharpened and practiced to the highest degree, rejects, selects, knots together ... out of many beginnings. He who selects less rigorously and likes to give himself up to his imitative memory can, under the right circumstances, become a great improviser; but artistic improvisation is something very inferior in relation to the serious and carefully fashioned artistic idea. All great artists have been great workers, inexhaustible not only in invention but also in rejecting, sifting, transforming, ordering. 973

S: Ah, Alcibiades 1 and 2, eh? Beware of cheap imitations. Do you think we'd appear as cheap imitations if someone were writing this down? Sorry, the thought keeps recurring what with me being for all eternity, for most people that is, a figment of Plato's imagination? Sometimes I think the only respite I get in regard of living my own life is when he gets one of his writer's blocks. I tried once when he was having one of these episodes to discuss the legacy he was creating for me. Never again. Forgive me if I've already said. Couldn't tear my eyes away from his finger - nails – like talons. Never done a day's work in his life of course. And then he puts his head on one side just like a hawk. "So what are you after then? An apology?" And then he exclaims, "Then that's what you'll get!" and begins to roar. I mean – really roar with laughter, as if he's said something hilarious? I felt as if I were somehow feeding him raw meat.

A: Hmm, if productive power has been blocked for a time and prevented from flowing out by an obstruction, there occurs in the end an effusion so sudden it appears that an immediate inspiration without any preliminary labour, that is to say a miracle, has taken place. This constitutes the familiar deception with whose continuance the interest of all artists is, as aforesaid, a little too much involved. The capital has only been accumulated; it did not fall from the sky all at once. Similar apparent inspiration is also to be found in other domains, for example in that of goodness, virtue, vice. 974

S: Typical! With you, all nourishment comes with vinegar. Let's not get side--tracked. This old prune has heard tell from you much about creation and appreciation of beauty, but naught of judgment of it.

A: Did I not say a while ago concerning the origin of the beautiful and the ugly that what instinctively repels us, aesthetically, is proved by humanity's longest experience to be harmful, dangerous, worth of distrust: the suddenly voiced aesthetic instinct [in disgust, e.g.] contains a judgment? 975

S: Come on now; nail your colours to the mast! First you tack one way, then the other. Which has primacy with you here: the epistemic or the aesthetic?

A: My thought is that aesthetic taste was first bred as an epistemic ability. Forget our appreciation of art in the usual sense; all that is secondary, derivative. Nothing is more conditioned, let us say narrower, than our feeling of beauty. Whoever would think of it apart from the pleasure of humans in humans, would immediately lose ground and footing. 976 Doesn't Plato say much the same: all beauty incites procreation, - ... just this is the proprium of its working, from the most sensual up to the most spiritual? 977

S: A moment? Beauty rouses thoughts of procreation by stimulating your Rausch, and all this rooted in sexuality: is that it?

A: Everything perfect and beautiful works as unconscious reminders of that enamoured state and its way of seeing -every perfection, all beauty of things reawakens through contiguity the aphrodisiac bliss. 978

S: As you well know this particular old prune advocates a search for the beauty within.

A: What can I say other than it is the body that speaks here. Just as only the human is beautiful, so, too, nothing is ugly except the degenerating human being. In the ugly, one hates the decline of his type. Here he hates out of the deepest instinct of the species; ... it is the deepest hatred there is. It is by virtue of this that art is deep. 979 Ugliness signifies the decadence of a type, contradiction and lack of co-ordination between the inner parts - signifies a decline in organizing strength, in "will", to speak psychologically. 980

S: Don't let's resort to euphemism.

A: The aesthetic judgments [taste, displeasure, disgust, etc.,] are what make up the ground of the table of goods. This in turn is the ground of moral judgments. 981

S: But these "aesthetic judgments" of yours hardly qualify as proper thoughts. If what you say about the inciting of Rausch is true, they are more like feelings?

A: We have a "nose" for this sort of thing. Remember it is the body that judges here; probably, early doors, these aesthetic judgments were also epistemic judg-ments designed to pick out the fittest mate. Thus the beautiful and the ugly are rec-ognized as conditioned; namely with regard to our under most preservation values; to want to posit a beautiful and an ugly apart from that is senseless. 982

S: With all due respect, where is the heat and fire of the erotic in this?

A: I was coming to that. Once the aesthetic drive is at work, a whole host of other perfections, originating elsewhere, crystalize around "the beautiful one". It is not possible to remain "objective", or to suspend the interpretive, additive, completing, poetizing force. 983 A man sees a woman and, as it were, makes her a present of everything preferred, so the sensuality of the artist lays into one object anything else he honours and esteems - in this way he perfects an object. 984

S: And thus it is that the lover begins to "lie", is that it?

A: Quite so. Aesthetic judging cedes place to aesthetic enjoying; whereas the for-mer judged fitness, the latter excites sexual pursuit - feeling eclipses the body's judgment. Rausch delights in beautifying the chosen one far beyond that original judgment. Isn't this what every lover does: make of the lover the heart of his world? Does one want astonishing proof of how far the transfiguring power of Rausch goes? "Love" is this proof ... Rausch will be finished with reality in such a way that the cause of love is extinguished in the consciousness of the lover, and something else seems to find itself in its place - a vibrating and glittering of all the magic mirrors of Circe. 985

# CHEWING THE CUD

S: Isn't that the truth of it. Last night when I caught a glimpse of what lay beneath Charmides' robe I nearly lost ... This passionate fixation? This partiality? It's not a straightforward lying is it? I mean, one lies not in seeing beauty that isn't there, but in amplifying, embroidering, this particular beauty to the exclusion of all others?

A: Yes. You seem to be in agreement with me?

S: Not at all. To be sure, many experience this as you say. But for me this initial state of affairs is merely the prelude to searching for the beauty within. All this seems rather to flag up the weakness of your perspectival view of reality. The intense partiality at play in being "in love" is such that any would be countervailing measures such as widening the perspective to include others or acknowledging the blinkered nature of the current perspective would be tantamount to an acknowledgement that the other's charm had been dispelled.

A: Point taken, is the world beautified by the fact that man takes it for beautiful? He has humanized it: that is all. But nothing, quite nothing, guarantees us that man should furnish the model of beauty. Who knows what he may look like in the eyes of a higher judge of taste? 986 Anyway, let us not forget the creative aspect of aesthetics. The lovers can enhance and perpetuate their charms through self-beautifying. This is not simply a matter of giving nature a helping hand for as I said we are already primed by nature to seek fitness in the other. Grooming, ornament, dress serve to create and enhance the impression of ascending life, not least procreative desirability.

Woman, conscious of man's feelings concerning women, assists his efforts at idealization by adorning herself, walking beautifully. 987If women had been as devoted to the beauty of men, it would in the end be the rule among men to be beautiful and vain - as it is now the rule among women ... It shows the greater and soberness of women [perhaps also their deficiency in aesthetic sense], that women also accept ugly men; they look more at what matters here: protection, maintenance; men more at the beautiful appearance. 988

S: Men are ever more likely to be gulled by such "lies", it is true. Hipparete gait is tantamount to a provocation compared to Xanthippe's matronly ambulation.

A: Woman learns how to hate...

S: .." to the extent that she unlearns how - to charm". 989 I remember.

349

A: Men are more easily duped by such sexual "lies". Natural selection already favours those who are healthy, so the sexes are predisposed to try to appear more healthy, and thus each will try to manipulate the other's aesthetic judgment it seems to me. Nature strives to arrive at beauty: if this is achieved somewhere, it concerns itself with propagating it. 990

S: Wait up. Just to be clear about this? This judging comes first; the creating and enjoying aspects are secondary? But we are mistaken in thinking that beauty is just there, so to speak? Rather nature in terms of preservation and procreation, has set us up to seek out fitness in regard of potential mates and this Raucsh of yours is the excitement aroused in us that conduces us to accomplish this?

A: Correct, as far as the initial phase is concerned.

S: "Initial phase"?

A: We are social animals, as well. Remember? As such the social practices aim to modify our more deep-seated natural behaviour and values toward ends determined by herd values.

S: Ah, yes. Your contention that our usual practice of explaining what we do in terms of motives misleads us; our actions being far from transparent to us?

A: As members of the herd our behaviour is already selected for certain outcomes independently of whether we as individuals choose these outcomes. Social practices, like inbred drives, derive their meanings and ends from what has gone on before. Thus the social practices in which I participate have ends determined not by my motives and intentions but by that history of which I am, to various degrees, ignorant.

S: Yes, yes; hence the need for recourse to your genealogy to clarify this. But how does this bear on the issue of aesthetics? Judging by your demeanour there is something more at stake here. Why don't you just come out with it?

A: I wanted to make sure that I was taking you with me. All right, I'll say it. Art is the only superior counter-force against all will to denial of life, as the anti-Christian, anti-Buddhist, anti-nihilistic, par excellence.991 An artistic servitude in service of the ascetic ideal is therefore the most genuine artist-corruption there can be, sadly also one of the most common. 992 Herding requires us to be more similar to one another and therefore a constraining of the very bodily instincts that induce us to seek selfish pleasures; it is predisposed to an ascetic ideal.

S: So, we are back once again with culture and civilization; civilization as taming?

A: And the nefarious effects of your campaign against the arts, for after you the virtuous hero must be a dialectician; thereafter there must be a necessary, visible connection between virtue and knowledge, faith and morality. 993
The herd-human will have the value feeling of the beautiful through different things than will the exceptional or overman. 994

S: It's all very well your getting impatient and caustic with me, but if you really want me to understand you're going to have to rein in your temper and supply me with something other than sarcasm. Once upon a time that dirty dog, Diogenes gatecrashed a party at Plato's house. Ostentatiously trampling upon Plato's new carpets he declaimed to the appalled throng, "Behold, I walk over Plato's pride!" "Yes", said Plato, "with pride of another sort".

A: Espied scraping vegetables, Plato whispered to him that he could avoid such menial labour by joining Dionysius' entourage. To which Diogenes, equally discreet, replied that, he, Plato, wouldn't have to be part of Dionysius' gang if he was not too proud to scrape vegetables. Yes, I've heard the stories. Asked what sort of man Diogenes was, Plato replied, "Socrates, with a screw loose". Sorry, it's been a long day. No, that's a lame excuse in itself. You are right. I apologize. Look at it this way. Generally speaking herd imperatives will try to appropriate art for the purposes of moralizing us so as to better to cement group identity. To this end they will seek to revise the criteria for "beauty" to which Rausch and aesthetic judgments in general are responses. Your arguments for the exclusion of the poets from the ideal society are a case in point, not content with challenging what tradition has instantiated you also want to impose your own moralized outlook on artistic production.

S: Tradition?

A: Tradition takes the former self-beautifying practices and transforms as a means of fostering unity among the herd. Art begins to assume a public face and becomes a means of displaying the customs and practices of the group. The aesthetic state has an over-richness of means of communication, together with an extreme receptivity for stimuli and signs. It is the high point of communicativeness and transmissiveness between living beings, - it is the source of language. 995

The change in general taste is more powerful than that of opinions. Opinions, along with all the proofs, refutations, and the whole intellectual masquerade, are merely symptoms of the change in taste and most certainly not what they are still often supposed to be, its causes.

What changes the general taste? The fact that some individuals who are powerful and influential announce without any shame, this is ridiculous, this is absurd, in short, the judgment of their taste and nausea; and then they enforce it tyrannically. Thus they coerce the many, and gradually still more develop a new habit, and eventually all a new need. 996

S: And we moralists, what do we contribute to this end?

A: A bad conscience. Art becomes the means by which religions teach that the appetites of the body are evil and the sufferers are themselves to blame for this. Art begins to be subverted by the ascetic ideal. The beautiful is re-fashioned as what is morally good. It is no longer the beauty of the body that we should admire, but rather that of the character or soul. Ergo, we must use our power of moral reasoning to judge the beautiful, which in its turn means that what is beautiful must meet one, and only one standard. And since this moral reason is independent of all instincts and interest, beauty becomes, as Zopy puts it, a kind of disinterestedness. Contempt for "naturalness", for desire, the ego: an attempt to understand the highest spirituality and art as consequence of a depersonalization and as desinteressement.997

S: Couldn't have put it better myself; exactly as it should be; Art as a bromide, as a means of quieting your Rausch. Instead of activating and energizing the other drives, as you might put it, and sexuality in particular, a moralizing art seeks to deaden them and divert them from their natural objects.

A: But don't you see if you demand art when you are sick you make sick the artists? 998 Such artists will create for the most part out of lack or deficiency rather than the abundance of the healthy artist. A fat lot you understand. A moralized art can still evoke Rausch, still excite the drives, but wear them out by a false strengthening of the will and feeling.

S: How so?

A: Romanticism. Every art, every philosophy may be viewed as a remedy and an aid in the service of growing and struggling life; they always presuppose suffering and suffers. But there are two kinds of suffers: first, those who suffer from the over-fullness of life - they want a Dionysian art and likewise a tragic view of life, a tragic insight - and then there are those who suffer from the impoverishment of life and seek rest, stillness, calm seas, redemption from themselves through art and knowledge, or intoxication, convulsions anaesthesia, and madness. All romanticism in art and insight corresponds to the dual needs of the latter type ...

He that is richest in the fullness of life, the Dionysian god and man, cannot only afford the sight of the terrible and questionable but even the terrible deed and any luxury of destruction, decomposition, and negation. In his case, what is evil, absurd, and ugly seems, as it were, permissible, owing to the excess of procreating, fertilizing energy that can still turn any desert into lush farmland. Conversely, those who suffer most and are poorest in life would need above all mildness, peacefulness, and goodness in thought and deed - if possible, also a god who would be truly a god for the sick, a healer and saviour; also logic, the conceptual understanding of existence - for logic calms and gives confidence - in short, a certain warm narrowness that keeps away fear and encloses one in optimistic horizons.

Thus I gradually learned to understand Epicurus, the opposite of a Dionysian pessimist; also the "Christian" who is actually only a kind of Epicurean - both are essentially romantics - and my eye grew sharper for that most difficult and captious form of backward inference in which the most mistakes are made: the backward inference from the work to the maker, from the deed to the doer, from the ideal to those who need it, from every way of thinking and valuing to the commanding need behind it.

Regarding all aesthetic values I now avail myself of this main distinction: I ask in every instance, "is it hunger or superabundance that has here become creative? At first glance another distinction may seem preferable - it is far more obvious - namely the question whether the desire to fix, to immortalize, the desire for being prompted creation, or the desire for destruction, for change, for future, for becoming. But both of these kinds of desire are seen to be ambiguous when one considers them more closely; they can be interpreted in accordance with the first scheme that is, as it seems to me, preferable. The desire for destruction, change, and becoming can be an expression of an overflowing energy that is pregnant with future [my term for this is, as is known, Dionysian]; but it can also be the hatred of the ill-constituted, disinherited, and underprivileged, who destroy, must destroy, because whatever exists, indeed all existence, all being, outrages and provokes them. To understand this feeling, consider our anarchists closely.

The will to immortalize also requires a dual interpretation. It can be prompted, first, by gratitude and love; art with this origin will always be an art of apotheoses, ... But it can also be the tyrannical will of one who suffers deeply, who struggles, is tormented, and would like to turn what is most personal, singular and narrow, the real idiosyncrasy of his suffering, into a binding law and compulsion - one who, as it were, revenges himself on all things by forcing his own image, the image of his torture, on them, branding them with it. ...

[That there still could be an altogether different kind of pessimism, a classical type - this premonition and vision belongs to me as inseparable from me, as my own and my quintessence; only the word "classical" offends my ears, it is far too trite and has become round and indistinct. I call this pessimism of the future - for it comes! I see it coming! - Dionysian pessimism. 999

S: Well that was a load off.

A: We always express our thoughts with the words that lie to hand. Or, to express my whole suspicion: we have at any moment only the thought for which we have to hand the words. 1000

S: Ha, ha. You'd be the last to be at a loss for words, that's for sure.
At risk of appearing stolid, the only words I have to hand are: what in heaven's name has all this to do with love?

A: You still don't get it, do you? One last time; love as you think of it seeks an ideal characterized by eternity without change, good without bad, the spiritual shorn of the physical. It culminates in a Romanticism, which takes two forms: either escape through withdrawal through quietude, or else a frenzy of self-destruction. The vehemence of the latter is result of exhaustion, impoverishment of life rather than any self-proclaimed vitality.

S: Yes, yes. There is no need for you to repeat yourself.

A: Romanticism in terms of spirit is no more than a late manifestation of that Platonism of the people whereby you and yours set about turning the denial of life into a moral duty, setting us against ourselves. 1001 Inciting us to damn all that has to do with the world, with the body, with the assertion of our natural power and strength, and to value in its stead humility, selfless and their cognates. A short step from here and you get the invention of a god who saves the weak and punishes the strong, and the intention of that free will through which we are supposedly at liberty to repudiate the very desires that make us the creatures we are. We can no longer conceal from ourselves what is expressed by ... this hatred of the human, and even more of the animal, and more still of the material ... this longing to get away from all appearance, change, becoming ... all this means - let us dare to grasp it - a will to nothingness, an aversion to life, a rebellion against the most fundamental presuppositions of life ...1002

# CHEWING THE CUD

S: And this hatred of the real as you see it? You still haven't said. What has that to do with love?

A: Put it this way then: the will to nothingness, the attempt to repudiate this world, is what has animated, and continues to animate, the attempt of "Judeo-Christian" civilization and - and its an important "and" - its secular successors. Not only this either, for a particular conception of love is informed by this and lies at the very heart of it.

S: Play fair now. I know you think Plato and I instigated this, but you can't hold us entirely responsible for what others then drew by way of their own imperatives from our work. A little knowledge can be a dangerous thing; who knows what some half-educated tyrant might, should circumstances prove propitious, draw from your championing of "higher men"? So tell me why anyone would seek meaning by willing nothingness, as you put it?

A: Out of fear of suffering. Take it from me, the historical record will show that on innumerable occasions this fear has gotten out of hand with the result that the will turns against life itself. The upshot? A culture obsessed with eradicating the causes of suffering, the very sight and reality of suffering. An impossible and self-defeating aim that strikes at the very heart of what makes us the creatures we are. And there's the rub it is not only the religion that pursues this insane ambition, but whatever it spawns by way of science and ethics and politics. The whole shooting match is intent upon eradicating as far as possible all risk and danger so as to bring about a state of anodyne well-being. All of this fostered by ressentiment in respect of suffering, of those who are strong and make us feel weak, and loss, those multifarious losses to which all life is prey. Don't you see? One value has come to dominate here, and especially in regard of love: that of pity for suffering?

S: Well, I begin to see how this all hangs together in your mind and why you laboured the point earlier in the day. All the same, I want to ask: leaving aside your suspicions about pity as a form of power, amidst all the selfishness and what-not isn't it a source of hope that we are sometimes moved by the sufferings of others even if not always or as often as we should perhaps be?

A: One simply knows nothing of the whole inner sequence and intricacies that are distress for you or me. 1003 When we see somebody suffer, we like to exploit this opportunity to take possession of him; those who become his benefactors and pity him ... call the lust for possession that he awakens in them "love"; and the pleasure

355

they feel is comparable to that aroused by the prospect of a new conquest. 1004 All such arousing of pity ... is secretly seductive, for our "own way" is too hard and demanding and too remote from the love and gratitude of others, and we do not really mind escaping from it - and from our very own conscience - to flee into the conscience of the others and the lovely temple of the "religion of pity". 1005

S: I know, I know. We flee into our neighbour from ourselves and would like to make a virtue of that. 1006 No need to reiterate it all. Identic memory, or close to. A bit patchy of late, I'll admit. Still some might say you've a heart of bronze to go with that shield of yours.

A: Come, lets not loose our aim at this critical juncture. The quarry is in sight. Pity is not an isolated question mark. It was precisely here that I saw the great danger to mankind, its sublimest enticement and seduction - but to what? to nothingness? 1007The love that issues from this moral universe of pity of pity is one mired in ressentiment and hatred. The profoundest and sublimest kind of hatred, capable of creating ideals and reversing values, the like of which has never existed on earth before - there grew something equally incomparable, a new love, the profoundest and sublimest kind of love. 1008 From what other trunk could it have grown, if not that of the Judeo- Christian tradition? 1009

S: But surely all would agree that love is the affirmative passion?

A: Indeed. Here love comes to repudiate the world and all that conduces to human well-being. This ideal of love represents a thirst for revenge against the world; it is its triumphant crown spreading itself farther and farther into the purest brightness and sunlight, driven as it were into the domain of light and the heights in pursuit of the goals of hatred ... Jesus of Nazareth, the incarnate gospel of love, this "redeemer" who brought blessedness and victory to the poor, the sick, and the sinners - was he not this seduction in its most uncanny and sublimest form...? 1010

S: You can't kid a kidder. Well, second thoughts, perhaps you can? But does my weather vane detect a half irony in that?

A: "Weather vane"?

S: I've always known which way a man bends.

A: Maybe, but your weather vane is all to cock in this instance. You've clearly had me arse about face!

# CHEWING THE CUD

S: Oh, how I wish!

A: You're incorrigible!

S: And I'll be inconsolable too, if I don't get my way.

A: I pity you. Just when I thought we had got beyond all that!

S: I suppose you wouldn't fancy taking pity on me, just this once?

A: I'd like to shove your irony where the sun doesn't shine!

S: There's always a fair few lads down the docks that are partial to that.

A: What's that you are doing with your hand?

S: Don't you recognise a duck's bill when you see one? Ha, ha. If you could see your face? Sorry. We'll be within sight of the city walls soon. Last chance. The mood waxes and wanes these days. Have to strike when the iron is hot, so to speak, or not at all. It's very far from plain sailing to be pursuing a younger man at my age.

A: How many times? Not interested!

S: Charmides, I mean. People think as the older party as the senior of the two that you call the shots, that you're in control. Its not like that; there are so many indignities one has to endure. Charmides for all his lack of years is far from innocent, and it is not I who has corrupted him. Precocity sometimes come clad in malice. He's all too keen to tell me what his friends want to know about our liaison: "Do I smell?", "What does it feel like to have stroke wrinkled flesh?", "Does he slobber when he kisses you?" And they all mouth, the adults that is, the same inanities when you attempt to explain: "On the bright side, you are only as old as the boy you feel; snigger, snigger". Absolute rubbish! You don't feel like a teenager again; quite the contrary you feel the difference in age every second of the encounter and in myriad ways. Sorry. Rambling now. Some people tell me they are too busy living their lives to engage in philosophy. Sometimes I get to wondering whether I've been too busy doing philosophy to have properly lived mine. Anyway, your half irony, or whatever it was?

## CHEWING THE CUD

A: You know that you've said all that before?

S: At my age I'm always relieved to hear that I've said something only twice, but then that's a problem I wouldn't want to burden you with. Anyway, the half irony - less I forget?

A: History teaches that the branch of a nation that preserves itself best is the one in which most men have, as a consequence of sharing habitual and un-discussable principles; that is to say as a consequence of their common belief, a living sense of community. Here good, sound custom grows strong, here the subordination of the individual is learned and firmness imparted to character as a gift at birth and subsequently augmented. The danger facing these strong communities founded upon similarly constituted firm-charactered individuals is that of the gradually increasing inherited stupidity such as haunts all stability like its shadow.

It is the more unfettered, uncertain and morally weaker individuals upon whom spiritual progress depends in such communities: it is the men who attempt new things and, in general, many things. Countless numbers of this kind perish on account of their weakness without producing any very visible effect; but in general, and especially when they leave posterity, they effect a loosening up and from time to time inflict an injury upon the stable element of the community. It is precisely at this injured and weakened spot that the whole body is as it were inoculated with something new; its strength must, however, be as a whole sufficient to receive this new thing into its blood and assimilate it.

Degenerate natures are of the highest significance wherever progress is to be effected. Every progress of the whole has to be preceded by a particular weakening. The strongest natures preserve the type; the weaker help it to evolve. - Something similar occurs in the case of the individual human being: rarely is a degeneration, a mutilation, even a vice and physical or moral damage in general without advantage in some other direction. The more sickly man, for example, will if he belongs to a warlike and restless race perhaps have more inducement to stay by himself and thereby acquire more repose and wisdom, the one-eyed will have one stronger eye, the blind will see more deeply within themselves and in any event possess sharper hearing.

To this extent the celebrated struggle for existence does not seem to me the only theory by which the progress or strengthening of a man or a race can be explained. Two things, rather, must come together: firstly the augmentation of the stabilizing force through the union of minds in belief and communal feeling; then the possibility of the attainment of higher goals through the occurrence of degenerate natures and, as a consequence of them, partial weakening's of the stabilizing force; it is precisely the weaker nature, as the tenderer and more refined, that makes any progress possible at all. ...That said, the dangerous companion of all duration, established authority, will, to be sure, usually resist it. 1011

S: Well, what do you know? After all that stuff celebrating the exploitation and appropriating of the strong, the man concedes we are sometimes ennobled through degeneration? I never thought I'd live to see the day!

A: It's your preconceptions about me that are being up-ended here, and nothing whatever about what I've been arguing. Human kind in the direst of circumstances will strive flourish, and invent imaginary worlds, if need be, in order to do so. Indeed Christian self-cruelty is a case in point. It has figured as the very womb of all ideal and imaginative phenomena, unearthing an abundance of strange new beauty and affirmation. 1012 Suffice to say, it was the fires of ressentiment that it stoked that first made human beings really interesting. 1013

S: Of course you speak here again from the vantage point of your rear-view mirror, not that I'm denying a certain logic to what you say. Oh, where is Plato? It would be interesting to know what he'd make of this. Have you noticed, he's never around when you need him? I could have done with his presence at the symposium the other night.

A: I've noticed that where you are, he isn't.

S: Yes, its almost as if he's ashamed to be seen with me in public. Still, be that as it may we've a little way to go - with the argument I mean. You've given me the negative, as you see, it with love. What of the positive? Even a heart of bronze must yield sometime?

A: Self-love. Love of fate.

S: And what's to stop the first from being a prescription for complacent self-indulgence.

A: Perhaps you should read what I've written about the demands of a severe nobility. 1014 One thing is needful: that a human being should attain satisfaction with himself ... Whoever is dissatisfied with himself is continually ready for revenge. 1015 What does not have its roots in a severe self-love is rooted in hatred - hate of oneself and hatred for others.

S: And love of fate?

## CHEWING THE CUD

A: One is a piece of fatefulness, one belongs to the whole, one is in the whole. You cannot love another separate from the whole, since she is a part of, a product of the whole of existence. The fatality of her essence is not to be disentangled from the fatality of all that has been and will be. S/he is not the result of a special design, a will, a purpose; s/he is not the subject of an attempt to attain to an "ideal of [wo]man" or an "ideal of happiness" or an "ideal of morality" - it is absurd to want to hand over [her] nature to some purpose or other. 1016

S: Not something with which to charm Hipparete, You're telling me you didn't give her the speech about "the dragon guarding his golden hoard"; that she didn't want to hear how to you as her lover "the whole rest of the world appears indifferent, pale, and worthless"?

A: Well I'd bet money Xanthippe's left ear isn't burning at this moment.

S: Hmm, I'm with Antisthenes on that one. We were discussing it last week. You know what he said to me? "I'd rather lose my mind than lose myself in pleasure". 1017

A: A right bundle of fun, he sounds. A sore disappointment to Gorgias, I'd bet. Anyway, if you are going to quote me back at myself, you might finish the quote. "One comes to feel genuine amazement that this wild avarice injustice of sexual love has been glorified and deified so much in all ages - indeed, that this love has furnished the concept of love as the opposite of egoism while it actually may be the most ingenuous expression of egoism". 1018 Maybe it is an illusion that love is perfected cloistered from the world; a noble love welcomes chance and necessity' rather than searches for safeguards from them.

    Love of fate - you see? I want to learn more and more to see as beautiful what is necessary in things; then I shall be one of those who makes things beautiful. Amor fati: let that be my love henceforth! I do not want to wage against what is ugly. I do not want to accuse; I do not even want to accuse those who accuse. Looking away shall be my only negation. And all in all and on the whole: someday I wish to be only a Yes-sayer. 1019

S: You say this, but tradition has the burden of proof on its side.

A: What first has to have itself proved is of little value. 1020

S: Don't make me. Even a novice would be wise to such a claim.

A: Wise you say? What do know of wise? To have to combat one's instincts - that is the formula for decadence: as long as life is ascending, happiness and instinct are one. 1021 In every age the wisest have passed the identical judgment on life: it is worthless ... Everywhere and always their mouths have uttered the same sound ... a sound full of doubt, full of melancholy, full of weariness with life, full of opposition to life... What does that prove? What does it point to? - Formerly one would have said, "Here at any rate there must be something true! The unanimity of the wise is proof of truth."
Shall we still speak thus today? Are we allowed to do so? "Here at any rate there must be something sick" - this is our retort: one ought to take a closer look at them, these wisest of every age! Were they all of them perhaps no longer steady on their legs? Belated? Tottery? Decadents? Does wisdom perhaps appear on earth as a raven, which is inspired by the smell of carrion? ...

S: You are all the same - you and yours. Think you have all the answers, but you don't! Ignorance dressed up as arrogance is all it is. Have I have not proved it time and again? At my apogee there was a fellow called, ... No. Gone now. Anyway, he used to lay bets on my reducing some supercilious scion or other to a mute or else to apoplexy. For a time I became quite the plebeian champion. Of course, the crowds have dwindled since; the fathers having warned their sons off of competing with me. Victim of my own success you might say; no point in dwelling on past glories though. Look we are within sight of the city walls again; a last chance to trip you up.

A: How's that?

S: You know where I stand, but as to you? What's the more important: art or truth?

## CHAPTER 15
### Of art, and time drawing near

A: Ah yes, art in which precisely the lie is sanctified, and the will to deception has a good conscience at its side, is much more fundamentally opposed to the ascetic ideal than is science. 1022

S: So what are you claiming here: that the will to truth is itself part of the ascetic ideal?

## CHEWING THE CUD

A: Yes. The lie - and not the truth - is divine. 1023

S: Forgive me saying, but your attempt to present yourself as the mirror image of Plato and I would have you court perversity here. Whereas for the sake of knowledge we are prepared to curtail the production of art, you seem set upon the contrary

A: If we had not welcomed the arts and invented this kind of cult of the untrue, then the realization of general untruth and mendaciousness that now comes to us through science - the realization that delusion and error are conditions of human knowledge and sensation - would be utterly unbearable. Honesty would lead to nausea and suicide. But now there is a counterforce against our honesty that helps us to avoid such consequences: art as the goodwill to appearance. We do not always keep our eyes from rounding off something and, as it were, finishing the poem; and then it is no longer eternal imperfection that we carry across the river of becoming - then we have the sense of carrying a goddess, and feel proud and childlike as we perform this service. As an aesthetic phenomenon existence is still bearable for us, and, ... 1024

S: Can I stop you there?

A: Obviously you can, and have!

S: Don't get prissy; I leave it to Plato to correct my grammar. More importantly you said bearable, not justified. If memory serves, early on you claimed: "It is only as an aesthetic phenomenon that existence and the world are eternally justified". 1025

A: And your point is?

S: They are not the same thing at all.

A: Grant me a little license will you? It's not as if you and Plato always sing the same song. One allows that it is a work in progress. Same for me. Early doors I favoured art over truth and then changed my mind; now I more inclined to my original view though with certain caveats. May I finish what I was saying?

S: Aren't you the prickly one?

A: The meeting? Haven't I been more than generous with my time?

362

# CHEWING THE CUD

S: Please.

A: As an aesthetic phenomenon existence is still bearable for us, and art furnishes with eyes and hands and above all the good conscience to be able to turn ourselves into such a phenomenon. At times we need a rest from ourselves...

S: Not half.

A: What was that? I was lost in concentration.

S: Nothing.

A: ... A rest from ourselves by looking upon, by looking down upon, ourselves and, from an artistic distance, laughing over ourselves or weeping over ourselves. We must discover the hero no less than the fool in our passion for knowledge; we must occasionally find pleasure in our folly, or we cannot continue to find pleasure in our wisdom. Precisely because we are at bottom grave and serious human beings - really more weights than human beings - nothing does us as much good as a fool's cap: we need it in relation to ourselves - we need all exuberant, floating, dancing, mocking, childish, and blissful art lest we lose the freedom above things that our ideal demands of us. It would mean a relapse for us, with our irritable honesty, to get entirely involved in morality and, for the sake of the over-severe demands that we make upon ourselves in these matters, to become virtuous monsters and scare-crows. We should be able also to stand above morality - and not only to stand with the anxious stiffness of a man who is afraid of slipping and falling at any moment, but also to float above it and play. How could we possibly dispense with art - and with the fool? - And as long as you are in any way ashamed before yourselves, you do not yet belong with us. 1026

S: That last bit I'll ignore; you seem to have mistaken me for one of your neo-phytes. Don't get me wrong. Its not that I'm uninterested in what these neophytes of yours are to be encouraged to think about art, especially as free spirits. I take as read that according to your schema these people will otherwise be co-opted into a socially moralized, that is to say an art constrained by the imperatives of herd soli-darity. As to the idea of art as a form of recuperation, well that's rather hackneyed; it's also, often - to use your vocabulary - a passive form of recreation. On that most would agree, even if not for quite the reasons you give. You know what's suddenly struck me; your relative indifference to the actual products of artistic endeavour. My omission, in part, I guess. My father tends to loom large when it comes to this topic. He blocks out the light, so to speak. Still I'd be right in thinking that it is the process itself that excites your interest rather than the product?

A: More still the affirmations and values of the artistic type. Yes. Art, in which precisely the will to lie is sanctified and the will to deception has a good conscience, is much more fundamentally opposed to the ascetic ideal than science: this was instinctively sensed by Plato, the greatest enemy of art Europe has yet produced. Plato versus Homer: that is the complete, the genuine antagonism - there the sincerest advocate of the "beyond", the great slanderer of life; here the instinctive deifier, the golden nature. 1027

S: Perhaps I shouldn't say this; this hyperbole of yours. Well ... it can sound slightly crazed. It can be, well, rather intimidating, rather off-putting.

A: I dare say. Sometimes I feel I'm running out of time. I won't get finished what it is I've got to say - that and the fact that few care to listen.

S: If it's any consolation, my string is probably a lot shorter than yours. That's another thing about old age, for the first time in your life you get to stand outside of yourself - to witness the whole thing as you were a third party. I remember waking up one day feeling like someone had thrown a switch, turned down the volume. All the clamour that had previously drowned out the why and wherefore of what I was doing with my life had just died away. It wasn't that the same drives - to use your terminology - had ceased to operate. I just knew that from there on in I would view them with a colder eye. At one and the same time, I felt empowered and a real sense of loss.

Old age is very different to middle age. With that you can be more tha halfway through it, before you realize that you are in it. What's that look on your face? Alarm? Discomfort? Should I not be speaking of these things? Is everything telling you that you would rather not know what you cannot in fact, at present know? You talk too easily about fate, my friend. Not nice to have your chain yanked, is it?

And that's another thing. You get tired; so very tired of it all. You find yourself losing interest. There was a time when I could give you the name of every lyre player here in Athens.

A: Surely that's only to be expected? You can't expect the concerns of every hot-blooded lyre player to continue to speak to you across the generations?

S: No, I suppose not. It's not just the one thing though. There's just so much that you used to do, that year upon year you find yourself no longer doing, no longer even interested in doing. Some days it seems as if, unnoticed and unannounced, you are quietly collapsing in yourself. You want to take yourself in hand, but you find it next to impossible to convince yourself there can be anything new under the sun - and so the doors on the world continue to close.

A: But your appetite for this verbal cut and thrust remains undimmed. That's no small thing.

S: Ah, but is it? You clearly think you can bring me round to your way of thinking. And, no, it's not that I'm passing judgment on the arguments. It's just that I've lived with my beliefs so long that they are who I am. I can't see that changing. For better or worse, I can do no other than play the hand I've got, run down whatever's left of the string. That's not to say I won't continue to play my part here.

Where were we? Oh yes, I remember. Well, at the least you have the option of committing it all to paper. Who knows it might even evade the gnawing criticism of the mice if you are lucky. Chin up, as the Stoics are wont to say; lets see if I can be of help? Let's begin with you clarifying that remark about science not being opposed to the ascetic ideal. I'm sure Democritus would have something to say about that.

A: Indeed he would, but he would nonetheless be mistaken in thinking science to be the liberating force. It is rather scientific methods that comprise a declaration of war and triumph against theology and morality. 1028

S: But Democritus is interested in results, in uncovering truths as he sees it.

A: No doubt, but the pathos that one has the truth now counts for very little in comparison with that other, gentler and less noisy pathos of seeking truth that never wearies of learning and examining anew ... for the scientific spirit rests upon an insight into method, and if every method were lost all the results of science together would not suffice to prevent a restoration of superstition and nonsense. 1029 Truth is not simply to be found: the spirit of all severe, of all profoundly inclined, spirits teaches the reverse. At every step one has to wrestle for truth. 1030 Unconcerned, mocking, violent - thus wants us: she is a woman and always loves only a warrior. 1031 Truth, that is to say, the scientific method, was grasped and promoted by those who divined in it a weapon of war - an instrument of destruction. 1032

S: There's no peace of mind to be had around you, that's for sure.

# CHEWING THE CUD

A: If you take what I'm saying to heart, then you will never pray again, never adore again, never again rest in endless trust; you do not permit yourself before any ultimate wisdom...; no resting place is open any longer to your heart, where it needs to find and no longer seek; you resist any ultimate peace; you will the eternal recurrence of war and peace. 1033

S: Yours would be a hard bed to lie upon. How are your hands? Hot, or cold? My mother used to say, "Cold hands, warm heart". I used to worry that mine were always warm.

A: Perhaps you were meant to?

S: Why you ... I'll have you know my mother was...

A: But the question is: "Did you? Did you know your mother? Were we to attempt to storm your citadel one day, I might wonder if that remark was in fact a curse. Keep your eye on the argument! It is not the victory of science that distinguishes the nineteenth century, but the victory of scientific methods over science. 1034

S: It takes that long?

A: Longer still for the light to dawn. The most valuable insights are discovered last; but the most valuable insights - to repeat - are the methods.1035 Alas, a new force can only appear and appropriate an object by first putting on the mask of the forces which are already in possession of the object. 1036

S: Another dig at my daemon and me. Self-preservation. Needs must. [Begins to jig]. "Well you can tell by the way I walk, I'm a woman's man: no time to talk. Music loud and women warm; I've been kicked around since I was born. You can love me either way...; I'm going nowhere ... somebody help me. Ah, ha, ha, ha, staying alive." 1037

A: What on earth was that?

S: Sorry. Not me at all. Not a description of Xanthippe I recognize either. Must have been my daemon. Catches me on the hop sometimes. "Hop" – get it? Quite out of breathe now. I didn't even know I could dance like one of your free spirits.

A: Is that what you call it?

# CHEWING THE CUD

S: Not so fast. Slow down! Need to catch my breath. Most people, you know, think of old age as a period of gentle, but remorseless decline. Not something I hold with. Death is always hovering over our lives. From time to time he bites great chunks out of our life; thereafter a period of normalcy such that one, foolishly, persuades oneself that the first episode was just that and presaged nothing more. Hence why people are able to persuade themselves they age gradually, that by plucking the odd grey hair from an eyebrow they will somehow slow down and manage the signs of decline if not the substance of it. It's not like that though: one ages quite literally over-night.

A: Can we get on now?

S: Out of step with all stuff of about ascending lines, eh? It's a philosophy for young; stick around and you'll see.

A: Firecracker. Didn't I say? Going to burn up hard and bright.

S: Hmm, no one would argue that the fuse is other than short. Before you do ... we were, or rather you were, discussing the limitations of the scientific outlook?

A: You know the more I become aware of those omnipotent art-drives in nature, and in them the ardent longing for illusion, for redemption through illusion, the more I feel myself impelled to the metaphysical assumption that the truly existent and primal unity, as the eternally suffering and contradictory, also needs the rapturous vision, the pleasurable illusion, for its continuous redemption. 1038

S: "Art drives in nature"?

A: Yes. Art is not just a human artefact; it divulges the world's meaning and significance. What is saved by art is not only human meaning, but life. 1039

S: Wouldn't that require we clip the wings of your "creators", and the reach of their ambition.

A: Can we put them to one side for a moment? The chiaroscuro is important.

S: Don't try to blind me with science? As with that glade over yonder, I need both the light and the shade to see it in its proper relief.

A: Exactly.

367

# CHEWING THE CUD

S: So why attempt to blind me with science?

A: I forgot...

S: Putting "creators" to one side; these memory lapses of yours? Are they something recent? Maybe you are under stress? If you were my age it would probably be a sign of...

A: Oh, for God's sake. Must you always get hold of the wrong end of the stick?

S: What stick's that then? Its the devil's own work trying to figure out what you mean sometimes.

A: I give up. Another instance where you and Plato get it wrong, I was going to say. Books 2, 3 and 10, Plato, if not you as well, attacks tragic poetry on the grounds that it falsely portrays the divine as unstable, dark, immoral, unjust; this not because the sensual pleasures of the arts seduce us to the bodily life, or not just. No, what is it he says in Book 3?

S: The flaw in tragedy is the unrequited suffering of good people. So?

A: The Apollonian is not to do with reason, but with aesthetic form. The apparent world is not a fiction [the "true world" is] but a livable truth. The alternative to appearance is not a "true world" but no world. Apollonian individuation seeks not to deliver us from pain, but rather from life-denial. 1040

S: I don't follow.

A: Both forces must unfold their powers in strict proportion. On its own the Dionysian threatens nihilism and pessimism, Apollonian art permits to find delight in individuals, to satisfy our sense of beauty which longs for great and sublime forms. Although Dionysus in the end holds sway because of the tragic limits that pertain to life's forms, in tragedy the two deities have parity. 1041

S: And these "art drives in nature"?

A: The Apollonian and Dionysian are artistic energies that burst forth from nature herself. Art, quite simply, is an imitation of these creative forces in nature. And in

368

answer to your question: no, art is not rooted in the individual will and the subjectivity of the artist. Humankind are not the true authors of this art world. 1042

S: If so, then ... No, I'll mull that over. In the meantime, could we...?

A: Yes, I was going to say. Truth ...., truth does not count as the supreme value-measure ... The will to appearance, to illusion, to deception ... here counts as deeper, more primal, more metaphysical than the will to truth. 1043 In the main, I agree more with the artists than with any philosopher hitherto: they have not lost the scent for life, they have loved the things of "this world" - they have loved their senses. To strive for "de-sensualization": that seems to me a misunderstanding or an illness or a cure, where it is not merely an hypocrisy or self-deception. I desire for myself and for all who live, may live, without being tormented by a puritanical conscience, an ever greater spiritualization and multiplication of the senses; indeed we should be grateful to the senses for their subtlety, plenitude and power and offer them in return the best we have in the way of spirit...: it is a sign that one has turned out well when ... one clings with ever greater pleasure and warmth to the things of "this world". 1044

S: Forgive my saying, but you never met my father.

A: Perhaps I should enter a caveat: it is not the artist but rather the "artist-philosopher" who creates at this cultural level. 1045

S: You not then advocating some sort of return to a primordial state?

A: There is no going back, and that doesn't mean art is a seduction to untruth in your terms. Art affirms the active powers of creation and transformation; it stands opposed to the ascetic demand for the extirpation of the passions, to the scientific deadening of the receptive faculties. Perspective? Interpretation? You see? All life rests upon semblance, art, deception, points of view, and the necessity of perspectives and error. 1046

S: At last, you admit it. You side with falsehood and lies.

A: Polemic against you Platonists, and others, who go in search of absolute truths and for whom art is a mere diversion. Where's your sense of irony when you need it most? To say it again, there would be no life at all if not on the basis of perspective estimates and appearances; and if, with the virtuous enthusiasm and clumsiness of some philosophers, one wanted to abolish the "apparent world" altogether - well, supposing you could do that, at least nothing would be left of your "truth" either. Indeed, what forces us at all to suppose that there is an essential opposition of "true" and "false"? Is it not sufficient to assume degrees of apparentness and, as it were, lighter and darker shadows and shades of appearance - different values, to use the language of painters? 1047

S: Don't think you can hoodwink me; the substitution of an aesthetic conception of value for a moral one in that aesthetic analogy.

A: I don't deny it. The thing is that the aesthetic point of view is intolerant of any final or totalizing view of reality; it accepts that there is no way to capture the interpretive multiplicity of existence. Though the artist accepts creation necessarily takes place within the constraints of style and perspective, this rather acts as a spur to ever new experimentation and innovation. In like manner the artistic Socrates of the future will find in art a necessary correlative of, and supplement for science.

So many things have to come together for scientific thinking to originate; and all these necessary strengths had to be invented, practiced, and cultivated separately. As long as they were still separate, however, they frequently had an altogether different effect than they do now that they are integrated into scientific thinking and hold each other in check. Their effect was that of poisons; for example, that of the impulse to doubt, to negate, to wait, to collect, to dissolve. Many hecatombs of human beings were sacrificed before these impulses learned to comprehend their coexistence and to feel they were all functions of one organizing force within one human being. And even now the time seems remote when artistic energies amid the practical wisdom of life will join with scientific thinking to form a higher organic system in relation to which scholars, physicians, artists, and legislators - as we know them at present - would have to look like paltry relics of ancient times. 1048

S: Let me see if I've got this straight. The philosopher's task is to create new values? 1049 He is required to do this because the drives, habits, dispositions, that currently guide his thought and behaviour are the expression of values given by a combination of nature and societal conditioning that are prey to nihilism?

A: Yes, the question is: can you give yourself your evil and your good and hang your own will over yourself as a law? Can you be your own judge and avenger of your law? 1050

S: I'm still rather of a mind that if we don't hang together we will surely hang separately, or at least that's what my daemon prompts me to say. 1051 But be that as it may. You say we should take our lead from the artists?

370

# CHEWING THE CUD

A: All this we should learn from the artists while being wiser than they. For with them this subtle strength [making beautiful] usually ends where art ends and life begins; but we will be poets of our lives, and in the smallest and everyday things first. 1052

S: My father wouldn't thank you for that "wiser than they", but I do - on behalf of my mother, God rest her soul. If ever there was anyone who was unlucky in love, it was she. Strange how certain things run in families? Can't honestly say I've been any luckier, neither with Xanthippe, nor latterly with Charmides. No matter how much altruism you attempt to embody in thought and deed it seems to rebound on you.

A: Perhaps love is the last place you should be looking for equality. Often it seems a ceaseless struggle to decide who will command. Remember though the lessons of last night. The lot of you come at it from a position of lack, or alternatively from loss. What if love is fraught with danger, - not in the sense of being carried away by passion. This strikes me as only an effect. What if Aristophanes has got the splitting apart the wrong way around? What if the real danger is that what comes to it as whole, as self-sufficient, is so easily subject to fissure?

S: Trust you to play the devil's advocate. Is there no innocence, no goodness, no fellow feeling, or kindness you won't call into question, or sully with your suspicions?

A: Ah, is it all too much for you and yet, not enough? I'll say it again, and just the once. One thing is needed. To "give style" to one's character - a great and rare art! It is practiced who surveys everything that his nature offers of strengths and weaknesses, and then fits them into an artistic plan, until everyone appears as art and reason, and even the weaknesses delight the eye. 1053

S: Forgive the repetition, but there really is no going back, no way of re-establishing what once was?

A: No. Towards new philosophers, there is no choice; towards spirits strong and original enough to give the impulse for opposite evaluations and to revalue and invert "eternal values". 1054

S: Giving "impulse for opposite valuations"? Am I right to infer that all this self-creation is not after for the benefit of the few?

# CHEWING THE CUD

A: Oh, you humans, there sleeps for me in the stone an image, the image of images! Oh, that it must sleep in the hardest, ugliest stone! .../ The beauty of the overman came to me as a shadow. 1055

S: That'll be your daemon speaking again? "Overman"?

A: Let's not get hung up on terminology; "free spirit" to you.

S: A malicious mind can do a lot of damage with a careless word; from what I hear some treacherous tongues are putting it about that I don't love Athens half as much as they. Speaking of which: this new philosopher of yours? You imply he will be a legislator of new values.

A: An "artistic" Socrates, - yes?

S: How would that work? There's precious little in what you've said that's supportive of the usual notions of communality in this area?

A: Not in how a soul draws near another, but in how it distances itself from it, do I recognize its kinship and commonality with the other. 1056 The weaker presses itself to the stronger, from a nourishment need; it wills to slip under it, if possible to become one with it. The stronger, on the contrary, fends off from itself. 1057

S: My very point.

A: Hah, that's the problem here; you don't read enough. That's why your legacy will be forever contested; someone else will have written it. Your innate conservatism locks you into an oral tradition that's on the wane. If you cared to read my books you'd see that are not just simply the medium by which I hope to make myself known to posterity, they are also the means by which I disclose the values by means of which I have re-made myself in hope that others will do likewise and thus propagate those values. To this end my books are self-consciously literary and avail themselves of certain genres.

S: Assuming these readers are out there.

A: It's not just any reader I want; its slow readers, careful readers, I need. A first requirement, you see - ruminators. To read my work one needs to be a cow, at any rate not a modern man.

372

# CHEWING THE CUD

S: Oomph, I've been looking at you cow-eyed all day; fat lot of good it has done me! Joke! See what you saying about reading your stuff. I can see the page: all those tricks and traps so artfully designed to slow the reader down, to oblige him to pay attention; all those italics, inverted commas, surprise questions, and thoughts that trail off unexpectedly impelling the reader to complete them, to say nothing of the hidden meanings, the double meanings.

A: How would you know that if you hadn't already...

S: It's a strange bird you seek. Even now most want their reading to be quick, short and to the point. They resent reading that steals their time. They lack the stomach necessary for chewing the cud. Speaking of regurgitation reminds me; I was going to say, or rather ask: by your own mouth there can be no blueprint, no template for this self-fashioning?

A: True. Freedom as a self-creator is the goal. As a singularity, as opposed to a societally constituted "individual", there can be no formula or set of rules that can specify how one comes to be such. You can only do this by display or example, such as - if I may say so? - you do in your own inimitable fashion. As I said hitherto there have been no artistic-philosophers. Quite simply, I aspire to exemplify through my books what you seek to do through your daily practice.

S: Give me a moment to collect my thoughts. All these compliments; I'm not used to them, especially from you. Most disconcerting. Now, it seems you are in danger of bending the stick too far, in respect of the both of us I might add. All this artistic creation doesn't take place *ex nihilio* as it were. We are surely as much as artists - truth-seekers, even your so-called free spirits? And yes, you need not re-iterate the stuff about there being no absolutes, but there are nonetheless truths that inform, underpin, and make your creative acts what they are?

A: What are you getting at? The aesthetic whilst it affirms sensuousness, creativity, becoming, etc., cannot take the place of science as the one true theory. That's the point: it throws into question the idea of there being a single totalizing account. The purpose of the genealogy -To take leave of all faith and everyday certainty, to have done with a will to truth that ultimately prefers even a handful of certainty to a whole cartload of beautiful possibilities. 1058

S: I know, I know; to set sail on new seas, etc. Its not as if you go lacking a compass, is it?

# CHEWING THE CUD

A: What do you mean?

S: If you'd stop asking me what I mean I'd tell you! Your genealogy, for a start? It is surely, from one angle, a story of the epistemic constraints on self-creating. For freedom's project to be advanced certain truths have to be grasped about how and why it has been retarded. It's not as if all perspectives in this matter would of equal worth. Some are clearly of more worth than others, more pertinent, more germane when it comes the issue of self-creation. If I'm to give my past deeds a new meaning by re-fashioning them in the light of a new and different future, it is surely of the first importance that I refuse the easy option of lying them away?

A: Strength, freedom through the force and super-force of the spirit, proves itself through scepticism. 1059

S: That's not quite it, is it? To be sure, to build anew you must first demolish existing structures and then clear the ground. But the higher health you are seeking to promote requires that the older values are not simply consigned to the scrapheap, or, again to use your language, "extirpated". Such "extirpation" of previous evils, say, would surely signal that past "mistakes" were being repeated? The creative aspect of your aesthetic approach surely demands that these older values are reshaped so that they are absorbed into the new dispensation so as to be turned to better account?

A: Quite so. As I said a few moments ago all this requires a new conception of truth and knowledge. The philosopher-artist will only appear after the "re-valuation of truth". "Purification of taste" can only be the result of a strengthening of the type. Our society of today only represents culture; the cultured man is lacking. The synthetic man is lacking, in whom the various forces are unhesitatingly harnessed for the attainment of one goal. 1060

S: Let's stick with the question of truth for the moment; I'll come to the issue of taste. However much you want your philosophers of the future to exemplify their new ideal, it seems that they still have need of the truth albeit that cannot avail themselves of an absolute truth. From what you say this new ideal must incorporate the sceptical insights generated by your genealogy in respect of ascetic and herd values. Furthermore this truth needs to reflect not just the thoughts, desires, and behaviour I actually have, for I need, in addition, to be able to see through the specific values I have willy-nilly inherited if I am to re-shape and re-value them to my own ends.

A: A fair summation. Order of rank: - What is mediocre in the typical man? That he does not understand the necessity for the reverse side of things: that he combats evils as one could dispense with them; that he will not take the one with the other - that he wants to erase and extinguish the typical character of a thing, a condition, an age, a person, approving of only one part of their qualities and wishing to abolish the others. The "desirability of the mediocre" is what we others combat: the ideal conceived as something in which nothing harmful, evil, dangerous, questionable, destructive would remain. Our insight is the opposite of this: that with every growth of man, his other side must grow too; that the highest man, if such a concept be allowed, would be the man who represented the antithetical character of existence most strongly, as its glory and sole justification - Commonplace man can represent only tiny nook and corner of this natural character: they perish when the multiplicity of elements and the tension of opposites, i.e., the preconditions for greatness in man, increases. That man must grow better and more evil is my formula for this inevitability -

Most men represent pieces and fragments of man: one has to add them up for a complete man to appear. Whole ages, whole peoples are in this sense somewhat fragmentary; it is perhaps part of the economy of evolution that man should evolve piece by piece. But that should not make one forget for a moment that the real issue is the production of the synthetic man; that lower men, the tremendous majority, are merely preludes and rehearsals out of whose medley the whole man appears here and there, the milestone man who indicates how far humanity has advanced so far. It does not advance in a straight line; often a type once achieved is lost again ... 1061

S: Are you deliberately trying to throw me off the scent, by raising my ire in regard of your denigration of the herd animal?

A: No denigration: I've said as much throughout the day - the herd should be allowed its pleasures. Breeding, too, is aesthetic work. Aesthetic and epistemic work, that is. Although as I've already said, even now the time seems remote when artistic energies and the practical wisdom of life will join with scientific thinking to form a higher organic system in relation to which scholars, physicians, artists, and legislators - as we know them at present - would have to look like paltry relics of ancient times. 1062

Forgive me for raking over things already said, but I'm not sure you've heard me. We face a momentous choice between that of culture and that of politics. Indeed some might say you two have already cast the die in favour of politics, that is to say the claims of justice.

S: And all to the good.

A: But is it; - That the urge for justice should be allowed to swamp all other ideas; that the cry of compassion be allowed to demolish the walls of culture? 1063

S: Imagine: little old me, as a stick of dynamite? Oh yes, I like that.

A: Of course you do; you and your "eternal" values. You can take the rabble out of the gutter, but not the gutter out of the rabble! Individual identity and liberty, for the likes of you, is always a given - something discrete from history and culture.

S: Don't let's fall out; we are nearly home. Let's not go back over old ground. I was merely trying to establish a case for the continuing importance of truth even for your free spirits. I rather fancy that I might nonetheless have saved my best till last. Let's see if a final fling might knock you off your perch?

A: Do your worst; I wouldn't have it any other way.

S: As I recall we were discussing a while back whether you considered life was justified - your original view - or made bearable [a lesser claim] by its being seen as an aesthetic phenomenon. Let's assume I'm persuaded that the "moral" view of life is suspect. My question to you is: is the recuperative aspect of art sufficient for your purposes? I'll answer for you. Whilst the answer is yes in respect of making life bearable, such an answer clearly arises from our position of spectators. In other words it fails to address how it is we come to formulate an aesthetic response to life: a response that you clearly want to advocate?

A: All life is dispute about taste! Taste: that is equally weight and scales and weighed; and woe to any living thing that wills to live without dispute about weight and scales and weighing. 1064

S: Taste?

A: Well, smell if you like.

S: Smell? As in "I smell a rat"?

# CHEWING THE CUD

A: It's your physiognomy Socrates; you can smell what's in front of you, but not what's right under your nose.1065 I? I have a subtler sense of smell for the signs of ascent and decline than any human being has had, I am the teacher par excellence for this, - I know both, I am both. 1066 I possess a perfectly uncanny sensitivity of the cleanliness-instinct, so that I physiologically perceive - smell - the "entrails" of every soul. 1067

S: Hygiene again, is it you arrogant so and so? Not all of us can afford the perfumes and body lotions that the spa has on offer. Just because the gods have blessed you with a body and social cache that allows you to strut your stuff as the implacable and undaunted warrior-hero doesn't entitle you to put on additional airs and graces.

A: I'll have you know I'm very comfortable in this body, born to it I might say.

S: In another life, you might find yourself saddled with a puny frame, half-blind and riddled with what I don't know what, then how ridiculous will all this bombastic preening sound?

A: It was a public space this morning. Isn't that what the demos craves - public spaces?

S: Not public spaces rendered private spaces by cost.

A: *Sans fare rien*, to me. You can't wash "rabble" off, however hard you try.

S: And just as I was warming to you again.

A: Nothing personal. Just saying my greatest danger is disgust at humans, at "rabble". 1068 When all is said, what is the greatest experience you can have? It is the hour of the great contempt; the hour in which even your happiness arouses your disgust, as well as your reason and your virtue. 1069

S: "Reason and virtue"?

A: Of course this last is a bridge too far for your ilk. Even so, you must have sampled a flavour of this some time. Aestheticism can find itself yoked to the "will to truth" at this juncture. You look puzzled. Think back to "The Republic"? All that animus directed at the threat of democracy. Was that not occasioned by a nihilistic despair at the "smallness" of all human beings? 1070

377

## CHEWING THE CUD

S: Not for the first time I object to being yoked to everything Plato said.

A: Oh, come now. You can't start playing the innocent this late in the day. A close reading of even the earlier dialogues reveals you as one who believes human kind to be mired in the deepest ignorance, regardless of that sleight of hand whereby for reasons of personal safety you adopt the guise of one knowingly ignorant. Hypocritical, that's what it is. A Socratic argument always smells of the rabble. 1071

S: Let me tell you now! I'm fast revising my opinion of democracy. High and mighty you may be, but under it I've a right to be heard!

A: Rights? Equal rights? Just so much pissing in the wind, if you ask me? Besides I've not abrogated your write to give me earache, nor would I. But let's be clear, between you and me, I reckon you have earned it. Now let me press my point, and then you may make your objection. Pity smells of the rabble. 1072 Our inbred taste has been given a bad conscience by morality. I say, listen ... to the voice of the healthy body: this is a more honest and purer voice. 1073 It is imperative that we learn to judge "ugly" all that inclines us to think and do the same as others, as the herd, and not simply those facts that might be adduced against the working of herd morality. There are many who threw away their last value, when they threw away their servitude. 1074 We must, perforce, hone our aesthetic judgment against all things that smack of the herd and herd values: whatever reminds us in the least of degeneration ought to cause in us the judgment of "ugly". 1075

S: That's what I'm trying to say. Your defence, your advocacy, of life lived as an aesthetic phenomenon comes down to this - your visceral distaste for - well my way of living and thinking. And this as the prelude to what - your proselytizing? ...

A: In favour of my tastes, the tastes of my free spirits; one needs taste for freedom, for the purposes of engaging in genealogy.

S: As I remember talking about "one" as a kid was enough to get this one beaten up.

A: Every animal abhors just as instinctively and with a subtlety of smell that is "higher than all reason", every kind of disturbance or hindrance that lies or could lie in its path towards the optimum. 1076

S: The little shits would have been glad to know that.

A: You are not hearing. It is not enough just to propound the idea of the aesthetic concept. Taste is not just a matter of conscious deliberation; it has to be incorporated in the body's drives. The aesthetic concept of the great and the sublime: the task is to educate this. 1077We just don't know what a body is capable of, remember? It is not sufficient to provide, as it were, a aetiology of our current values. The values that shape our behaviour do their work unconsciously; if we are to curb their influence then we must seek ways of incorporating our sights at the lower level by listening to the judgments of our bodies in respect of health, diet, climate and other matters. Aesthetic taste is critical as, unlike reason, it can act as a guide in this regard. A well-rounded individual has a taste only for what is good for him. 1078

## CHAPTER 16
## Summation: Time And Tide ...

S: Sorry, just gathering my thoughts. You know what I have here are still a lot of loose strings. I can make out the warp and woof of this philosophical carpet of yours, but as to the detail of its design - ...well? Not only am I unclear   as to what exactly you mean by terms such as freedom, necessity, truth, will to power, etc., but I can't see how they fit together, what kind of unity that they comprise? I'm right to think there's a picture here?

A: Over immense periods of time the intellect produced nothing but errors. A few of these proved to be useful and helped to preserve the species: those who hit upon or inherited these had better luck in their struggle for themselves and their progeny. Such erroneous articles of faith, which were continually inherited, until they became almost part of the basic endowment of the species, include the following: that there are enduring things; that there are equal things; that there are things; substances, bodies; that a thing is what it appears to be; that our will is free; that what is good for me is also good in itself. It was only very late that such propositions were denied and doubted; it was only very late that the truth emerged - as the weakest form of knowledge. It seemed that one was unable to live with it: our organism was prepared for the opposite; all its higher functions, sense perception and every kind of sensation worked with those basic errors which had been incorporated since time immemorial. Indeed, even in the realm of knowledge these propositions became the norms according to which "true" and "untrue" were determined - down to the most remote regions of logic. 1079

S: O.k. there ensues a fight for knowledge.

379

A: Not just that. Knowledge became a piece of life itself, and hence a continually growing power - until eventually knowledge collided with those primeval basic errors: two lives, two powers, both in the same human being. A thinker is now that being in whom the impulse for truth and those life reserving errors clash for their first fight, after the impulse for truth has proved to be also a life-preserving power. Compared to the significance of this fight, everything else is a matter of indifference: the ultimate about the conditions of life has been posed here, and we confront the first attempt to answer this question by experiment. To what extent can truth endure incorporation? That is the question; that is the experiment. 1080

S: Where are you going with this?

A: What, if some day or night a demon were to steal after you into your loneliest loneliness and say to you: "This life as you now live it and have lived it, you will have to live once more and innumerable times more; and there will be nothing new in it, but every pain and every joy and every thought and every sigh and everything unutterably small or great in your life will have to return to you, all in the same succession and sequence - even this spider and this moonlight between the trees, and even this moment and I myself. The eternal hourglass of existence is turned upside down again and again, and you with it, speck of dust!"

Would you not throw yourself down and gnash your teeth and curse the demon who spoke thus? Or have you once experienced a tremendous moment when you would have answered him: 'You are a god and never have I heard anything more divine". If this thought gained possession of you, it would change you as you are or perhaps crush you. The question in each and every thing: "Do you desire this once more and innumerable times more?" would lie upon your actions as the greatest weight. Or how well disposed would you have to become to yourself and to life to crave nothing more fervently than this ultimate eternal confirmation and seal? 1081

S: Where did that come from?

A: My thought of thoughts? 1082 What do you think?

S: How would I answer?

A: More, could you answer - believing as you do?

S: Who could do other than say, "No"?

## CHEWING THE CUD

A: Only those well-disposed to themselves and life : that's the point of the test. Only those who can love fate can rise to the challenge. As an existential challenge, in regard of life affirmation - life affirmation as opposed to life enhancement, remember? - It serves to sort the wheat from the chaff. All those who see time as the enemy, who seek succour from its tragic effects: the consolations of another world the other side of death, or else cling to a belief that the alienation of this present world can be surmounted such that peace may be achieved on earth. Eternal recurrence is my formula for the redemption of time and becoming.

S: Speaking for myself, doesn't this eternal recurrence of yours make moral repugnance futile? What I mean to say is that affirming the repetition of everything implies that I must accept the repetition of even the most horrendous of things that have happened before. On the face of it, you would seem to have bound yourself to an all-encompassing determinism. A determinism that would seem to have dire consequences for yet other of your stated views: those of free will, the sovereign individual, the creativity of such, and that's just for starters. It would appear that the whole skein is now caught in an impossible tangle.

A: Affirming everything is not tantamount to approving everything. Before you dismiss this out of hand, let us first see if we can unravel what appears to you as knots. Many of these I shall argue are the result of your commitment to a particular and perversely peculiar perspective on the world; and before you start accusing me of insulting you, I want to add that this view is, in fact, pervasive.

S: Carry on.

A: Let's begin with necessity, and let us begin by acknowledging that there are no laws in nature. There are only necessities. 1083 Occurrence and necessary occurrence, is for me, a tautology. 1084 Necessity does not follow from the force of law but from the absence of law. 1085 A state is what is rather than something else; an occurrence cannot be otherwise. 1086 There are no alternatives. There is no other mode of action whatever; and the "world" is only a word for the totality of these actions. 1087

S: There is only the present?

A: Not a pure "present, - no. All occurrences are temporally structured. I'll explain in relation to will to power.

# CHEWING THE CUD

S: But if there is no alternative, aren't we then just fated in the sense of bound to having to resign ourselves to the inevitable?

A: We've been here before. Death, change, age, as well as procreation and growth, are for them objections - refutations even. What is does not become; what becomes is not ... Now they all believe, even to the point of despair, in what is. 1088 To crave nothing more fervently? Living on earth is worthwhile: one day, one festival with Zarathustra, taught me to love the earth. "Was that life?" I want to say to death. "Well then! Once more!" 1089   Revaluation of values, yes? Becoming, not being. One cannot assert the value of becoming by wishing its eternity, since one cannot wish the permanence of what essentially involves change. One can, however, wish the eternal recurrence of becoming.

Contempt, hatred for all that perishes, changes, varies - whence comes this valuation of that which remains constant? ... Happiness can be guaranteed only by being; change and happiness exclude one another. 1090 Life affirmation is only possible if I hold no life negating values.

S: And were I to ask what sort of value can underwrite this revaluation of values, you would answer what?

A: Isn't becoming the rudimentary feature of the will to power? Will to power as an "agonistic" force field. There are no stable identities such as the binary thinking you champion envisages; hence perspectivism in lieu of the traditional norms of uniform and immutable truth. Will to power where any state is partially constituted by its "contest" with some counterforce; will to power as the drive to overcome resistances? The world- as a network of such tensions? Will to power can only manifest itself against resistances; therefore it seeks that which resists it. 1091
S: As expropriation, annihilation, etc. I recall.

A: No.

S: You said as much.

A: There is no annihilation in the sphere of the spirit. 1092 Your mistake here is in persisting in seeing power as "instrumental" for any resultant state, whether it be self-preservation, pleasure, knowledge, or whatever. These are merely the epiphenomena of power, of a drive to overcome something. Power is overcoming something, of annihilating it. You persist in seeing it in respect of individual states. Will to power is a force field of tensions within which individuals assume form by searching for other sites of power that they might overcome. Life is that which must always overcome itself. 1093 The moral of my story is: "Don't win the lottery!" The will to power demonstrates that measuring life by "happiness" is an error. Dissatisfaction and displeasure are the motors that drive overcoming. 1094 Sheer self-satisfaction drain the well of life's energy.

S: Is that what they call dry humour?

A: I'm serious. What of all that we prize in terms of culture, our science, our art, our intellectual accomplishments, did not originate in dissatisfaction, or the desire to overcome something?

S: That's as may be. Can we get back to necessity? A few moments ago you criticized my view of power as instrumental in respect of outcomes, and then argued we ourselves as individuals are the loci of competing wills to power. If this is so, it would seem to render any notion of us as free as somewhat nugatory and your "sovereign" individual a paper tiger?

A: Ah, creation - that is the great redemption from all suffering, and life's growing light. But that the creator may be, suffering is needed and much change. Indeed, there must be much bitter dying in your life, you creators. Thus are you the advocates and justifiers of all impermanence. 1095

S: Let me stop you there. Impermanence'?

A: Yes. The total character of the world ... is in all eternity chaos - in the sense not of a lack of necessity but a lack of order, arrangement, etc. 1096My world, the world as I see it, has a "necessary" and "calculable" course, not because laws obtain in it, but because they are absolutely lacking, and every power draws its ultimate consequences at every moment. 1097 As I said earlier, one is necessary, one is a piece of fatefulness, one belongs to the whole; there is nothing which could judge, measure, compare, or sentence our being, for that would mean judging, comparing, or sentencing the whole. But there is nothing besides the whole! That nobody is held responsible any longer, that the mode of being may not be traced back to a causa prima, that the world does nor form a unity either as a sensorium or as a "spirit" - that alone is the great liberation; with this alone is the innocence of becoming restored. 1098

If becoming could resolve itself into being or nothingness ... then given infinite time this state must have been reached. But it has not been reached: fro which it follows that it cannot and will not be reached. 1099

# CHEWING THE CUD

I seek a conception of the world that takes this fact into account. Becoming must be explained without recourse to final intentions; becoming must appear justified at every moment [or incapable of being evaluated; which amounts to the same thing]. ... "Necessity" not in the shape of an overreaching, dominating total force, or that of a prime mover - even less as a necessary condition for something valuable. To this end, it is necessary to deny a total consciousness to becoming, a "God". ... Fortunately such a summarizing power is missing [- a suffering and all-seeing "God", a "total sensorium" and "cosmic spirit" would be the greatest objection to being]. More strictly one must admit nothing that has being - because then becoming would lose its value and actually appear meaningless and superfluous.... Becoming is of equivalent value every moment; the sum of its values always remains the same; in other words, it has no value at all, for anything against which to measure it and in relation to which the word "value" could have any meaning, is lacking. The total value of the world cannot be evaluated. 1100

S: Hence the "eternal return"? I think I'm beginning to see how this all fits together in your mind. What was it your Zarathustra said about the gods being dice players and the earth being their table?

A: Those iron hands of necessity which shake the dice-box of chance play their game for an infinite length of time, and we ourselves shake the dice-box with iron hands, ... we ourselves in our most intentional actions do no more than play the game of necessity. 1101 Everything in the natural world, do you see, ourselves included, are combinations that have turned up in this game of chance? But, and this is the point,, this chance is not opposed to necessity. Whilst the throw of the dice is an act of freedom, it is helpless when it comes to determining the resulting combination. This is left to necessity. Of course, retrospectively we might determine the conditions and forces that led to a particular result, but no prospective inference will enable us to determine the outcomes of future throws. Each of these will, once again, affirm both necessity and chance.

S: But what then of "freedom", in your scheme of things? It is assuredly something altogether more attenuated than is commonly supposed? And, if so, doesn't this make that injunction of yours to become what you are somewhat paradoxical?

A: There's not a lot that slips through your net, is there?

S: Even if I say so myself, I've made a meal of many a man, but only metaphorically speaking, and only for their ultimate benefit. No harm, me.

# CHEWING THE CUD

A: Strange that, many a one tells me of being eaten alive, and that their revenge will be eaten, sooner or later, cold.

S: I'm surprised you pay it any heed; it's not called trumpery for no reason. As I've told anyone who cares to listen: if I'm in want of fresh air, all I have to do is to stand up-wind of Miletus, Anytus, Lycon and the rest of their cronies.

A: Have a care, my friend. It is but a short step from trumpery to trumped up charges.

S: Come. Don't look so solemn. What could they bring against me? Have I not always sought the greater good of my city and fellow Athenians? Athenian through and through am I; it's not about having the courage to challenge my own convictions.
A: As with a snake that must slough off its skin if it is not to die, he who has convictions must …

S: It's more a question of having the courage of my convictions so that I might carry my fellow Athenians with me. The only harm that could befall me would be to be separated from my beloved. If there is a paradox here, it is you. Well-born you might be, having nestled in the very bosom of Athenian glory somehow you speak and sing as if you were a barbarian, an outsider, a cuckoo in the nest. It's that alien note that alarms the ears of some.

A: Lichtenberg says that, "A good metaphor is something the police ought to keep an eye upon", you know? Not that I'd want it mooted abroad, I'll confess. Even at the best of times, the applause has always rung hollow to me. Anyway, less of me; we were talking of you, my friend. You should consider whether those who lack power over themselves don't often compensate by seeking it over others?

S: Enough, I'm not going to worry my pretty little head over trifles. What we are speaking of here is far more important. Freedom? You were about to tell me?

A: One further thought about "necessity"; it will save us time. Necessity is of a piece with my thought of the "eternal return"; it obliges us to attend to events as they occur in contrast to the nihilistic implications that follow from wanting life to be other than it is. Moreover, the love of fate - not simply it's acceptance, or recognition, since these imply being merely fated. Causal and teleological thinking mandate in their differing ways a closed future. Immediacy of occurrence entails an open future.

# CHEWING THE CUD

S: And this frail, orphan waif is your freedom?

A: Try thinking of it this way, then. Freedom is more often than not counter-posed to scientific determinism.

S: But you've already ruled out any self-caused freewill.

A: I know. I repudiate the desire for control that animates both determinist and freewill conceptions. Chance - the necessity of occurrence minus any natural law or a self that transcends such nature. You keep wanting to talk of freedom as if it were a power or faculty residing in a "subject". Think instead of the agonistic formation of the will to power. The measure of freedom can only be calculated according to the resistance overcome. There are only strong and weak wills; wills defined by their scope for agonistic practice and experimentation. We are at the same time the commanding and the obeying parties. 1102

S: Yes, yes. So you have said, but what I don't get is how such action is then ours?

A: Agency and constraint are conjoined, don't you see? What we participate in is always broader than what lies within our initiative or control. Think of what Heraclitus says of the play of children.

S: Can we keep him out of this?

A: Think of games. There is agency, but this is constrained by the other players who like us agree to play on the basis of pre-established rules. Like actors in a play we are both free and constrained by a script and our interaction with the other members of the troupe. One is necessary, one is a piece of fatefulness, one belongs to the whole, one is in the whole. 1103

S: All right, but this would seem to entail a radical downsizing of all talk of sovereign individuals, and their scope for creativity. Before you address that, one other thing; this dictum of yours: "become who you are". How does that work? On the face of it, it would seem to entail a becoming that isn't controlled by external causes or purposes. At one and the same time the dictum implies that the horizon for such action is very limited? You'll forgive the impertinence, but one might think one is not really free to be other than one is?

A: Ha, ha. Very astute, I agree.

## CHEWING THE CUD

S: But, I thought that ..

A: Thought you had got me? You are right; one may not be free to be other than one is, but that's not to say we aren't free in relation to other forces that would control or impede us. Self-affirmation is saying yes to what one is together with all the relations of tension that comprise becoming what one is.

S: And creativity?

A: It needs to be looked at through the same prism. Where creation is concerned, it is life as a whole that advances through such acts. 1104 All that romantic nonsense about the artist creating *ex nihilio*, out of his own depths alone, is just that - romantic nonsense. It is a kind of surplus energy that breaks forth here. Here, again, it is necessity that is at work - not as causal process, but active becoming. We want to become what we are - human beings who are new, unique, incomparable who give laws to themselves, who create themselves. To that end we must become the best learners and discovers of everything that is lawful and necessary in the world: we must become physicists in order to be able to be creators in this sense. 1105

S: Nonetheless, not an activity for all?

A: Indeed. Creativity is a dancing in chains; only he few have the strength and ability.

S: The romantic view, again. The artist as a wild, free, spirit.

A: Creative freedom is not at all like that. It needs fetters, structures to prepare and bring to fruition departures from the norm. It takes a special strength. As I said before, artists seem to have more sensitive noses in these matters - no offense - knowing only too well that precisely when they no longer do anything "voluntarily" but do everything of necessity, their feeling of freedom, subtlety, full power, of creative placing, disposing and forming reaches its peak - in short, that necessity and "freedom of the will" then become one in them. 1106
    Such a spirit who has become free stands amid the cosmos with a joyous and trusting fatalism, in the faith that only the particular is loathsome, and that all is redeemed and affirmed in the whole - he does not negate anymore. Such a faith, however, is the highest of all possible faiths: I have baptized it with the name of Dionysus. 1107

It's getting late, and I can't remember if I've said this. On occasion life reaches out to us. It might only be for a fleeting moment, but there and then you must grab her back!

S: All very well for your sort. All life has ever given me is the back of her hand.

A: And therein lies the difference between you and I. You fight life as a rear-guard action.

S: What would you know of the requirements of prudence?

## EPILOGUE
### No, "At The Eleventh Hour"

A: You've not said a word for the last ten minutes and we are nearly at the gate. What do you think?

S: Is that it? There's no more in your locker?

A: What do you mean, "Is that it"?

S: I don't think it is enough. Two minutes. Let's sit here. They won't close the gate on you. Everyone recognizes that robe. Me? That might be a different matter the way things are going.

A: "Not enough"?

S: It's not clear to me how it is you think we ought to live. Don't get me wrong about this? I'm not denying for a moment that your criticisms of my outlook lack weight, especially those concerning the death of god and the concerns about the rise of nihilism. It is curiously apt don't you think that we two have spent the day outside of the city walls discussing all this, whilst those inside have gone about their business with hardly a thought for our sort of concern? No desire there for your thoughts of derring-do. Peace, pleasure, comfort, security are their watch-words.

A: Well that's democracy for you. Where nothing is heard, nothing is there. The filtering process - the will to ignorance? Society's means of controlling the flow of new information so as to ensure that its culturally sanctioned convictions about human nature are not swamped; the same mechanism is at work within the individual. The unbending of the bow, to insure that spirit should not experience itself so readily as "need". 1108

S: Nothing like a military metaphor to add a certain frisson, eh?

A: One error after another is calmly put on ice: the ideal is not refuted - it freezes to death-. 1109

S: Ha, ha. As I shall if we don't get indoors soon. Not so weather-proof as when we were first on campaign.
A: You can have my robe if you like. I don't actually need it.

S: Thanks, but no thanks. Can't have people thinking I'm bought and paid for; that would be dangerous in my position.

A: That one has the will to self-responsibility. That one preserves the distance that divides us. That one has become indifferent to hardship, toil, and privation, even to life. The one who has become free ... spurns the contemptible sort of well being dreamed of by shopkeepers, Christians, cows, women, Englishmen and other democrats. The free man is a warrior. 1110

S: That was all a long time ago.

A: I'm just saying: one should seek the highest type of free man where the greatest resistance is constantly being overcome. 1111

S: Danger, strength, overcoming; its become a familiar litany. It still begs the question of how we ought to live. And don't tell me again that there is no template, no blueprint - that each must find his way.

A: Amor fati then? - to see everything as necessary. One should not only bear it, one should love it. Amor fati - that is my innermost nature.1112 Learning to see the necessary as beautiful. To love life again; only, one loves differently ... It is the love of a woman who makes us doubt. 1113

S: Well Xanthippe fits the bill there, if it's a case of loving someone whose love for us is continually in doubt. I've got a pie waiting for me but whether as a prop in a farce by Aristophanes I won't know until I get through the door. Can we get on?

# CHEWING THE CUD

There have been a couple of things that have been troubling me. They bear on each other, and fatalism's one. There are others, but time is short.

This stuff about fatalism? I'm afraid I remain unconvinced. Once again I'm left with more questions than answers. How could one come to love one's fate? Moreover, what exactly is this fate that one is supposed to love?
You don't need me to tell your life can be cruel; oft times one is faced with having to play the hand one has been dealt rather than the one that one have chosen. How on earth is one to love such arbitrary suffering? It is not as if those who are seemingly well-blessed fare any better; you, yourself, talk of us higher types - sorry, couldn't resist that - being no more than sacrificial lambs? All of which brings us back to tragedy, and the tragedy of it all. Not much succour to be had there save the implicit urge to mimic the actions of certain doomed heroes and heroines, but then most of us are not such. I'd ban it, myself.

A: Haven't I made it plain that I hold no truck with any common or garden determinism: that I have foresworn any notions of the pre-ordained or predestined? Am I not the one who proclaims that one should become who one is? That is far from a counsel to throw oneself beneath the wheels of the juggernaut of fate, leastways as you conceive of it?

S: But that only brings us to my second cavil: the "self" who is to affect this rescue. In all my days, never have I witnessed a more devastating attack. I'm not even sure that anything has been left standing. And I'm the one who prides his self on knowing nothing, but in my case there is at least a self to know nothing about. It's not just that you've blown grievous holes in the pretensions of consciousness, but that the miasma of suspicion you have raised about our selves is such that hitherto it will be hard to see our selves as other than mired in self-deception and self-deceit. We knowers are unknown to ourselves, and all that. A pretty little compliment, I know, but one for all that carries its own sting its tail for your philosophy since it raises the question once again of whether you have argued us into an impasse?

A: Let looking away be my only negation.

S: With respect, there you go again. It's not enough. You've got this meeting about the proposed invasion to attend. You can't tell me that you are going to sit around and see what happens, wait upon the body, your drives, your destiny to see what they tell you to do.

A: Now you are being ridiculous.

# CHEWING THE CUD

S: Am I? To borrow one of your many metaphors, it won't be plain sailing - the meeting, I mean. But I'm sure you'll prove to be rather than a mere pilot in a vessel, 1114 much less "no helmsman at all" 1115

A: Have we ever complained because we are misunderstood, misjudged, misidentified, slandered, misheard, and not heard? Precisely this is our fate - oh for a long time yet! let us say, to be modest, until 1901 - it is our distinction; we ... Why are you smirking? We should not honour ourselves sufficiently if we wished that it were otherwise. We are misidentified - because we ourselves keep growing, keep changing, we shed our bark, we shed our skins every spring, we keep becoming younger, fuller of future, ... 1116

S: That's a joke - the date whatever it signifies? There's a watershed here that you know nothing about.

A: What "watershed"?

S: Its all future for you. You count time forward from some beginning or other. You know you have become old when you start counting time in the reverse, in terms of how long you've got left. You are not old enough to know what disappointment and disillusion really are. Ambition burns too brightly for you to see the shadows it throws. Not that this has much to do with the impasse we are discussing.

A: I was merely acknowledging that we have it in us to change our outlook, even if our room for manoeuvre is limited; after all is said, done, - our character is our fate. 1117Everyone has his good days when he discovers his higher self; and true humanity demands that everyone be evaluated only in the light of this condition and not merely in the light of his workaday un-freedom and servitude. 1118

S: Where did that come from? You are no different from those Utilitarian's: you'd sell your granny, and everyone else's for the sake of producing one of your higher men!

A: Infamy! Infamy! He's got it in for me!

S: We are just going in circles here. Heraclitus leaves me in the dark. Perhaps his take on fate is different again? To be sure there appear to be elements of our character that are set in stone, but that said we are faced with the initial problem once again. And whilst it is easier to state than resolve, the question at issue is how one might best live in light of it? You seem to think that our tragedians hold the key in

391

holding in some fruitful tension a deeply pessimistic view of life and the world and a transformative joyful desire to live life to the full.

For myself I'm left wondering whether we are merely being moved, exhorted to embrace a life built upon grand aesthetic gestures. ...

A: Ah, but then prudence is your middle name. What truck would you want with a life without guarantees? What you love, above all else, about a person is their prospects. You know that one can only become a philosopher, not be one? As soon as one thinks one is a philosopher, one stops becoming one. Diogenes said when someone praised a philosopher in his presence: "How can he be considered great, since he has been a philosopher for so long and has never yet disturbed anybody?" 1119

S: And you would have us believe what? The more hopeless the cause, the more resolute the refusal of what the fates have decreed, the more heroic the deed?

A: Why not? Given that we knowers are unknown to ourselves, given the limitations of reason and reflection to shape a life, what other option is there than to suck it and see. It is incontestable that we are all related and allied to the saint, just as we are related to the philosopher and artist. The artist and the philosopher ... strike home at only a few, while they ought to strike home at everybody.

S: That's rather inelegant, not to say crude. It can't be at this late hour that you are denying you are an elitist? Can it?

A: Become who you are! "Conscience", my friend; be yourself! All you are now doing, thinking, desiring is not you yourself. The man who belongs to the mass needs only to cease being comfortable with himself. Anyone is capable of change at any time, but what is needed for this is the most difficult thing in the world. 1120 Many baulk at the first hurdle preferring to stick with what they already think they know.

S: Tell me about it, you are the genius!

A: It's our vanity that promotes the cult of genius, don't you think? The only way to keep the genius from aggrieving us is to think of him of him as being very remote from us, as a miracle? 1121

S: I was being ironical.

# CHEWING THE CUD

A: So was I. Zopy used to say, "What makes him {that is the great human being} great in all circumstances is the fact that he does not seek himself and his own interest ... He who is great recognizes himself in all and thus in the whole ... On account of this extension of his sphere, he is called great. Accordingly, that sublime predicate belongs by right only to the true hero in any sense and to the genius; it signifies that, contrary to human nature, they have not sought their own interest, and have lived not for themselves, but for all. 1122

S: Mores the pity you attended to the words and not the sentiment, but then we all know what you think about morality.
A: Clearly not. It is any rate certainly questionable whether this superstitious belief in genius, in the privileges and special abilities of the genius, is of any benefit to the genius himself if it takes root in him. It is in any event a dangerous sign when a man is assailed by awe of himself, ... when he comes to regard himself as superhuman. The consequences that slowly result are: the feeling of irresponsibility, of exceptional rights, the belief that he confers a favour by his mere presence, insane rage when anyone attempts even to compare him with others, let alone to rate him beneath them, or to draw attention to lapses in his work. Because he ceases to practice criticism of himself, at last one pinion after the other falls out of his plumage: that superstitious belief eats at the roots of his powers ... For the great spirits themselves it is therefore probably more beneficial if they acquire an insight into the nature and origin of their powers, if they grasp, that is to say, what purely human qualities have come together in them and what fortunate circumstances attend them. 1123

S: I'll not ask who that was about, however that all sounds both anti-elitist and highly moral?

A: But not moral, in the sense of putting others first. What have I to do with all that cant about "regarding the end of humanity in one's own person"? No, for me the cultivation of one's higher self is a precondition of the furtherance of one's capacity for genuine, and as psychologist I emphasize the genuine, responsiveness to the needs and claims of others.

S: Psychology aside, have I been missing something here all along?

A: Fundamentally, my term immoralist involves two repudiations. First, I repudiate a type of man that has so far been considered supreme ... And then I repudiate a type of morality which has attained validity and come to dominate as [if it were] morality itself - the morality of decadence or, more concretely, Christian morality. It is admissible to consider the latter contradiction the more decisive one. 1124

S: So morality still has a role to play? But doesn't that sit uncomfortably with those claims about life being only justified as an aesthetic phenomena. I noticed a few moments ago you were still yoking philosophers and artists - and saints as well.

A: Well, perhaps I'm a work in progress?

S: More a piece of work. Scratch that! That was uncalled for. Ever since that incident with the scallywag who caught me napping, I've been dogged with a sense of foreboding. I'm surprised it hadn't reached your ears. 'Felt like I'd lost my body armour, my "mask" – to use your terms – in one fell swoop. Weary.

A: Just because I've heard nothing, doesn't mean the jackals won't be circling. They all too quick when it comes to scenting wounded prey. There's always room enough for you on one of my ships if you are willing to tear yourself away from your beloved Athens.

S: Sorry. Second thoughts? Tell me something to lift my spirits.

A: It's a matter of educating humans to be human. The goal of culture is to promote the production of true human beings and nothing else. ... Let us reflect: where does the animal cease, and where does the human being begin? ... As long as anyone desires life as he desires happiness, he has not yet raised his eyes above the horizon of the animal, for he only desires more consciously what the animal seeks through blind impulse ... Usually we fail to emerge out of animalism; we ourselves are the animals whose suffering seems to be senseless. But there are moments when we realize this ... and we see that we are pressing towards the human as towards something that stands high above us. 1125

S: And the proximity of the philosopher, artist, and saint?

A: Every human being is accustomed to discovering in himself some limitation ... which fills him with melancholy and longing: ... as an intellectual being he harbours a profound desire for the genius in him. This is the root of all culture; and I understand by this the longing of the human being to be reborn as saint and genius. 1126

# CHEWING THE CUD

S: Wait up! Questions! If I understand you correctly ... ideally, all these "higher types" should beat in the one breast? An ideal, not to say a practice, that is very close - if you'll excuse my saying so - that is very close to Plato's?

A: There exists no more repulsive desolate creature in the world...

S: Oh, come on! You can't mean that!

A: I wasn't talking about Plato. No more repulsive and desolate creature than the human being who has evaded his genius and who now looks furtively to left and right, behind him and all about him. 1127

As regards Plato, and more especially his progeny, I feel bound to say if an ethical man finds that people want to admire him ... he must himself see that this holds a deception, an untruth. An ethical man must not let people admire him, but - through him - they must be urged to the Ethical. As soon as people are permitted to admire an ethical man they elevate him into a genius, i.e. put him on a different plane, and, ethically, that very thing constitutes the most horrible fallacy, for the ethical shall and must be universally human. An ethical man must constantly maintain, and inculcate in others, that every human being is as capable as he ... They want to admire him in order to be rid of him [i.e. the gad-fly sting of his existence] but the human feeling in him that makes him say: 'anyone can do it as well as I' calls forth hatred and makes people wish to have him at a distance.

Another result of this is that after he is dead they will honour him, as by then the sting inherent in his being their contemporary will have gone. The very objection to such an ethical man during his lifetime becomes a eulogy of him after his death. 1128

S: A rum state of affairs that would be.

A: Human beings are timid. They hide themselves behind customs and opinions. 1129 Hence why the writer should aim to defeat the expectations of his audience, to make the reading of his thoughts a discomforting experience. It is not instruction, but provocation, that I can receive from another soul. 1130

S: You know what I'm thinking? Your principle worry here is not nihilism, but indifference. To be sure nihilism is a concern. How could it not be if a dominant system of values collapses? And to be sure many will not be alive to the spectres that will continue to haunt the shadows long after the dearly departed has been laid to rest. Even so, it seems to me that this so-called "last man" of yours constitutes the main problem, in light of what you've just been saying. No, me thinks the problem is rather one of indifference.

A: Zarathustra might agree. He goes under thrice, and each time he fails to get a hearing. Three tragedies and a satyr play, don't you know?

S: The standard submission, so Euripides tells me. Is there no limit to your literary ambition? "Goes under"? Oh, never mind. What does it profit a man if he fails to provide others with a regulative principle?

A: As I said there is no once and for all, no revolutionary moment. Whatever I may create and however I may love it - soon I must oppose it and my love, thus my will wants it. 1131

S: So good riddance to the over-man? You know what I hear beneath all this fine words? A fear that the task is beyond all but a very few, and even amongst these you might be courting failure.

A: Perhaps. Perhaps we have become too weary to die; now we continue to wake and we live on - in burial chambers. 1132 Chronophobia - you and Plato set the bench-mark with a negative assessment of it in the "Phaedo"; the psychological aversion to time and becoming, that is? Its the bed-rock of the intellectual Chronophobia that runs like a seam through the subsequent history of western philosophy; hence the preoccupation with securing firm foundations - the search for truth and knowledge. The resolution of the problems of change, mortality, etc.,by way transposing time into eternity and becoming into being?

S: Yes, yes. Not that I've heard it called such. You know when my mother spent what little leisure time she had sewing, or even playing cards for that matter, she'd refer to it as "killing time"? This Zarathustra - what is he exactly?

A: You may well ask. Is he a promisor? - Or a fulfiller? - Or a conqueror? - Or an inheritor? An autumn? A plough? A ... 1133

S: I'm serious!

A: So, too, am I. Eternal return of the same? 1134

S: Sorry. That's a question?

# CHEWING THE CUD

A: An abysmal thought - the ceaseless return of the last man. More like an answer to your speculations about my state of mind.

S: Now who is rambling?

A: Am I? My children are near, my children. 1135

S: Alcibiades! You are beginning to alarm me. Are you saying its all been in vain?

A: Is it? Has it? We now know that the world wasn't made for us, or we for the world. We know that there is no God's eye view or vantage-point from which from which we can get outside of our history and survey the world, and thereby validate what we do. As a result we are left with an ambivalent heritage, not only in terms of the achievements of our kind that we nonetheless continue to value despite their stratospheric human cost, but also a much reduced confidence in our reflective capacities. Moreover, we now know there is no redemption to be sought and no guarantee that what we have done, let alone what will do, will come out well in the end.

And the bitter dregs? However much we may try to hang loose, to pretend we are not trying to run the whole show, at another level we will be, nevertheless, struggling might and main to keep the show on the road.

S: But doesn't that give the lie to all the talk of heroic deeds of derring-do?

A: Between you and me? Between headaches, I have my doubts.

S: Headaches?

A: Yes, they are getting more frequent of late. Real humdingers. They quite incapacitate me. Once or twice just lately, and no particular reason that I can discern, I've found myself reduced to tears - not that I would want that getting abroad.

S: I can understand that.

A: Can't put my finger on it, but its like I no longer belong here.

S: Here in Athens, you mean.

A: Yes, but more than that; both out of step, and out of time.

S: You and me, both.

# CHEWING THE CUD

A: Look - above your ankle. Your leg it's bleeding.

S: Its nothing. Must have caught it on a bramble. Skin's as thin as parchment these days. Meletus could write his charges on it.

A: Some say celebrity is a bit like a bubble in that at its zenith it sparkles with the colours of the rainbow, but past a certain point its skin thins and turns black - a sign that it is about to burst.

S: If I might interrupt? One last thought, before we part? The heroic posing? Haven't you burnt your bridges, cut off your own line of retreat? You speak as if those tragic heroes of yore constitute an exemplar, a role model. Strange to say, but you seem not taken account of the ramifications of all that caustic acid you have poured over all talk of intentionality self-knowledge. There was surely a certain naive cheerfulness with which your "heroes" greeted the dawn; a confidence in who they were and what they were about, even if they were to sooner or later to be made to pay a heavy price for this largely innocent hubris by the gods.

Although the picture you draw is one in which we are again exposed to the elements, one of a life lacking guarantees of comfort and security, there are important differences. The major characters must struggle with new burdens of radical self-doubt about who they really are, about their intentionality, and what it is they take themselves to be doing. Between a rock and a hard place, that's where you have left us. Ironic really, as you argue it the perils of over-egging our notions agency and burdening ourselves with an excessive sense of our own responsibility, in the end prove as great as those of despairing over our limitless capacity for self-deception and our exposure to the caprice of fate.

You know what is really required here? The writer of tragedy should also be a writer of comedy. [1136]

A: Indeed. Just that is my ideal: saying what is sombre through what is laughable. 1137 We are, after all, creatures of affects. Tragic creatures who must suffer a destiny which we are not free to choose; enslaved by illusion, by the tyranny of uncontrollable forces, by our desires, our feelings, our affects. Dionysis versa Apollo; the Apollonian as a temporary imposition of form; haven't we spent the day talking about that in one way or another?

S: Aye, that's the thing we keep coming back to: if as you claim we are creatures of affect, then our reality dances to a different "logic" to that of reason. Me - as a wallflower; could you picture it? An interesting day, but at my back I always hear, Time's winged chariot draw near. Sorry, off on one again. No coy mistress, Xanthippe.1138. If you don't mind, a last favour? A juicy morsel to chew on whilst I attempt to swallow Xanthippe's pie? How came you to all this?

A: I have been bitten by more than a viper's tooth; I have known in my soul ... that worst of pangs ... the pang of philosophy which will make a man say or do anything. And you ... all of you, and I need not say Socrates himself, have had the experience of the same madness and passion in your longing after wisdom. Therefore, listen and excuse my doings ... and my sayings.

But let profane and unmannered persons close up the doors of their ears. 1139.

S: Ha, ha, ha. That counts as a conquest of sorts. Next time though, I'll bring the poison just to be sure. Don't scowl! You can count on me to save you a drop! Are we not agreed that we philosophers are lovers, and that words are our means of seduction?

A: Ah, but remember. Love brings to light the exceptional and concealed qualities of a lover – what is rare and exceptional in him: to that extent it can easily deceive as to what is normal in him. 1140.

## Main Works of Friedrich Nietzsche

AC.    The Anti-Christ.
AOM    Assorted Opinions and Maxims.
BGE    Beyond Good and Evil.
BT     The Birth of Tragedy.
D      Daybreak.
EH     Ecce Homo.
HH     Human, All – Too – Human.
GS     Gay Science.
GM     On The Genealogy of Morals.
PTG    Philosophy in the Tragic Age of the Greeks.
TI     Twilight of the Idols.
WP     The Will to Power.
Z      Thus Spoke Zarathustra.

# Notes

## CHAPTER 1

1. An allusion Nietzsche's *The Wanderer And His Shadow*.
2. The party referred to being that of Plato's *Symposium*.
3. For a traditional discussion of the problem of "Universals" see J. Hospers': *Introduction To Philosophical Analysis*.
4. Dogs were not well thought of by the Greeks. Alcibiades is not only taunting Socrates in respect of his plebeian origins, but also spitefully suggesting some connection between Socrates and the Cynics whom both Socrates and Plato reviled.
5. Socrates, the Brazilian football team's captain of the 1980s.
6. "Only the day after tomorrow belongs to me. Some men are born posthumously", Foreword to *The Anti-Christ*.
7. Plato's *Phaedrus*.
8. The consensus is that the early dialogues give expression to the thoughts of Socrates; the later ones those of Plato.
9. See the *Republic* for example; especially the allegory concerning the cave.
10. A sobriquet that Socrates took pleasure from.
11. *Anti-Christ*, 43.
12. *Daybreak*, 95.

13. Socrates fought against the Persians and reputedly saved Alcibiades' life. Later Alcibiades, in turn, saved Socrates' life using his mount as a shield.

14. *Gay Science*, 357.

15. *Ecce Homo*, 1V: 8.

16. See the *Republic*.

17. See Plutarch.

18. See Plutarch.

19. According to Plutarch, Alcibiades once cut off the tail of his of his dog to ensure the Athenians had something to say about him for fear they might have worst to say about him otherwise.

20. EH,111

21. See here the writings of G. Leopardi.

22. A view first formulated by F. Dostoevsky.

23. TI, II1:1.

24. WP, 12.

25. GM, III 11.

26. R. Frost.

27. AC, 43

28. Like many, Socrates misunderstands the myth. The point is not that where there's life there's hope, but that hope as the last evil is retained in the box and thus persists as a means of torturing mankind; i.e., by proffering what is ultimately false hope.

29. Alcibiades' wife. Socrates is alluding to a notorious incident when Hipparete went to court to file for divorce and Alcibiades upon hearing of this went after her, picked her up, slung her over his shoulder, and carried her back home. Thereafter they are to have lived happily till she died some two or three years later.

30. BGE, 176.

31. WP, 732.

32.Plato's *Apology*.

33. Alcibiades was raised as a member of Pericles' household.

34. Plato: *Republic*, Bk. 1V and V1.

35. "Of all fair things the autumn, too, is fair": Euripides of Alcibiades, according to Plutarch.

36. Shakespeare, *Hamlet*.

37.Shakespeare, *As You Like It* – "a man gets to play many parts".

38. Shakespeare, *Hamlet*.

39. BT, 14.

40. Ditto.

41. Ditto.

42. Ditto.
43. BGE, 44.
44. WP, 32.
45. BT, *Preface*.
46. Oscar Wilde.
47. Shakespeare, *As You Like It*.
48. The rhetorical figure in question is an anaphora. The Sophists took money for teaching rhetoric rather than the truth. See "You talkin' to me?" by S. Leith.
49. D, 131.
50. Zophrus espouses the thoughts of Schopenhauer throughout the dialogue.
51. Z, 1: 22. "One repays a teacher badly if one always remains a pupil only".
52. A criticism leveled at Galiani, a personal favourite of Nietzsche's. See F. Steegmuller: *A Woman, A Man, And Two Kingdoms*.
53. D, 119.
54. *Wagner in Bayreuth*.
55. WP, 765.
56. WP, 368.
57. HH, 1.
58. Parmenides was the founder of the Eleatic School, which was based in Italy.
59. A. N. Whitehead once described the history of philosophy as footnotes to Plato.
60. BGE, 2.
61. WP, 539.
62. BT. *Preface*.
63. GS, 344.
64. Plato was a keen wrestler.
65. TI, *Reason*.
66. Schopenhauer's name has become synonymous with pessimism.
67. Schopenhauer was taken to court for pushing a gossip down the stairs outside of his apartment.
68. Schopenhauer, *The World as Will and Representation*, 2: 574.
69. Ditto, *Essays and Maxims*.
70. See Dienstag: *Pessimism*.
71. WP, 70.
72. BGE, 186.
73. A pastime of Schopenhauer's.
74. GM.
75. Harpocrates [Horus the child]. A god of Egyptian origin, usually represented as an infant with a finger held to his mouth.
76. Gracian: *The Pocket Oracle and the Art of Prudence*. 268.
77. Wilco: *The Album, You Never Know*.

78. Gracian, 267.
79. George Harrison and The Beatles.
80. See Steegmuller above.
81. Plato [Wikipedia unsourced].
82. AOM, Preface, 1.
83. Plato [Wikipedia unsourced].
84. WP, 12.
85. TI, *Four Great Errors*, 8.
86. WP, 6.
87. WP, 37.
88. WP, 12.
89. Plato: *Republic*. See also the writings of Leo Strauss.
90. Shakespeare: *King Lear*.
91. WP, 777.
92.  KGW, 8: 1:109.
93. BGE, 131.
94. WP, 853.
95. Ditto.
96. Phidias, architect of The Parthenon.
97. Phaenarete, Socrates' mother was a midwife. It was then common practice to expose the newborn.
98. GM, Preface.
99. HH 379.
100. Adapted from an episode of "The Simpson's".
101. Plato: *Phaedrus* – Socrates' last words. A cock was sacrificed to Asclius upon recovery from illness. Nietzsche reads this episode as implying that life itself was an illness for Socrates.
102. Various philosophers have raised this issue. See below.
103. WWR, 1: 194.
104. WWR, 2:584.
105. PP, 1:406.
106. Ditto.
107. WWR, 1: 86. The Metic in question is Aristotle.
108. Ditto.
109. WWR, 1:57.
110. See I. Soll in *Reading Nietzsche*, ed. By Solomon and Higgins.
111. One of Plato's similes.
112. Socrates' upturned nose and nostrils were frequently commented upon.
113. Steve Forbert: "It isn't going to be that way".
114. BGE, *Preface*.

115. Ditto.
116. Plato: *Phaedrus*.
117. TI, 2: 1.
118. Letter to Elizabeth, June, 1865.
119. BGE, 1.
120. Z, *On Free Death*.
121. Z, 11: 3.
122. GS, 338.
123. See W. Kaufmann' *Nietzsche*.
124. WP, 910.
125. D, 503.

## CHAPTER 2

126. GS.64.
127. GS.66.
128. Epicurus was known as the garden philosopher.
129. HH.389.
130. BGE, Interlude.
131. EH, 1:8.
132. AC.57.
133. Ditto.
134. x, 379.
135. AC, 57.
136. Pollyanna, the eternal optimist, and central character of a series of books for children - first authored by E. Porter.
137. Plato had hoped to persuade Dionysuis to put into practice his theories concerning the ideal state.
138. Shakespeare, "Henry IV".
139. See E. *Canetti: Crowds And Power*.
140. Plato, *Republic* : Part 10,Theory Of Art.
141. Ditto.
142. Glaucon, Plato's elder brother. His name is variously thought to suggest he was grey-eyed, bright-eyed, or owl-eyed.
143. The argument ad hominem [against the man]. A favourite weapon of Nietzsche's reflecting his conviction that a man's character determined the kind of beliefs he chose to hold.
144. References a famous contest held in Ancient Greece to find the painter best able to execute a still life.

145. Called at birth Aristocles, only later did he acquire the name Plato - meaning wide, and, perhaps a reference to his physique as a wrestler.
146. Plato, *Republic*: Part 10.
147. Glaucon figures prominently in several of Plato's dialogues.
148. Sir Walter Scott, *Marmian*.
149. Plato, *Republic*: Part 10.
150. Aristotle, *Poetics*: 49.
151. Plato, *Republic*: Part 10.
152. It is said upon his death, a copy of Aristophanes was found beneath Plato's pillow.
153. GM, 111:25.
154. WP, 820.
155. WWR, 1:185.
156. WP, 808.
157. Ditto.
158. Alcibiades is alluding to an incident in which Diogenes, on hearing of Plato's definition burst into the Academy carrying a plucked chicken shouting, " Look everybody, Plato's human being!"
159. A saying attributed to Diogenes.
160. Alcibiades is alluding to reports of a meeting between Alexander the Great and Diogenes. When Alexander asked if there was anything he could do for the philosopher, Diogenes - who lived in a barrel - merely asked that he move so as not to block the sun. The other allusion here is to another of Diogenes' sayings, "I am called a dog because I fawn on those who give me anything, I yelp at those who refuse, and I set my teeth at rascals.
161. See R.Dawkins: *The Blind Watchmaker*.
162. GM, 111:25.
163. AC, 14.
164. BGE, 230.
165. TI, Page 80.
166. BGE, 3.
167. GS, 333.
168. BGE, 36.
169. WP, 387.
170. Z: 1.
171. AC, 14.
172. Another saying attributed to Diogenes.
173. Ditto.
174. GS, 290.
175. WP, 821.

176. WP, 853.
177. WP, 134.
178. KGW, 7:3:210.
179. One of Socrates' most famous sayings.
180. Another of Diogenes' quotes.
181. Discordant concord of things: Horace, *Epistles*, 1:12,19.
182. GS, Bk1, 2.
183. Diogenes, see above.

## CHAPTER 3

184. See *Republic*, Part V11.
185. Ditto. An allusion to "The Simile of the Sun"; here Plato compares the Form of the Good to the Sun, and thereby what he regards as the Intelligible World [the proper subject matter of philosophy - the study of reality and truth - the Good] to the Visible World.
186. Ditto.
187. The allusion here is to "The Divided Line". A further development of the Sun simile, centering on the state of mind of the perceiver, Plato seeks to differentiate a hierarchy starting with intelligence at the summit, and then on down through reason, then belief to illusion at the bottom.
188. Ascribed above the entrance to Plato's Academy was the slogan: " Let no one who is not a geometer enter here".
189. Quotation of Plato's. Source unknown.
190. Although Pythagoras enrolled women, controversial in itself at the time, their curriculum seems to have been restricted to wifely duties. Plato took this a stage further acknowledging that women in the ideal state warranted the same education as men. See S.B.Pomeroy: *Goddesses, Whores, Wives, and Slaves*.
191. Ditto.
192. Quotation of Plato's. Location unknown.
193. Diogenes.
194. Ditto.
195. Ditto.
196. Nietzsche.
197. Plato .{source unknown].
198. WP, 37.
199. *Republic*, Part XI: The Myth of Er. Here Plato discusses the rewards that await the good man after death.
200. GS, 108.
201. WP, 579.

202. WP, 11.
203. EH, IV: 7.
204. WP, 428.
205. "Republic", ?
206. D, 139.
207. TI, VII:I.
208. WP, 258.
209. Xenophon: *Socrates*.
210. La Rochefoucauld: *Maxims*.
211. D, 103.
212. GS, 116.
213. Ditto.
214. BGE, 1
215. WP, 121.
216. BGE, 126
217. GS, 1.
218. BGE, 268.
219. GS, 21.
220. N; "Thoughts.
221. D, 132.
222. GM, Bk.1: 11.
223. BGE,262.
224. The allusion is to the sub-title of *Zarathustra* – "a book for everyone and no one".
225. BGE, 199.
226. *Republic*, 452.
227. See Pomeroy, op.cit.
228. BGE, 199.
229. HH, I: 96. HH, 2:89.
230. Z, 1:15.
231. GS, 117.
232. 911.18.
233. One of the most renown of the sayings of Socrates.
234. HH, 1:96,99.
235. GM.Bk.2: vi.
236. WP, 738.
237. GM, Preface.
238. GM, X11.
239. Ditto.
240. GS, 65.

241. Timandra- a courtesan with whom Alcibiades lived until his murder. The other reference here is to Pericles who likewise lived with a courtesan, Aphasia. In later life, after Pericles' death she became a madam.

242. Aristophanes, *Achilles*,526.

243. Aristotle. Op cit.

244. The telltale is Diogenes Laertes. Leontion, a companion of Epicurus, actually wrote philosophy. See Pomeroy.

245. Due to manpower shortages occasioned by war losses Athenian men were for a time encouraged to take a second "wife". See Pomeroy.

246. HH.413.

247. Actually O. Wilde, *Essays and Letters*, p,569.

248. IIH.413.

249. *Republic*, Introduction: Thrasymachus and the Rejection of Conventional Morality.

250. The allusion is to Hobbes: "Leviathan".

251. The Thirty Tyrants who seized power in late fifth century Athens killing thousands and driving others into exile, having severely curtailed democratic rights.

252. WP, 370.

253. WP, 372.

254. GS, 354.

255. BGE, 268.

256. Ditto.

257. GS, 116.

258. BGE, 32.

259. Pyrrho - the Greek Sceptic.

260. Actually quoting from *If* by Kipling.

261. WP, 434,437.

262. Actually the quote is from Chiang Tzu of whom Pyrrho would probably have never heard. Pyrrho did however accompany Alexander to the East where rumour has it he met with certain mystics.

263. Quote from Chiang Tzu again.

264. A favourite argumentive ploy of the early sceptic whose ultimate aim of bring about a state of *epokhe,* i.e. a suspension of judgment. The suspension of judgment is designed to free you from the need to find a definite answer to anything. *Epokhe* functions rather like a Zen koan, and, perhaps, not accidentally, like many a sage within this tradition, Pyrrho counseled a live of withdrawal.

265. Chiang Tzu.

266. BGE. 207.

267. BGE, 208.

CHAPTER 4

268. HH, 196.
269. GM, 11:XVI.
270. Ditto.
271. WP, 7.
272. WP, 492.
273. BGE, 88.
274. BGE, 113.
275. BGE, 95.
276. BGE, 111.
277. GS, 335.
278. Republic.
279. Ditto.
280. TI, *Socrates*.
281. "Homer's Contest".
282. Aristotle: *Nicomachean Ethics*.
283. UM: UDH.
284. C. Middleton: *Letters* ,in R. Solomon and K. Higgins ed., *Reading Nietzsche*.
285. GS, 247.
286. WP, 254.
287. GM. Preface 6.
288. See C. H. Kahn: *The Art and thought of Heraclitus*: L111.
289. *Alice in Wonderland*: C. Dodgson.
290. WP, 1006.
291. WP, 55.
292. TI, IV: 4 .
293. BGE, 9.
294. AC, 54.
295. GS, 297.
296. See introduction of "Alcibiades I and II": Plato and Jowett. - Authenticity as a function of length, seriousness, and other considerations.
297. The principal theme of Alcibiades II being the efficacy of prayer.
298. The allusion is also to Alcibiades' mother, Dinomache, who at his birth was attended by "a good-for-nothing woman-nurse", whereas a Persian queen would have availed herself of royal eunuchs. The author of " Alcibiades I" also refers to the frugality of Dinomache's wardrobe and the small landholding of he family.

299. See J. R. Seeley.: *Expansion of England*,1883.

## Chapter 5

300. BGE, 3.
301. D. Hume: *A Treatise Of Human Nature*.
302. WP, 254.
303"The Case of Wagner", E.H.
304. GS, 21.
305. Ditto.
306. Former British P.M. speaking of Lord Braintree, a former Cabinet Minister
307. GS, 328.
308. Ditto.
309. See Rev. M. L. King, or for the original expression of this sentiment Martin Luther himself.
310. WP, 377, 456.
311. XVI, 318.
312. AC, 55.
313. AC, 54.
314. Ditto.
315. BGE, 39.
316. AC, 50-51.
317. Ditto.
318. Said by Nietzsche as criticism of Wagner.
319. D, 90.
320. WP, 483.
321. GS, 121.
322. GS, 344.
323. Ditto.
324. Ditto.
325. BGE, 39.
326. Jesus Christ.
327. WP, 257.
328. WP, 918.
329. Ditto
330. Ditto.
331. AC, 2.
332. Z, 1:15.
333. BGE, 43.
334. EH, 1:7.

335. GS, 325.
336. Socrates quote.
337. Ditto.
338. GM. Preface 6.
339. BGE, 44.
340. Z, 11,2
341. WP, 216.
342. GS, 338.
343. Z, 111:12.
344. Ditto.
345. GM, 1:10.
346. Socrates [Wikipedia unsourced}.
347. Z, "War and Warriors".
348. WP, 48.
349. HH, 377.
350. HH, 406.
351. HH, 405.
352. HH, 402.
353. HH, 401.
354. HH, 398.
355.WP, 584.
356. G. Leopardi, p58.
357. HH, 404.
358. I. Kant; *Groundwork for the metaphysics of morals*, p 446,457,458.
359. D, 109.
360. WP, 387.
361. WP, 46.
362. See B. Reginster: *The Affirmation of Life*.
363. BGE, 231.
364. GS, 380.
365. TI, IV: 5.
366. TI, 11 2.
367. WP, 522.
368. WP, 461.
369. WP, 12.
370. GS, 301.
371. D, 210.
372. Quotes from the works of Terence.
374. Ditto.
375. Ditto.

376. Ditto.
377. Ditto.
378. Ditto.
379. Ditto.

CHAPTER 6

380. Socrates quote.
381. WP, 692.
382. TI, 1V: 3.
383. TI, VI: 7.
384. BGE, 21.
385. Aristotle, *Ethics*.
386. Plato: *Protagoras*, 352.
387. WP, 46.
388. TI, V: 5.
389. TI, VIII: 6.
390. WP, 84.
391. WP. 438.
392. BGE, 19.
393. GS, *Preface* 3.
394. GS, 166.
395. GS, 378.
396. GS, 174.
397. GS, 50.
398. GS, 52.
399. GS, 371.
400. GS, 3.
401. GS, 1:3.
402. Kant, GW, pp.436-7.
403. Ditto, p.421.
404. GS, 3:197.
405. GS, 4:335.
406.WP, 308.
407. O. Wilde.
408. D, 510.
409. WP, 309.
410. WP, 235.
411. WP, 886.
412. GS, 335.

413. WP, 886.
414. WP, 997.
415. BGE, 257.
416. See *Republic* and other dialogues.
417.WP, 886.
418.WP, 235.
419. GS, 370?

## CHAPTER 7

420. BGE, 19.
421. TI, "Maxims and Arrows": 4." *From the military school of life.* - What does not kill me makes me stronger".
422. BGE, 19.
423. Z,
424. GS, 347.
425. Ditto.
426. Heraclitus, LXXX11.
427. Ditto, LXXX111.
428. Ditto, LXV11.
429. WP, 642.
430. WP, 657.
431. WP, 660.
432. Heraclitus, CXXV.
433. BGE, 18.
434. TI, VI: 7.
435. BGE, 21.
436. Ditto.
437. GM, II: 2.
438. BGE, 19.
439. TI, IX: 41.
440. TI, IX: 38.
441. ix, 398.
442. WP, 705.
443. BGE, 29.
444. 7/542.
445. Culture and education were abiding concerns of Nietzsche's.
446. Z, V, 4."Man is a rope, tied between beast and overman - a rope over an abyss".
447. AC, 125.

448. Descartes, "Discourse".
449. GS, 347.
450. Z, 61.
451.VP, II: 227.
452. Ditto.
453. WP, 659.
454. GS, 305.
455. Written by Livingston and Evans.1956.
456. D, 570.
457. H.H. "The Wanderer",61.
458. J. P. Sartre: *Being and Nothingness*.
459. Wittgenstein. *Philosophical Investigations*.
460. Tennyson: *The Charge Of The Light Brigade*.
461. Shakespeare: *Hamlet*.
462. GM, 1:10.
463. GM, 11:12.
464. GM, 1:12.
465. Pelagius denied the doctrine of original sin.
466. Plato: *Republic*.
467. AC.1.
468. Z.: "The Stillest Hour".
469. GS, 62.
470. WP, 893.
471. WP, 121.
472. GS, 69.
473. GM, 111:7.
474. GS, 67.
475. Actually Montaigne: *Complete Essays*, p.647.
476. J. Austen: *Pride and Prejudice*.
477. GS, 227.
478. Eurubiuse on Origen." There are eunuchs who made themselves eunuchs for the sake of the kingdom of heaven". Matthew 19:12.
479. St. Paul, *Galations*, 3: 28.
480. St. Augustine, *Confessions*.
481. St. Augustine, *Contra Faustum*.
482. GM, 111.
483. Ditto.
484. Z, 1.
485. KSA, I: 798.
486. Ditto.

487. Ditto.
488. Aristotle: "Ethics".
489. BGE, 224.
490. Shakespeare: "As You Like It".
491. TI, 28.
492. Wounded during the battle, Alcibiades was saved by Socrates.
493. Z, 1:5. WS, 53.

## INTERLUDE

494. Aristotle.
495. The plague of 430BC. decimated Athens. The witticism belongs to Demonax - see "Lucian" in R. Dobbin's "The Cynic Philosophers".
496. Aristotle, *Ethics*.
497 Many of these people had been at the very centre of the Periclean cultural project that aimed to give expression to Athenian military power in terms of public works and the promotion of the arts.
498. BGE, 79.
499. TI, Maxim: 19.
500. BGE, 115.
501. BGE, 120.
502. BGE, 139.
503. BGE, 163.
504. BGE, 175.
505. BGE, 145
506. HH, 287.
507. BGE, *Preface*.
508. BGE, 136.
509. BGE, 166.
510. BGE, 153.
511. BGE, 187.
512. Z. op. cit.
513. O. Wilde.
514. Plato, *Gorgias*, 469c.
515. *Richard Wagner in Bayreuth*,1 :87.
516. BGE, 259.
517. Aristotle ?
518. BGE, 264.
519. Miletus acted as the prosecuting attorney at the trial of Socrates.
520. Antyus funded the prosecution.

521. Spoken by Achilles in Hades. Homer: *The Odyssey*.
522. *Republic*, Bk. 111.
523. *Symposium*.
524. Aeschylus, *Niobe*.
525.*Lamentations*, 3:38. Job, 2: 10.
526. *Symposium*.
527. L. Cohen, *A Thousand Kisses Deep*.
528. *Republic*, Bk. VI and VII.
529. D. Rumsfeld, former U.S. Secretary of State for Defense.
530. *Republic*, 433c.
531. GS, 301.
532. *The Laws*, 816.
533. Ditto.
534. K. Williams, *Carry on Caesar*.
535.*The Laws*, 935.
536. TI, 1:23.
537. D, 371.
538. BGE, 259.

## CHAPTER 8

539. R. Adams, *Firecracker*.
540. GS, 356.
541. GS, 361.
542. Ditto.
543. GS, 356,361.
544. GS, 356.
545. Ditto.
546. Ditto.
547. GM, 11:17.
548. GS, 35. Joint commander of the ill-fated Sicilian expedition along with Alcibiades.
549. See Plato's *Laches*.
550. Machiavelli.
551. Ditto.
552. See Thucydides. Greek island state invaded by Athens.
    Two schools of thought, then and since, as to the wisdom of this conquest.
    - notorious    for the cold brutality of the Athenian ultimatum.
553 Machiavelli.
554. Ditto.

555. Ditto.
556. Ditto.
557. Ditto.
558. J. Donne.
559. GM, 111:12.
560. WP, 678.
561. BGE, 11. Nietzsche's use of the concept "perspective" is vanishing small.
562. GM, 11:12.
563. WP, 500, 501.
564. BGE, 13.
565. GM, 111,12.
566. BGE, 12.
567. GM, 1. 13.
568. BGE, 12.
569. WP, 556.
570. WP, 490.
571. WP, 636.
572. Spinoza.
573. WP, 481.
574. WP, 254.
575.WP, 259.
576. Z, 2.
577. WP, 492.
578. WP, 556.
579. WP, 259.
580. WP, 966.
581. GM, 111:13.
582. GM, 111:12.
583. GM, 111:28.
584. WP, 228.
585. O. Wilde.
586. Plato, *Republic*.
587. WP, 579.
588. Ditto.
589. K. Mansfield.
590. BGE, 19.
591. GM, 111:12.
592. BGE, 19.
593. Aristophanes' *Wasps*.
594. Aristotle, *Poetics*.

595. GM, 1:13.
596. Ditto.
597. Ditto.
598. Ditto.
599. Ditto.
600.Ditto.
601. Ditto.
602. GM, II: 15.
603. Ditto.
604. "Schopenhauer as educator".
605. IIII, 2:211.
606. EH, I.
607. TI, "Maxims".
608. "Schopenhauer as educator".
609. BGE, 42.
610. BGE, 30.
611. D, 62.
612. Contra Wagner.
613. D, 30.
614. D, 106.
615. D, 107.
616. Z, *The Three Metamorphoses*.
617. BGE, 45.

## CHAPTER 9

618. EH, IV: 8.
619. GM, 1
620. Ditto.
621. Ditto.
622. GM, 1:13.
623. Ditto.
624. Ditto.
625. Ditto.
626. See HH, and TI.
627. VP.11, 227.
628. Ditto.
629.GM, 11:12.

630. WP, 676.
631. WP, 657.
632. WP, 962.
633. BGE, 259.
634. GM1: 6
635.  GM, 111:15. GS, 359.
636. GM, 111: 14.
637. GM, 1:10.
638. GM, 111:14. WP, 179.
639. Ditto.
640. GM, 111:15.
641. GM, 11:17.
642. GM, 11:16.
643. Ditto.
644. GM, 111:11.
645. Ditto.
646. GM, 1:10.
647. GM, 11:22.
648. GM, 11:17.
649. GM, 11:16.
650. GM, 11:16.
651. BGE, 3.
652. BGE, 62.
653. AC, 57. BGE,  229.
654. AOM, 34.
655. GM, 111,28.
656. BGE, 203.
657. KSA, 13: 11.
658. Nietzsche's opponent in respect of Christian theology is less Christ than the Pauline doctrine that came to dominate church teaching.
659. GM, 111:28.
660. BGE, 1.
661. V.P.107.
662. M.Twain.
663. GS, 344.
664. GM, 111:27.
665. BGE, 230.
666. GS, 276.
667. EH. *Why I am so clever*.
668. T.I. *Socrates*, 9.

669. Ditto.
670. T.I. "Socrates", 10.
671. GS, 335.
672. GS, 276.
673. BGE, 21.
674. Ditto.
675. BGE, 188.
676. BGE, 21.
677. BGE, 188.
678. GS. 276.
679. Ditto.

## CHAPTER 10

680. HH.420.
681. Ditto.
682. GS.71.
683. Actually said by Goethe.
684. GS, 60.
685. GS, 59.
686. GS, Ditto.
687. D.346.
688. Nietzsche, himself, was brought up in a house full of women.
689. WP, 808.
690. HH, 415.
691. WP, 807.
692. Z, "Of old and young women".
693. BGE, 86.
694. HH, 276.
695. HH, 553.
696. TI, *Maxims*: 13.
697. BGE, 175.
698. BGE, 79.
699. BGE, 67.
700. BGE,
701. WP, 864.
702. GS, 56.
703. BGE, 3. BGE, 17.
704. BGE, 6.
705. D, Preface, 5. BGE, 229.

706. BGE, 230.
707. Ditto.
708. BGE, 231.
709. Ditto.
710. Ditto.
711. Ditto.
712. BGE, 237.
713. Ditto.
714. BGE, 84.
715. BGE, 165.
716. BGE, 226.
717. GS, 58.
718. BGE, 136.
719. GS, 68.
720. BGE, 148.
721. TI, 3:1.
722. TI. *Maxims*, 27.
723. GS, 363.
724. See Aristophanes: *Lysastrata*.
725. EH, 4:5.
726. GS, 176.
727. GS, 368.
728. BGE*, Prelude*.
729. D, *Preface*, 5.
730. TI, 38.
731. Z, 1V:13.
732. GS, 343, BGE, 230.
733. WP, 339.
734. TI, 5:6.
735. BGE, 232.
736. BGE, 239.
737. WP, 354.
738. WP, 355.
739. WP, 871.
740. WP, 877.
741. WP, 280.
742. WP, 53.
743. WP, 80.
744. WP, 926.
745. WP, 858.

746. WP, 926.
747. BGE, 153.
748. WP, 928.
749. EH, 1V: 8.
750. WP, 966, *Letter to Lou Salome.*
751. BGE, *Preface*
752. WP, 926.
753. BGE, 153.
754. TI.p.16.
755. GM, *Preface*. BGE, 62
756. GS.88.
757. See Aristotle *Poetics.*
758. HH, section 2.
759. See K. Oliver.
760. Ditto.
761. WP, 28.
762. D, 430.
763. BGE, 232,
764. WP, 584.
765. See K. Oliver.
766. HH, VII, P.305.
767. BT, 38.
768. KSA, 123.
769. GS, 107.
770. TI. 5: 3.
771. GS, 377.
772. WP, 385.
773. WP, 1067
774. *The Case of Wagner.*
775. Originally from Goethe's *Faust*, part 2 – "man is a coward in face of the eternally feminine".
776. TI, P.5.
777. HH, 11. BT. 15.
778. GS, 339.
779. WP, 804.
780. TI, P, 5.
781. GS, 339.
782. WP, 804.

## CHAPTER 11

783. GS, *Preface* 3.
784. WP, 224.
785. GS, 283.
786. WP, 1052.
787. Disgusted with all things German, Nietzsche wondered as breakdown took hold whether he might have been Polish by birth.
788. EH, 11: 10.
789. Z, 111: 11.
790. EH. *Preface*, 2.
791. TI, X, 4.
792. Z, 11: 12.
793. Z, 11: 2.
794. GS, 370.
795. BGE, 295.
795. GS, 370.
796. Bob Dylan, "Love minus zero/no limit" from "Bring it all back home".

## CHAPTER 12

797. See C.H.Kahn: *The Art And Thought Of Heraclitus*.
798. Ditto.
799. Plato; *The Sophist*.
800. See Kahn above.
801. Heraclitus was reputedly fond of watching children play.
802. PTA.II.
803. See *Parmenides*.
804. TI, *Reason*, 2.
805. See Plato: *Timaeus* for the distinction between being and becoming. TI. Reason 6.
806. See Kahn, op. cit.
807. Ditto.
808. TI; *Reason*.
809. *On Truth And Lies*. P 84.
810. WP. 493.
811. SE.3.
812. GM.111: 25.
813. Kant. *Critique of Pure Reason*, p. 257.
814. WP, 520.

815. TI. *World,* 6, *Reason*, 2.
816. WP.567.
817. WP.552.
818. Lecture notes on the Pre-Socratics. See Breazeale's Introduction to *Philosophy and Truth*.
819. TI. *Reason*, 6.
820. PTA.12.
821. WP.568.
822. PTA.6.
823. GS.2.
824. Spinoza's formula: Chaos v Nature. See KSA,9:11.
825. GS.109.
826. WP.708.
827. BGE, 146.
828. G. Berkeley; *A Treatise Concerning The Principles Of Human Knowledge*.
829. GS.109.
830. WP.552.
831. WP.1066.
832. WP.708.
833. Demosthenes was logographer before his interests turned to politics. Democritus, in addition to speculating about the existence of atoms, advocated cheerfulness as a virtue to be cultivated.
834. GM.111: 9.
835. GS.2.
836. GS.54.
837. BGE.36
838. KSA.11: 26.
839. AC. 14.
840. BGE, 12.
841. TI, *Reason*: 5.
842. WP, 715.
843. WP. 636.
844. WP.492.
845. WP.633,
846. WP.715.
847. D, 49.
848. AC. 14.
849. GM.12.
850. AC, 4.
851. HH. 9.

852. WP. 684.
853. BGE. 13.
854. GS. 349.
855. Z. *Prologue*,1
856. Z.2.
857. GM.11: 17.
858. WP.668.
859. BGE.262.
860. WP. 656.
861. GS. 285.
862. WP. 655.
863. GS. 109.
864. BGE. 36.
865.WP. 619.
866. GS. 115.
867. WP. 692.
868. BGE. 259.
869. BGE. 260.
870. GM.11: 11.
871. WP. 635.
872. WP, 643.
873. GM.111: 24. GM.11.
874. Z.1.
875. BGE. 36.
876. BGE. 30.
877. Ditto.
878. GS. 374.
879. BGE. 22.
880. GS, 341.
881.WP. 862.
882. Z.1V: 19.
883. D, 28.
884. Ditto.
885. TI. *The Hammer Speaks*.
886. Z.11: 20.
887. Z.111: 12.
888. Z, *Prologue*, 3.
889. Z. 1V: 19.
900. WP.585.
901. Z.11: 19.

902. EH. 11: 10.
903. WP. 1052.
904. Ditto.
905. GS. 283.
906. GS, *Preface,* 3.
907. WP.481.
908. Z.1.
909. AC.14.
910. Plato: *Apology*, 38a.
911. GM, *Preface*.
912. Plato, *Apology*, 33b.

## CHAPTER 13

913. Plato: *Symposium,* p,209
914. Ditto, p,212.
915. See *Cratylus,* 400; *Gorgias*, 493; *Phaedrus*, 250.
916. Stalin would be an example, but far from the only one.
917. Plato: *Sym*,192. A punishment for human hubris, but one that preserves humanity; the gods having need of human kind, as much as human kind needing the gods.
918. A copy of Aristophanes, or so the story goes.
919. A claim made by F. Engels in describing how the rise of private property led to the social demotion of women.
920. BGE, Part 7.
921. Not quite what Empedocles argues.
922. GS, 334.
923. Plato, *Sym*, p, 203.
924. Ditto, p, 211.
925. TI, 9: 19.
926. WP, 341.
927. WP, 804.
928. WP, 48.
929. WP, 804.
930. WP, 176.
931. WP, 296.
932. WP, 777.
933. D, 335.
934. WP, 453.
935. GS, 363.

936. GS, 59.
937. HH, 406.
938. GS, 14.
939. GS, 279 [footnote].
940. *Magna Moralia* 1213a.
941. GM, *Preface*.
942. Aristotle, *Nicomachian Ethics*,1165.
943. Ditto, 1156.
944. Ditto, 1105a.
945. Ditto, 1159.
946. Ditto, 1159.
947. BT, 14.
948. WP, 853.
949. BGE.167.
950. GM, 111: 25.
951. D.309.
952. D, 269.
953. GS, 338.
954. The Greeks reputedly lost 200 men to the Persian's 6400.
955. HH, 287.
956. WP, 357.
957. Plato: *Symposium*, p, 212b.
958. BT.5.

CHAPTER 14

959. GM.111: 25.
960. HH, 491. GS, 344.
961. BT.5.
962. Ditto.
963. HH, *Preface*.
964. WP. 598.
965. WP, 800.
966. WP, 826.
967. WP, 811.
968. WP, 802.
969 TI, IX: 9.
970. WP, 801, 811.
971. WP, 801.

972. WP, 804.
973. HH, 1: 155.
974. HH, 1:156.
975. WP. 804.
976. TI, ix: 19.
977. TI. ix: 22.
978. WP. 805.
979. TI, ix: 20.
980. WP. 800.
981. [9.11 [78],1881].
982. WP. 804.
983. Ditto.
984. WP, 806.
985. WP, 808.
986. TI, ix:19.
987. BGE, 232.
988. 7.7.121.
989. BGE, 84.
990. 7.7. [121].
991. WP, 853.
992. GM, III: 25.
993. BT.14.
994. WP. 804.
995. The anecdotes come from D. Laertes ,6. WP, 809.
996. GS, 39.
997. WP, 30.
998. D, 269.
999. GS, 370.
1000. D, 256.
1001. GM, III: 14.
1002. GM, III: 28.
1003. GS.338.
1004. GS, 14.
1005. GS, 338.
1006. Z, 1: 16.
1007. GS, *Preface*, 5.
1008. GM, 1: 8.
1009. Ditto.
1010. Ditto.
1011. HH, 224.

1012. GS, II: 18.
1013. GS, I: 6.
1014. See BGE.
1015. GS.290.
1016. TI. 'Four Errors': 8.
1017. Antisthenes - friend of Socrates, student of the Sophist, Gorgias, and reputed by some as the founding father of the Cynics. See Diogenes Laertes, 6:3.
1018. GS, 14.
1019. GS, 276.
1020. TI, *The problem of Socrates*, 5.
1021. Ditto, 11.

## CHAPTER 15

1022. GM, III: 25.
1023. WP, 1011.
1024. GS, 107.
1025. BT, 5.
1026. GS, 107.
1027. GM, III: 25.
1028. AC, 59.
1029. HH, 633, 635.
1030. AC, 50.
1031. Z, 1.
1032. WP, 457.
1033. GS, 285.
1034. WP, 466.
1035. AC, 13.
1036. G. Deleuze: *Nietzsche and Philosophy*, 5. GM, III: 10.
1037. Bee Gees: *Staying Alive*.
1038. BT, 4.
1039. BT.7.
1040. WP, 568.
1041. BT.2
1042. BT.5.
1043. WP, 853.
1044. WP, 820.
1045. WP, 759.
1046. GS, 54.BGE, 2:34.

1047. BGE, 34.
1048. GS, 113.
1049. BGE, 211.
1050. Z, 1: 17.
1051. Ben Franklin.
1052. GS, 299.
1053. GS, 290.
1054. BGE, 203.
1055. Z, ii: 2.
1056. HH, 11: 252.
1057. WP, 655.
1058. For rumination see GM, Preface. GS, 347. BGE, 10.
1059. AC, 54.
1060. WP, 883.
1061. WP, 881.
1062. GS, 113.
1063. Homer's Contest.
1064. Z, ii: 13.
1065. Reputedly Socrates' nose was so upturned that his nostrils faced the world.
1066. EH, 1; 1.
1067. EH, 1:8.
1068. Ditto.
1069. Z, i, P.3.
1070. Plato: *Republic*
1071. BGE, 190.
1072. EH, i:4.
1073. Z, i: 3.
1074. Z, i: 17.
1075. TI, ix: 20.
1076. GM, iii: 7.
1077. P and T, 157.
1078. EH, i: 2.

## CHAPTER 16

1079. GS, 110.
1080. Ditto.
1081. GS, 341.
1082. KSA, 9: 496.
1083. GS, 109.

1084. WP, 69.
1085. BGE, 22.
1086. WP, 552, 631.
1087. WP, 567.
1088. TI, 111: 1.
1089. Z, 4: 19.
1090. WP, 585.
1091. WP, 567. EH, 1: 7.
1092. WP, 588.
1093. Z, 11, 12.
1094. WP, 696, 704.
1095. Z, 11, 2.
1096. GS, 109.
1097. BGE, 22.
1098. TI. *Errors*, 8.
1099. WP, 1066.
1100. WP, 708.
1101. TI, 9:38.
1102. BGE, 19.
1103 TI, 6: 8.
1104. TI, 9: 33.
1105.GS, 335.
1106. BGE, 213.
1107. TI, 9: 49.

## EPILOGUE

1108. EH, *Why I Write Such Good Books*. BGE, P.4
1109. GS, 56.
1110. TI, 38.
1111.  Ditto.
1112. AC. *The case of Wagner*, EH: 1
1113.  Ditto, EH: 4.
1114. Descartes.
1115. GS.360.
1116. GS.371.
1117. Heraclitus, op. cit.
1118. H.H.1: 624.
1119. SE, p.194.
1120. SE, p, 127.

1121. SE, p.154.
1122. Schopenhauer: *The World as Will and Representation*,2 :p.385
1123. HH.1: 164.
1124. EH.111: 4.
1125. S.E. pp. 157 - 164.
1126. S.E.p142.
1127. S.E.p.128.
1128. Actually S. Kierkegaard; *The Diary of Soren Kierkegaard*, p.11
1129. S.E.p.127
1130. Actually R.Emerson: *Essays and Lectures* - "Divinity School Address."
1131. Z, pp89.
1132. Z, p, 106.
1133.Z.p.110.
1134. Z.p.127.
1135. Z.p.266.
1136. Socrates' last thought in the *Symposium*. See the title page of *The Case of Wagner*.
1137. Parodying Horace, Nietzsche's self-confessed stylistic ideal.
1138. A. Marvell: "To My Coy Mistress".

1139. Plato's Alcibiades in his *Symposium*. Also the last quotation in W .Kaufmann's *Nietzsche: Philosopher, Psychologist, Antichrist* - the great beginning of Nietzschean scholarship.
1140. BGE, 163.

\*\*\*\*\*

Lightning Source UK Ltd.
Milton Keynes UK
UKOW03f2024040813

214860UK00003B/109/P